HIGHLAND ODISHA

DR BISWAMOY PATI
(1955–2017)
Photograph courtesy: Dr Manu Sehgal

HIGHLAND ODISHA

Life and Society
Beyond the Coastal World

edited by

UWE SKODA
BISWAMOY PATI

PRIMUS
BOOKS

PRIMUS BOOKS
An imprint of Ratna Sagar P. Ltd.
Virat Bhavan
Mukherjee Nagar Commercial Complex
Delhi 110 009

Offices at CHENNAI LUCKNOW
AGRA AHMEDABAD BENGALURU COIMBATORE DEHRADUN GUWAHATI HYDERABAD
JAIPUR JALANDHAR KANPUR KOCHI KOLKATA MADURAI MUMBAI PATNA
RANCHI VARANASI

First published 2017

ISBN: 978-93-84082-97-0 (hardback)
ISBN: 978-93-84092-33-7 (POD)
ISBN: 978-93-84092-34-4 (e-book)

Published by Primus Books

Lasertypeset by Sai Graphic Design
Arakashan Road, Paharganj, New Delhi 110 055

Printed and bound in India by Replika Press Pvt. Ltd.

In memory of

BISWAMOY PATI

colleague, teacher and friend

Contents

Preface

The idea of this volume emerged as we reached the end of the second Odisha Research Project (ORP-II) in 2005, but it took a rather long time to conceptualize the book project. Since almost all projects were funded, directly or indirectly by the German Research Foundation (DFG) through ORP-II, we would like to thank, first and foremost, the DFG for their generous support over many years, but also Professor Hermann Kulke who was the coordinator of ORP-II.

All anthropological projects assembled in this volume were conducted at the Ethnologie-Institut (Department of Social Anthropology) of Freie Universität Berlin under the guidance and supervision of Professor Georg Pfeffer to whom we are grateful as much for his constant encouragement, and advice as for his critical comments.

Unfortunately, it is impossible to thank all our friends, colleagues and interlocutors here though each and every project benefitted immensely from their individual involvement. However, we would like to single out at least one institution for its outstanding commitment, namely, the Department of Anthropology, Sambalpur University, Burla, where its former Head, Professor Deepak Kumar Behera and his students and now colleagues Rashmi Pramanik, Manto Pradhan, Minaketan Bag and many others took a keen interest in this work, contributed to the research and readily offered a helping hand when required.

Last, but not the least we would like to put on record our appreciation of the anonymous reviewers for their insightful comments and critical remarks which have helped shape this volume.

1 Highland Odisha
Life and Society Beyond the Coastal World

UWE SKODA AND BISWAMOY PATI

Fifty-five years ago anthropologist F.G. Bailey (1960) encountered a complex structural coexistence of frames of reference—'Tribe, Caste and Nation' among Konds in Odisha that 'induced an unusually large degree of "anomie"' and 'created an unusually extensive field of political choice' (ibid.: 243). More recently, and going beyond Odisha, historians P. Price and A. Ruud (2010) dwelt on the political segmentation that had emerged historically and argued that, even as a modern nation state, 'India can maintain high degrees of segmentation amidst vast expanses of porous central and state bureaucracies' (ibid.: xxii). While new orders evolve(d) transforming kingship as well as the state and leading to new 'little political systems' (Mitra 2001) in a democratic set-up, older 'frames' such as kingdoms, 'princely states' or clan divisions often show a remarkable resilience.

Within such a multi-segmented Odishan society with its multitude of domains, however, crucial dichotomies have (re-)appeared in various, often coexisting and overlapping avatars. The plain has frequently been contrasted with the highlands; Mughalbandi with Garhjats; directly with indirectly ruled territories; administrative capitals with periphery; coastal with (south-) western Odisha, or in its latest form, closely linked to discourses on development, Utkal with Koshal. These intersecting and intertwined oppositions and forms of 'othering', though rather fuzzy, have often been condensed to a notion of 'hinterland' as 'land behind' as well as 'land left behind' vis-à-vis a more prosperous, urbanized centre along the sea. As a result of such processes an(-)'other' Odisha beyond the coastal world, i.e. the largely Adivasi[1] populated highlands and ostensible backyard areas in coastal perspectives, has often been rather invisiblized. This volume inverts this point of view by assembling a range of chapters based on solid, deep ethnography and deliberately shifts the focus to the less visible and often misrecognized highlands of Odisha—thus questioning dominant, coastal-centric views and acknowledging a multitude of perspectives on Odisha beyond any simplified dichotomy.

Locating an(-)'other' Odisha: multi-segmented frames

Geographical-demographic conditions: highlands, plain and contact zones

A quick look at the topographical map (Map 1.1) indicates, Odisha—the Union State on the Bay of Bengal with a territory roughly of the size of Ireland—can be divided into or is often perceived as consisting of two parts. On the one hand, the highland mountain region and on the other, the coastal strip that include the foothills of the Eastern Ghats and Garhjat mountains surrounding the fertile plain-delta in the shape of a sickle and forming a natural barrier between the two areas as well as separating the coastal area from the rest of India. This basic geographical division has often been linked to divergent historical developments and cultural, linguistic and religious differences in Odisha leading to distinctive cultural imprints. However, the area beyond the fertile coastal plain could also be further subdivided geographically into three units—first, the region north of the river Mahanadi, which belongs to the Chotanagpur plateau; second, the central plateau south of the river; and third the

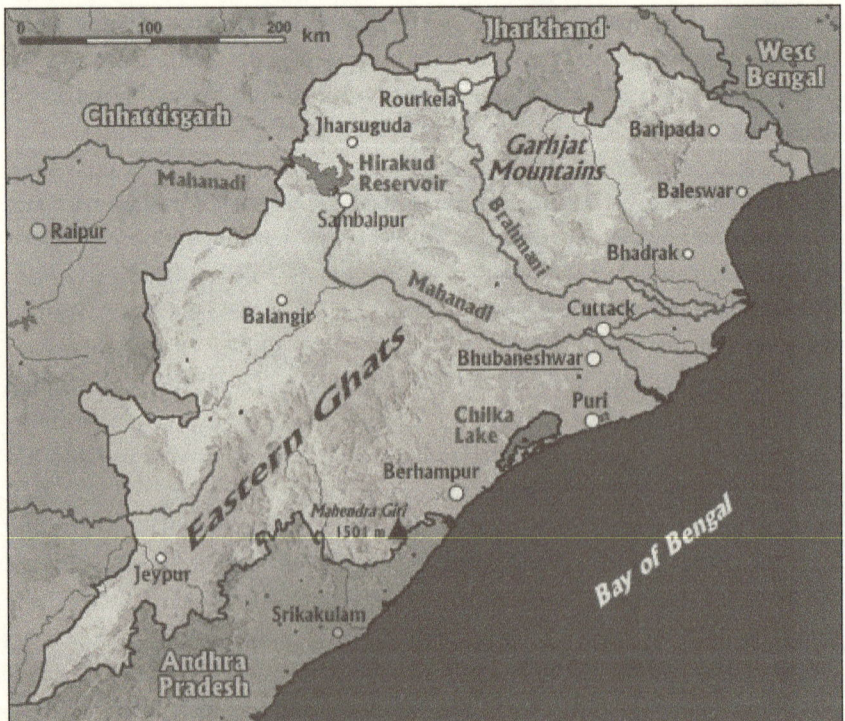

MAP 1.1: Topographic Map of Odisha (© Eric Töpfer)

adjacent foothills of the Eastern Ghats further south covered by dense forests. Settlements and centres along the rivers, and especially along the Mahanadi (and Brahmani) with important kingdoms, may also be considered forming a middle ground and contact zone between the plain and the highlands.

The mountain region of the Eastern Ghats with an average of over 1,000 m. in altitude runs in a semicircle along the coast. The lush forests of this range form almost one-third of the country and are predominantly inhabited by different indigenous groups known as Adivasis or Adibasis in Odia. The highest mountain of Odisha, the 1501 m. high Mahendra Giri, is also found here. Particularly these forested and relatively sparsely populated northern highlands of Chotanagpur continuing into Jharkhand and Chhattisgarh as well as parts of the Eastern Ghats are very rich in mineral resources, coal, etc. They were lately subjected to forms of often rather ruthless industrialization and dirty growth leading to fierce protests against mining projects such as Vedanta while defending the land and habitat.[2] In contrast, the soil of the coastal region known as Utkal, especially in the various river deltas (Mahanadi and Brahmani), is mainly made of fertile sediments. Not surprisingly, the Chilika plain, close to the Chilika Lake—India's largest salt water lagoon—is the most densely populated area of Odisha. However, population density is no guarantee against land alienation or land grabbing in favour of industrial projects either.

About half of Odisha's 36 million inhabitants live in the fertile coastal plain or on the banks of the river Mahanadi, flowing eastwards from the Chhattisgarh border into the Bay of Bengal through the centre of the province. The other half is settling in the western highlands. Almost 90 per cent of the population lives in villages, with most villages and a few large cities being situated in river valleys (including western Odishan centres of heavy industry such as Rourkela) and in the intensively cultivated lowlands yielding two to three harvests annually. The largest city and seat of government is the state capital Bhubaneswar, itself an ancient centre located in the plain-like area adjoining Cuttack from which it took over in 1948. Cuttack the political, military and administrative centre during the Mughal period and now considered the twin-city of Bhubaneswar, continues to remain an important commercial centre. Some of India's most famous antique temples in the coastal zone refer to an imperial past of Odisha. In addition to the sacred buildings in the plain (the main centres being Puri, Bhubaneswar and Konark) and in former little kingdoms, many temples in the highlands have instead been constructed relatively recently, a boom often linked to the rise of Hindu nationalism.

The relatively more remote forests and mountainous areas are the main settlement areas of the 'indigenous' populations. For administrative purposes, more than eight million people are classified as Scheduled Tribes (ST), that is, around 22 per cent of the total population of Odisha.[3] More than 60 indigenous ethnic groups are recognized and live mostly in the western and southern districts such as Sundargarh, Keonjhar, Mayurbhanj, Malkangiri and Koraput. The bigger Adivasi communities include millions of people and often settle across political boundaries of units such as Odisha while smaller ones may have only a few thousands of members. Their distinctive cults, ritual and economic practices are under pressure due to an internal colonization, globalization and particularly due to a rapid industrialization. Around dams or other industrial projects small enclaves of caste and class society have emerged as new contact zones. However, according to the census, Hindus constitute over 90 per cent of the population. The rest is divided among Christians, Muslims (mostly Sunnis) and 'other religions', and possibly Adivasis, though there is no such separate category in the census and many are simply subsumed under or identify with the category Hindu.

Historical trajectories

The just outlined geographical-demographic divisions clearly intersect with historically evolving processes of state-formation and diverse forms of colonial rule with an impact on the emergence of present-day Odishan identities. Without going into the details of ancient or medieval Odishan history here, it may suffice to indicate some later developments around the so-called feudatory or princely states separating 'western' Odisha under indirect rule from the strategically more important and therefore primarily directly ruled coastal Odisha.

These feudatory states of Odisha emerged and were acknowledged as such under colonial rule, but their evolution was a complex, at times even arbitrary process dating back at least to the period of Mughal rule when they used to be under their—often loose—overlordship, including their appointed governors (Subahdar). The Mughals conquering Odisha stepwise since 1576 subsequently divided it into two major constituents: on the one hand the Garhjat states, clusters of states and particularly one under the Sambalpur and Patna Rajas[4] in the hilly hinterland sometimes referred to as Sambalpur Garhjats,[5] and on the other hand Mughalbandi, the coastal plain (Map 1.2). This distinction between Mughalbandi, i.e.

areas under the more direct control of a Subahdar at the regional centre Cuttack, and Garhjat states in the north-western (and southern) part continued and still continues to influence regional identities. Though they were obliged to pay tribute to the Subahdar the Garhjat states under the control of little kings remained relatively independent—forming alliances with major Adivasi groups, appropriating and promoting their goddesses, etc. However, in 1751 the overlordship passed into the hands of the Marathas, namely the Bhonsle Rajas of Nagpur, and remained under their control until 1803 when the East India Company occupied the coastal belt—incorporating it into the Bengal Presidency after they had already occupied the southern Odishan coast in the early 1760s becoming part of the Madras Presidency subsequently. Though the Sambalpur Garhjat tracts were returned to the Marathas in 1806, they finally came under British control in 1818 and were officially ceded in 1826.

After 1803 the East India Company entered into engagements and treaties with chiefs, but the ultimate status of these states was determined only in 1888[6] and the situation remained relatively fluid, particularly up to the Great Uprising in 1857/58. Chiefs such as the ones in Banki (in 1840) and Angul (in 1848) were deposed for various reasons such as murder or the support of rebellions. In 1849, Sambalpur was seized—ostensibly under the doctrine of lapse. These annexations led to relatively discontinuous territories, resulting in the map of British India and the feudatory states in Odisha resembling a rag rug. Yet, after the Great Uprising or so-called Mutiny and revision of the British policy towards the native states it was this geographical patchwork structure with its dispersed boundaries that was more or less frozen.

These states or *mahals* varying considerably in size and revenue (e.g. Tigiria: 119 km², Mayurbhanj: 10989 km²) were either labelled generally by the British administration as 'native states' and in the later colonial period increasingly as 'princely states'—presumably to indicate as well as confer a status lower than the British crown. While 'princely state' was perhaps the most widely used term for kingdoms under British paramountcy, a range of other terms was synonymously used—often adding to a certain confusion rather than to an analytical sharpness. The central element constituting the 'feudal' relations between the native or 'feudatory' states and the British crown was the payment of a tribute linked to an inferior rank. This quality was particularly stressed and expressed in the term 'tributary state' used almost interchangeably with 'feudatory state'.[7] In the same way, semantically, Raja was more or less used like chief, though it was later qualified as 'ruling chief' or 'feudatory chief' to distinguish the heads of states from other title-holders, who,

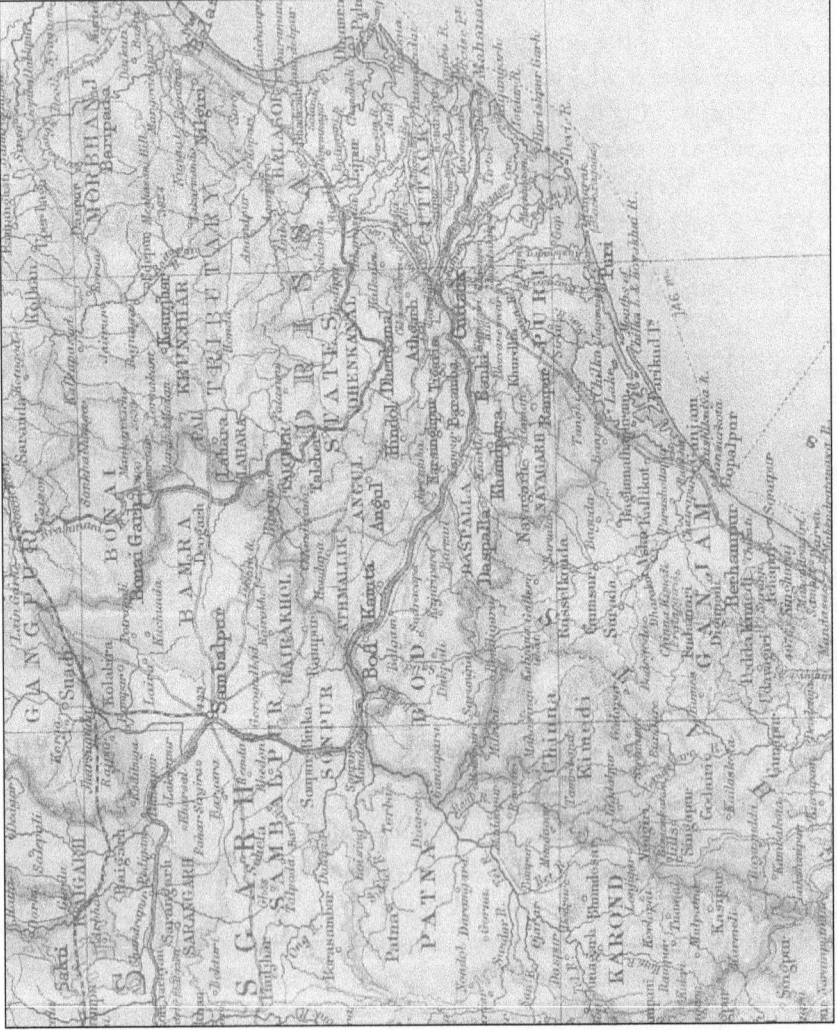

MAP 1.2: Feudatory/Tributary States of Odisha (map adapted from map of Central Provinces 1909)

though in charge of large estates, e.g. Koraput/Jeypore in the South, were never acknowledged at par with the north-western and central chiefs.

Thus, just like the rest of the subcontinent—and not unlike an earlier bifurcation during the Mughal rule—under the colonial regime present-day Odisha was divided into a British India, primarily the directly controlled territory along the coast (the latter districts of Puri, Balasore and Cuttack), and into an Indian or Native India,[8] an area under indirect rule, yet under the British crown. Such more autonomous kingdoms continued to exist as 'states' away from the colonial centres in relatively remote areas such as in the, at least initially, thick jungles and hills of the Eastern Ghats—the Odishan 'hinterland' from a coastal perspective, while more fertile and strategically more important territories that could be ruled cost-effectively were more likely to be conquered by the British.[9] Till today, the Odishan infrastructure reflects this orientation towards and connection to colonial centres including Calcutta, Bombay and Madras rather than the previous royal capitals—supplemented later only by including a few industrial centres.

A certain arbitrariness just mentioned in the evolution of the boundaries between British India and the feudatory states—and in fact, the evolution of Odisha as idea and province/Union State—depending on historical processes and contingencies, is mirrored and has been shaped by a shifting classification of those princely states. A number of them—notably the Garhjat States around Sambalpur—were initially administered as part of the South-Western Frontier Agency (formed in 1833), which was transformed into the Chotanagpur Division under a Commissioner in Ranchi (from 1854 onwards). However, after 1860 only few of them, e.g. Bonai and Gangpur remained under this division, while others (Bamra, Kalahandi, Patna, Rairakhol and Sonepur) became part of the Central Provinces. It was only in 1905, after the division of Bengal, that an administrative reform was initiated and all these seven states were attached to the Odisha Division and thus united with the other 17 Tributary States under a Commissioner in Cuttack. While the states were under direct supervision of the Commissioner, up to the reform, the office of Political Agent stationed in Sambalpur was created, under the Commissioner again, leading to a special status of the states in present-day western Odisha. In 1922 another administrative re-organization led to the formal abolition of the offices of Commissioner with regard to the states and the Political Agent was rechristened as Political Agent and Commissioner, Odisha Feudatory States and included the states of Sareikela and Kharsuan at that time as well—later part of Bihar and now Jharkhand.[10]

However, connections beyond Odisha did not cease, but were maintained, e.g. within a new administrative unit—the Eastern States Agency—formed in 1935 together with states in present-day Chhattisgarh and Jharkhand and elsewhere, while the directly ruled districts were first separated from Bengal by forming the Bihar and Orissa Province in 1912, and later in 1936 Odisha (Orissa) as a province in its own right emerged creating the first Indian province along linguistic lines and thus fulfilling demands by 'Odia nationalists', or perhaps 'regionalists', e.g. the Utkal Sammilani founded 100 years after the colonial conquest of the coastal centres. Only at the time of Indian independence and the subsequent merger of the princely states with the Indian Union Odisha with its contemporary boundaries was formed with initially 13 and later 35 districts—in many ways reflecting earlier state structures with royal capitals often becoming (sub-)district headquarters.

With independence and the subsequent merger of the feudatory states with the province of Odisha a century-old history came formally to an end—despite other visions such as the idea of turning the Eastern States Agency into a province. While some former princes joined the Congress, a greater number supported the Ganatantra Parishad, crucially founded with the help of former rulers, e.g. from Kalahandi and somehow perpetuating a distinctive Garhjat identity under changed political circumstances.[11] Though later merged with the Swatantra Party, it is certainly not just a coincidence that in 1967 Rajendra Narayan Singh Deo, former ruler and Maharaja of Patna-Bolangir, became the first Odishan Chief Minister not hailing from the coastal belt (in fact, only three out of 14 Chief Ministers since independence have not come from the plain).[12] Thus, in many ways the states and their past continued and continue to inform the imagination of former subjects as well as younger generations and may be used in future to articulate separate identities and political goals such as for a Koshal state.

'Distributing the spoils': Koshal, Utkal and beyond?

The historically determined cleavages within Odisha, converge with politically driven agendas and projects, to mobilize for a formation of a Koshal state which in turn date back at least to the period of late-colonial rule but have been boosted by the creation of new Union states such as Telengana in 2013. As a rational beyond the shared history, economic neglect of the 'hinterland' has often been cited by those championing this cause. While the mineral wealth is concentrated largely in the hills and highlands, the area, so they argue, is deprived of its due share while value is added in the plain.

A movement for the bifurcation of Odisha is slowly emerging with a multitude of organizational drivers such as Koshal Kranti Dal (KKD) demanding statehood for 10 districts in western Odisha and spearheading agitations, e.g. against Utkal Diwas (Odisha Day) considered a black day for western Odisha. While the creation of Koshal is not immanent the establishing of a 'Western Odisha Development Council' (WODC) can be considered a certain success for the Koshal supporters. Meant to remove imbalances and to alleviate the cleavage, its functioning also illustrates the differences of the two regions in economic terms. As WODC itself states:

Looking at the degree of development/backwardness of 10 Western Orissa districts, it can be said that out of 87 blocks only 5 blocks are developed, 25 are developing, another 25 are backward and 32 blocks are very backward, whereas in coastal districts 70 blocks are developed, 50 blocks are very backward out of total 227 blocks. Only 5.7% developed blocks [and] 36.78% very backward blocks are there in WODC districts. This is against 30.84% of the developed blocks [and] only 22.03% . . . very backward blocks in non–WODC districts.[13]

Apart from the fact of lagging behind economically, representatives of a Koshal movement also criticize a marginalization in cultural and linguistic terms. They demand that Kosli/Koshali/Sambalpuri should be fully recognized as a language by including it in the Eighth Schedule of the Indian Constitution rather than considering it a dialect of Odia.[14] This campaign plays on older prerogative and stereotyped classifications of coastal Odia as 'Kataki speech' (Cuttack speech) and Sambalpuri as 'Adivasi language' (Gochhayat 2013: 11) while downplaying an internal linguistic diversity in both cases.

Yet, the strategic claim for, or acknowledgement of a distinctive cultural identity of ten districts in western Odisha by KKD and WODC against a dominant coastal Odisha, however well-argued, often fails to address the position of southern Odisha and the fuzzy distinction between coastal/centre/plain versus western/highlands/periphery and serves as a reminder that we are confronted not only with a simplified opposition but rather a multitude of 'Odishas'. Thus, the volume questions hegemonic, often coastal-centred perspectives by shifting the focus westwards away from shores, but at the same time acknowledges a multitude of perspectives on Odisha that go beyond such a simplified dichotomy.

Researching Odisha and Highland Odisha

Hegemonic discourses on Odisha—inside as well as outside Odisha—have focused for a long time on the ostensible cultural centre in the coastal and delta area and here particularly on the cult of Lord Jagannath in the sacred centre Puri. In this dominant discourse Lord Jagannath, the Lord of the Universe, was elevated to a central symbol of Odia-identity at least from the nineteenth century onwards. Odia elites especially the leading representatives in and around the temple (Brahmins, rulers) identified the deity with the region, Odisha as land of Lord Jagannath, referring back to a putative glorious medieval past. However, this connection between Odia-ness and the cult of Lord Jagannath was also reinforced through academic scholarship in the 1960s and 1970s, i.e. in the context of the so-called first Orissa Research Project (henceforth ORP-I) funded by the German Research Council between 1969 and 1975 which—intended or otherwise—contributed to this image of Odisha as land of Lord Jagannath. The project led to the pioneering, interdisciplinary volume *The Cult of Jagannath and the Regional Tradition of Orissa,* ed. A. Eschmann, H. Kulke and G.C. Tripathi (1978), having a major impact on and facilitating an emerging distinctive regional historiography, rather than an imperialist or nationalist one. It also resulted in a range of substantial studies, articles and monographs—all related to aspects of the 'great' Jagannath temple tradition in Puri. Making use of widely discussed concepts of the 1960s and 1970s such as tribe-caste-continuum, Hinduization versus tribalization, Great versus Little tradition, or Sanskritization, for example, von Stietencron (1978a, b) analysed traditions within Hinduism, Eschmann (1978a, b; 1994 [1975]) focused on Hinduization, Pfeffer (1978) on settlements of Sasana Brahmins around Puri; Tripathi (1978) on the concept of Purushottama, Kulke (1978, 1979) on the aspect of state formation and legitimation and Roesel (1980) on pilgrimage.

Thus, ORP-I project decisively contributed to a dynamic research tradition in and on Odisha, particularly boosting a regional historiography. A range of historians, inspired by the project's focus, continued to work along those lines, while critically looking at its findings (Banerjee-Dube 2001; Mubayi 2005; Brandtner and Panda 2006; Nanda 2010; Sahu 2012; Dash 2012 et al.). Simultaneously some anthropological projects were carried out around, before and after ORP-I (e.g. Bailey 1957, 1960, 1963; McDougal 1963, 1964; Niggemeyer 1964; Seymour 1980;[15] Marglin 1989 [1985]; Freeman 1993 [1979]), enabling or prompting some mutual engagement. Subsequently, members of ORP-I continued with their interest in Odisha (e.g. Kulke 1993; Kulke and Schnepel 2001; Berkemer,

Frenz and Kulke 2003; Kulke and Skoda 2010; Pfeffer 1982, 2003; Mallebrein and von Stietencron 2008) and often facilitated follow-up projects carried out by a new generation of scholars. Partly these projects extended the work on the Jagannath cult by including aspect so far relatively neglected like the Nabekalevara rituals (Hardenberg 1999), partly these or simultaneously conducted projects (Boal 1982; Carrin-Bouez 1986; Nayak 1989; Parkin 1992; Berkemer 1993; Vitebsky 1993; Mallebrein 1996; Padel 1996; Schnepel 2002) slowly but surely shifted the focus away from the centres of the supposedly 'greater' tradition such as Puri towards relatively smaller centres or 'little kingdoms', their rules or Rajas including 'jungle kings'—initially often inspired by and taking into account the anthro-historical research of Cohn (2001 [1962]); Dirks (1987, 1992), but also anthropological approaches of Dumont (1980 [1966]) and others. Moreover, these rulers' subjects or Prajas, often Adivasis, their local deities, kinship systems and interrelations became central foci of research. Through these various smaller projects, an awareness increasingly emerged about the shortcomings of ORP-I in terms of overemphasizing the position of one deity, cult and its protagonists in a coastal centre vis-à-vis a multitude of competing centres, social groups and perspectives being rather relegated to the background. This insight culminated in a second Orissa Research Project (henceforth ORP-II, 1999–2005) meant to rectify this lacunae and introducing several paradigmatic shifts, while retaining a regional focus and arguing for the advantages of regional studies vis-à-vis looking at a towering entity such as India at large.

The continuity was contrasted with a decisive reorientation during ORP-II, i.e. away from a privileged religious and political centre to the periphery/-ies—peripheral being understood in a horizontal, geographical way as 'hinterland', but also in a vertical, socio-political sense as being marginal(ized) with a range of combinations and overlaps possible. A centre was not understood as a monolithic entity, but as a position open for contestation and being embedded in a wider power-configuration involving competing temples, agents and perspectives.

Furthermore, ORP-II also advocated a bottom-up perspective in order to supplement the previously dominant discourse represented by priests and kings. Taking clues from the French Annals school, the concept of microhistory and the subaltern studies group, a shift in Odishan studies from dominant to demiotic discourses was proposed to unearth other voices, even if only preserved as fragments. Agency as a certain ability to negotiate, however limited in case of marginalized individuals or communities, became a major concern for scholars involved in ORP-II, who were also increasingly less interested in texts and scriptures alone, but in the contexts of their production or circulation—including in ostensibly 'little' traditions. Texts were not only seen as documenting and expressing processes of negotiation within a culture, but rather as arenas with multiple and often contradictory traces of interests and power and even aktants within such process. Like other cultural artefacts, texts were considered as having object biographies with shifting meanings, were related to processes of appropriation and to (public) performances—legitimizing or challenging authorities. Lastly, the construction of identities, of connections as well as of boundaries between communities in Odisha was emphasized and processes of becoming, rather than being, took center-stage—particularly in relation to cultural encounters. The various volumes published by ORP-II—apart from more individual publications[16]—highlight these predominant concerns: *Text and Context in the History, Literature and Religion of Orissa* (ed. Malinar/Beltz/Frese 2006); *Periphery and Centre* (ed. Pfeffer 2007) symbolically inverting a standardized perspective; *Time in India: Concepts and Practices* (ed. Malinar 2007) and finally *Centres Out There?: Facets of Subregional Identities in Orissa* (ed. Kulke/Berkemer 2011) questioning and deconstructing a dominant regional identity by bringing in a multitude of traditions particularly at the margins, for example, in relation to conversion (Pati 2007) or 'stereotyped' princely states (Pati 2011).

As historian B.P. Sahu summarized the achievements of ORP-II in retrospective:

the picture of a neat, undifferentiated, coast centered (Jajpur-Bhubaneswar-Puri-Konark) hegemonic reality was being disturbed with the problematizing of several interrelated issues. . . . The ORP-II naturally to begin with envisaged the persistence of multiple centres, instead of the centre, and proceeded to decipher the network of interrelationships between them; with a band of young interdisciplinary scholars. The associated aspects of contestation and negotiation were given their due in the construction of the new complex narrative. (2013)

The present volume clearly emerged out of the ORP-II context with seven out of the eight contributors being directly involved in the activities and Pfeffer, leading this group of mostly younger scholars in Berlin, being also part of ORP-I. Most of the authors received funding for their doctoral and post-doctoral (particularly Hardenberg) research through ORP-II. Four anthropologists (Berger, Guzy, Skoda and Strümpell) who joined ORP-II as Ph.D. students moved on to post-doctoral projects later, while Reichel began her research at the end of, but nevertheless in the environment of the ORP. Thus, the contributions share and reflect some of the central ORP concerns especially by focusing on 'indigenous' people, identifying themselves often as Adivasis and being classified by the State as Scheduled Tribes. Several scholars conducted their field research either among Adivasi communities such as the Ho, Gadaba or Dongria Kondh or in settings of cultural encounters.

In this way, for their projects they could use insights from a few early ethnographers who had worked in the Odishan 'hinterland' or adjacent areas—notably the early work of lawyer-turned-ethnographer S.C. Roy, for example, on the Munda (1912), Oraons (1915) or Hill Bhuiyans (1935); or the early anthropological work of V. Elwin (e.g. 1944, 1950, 1954, 1955) among the Bondos or Saoras and Fürer-Haimendorf (1943, 1979). Similarly, they also took advantage of the aforementioned research of F.G. Bailey (recently also re-studied by Otten[17]) and Niggemeyer carried out subsequently—without in any way confining their projects to the earlier ethnographic standards of those pioneering scholars who initially aimed at covering communities in their entirety.

Unlike the earlier ethnographers anthropologists of this Berlin group within the larger ORP focused on specific questions and topics. While Pfeffer focused on the larger structural framework and social order across communities and particularly kinship systems; Strümpell and Skoda conducted their research in contact zones between caste and tribal society—the former in relation to industrial settlements as enclaves (a power plant and later a major steel plant), the latter on interactions between migrant peasants turned landlords, Adivasi village founders as well as other (Adivasi) migrants. Moreover, Berger looked at the role of food and food transactions among and beyond Gadabas; Hardenberg studied the 'infamous' meriah or buffalo sacrifice among Dongria Kondhs—often linked to human sacrifice and as such a major topos for a supposedly civilizing colonial rule, though never studied in detail; Guzy concentrated on Mahima Dharma as an indigenous religious movement increasingly successfully proselytizing among Adivasis, thus also engaging with and building on Eschmann's earlier work,[18] but also later on music traditions in western Odisha; and Reichel investigated concepts of dying and death among Hos.

However, while the above-mentioned collaborative ORP-II-volumes were, in line with the overall project, interdisciplinary the anthropological research projects and the productive Berlin environment out of which they emerged were never introduced in and themselves made visible through a more distinctive collection—here supplemented with a historical chapter. Thus, the aim of this compilation is also to present a set of projects conducted more or less simultaneously at Freie Universität

Berlin that have mutually influenced each other through spatial and intellectual proximity paired with an emphasis on in-depth field research.

Deep ethnography in and on Odisha— making other cultures visible

The volume does not only focus on the relatively invisiblized Odishan highlands in the West and South, often perceived as 'hinterland', but also brings together contributions based on long-term anthropological and historical research which may be best characterized as 'deep ethnography'.[19] All authors have a lasting and deep-rooted engagement with their interlocutors and immersed into their respective fields involving a profound respect for other cultures and facilitating a subtle and nuanced rather than gross or shallow ethnography. Instead of a grab-and-run approach they have been committed to their respective projects for years—despite academic or bureaucratic hurdles and funding problems. Thus, the intensity as well as extensity are clearly visible and stand out in times of increasingly shorter field 'visits' and an inflationary use of the term ethnography.

Based on field work and participant observation, but also including oral traditions, archival materials, and the work of a range of scholars that negotiate the region and the people, this book brings to life a set of diversities that together make this work meaningful. However, the different contributions that together constitute this volume do not approach the problem from any single vantage point or theoretical perspective. In fact, what is attempted is to combine different ways in which the 'indigenous' people or 'tribes' of the highlands of Odisha can be studied.

As the first chapter, Biswamoy Pati's 'Survival, Interrogation and Contests: Tribal Resistance in Nineteenth-Century Odisha', while noting the logic of upper caste hegemony, points to the 'Otherisation' of the non-coastal tract. Focusing on the shifts and changes unleashed through the process of colonization that had an intimate association with the collaborating internal exploiting classes, it highlights the manner in which this impacted the tribals. This chapter delineates the level of fluidities when it comes to differentiating between the tribals and the outcastes (or untouchables) and tells us about the social history of resistance that is projected holistically over the period 1840s and 1890s.

The next chapter, Georg Pfeffer's 'Tribal Social Structure in Odisha', takes up a category of people of the region who have been stereotyped differently right up to the present-day. Pfeffer questions both the undefined

'Western universalism' that tends to locate the tribals as individuals 'within the familiar administrative setup', as well as the efforts of the method of 'Hindu universalism' that sees them as parts of caste groups, and hence as Hindus. On the basis of 'academic anthropology' it engages with the social order of the tribes to historicize a set of people, even as it contests and critiques their labelling.

Peter Berger's 'Feeding, Sharing and Devouring: Alimentary Rituals and Cosmology in Highland Odisha, India' focuses on the Gadabas, a tribal community of Koraput in south Odisha. It weaves in certain features of Gadaba society associated with the indigenous notion of cosmology or divine social order known as *niam*. This chapter takes up food as an entry point and engages with feeding/eating, sharing and devouring, to tell us about a set of complex relationships of the Gadabas.

The next chapter, Eva Reichel's 'On Death and the Ho's Relationship with their Dead' explores ways of mourning their dead of the Ho tribe. Taking the universal bio-physiological phenomenon of death Reichel tells us about the culture specific features associated with the Ho. The effort blends anthropological theory and rigorously conducted fieldwork in Jharkhand and Odisha over 2004 and 2012. As delineated, dying in Ho country is seen as a cultural affair and burying and mourning a social, non-individual matter beyond biological givens. Moreover, by sub-classifying death, an effort is made to keep aloof from 'deviant' deaths.

Roland Hardenberg's '"Juniors", "Exploiters", "Brokers" and "Shamans": A Holistic View on the Dombo Community in the Highlands of Odisha', delineates a rather complex problem associated with the socially excluded untouchables—Dombos/Panos—and their interaction with the different Kond tribals of western Odisha. The author captures the interdependence and coexistence of both, including the role of the Dombos/Panos as intermediaries and middlemen of the Konds, even as he articulates the changes in the stereotypical image of the Dombos/Panos that sustains the hierarchy of 'purity' and 'pollution' in tribal cultures.

The next chapter, Lidia Guzy's '*Thea-phony* in Western Odisha', examines the important position of music associated with the marginalized musicians, especially the Ganda village musicians and other non-Brahmin priest-musicians in the local society of the Boro Sambar region of western Odisha. As outlined, these musicians play a crucial role in the socio-religious life of the region, besides being mediators between diverse social groups as well as the clients of present-day. As suggested, the specific cultural identity and memory of the region are transmitted and preserved through particular local musical traditions. It is in this context that it is vital to grasp the local knowledge and the value/belief system the Bora Sambar region through an analysis of the ritual music.

Uwe Skoda's 'Pioneers of the Plough: Aghria-Peasants in North-Western Odisha in an Anthro-historical Perspective', the next chapter focuses on the process of migration of a peasant caste from the north-western parts into the ex-princely states of western Odisha. What is highlighted is that this coexisted with their pivotal role in agricultural expansion under the aegis of colonialism and the emerging princely order. This transformed the region through the clearing of the forests and promoting plough-related rice cultivation and saw politico-economic changes, especially though increased revenue generation and collection, and the emergence of a 'regional society'. As argued, the plough emerges as a metaphor both as a prime agricultural instrument and as a major component of early revenue measurement, especially in a context when the land itself was surveyed differently.

Finally, Christian Strümpell's 'A Steel Town in the "Wilderness": Industry, State and Empire in Western Odisha', takes up the country's first public sector undertaking, the 'steel city' of Rourkela for scrutiny. Exploring the 'ideas' related to this project of the post-colonial Nehruvian state, Strümpell explores the growth of similar urban industrial clusters as symbols of modernity. His effort seeks to study how far such centres succeeded in integrating India's internal 'hinterland' with the new post-colonial nation-state. His exploration critically evaluates this quest to accommodate citizens who could transcend divisive identities of caste, community, and language-based ethnicity in the enclaves of 'modernity' like Rourkela, that could be then integrated with the new nation-state.

Notes

1. The volume focuses primarily on communities variously described as Adivasis ('original settlers'), indigenous peoples or tribes. Keeping in mind the various (dis-)advantages of these terms, their historical usages, etc. the editors of this volume have left it to the individual authors to work critically with any of them rather than imposing any misplaced terminological uniformity. Thus, we use and retain 'indigenous', 'tribal' and 'Adivasis' in a rather fluid manner fully aware of the different terminologies used in various parts of the world, the multitude of meanings attached to them and the problems associated with defining terms such as 'Adivasi'.

2. A body of literature studying and analysing 'development projects' in Odisha and the related drive to acknowledge and implement land and forest rights has recently emerged. See Padel (2009, 2010) and more recent contributions

from Oskarson (2010) and Shutzer (2013). Also the earlier work of Banik (2007) could be mentioned here.

3. http://censusindia.gov.in/Tables_Published/SCST/dh_st_Odisha.pdf, accessed on 4 November 2010.

4. Impey (1958 [1863]) and others have pointed out that a number of states—sometimes 18 is given as a figure—were under the loose overlordship of Patna and Sambalpur (the latter soon eclipsing the older line in Patna). These Garhs are: Phuljar, Sarangarh, Sakti, Raigarh, Bonai, Gangpur, Bamra, Boud, Athmallik, Rairakhol, Sonepur, Bargarh, Khariar, Boro Sambar, Chandarpur and Bindanawagarh.

5. Cobden-Ramsay 1982 [1910], 28.

6. It took till 1888 that the status of the so-called tributary mahals of Odisha was finally clarified. The High Court in Calcutta ruled that 17 states—namely Athgarh, Athmallik, Baramba, Baudh, Daspalla, Dhenkanal, Hindol, Keonjhar, Khandpara, Mayurbhanj, Narsingpur, Nayagarh, Nilgiri, Pal Lahara, Ranpur, Talcher, and Tigiria—did not form part of British India—a view subsequently accepted by the Secretary of State for India. Soon afterwards in 1891 the same status was conferred to the states of the Chotanagpur Division (Gangpur, Bonai) and new treaties (*sanads*) were issued to them as well specifying their position vis-à-vis the British, their powers and tribute. At the same time the disputes and uncertainties about the status of former kingdoms as states or estates (*zamindaris*) were more or less resolved from the British point of view eager to order society unambiguously and kingdoms such as Pal Lahara were acknowledged as tributary states despite claims that it used to be a dependent zamindari of Keonjhar state. In other cases the *zamindari* status was confirmed and maintained, e.g. in the case of the Khurda Rajas. Cobden-Ramsay 1982 [1910]: 27.

7. States such as Sareikela exempted from paying tributes were classified as 'Political States'.

8. Copland 1987 [1982].

9. This remoteness of relatively secluded kingdoms in terms of thick jungles has been expressed recently in the term 'jungle kings' (Schnepel 2002)—reminiscent of former kingdoms further north classified by the colonizers as 'Jungle Mahals'. See Schnepel, B., 2002.

10. On the administrative reforms and classifications see C.U. Aitchison, 1930.

11. Bailey 1959.

12. Richter 1978, Gochhayat 2013: 11.

13. See for example http://www.wodcorissa.org/about.htm, accessed on 30 November 2014.

14. See for example http://www.ekoshal.com/about-koshal/, accessed on 30 November 2014.

15. Seymour's research was tied to the wider Harvard-Bhubaneswar Project running from 1962 to 1973. See Seymour 2013.

16. See for example Berger 2002, 2007; Berger, Hardenberg et al., 2010; Otten 2006; Otten and Skoda 2014; Strümpell 2008; Skoda 2005; Guzy 2002; Mallebrein and Guzy 2004; Banerjee-Dube and Beltz 2008; Hardenberg 2000, 2005; Ahuja 2009.
17. See https://www.soas.ac.uk/anthropology/rural-change-and-anthropological-knowledge-in-post-colonial-india/, accessed on 5 September 2015.
18. On Mahima Dharma see also the work of Banerjee-Dube and Beltz (2008) related to the ORP.
19. On the earlier use of the term 'deep ethnography' see for example Pryor 2004, Brick 2013.

References

Ahuja, R., *Pathways of Empire: Circulation, 'Public Works' and Social Space in Colonial Orissa, c.1780–1914*, Delhi: Orient BlackSwan, 2009.

Bailey, F.G., *Caste and the Economic Frontier: A Village in Highland Orissa*, Manchester: Manchester University Press, 1957.

———, *Tribe, Caste and Nation: A Study of Political Activity and Political Change in Highland Orissa*, Bombay: Oxford University Press, 1960.

———, *Politics and Social Change: Orissa in 1959*, Berkeley: University of California Press, 1963.

Banerjee-Dube, I., *Divine Affairs: Religion, Pilgrimage, and the State in Colonial and Postcolonial India*, Shimla: Indian Institute of Advanced Studies, 2001.

Banerjee-Dube, I. and J. Beltz, *Popular Religion and Ascetic Practices, New Studies on Mahima Dharma*, New Delhi: Manohar, 2008.

Banik, D., *Starvation and India's Democracy*, London: Routledge, 2007.

Berger, P., 'The Gadaba and the "non-ST" Desia of Koraput', in *Contemporary Society: Tribal Studies*, ed. G. Pfeffer and D.K. Behera, vol. 5, New Delhi: Concept Publishing Co., 2002, pp. 57–90.

———, *Füttern, Speisen und Verschlingen. Ritual und Gesellschaft im Hochland von Orissa, Indien*, Berlin: Lit, 2007.

Berger, P., R. Hardenberg, E. Kattner and M. Prager, eds., *The Anthropology of Values: Essays in Honour of Georg Pfeffer*, New Delhi: Pearson, 2010.

Berkemer, G., *Little Kingdoms in Kalinga: Ideologie, Legitimation und Politik Regionaler Eliten*, Stuttgart: Franz Steiner, 1993.

Berkemer, G., M. Frenz and H. Kulke, *Sharing Sovereignty: The Little Kingdom in South Asia*, Berlin: Klaus Schwarz, 2003; Delhi: Primus Books, 2015.

Boal, B.M., *The Khonds Human Sacrifice and Religious Change*, Warminster: Aris & Phillips, 1982.

Brandtner, M. and S.K. Panda, eds., *Interrogating History: Essays for Hermann Kulke*, Delhi: Manohar, 2006.

Carrin-Bouez, M., *La fleur et l'os. Symbolisme et rituel chez les Santal*, Paris: Editions de l'École des Hautes Études en Sciences Sociales, Cahiers de l'homme. Nouv. Ser. 16/a, 1986.

Cobden-Ramsay, L.E.B., *Feudatory States of Orissa*, Calcutta: KLM, 1982 [1910].

Cohn, B.S., 'Political Systems in Eighteenth-Century India: The Banares Region', in *An Anthropologist among the Historians and other Essays*, Delhi: Oxford University Press, 2001 [1962], pp. 483–99.

Dash, K.C., 'Inventing Odisha', in *Odisha Review*, April 2012, http://odisha.gov. in/e-magazine/Orissareview/2012/April/Aprilreview.htm, accessed on 5 September 2015.

Dirks, N.B., *The Hollow Crown: Ethnohistory of an Indian Kingdom*, Cambridge: Cambridge University Press, 1987.

———, 'From Little King to Landlord: Colonial Discourse and Colonial Rule', in *Colonialism and Culture*, ed. N.B. Dirks, Ann Arbor: The University of Michigan Press, 1992, pp. 175–208.

Dumont, L., *Homo Hierarchicus: The Caste System and Its Implications*, Chicago: Chicago University Press, 1980 [1966].

Elwin, V., 'Notes on a Kondh Town', *Man in India*, vol. 24, no. 1, 1944, pp. 40–50.

———, *Bondo Highlander*, Bombay: Oxford University Press, 1950.

———, *Tribal Myths of Orissa*, Bombay: Oxford University Press, 1954.

———, *Religion of an Indian Tribe*, Bombay: Oxford University Press, 1955.

Eschmann, A., 'Hinduization of Tribal Deities in Orissa: The Sakta and Saiva Typology', in *The Cult of Jagannath and the Regional Tradition of Orissa*, ed. A. Eschmann, H. Kulke and G.C. Tripathi, Delhi: Manohar, 1978a, pp. 79–97.

———, 'The Vaisnava Typology of Hinduization and the Origin of Jagannatha', in *The Cult of Jagannath and the Regional Tradition of Orissa*, ed. A. Eschmann, H. Kulke and G.C. Tripathi, Delhi: Manohar, 1978b, pp. 99–117.

———, 'Sign and Icon: Symbolism in the Indian Folk Religion', in *Religion and Society in Eastern India*, ed. G.C. Tripathi and H. Kulke, Delhi: Manohar, 1994 [1975].

Eschmann, A., H. Kulke and C.G. Tripathi, eds., *The Cult of Jagannath and the Regional Tradition of Orissa*, New Delhi: Manohar (South Asian Studies. 8), 1978.

Freeman, J., *Untouchable: An Indian Life History*, Delhi: Harper Collins, India, 1993 [1979].

Fürer-Haimendorf, C.V., 'Megalithic Ritual among the Gadabas and Bondos of Orissa', *Journal and Proceedings of the Asiatic Society of Bengal, Third Series*, vol. 9, 1943, pp. 149–78.

———, *The Gonds of Andhra Pradesh: Tradition and Change in an Indian Tribe*, New Delhi and Bombay: Vikas, 1979.

Gochhayat, A., 'Statehood Demands after Telengana: Politics of Agitation in the Koshal Region in Odisha', *Journal of Research in Humanities and Social Science*, vol. 1, no. 3, 2013, pp. 8–12.

Guzy, Lidia J., *Baba-s und Alekh-s. Askese und Ekstase einer Religion im Werden. Vergleichende Untersuchung der asketischen Tradition Mahima Dharma in zwei Distrikten Orissas (Dhenkanal und Koraput)/östliches Indien*, Berlin: Weißensee Verlag (Berliner Beiträge zur Ethnologie. 1), 2002.

Hardenberg, R., *Die Wiedergeburt der Götter. Ritual und Gesellschaft in Orissa*, Hamburg: Kovac, 1999.

————, *Die Ideologie eines Hindu-Königtums. Struktur und Bedeutung der Rituale des Königs von Puri' Orissa/Indien*, Berlin: Arabisches Buch (revised version published 2007 *König ohne Reich. Rituale eines Königtums in Orissa*, Schiler Verlag), 2000.

————, *Fierce People of the Mountains: Society, Ritual, and Cosmology of the Orissa Hills* (Habil), 2005.

Impey, H.B., 'Notes on Gurhjat State of Patna', *The Orissa Historical Research Journal*, vol. 2, no. 2, July 1958 [1863].

Kulke, H., ' "Juggernaut" under British Supremacy and the Resurgence of the Khurda Rajas as "Rajas of Puri"', in *The Cult of Jagannath and the Regional Tradition of Orissa*, ed. A. Eschmann, H. Kulke and G.C. Tripathi, Delhi: Manohar, 1978, pp. 345–58.

————, *Jagannātha-Kult und Gajapati-Königtum. Ein Beitrag zur Geschichte religiöser Legitimation hinduistischer Herrscher*, Wiesbaden: Franz Steiner, 1979.

————, *Kings and Cults: State Formation and Legitimation in India and Southeast Asia*, Delhi: Manohar, 1993.

Kulke, H. and B. Schnepel, eds., *Jagannath Revisited*, New Delhi: Manohar, 2001.

Kulke, H., N. Mohanty and D. Pathy, eds., *Imaging Orissa*, New Delhi: Prafulla, 2013.

Kulke, H. et al., eds., *State, Power and Violence*, Wiesbaden: Harassowitz, 2010.

Kulke, H. and G. Berkemer, eds., *Centres out there? Facets of Subregional Identities in Orissa*, Delhi: Manohar, 2011.

Mallebrein, C., 'Dantesvari, the Family Goddess (kulsvamini) of the Rajas of Bastar, and the Dasahara-Festival of Jagdalpur', in *Wild Goddesses in India and Nepal. Proceedings of an International Symposium Berne Zurich, November 1994*, ed. A. Michaels, C. Vogelsanger and A. Wilke, Bern, 1996, pp. 483–511.

Mallebrein, C. and H.V. Stietencron, *The Divine Play on Earth: Religious Aesthetics and Ritual in Orissa*, India and Heidelberg: Synchron Publishers, 2008.

Marglin, F.A., *Wives of the God-King: The Rituals of the Devadasis of Puri*, Delhi: Oxford University Press, 1989 [1985].

McDougal, C.W., 'The Social Structure of the Hill Juang', unpublished dissertation, The University of Mexiko; Ann Arbor: University Microfilms, 1963.

————, 'Juang Categories and Joking Relations', *Southwestern Journal of Anthropology*, vol. 20, 1964, pp. 319–45.

Mitra, S.K., 'Kashipur Revisited: Social Ritual, Electoral Politics and the State in India', in *Jagannath Revisited*, ed. H. Kulke and B. Schnepel, New Delhi: Manohar, 2001, pp. 333–62.

Mubayi, Y., *Altar of Power: The Temple and the State in the Land of Jagannatha*, Delhi: Manohar, 2005.

Nanda, C.P., 'Rethinking "Politico-Ritual States": Sitting on the Lap of a Bhuiyan: Coronation Ceremonies in Keonjhar', in *State, Power and Violence*, ed. H. Kulke et al., Wiesbaden: Harassowitz, 2010, pp. 725–44.

Nayak, P.K., *Blood, Women and Territory: An Analysis of Clan Feuds of Dongria Kondhs*, New Delhi: Reliance, 1989.

Niggemeyer, H., *Kuttia Kond. Dschungel-Bauern in Orissa*, München: Renner, 1964.

Oskarsson, P., The Law of the Land Contested: Bauxite Mining in Tribal, Central India in an Age of Economic Reform, 2010 <https://ueaeprints.uea.ac.uk/20537/1/Oskarsson_Law_of_the_Land_PhD_Thesis.pdf>, accessed on 5 September 2015.

Otten, T., *Heilung durch Rituale. Vom Umgang mit Krankheit bei den Rona im Hochland Orissas, Indien*. Inaugural-Dissertation, eingereicht an der Freien Universität Berlin. Veröffentlichung in der Serie *Indus*, Georg Pfeffer, Frank Heidemann und William Sax, eds., Münster, Berlin: LIT Verlag, 2006.

Otten, T. and U. Skoda, eds., *Dialogues with Gods: Possession in Middle Indian Rituals*, Berlin: Weissensee Verlag, 2014.

Padel, F., *The Sacrifice of Human Being: British Rule and the Konds of Orissa*, Delhi: Oxford University Press, 2001 [1996].

———, *Sacrificing People: Invasions of a Tribal Landscape*, Hyderabad: Orient BlackSwan, 2009.

Padel, F. and S. Das, *Out Of This Earth: East India Adivasis and the Aluminium Cartel*, Hyderabad: Orient BlackSwan, 2010.

Parkin, R., *The Munda of Central India: An Account of their Social Organization*, Delhi: Oxford University Press, 1992.

Pati, B., 'Identity, Hegemony, Resistance: Conversions in Orissa 1800-2000', in *Periphery and Centre: Studies in Orissan History, Religion and Anthropology*, ed. G. Pfeffer, Delhi: Manohar, 2007, pp. 417–42.

———, 'Interrogating Stereotypes: Exploring the Princely States in Colonial Orissa', in *Centres out there? Facets of Subregional Identities in Orissa*, ed. H. Kulke and G. Berkemer, Delhi: Manohar, 2011, pp. 327–46.

Pfeffer, G., 'Puri's Vedic Brahmins: Continuity and Change in their Traditional Institutions', in *The Cult of Jagannath and the Regional Tradition of Orissa*, ed. A. Eschmann, H. Kulke and G.C. Tripathi, Delhi: Manohar, 1978, pp. 421–38.

———, *Status and Affinity in Middle India*, Wiesbaden: Steiner (Beiträge zur Südasienforschung. 76), 1982.

———, *Hunters, Tribes, Peasants: Cultural Crisis and Comparison. Ambedkar Memorial Lectures*, Bhubaneswar: NISWASS, 2003.

———, ed., *Periphery and Centre: Studies in Orissan History, Religion and Anthropology*, Delhi: Manohar, 2007.

Pfeffer, G. and D.K. Behera, eds., *Contemporary Society: Tribal Studies*, vol. 5, New Delhi: Concept Publishing Company, 2002.

Price, P. and A.E. Ruud, eds., *Power and Influence in India: Bosses, Lords and Captains*, New Delhi: Routledge, 2010.

Richter, W.L., 'Traditional Rulers in Post-Traditional Societies: The Princes of India and Pakistan', in *People, Princes and Paramount Power*, ed. R. Jeffrey, Delhi: Oxford University Press, 1978, pp. 329–54.

Roesel, J., *Der Palast des Herrn der Welt. Entstehungsgeschichte und Organisation der indischen Tempel- and Pilgerstadt Puri*, München: Weltforum Verlag, 1980.

Roy, S.C., *The Mundas and their Country*, Calcutta: Kuntaline Press, 1912.

———, *The Oraons of Chota Nagpur*, Ranchi, 1915.

———, *The Hill Bhuiyas of Orissa*, Ranchi: Man in India Office, 1935.

Sahu, B.P., *Passages to India: Odisha as the Focus of Historical Interest*, Lecture presented to International Humboldt-Kolleg, 'Reviewing Indo-German Cultural Contacts in the 21st Century', Centre of German Studies, Jawaharlal Nehru University, New Delhi, 23–24 September 2013 (unpublished manuscript).

———, *Changing Gaze: Regions and the Construction of Early India*, Delhi: Oxford University Press, 2012.

Schnepel, B., *The Jungle Kings: Ethnohistorical Aspects of Politics and Ritual in Orissa*, Delhi: Manohar, 2002.

Seymour, S., 'The Harvard-Bhubaneswar, India Project', *Asian Man: An International Journal*, vol. 7, nos. 1–2, 2013, pp. 1–8.

———, ed., *The Transformation of a Sacred Town: Bhubaneswar, India*, Boulder: Westview Press, 1980.

Shutzer, M., 'The Practice of Custom in India's Recognition of Forest Right's Act: Case Studies from Kalahandi, Odisha', *Samaj*, vol. 7, 2013 (The Ethics of Self-Making in Postcolonial India), <https://samaj.revues.org/3623>, accessed on 5 September 2015.

Skoda, U., *The Aghria: A Peasant Caste on a Tribal Frontier*, Delhi: Manohar, 2005.

Stietencron, H.V., 'Early Temples of Jagannatha in Orissa: The Formative Phase', in *The Cult of Jagannath and the Regional Tradition of Orissa*, ed. A. Eschmann, H. Kulke and G.C. Tripathi, Delhi: Manohar, 1978, pp. 61–78.

———, 'The Advent of Visnuism in Orissa: An Outline of its History According to Archaeological and Epigraphical Sources from the Gupta Period up to 1135 AD', *The Cult of Jagannath and the Regional Tradition of Orissa*, ed. A. Eschmann, H. Kulke and G.C. Tripathi, Delhi: Manohar, 1978, pp. 1–30.

Strümpell, C., '"We Work Together, We Eat Together": Conviviality and Modernity in a Company Settlement in South Orissa', *Contributions to Indian Sociology*, n.s., vol. 42, no. 3, 2008, pp. 351–81.

Tripathi, G.C., 'On the Concept of Purusottama in the Agamas', in *The Cult of Jagannath and the Regional Tradition of Orissa*, ed. A. Eschmann, H. Kulke and G.C. Tripathi, Delhi: Manohar, 1978, pp. 31–60.

Vitebsky, P., *Dialogues with the Dead: The Discussion of Mortality among the Sora of Eastern India*, Cambridge: Cambridge University Press, 1993.

2 Survival, Interrogation and Contests
Tribal Resistance in Nineteenth-Century Odisha

BISWAMOY PATI

Historians working on the oppressed, normally overlook several aspects of resistance since they do not take into account diversities associated with both social history and resistance. Colonial Odisha's history is no exception and in fact upper caste hegemony, combined with an utter insensitivity and the 'Otherisation' of the non-coastal tract has reinforced this in a significant manner. In fact, it would not be irrelevant to mention here that the culture of resistance of the tribals in the hills of western Odisha remains invisibilized unless one is particular about situating it within the paradigms of social history. At the same time, resistance can never be located mono-dimensionally since it is an interactive process. It is here that historians have to grasp several intricate and interrelated components connected to what one might call the social history of resistance.

The suddenness related to the changes that colonialism enforced on the region over the nineteenth century provided the contextual setting of this vital dimension. The introduction of private property in land reinforced the position of those who owned land (viz., the princes and *zamindars*) vis-à-vis the marginal sections of the tribals and led to the polarization of caste / class relations. Alongside, it meant the rise of a host of features associated with a rapid process of social differentiation; the rise of 'internal' exploiters (viz., the moneylenders along with the princes and the *zamindars*); land displacements; the loss of forest and water resources; the 'meriah' wars against the Kandhas in the hills (that were very much like the search for the proverbially non-existent Weapons of Mass Destruction in Iraq); the criminalization of tribes; and the emergence of a 'monster' in the form of the market, etc.

Some other features need to be delineated about this chapter. One needs to perhaps underline the level of fluidities when it comes to differentiating between the tribals and the outcastes (or untouchables).

Moreover, the effort to demarcate the three components related to (1) survival strategies, (2) interrogations, and (3) contestations of the tribals that are highlighted form a part of an exercise to locate the culture of resistance holistically over the period of 1840s and 1890s.

Survival Strategies

As far as the tribals were concerned, shifting cultivation was one of the major components that emerged as a response to this context. At the same time, historians like David Ludden (1994) are strikingly silent about this method of cultivation.

While talking about tribals one of the standard assumption seems to trace them as 'ancient people'—the 'original inhabitants'—residing in the forests and mountains, who loved this method of cultivation. Besides marking the triumph of colonial anthropology, such positions tend to stereotype a large section of the people who not only lost their lands but were at different points of time pushed into the forested/mountainous interior. Given the complexity of the context we have outlined, it is in fact quite usual to come across references to a fractured tribal reality. Thus, in the case of Kalahandi we come across references to two chief categories of tribals—those living in the open country who were called Kotchriah Kandhas and the Pahariah or Dongariah (viz., *pahar* = hill; *dongar* = shifting cultivation) Kandhas. In fact, the colonial establishment clearly admired the Kotchriah Kandhas (Senapati and Kuanr 1980: 473). Similarly, in Mayurbhanj we are told about two classes of people—the Deslog comprising Santals, Bhumijs, Kols and Hos and the Hatuas, which included Hindu Goalas, Chasas and Mahantis (Senapati and Sahu 1967: 75). Severe problems and pressures saw a large section of the tribals taking up shifting cultivation. This was adopted not because it was 'dear to their heart' as felt by colonial officials (Ramdhyani 1942: 109) but because they had lost control over the tracts they had cleared due to their large-scale desertions and displacements, and also because there was no other alternative. New ideas and concepts were invented to negotiate the changed situation. Thus, one comes across the Kandhas of the Jeypur *zamindari* who had most probably started using either hoes or wooden ploughs to loosen the soil and sow the seeds in this context. Perhaps they had invented oral traditions to justify this. As expressed, the use of the iron plough was discouraged since it would hurt 'mother earth' (Pati 1990: 986–8). Interestingly, on being told time and again to stop Meriah sacrifice by Campbell, the Kandha leaders had responded by saying that they 'were not beasts' (Brandstadter 1985: 179). In fact, given the context, it is highly possible that some of them adopted shifting cultivation as a protest for being labelled in this manner.

Shifting cultivation witnessed the beginnings of a shift away from rice production, even though different varieties of rice were grown by the Kandhas (Campbell 1861: 244; and MacPherson 1842: 49). After all, clearing the forests for cultivation, the problem of cultivating on hilltops and water constraints led to a greater dependence on dry crops like *mandia* (millet), *ragi*, *kotkee*, etc. Alongside, what is essential to grasp here is that the shifting cultivator's diet also began to shift—from one that was based on rice, to dry crops. This also implied drinking *mohwa* that was distilled from the *mohwa* tree instead of *handia* that was made from rice and which was their common drink (Campbell 1861: 19). Thus, one observes a shift in the dietary pattern as well. Hence, what needs to be emphasized is that like shifting cultivation their food habits changed in response to forces which were largely external to their existence, and over which they had very little control. And, in this sense, their re-orientation to these changes needs to be perhaps seen as a part of their survival strategy that epitomized resistance.

In fact, resistance needs to be perhaps located in the very act of practising *podu*, *dongar*, *kumri* and *jhum*. Interestingly, the tribals encountered two contradictory features—one that sought to enforce a tax on shifting cultivators in areas that were not surveyed and as a result was not clearly defined (and had to be calculated on the number of hoes or ploughs owned) and the other that saw efforts to prevent and discourage it. This created the suspicion that taxes would be enforced anytime. It was this component that perhaps determined the way tribals wanted to remain in isolation and felt insecure about the construction of roads. Thus, in 1865 some Kandhas of Parliakhemedi feared that 'this was the first step towards introducing an assessment on their lands' (23 December 1865, File no. 1344 G/2, Odisha State Archives, Bhubaneswar, hereafter OSA) and in 1872 some of them 'carelessly allowed two Government wooden bridges to be burnt' when 'firing the jungles' (6 January 1876, File no. 1845 G/7, OSA). This 'carelessness' is difficult to accept; incidentally the bridge was re-built by them. This preference for living in isolation perhaps also explains the possible reluctance of the Sauras to work on a regular basis in order to make them work on roads in order to gain access to the forests (6 January 1876, File no. 1845 G/15, OSA).

On occasions the response of the tribal folk provides fascinating forms of subversion, wherein components drawn from the colonial administrative system were almost turned upside down. Thus, an argument that justified such action worked on the strategy that some tribals located themselves as 'independent'. In fact, as late as 1877, colonial administrative reports mentioned how the Kandhas did not owe allegiance to any rajahs (Anon 1877: 29). Some others preferred to occasionally offer vegetables to the chiefs or touring officials (Campbell 1861: 254), perhaps as bribes to avoid assessments. Consequently, these features were intimately involved with the survival strategies of the tribals that were aimed at retaining the access to the forests and also to resist the effort to assess and tax the shifting cultivators.

At the same time, some tribals like the Sauras in the Parliakhemedi hill tracts were allowed to continue with *kumri* and cut timber for domestic and agricultural purposes in order to avoid the development of any discontent among them (24 November 1881, Judicial Department, Accession no. 1434 G/9, OSA). Moreover, on occasions the idea of taxing shifting cultivators was dropped. Thus, the proposal to tax the Khaira tribals of Mayurbhanj (in 1899), who carried out shifting cultivation 'extensively', was dropped by the chief as it would 'cause dissatisfaction among' the Khairas (*Report on the Tributary Mahals of Orissa, 1899–1900*, 1900: 14; *Report on the Tributary Mahals, 1900–1901*, 1901: 12).

The survival strategies also saw the phenomenon of shifting identities. We have already mentioned the implication of the agrarian settlements. Thus, these agrarian settlements polarized the class/caste system, with the poorer sections of the tribals emerging as agricultural labourers. These features created the space for shifts and changes leading to religious conversion to Brahminical Hinduism, with the affluent sections getting themselves incorporated within the brahminical order and the poorer sections emerging as tribal agricultural labourers or as outcastes (Pati 2003).

One should refer to the importance—the relevance as well as the limitations—of the concepts of Sanskritization and Hinduization while dealing with conversions. Sanskritization was a route through which low castes were able to rise—over one or two generations—to a higher position in the hierarchy by adopting vegetarianism and teetotalism, and by Sanskritizing their ritual and pantheon. One can agree with this as long as it accepts that such shifts were linked to some degree of upward economic movement and is not seen as a mono-dimensional, non-interactive process. Thus, as argued this was possible, especially for those in the middle regions of the hierarchy (Srinivas 1952: 30). This perhaps implies some degree of affluence that needs to be stressed. I would like to refer here to the 'diffusion model' (Weber 1967: 30–31). The basic problem with this 'model' is that it locates this as a one-way process, involving the Hinduization of tribal beliefs.

Another problem inherent in this formulation is that it does not see the level of violence inflicted on the tribals and their ideas. In fact, even sensitive socio-anthropological studies sometimes categorically assert that Hindu civilization did not on the whole seek to convert or displace tribals, although they agree that conflicts were frequent, and tribes were forced to retreat to the 'remotest areas', viz., the forests and mountains (Padel 1995: 17). Taken together, these contradict the 'civilizational' claims of Hinduism. This right-wing position veils the basic components of terror and violence directed against the Adivasis and outcastes by Brahminical Hinduism. In fact, if anything, the opposite seems to be the case. A very superficial survey of some of the available land settlement *Reports* of the Temporarily Settled Areas of Cuttack, Puri and Balasore, the princely states and some of the major *zamindaris* illustrates the rather serious fall-out of the agrarian interventions and the expansion of cultivation, especially the way they polarized social relations (Pati 1993: Chapter 1). These had a bearing on the conversions since the land settlements entailed a set of complex negotiations with the tribals. The specificities of the context are perhaps reflected in the way the Ranas of Jeypore wore the 'sacred thread' and believed that they had bought the right to do so from the Maharaja of Jeypore (Senapati and Sahu 1966: 110). What deserves emphasis is the significance of this language of exchange that was applied to the sacred realm. We also witness the Gonds of Sambalpur inventing new legends to relocate themselves within the framework of Brahminical Hinduism, and the Gond *zamindars* wearing the 'sacred thread' (O'Malley 1932: 70; Senapati and Mohanty 1971: 117). Here one can also mention the Kandhas of Ranpur state who preferred to be identified as 'Oriya Kandhas', that indicates an allied component of the process—Oriyaization (Singh 1963: 10). These practices not only implied a degree of Hinduization, but also a strategy to cope with the shifts and changes by getting incorporated into the brahminical order.

The relatively affluent Adivasis claimed Khandayat—the Oriya variant of Kshatriya—status. Khanda means a sword and Khandayat means sword-wielding. In fact, this caste accommodated a wide variety of the prosperous section of tribals as well. Thus, one witnesses, a level of Rajputization/Kshatriyaization/Oriyaization that converged with Hinduization, and affected the affluent sections of the tribals. Leading anthropologists like Bailey also see the Oriyas as migrants to the Kandha hills. As he puts it, in the 1950s, Oriyas were about three in every eight of the population, and he feels that they were probably fewer at the beginning of the century (Bailey 1996: 3). Although the question of Oriya migrants cannot be disputed, he cannot conceptualize of their emergence from among the Kandhas itself. Thus, the hillman/plainsman dichotomy is a feature haunting even sensitive scholars like him. What needs to be also grasped is a complexity where 'Oriyas'—besides being migrants— emerged from among the Adivasis in the pre-colonial and colonial period, as we have sought to demonstrate. Thus, castes like the Warrior caste that he refers to (Paikas or Khandayats) also emerged from among the Kandhas and other Adivasi groups. This in fact illustrates the process of conversions of Adivasis via Hinduization/Kshatriyaization/Oriyaization, and his reference to the Oriyas should also be seen as an extension of this process that was perhaps 'happening' even while Bailey was doing his field work in the area. Some of the references in the *Census Reports* offer clues to understand this process. For example, the first *Census* (1871–2) mentions the presence of 'numerous' Savaras in the Cuttack and Puri tract (Beverley 1872: 191) though this was not the case in the 1930s and 1940s. One also sees a very large increase of the Khandayat population—45.4 per cent (the largest for any caste)—between 1901 and 1931 in the Odisha Division and the Odisha States (Lacey 1933: 267). At the same time, a decline of the population of the Saoras (Savaras –4,807) and the Jatapu (–37,961) in the Jeypur *zamindari* between 1931 and 1941 is noticeable, although there is no serious reason to explain this. Thus, over the 1931–41 decade the Saora population went down from 57,325 to 52,518 and that of the Jatapu from 53,134 to 15,173 (Bell 1942: 26–7). One needs to grasp here that a large number of tribals identified themselves as Khandayats. Consequently, the connection between a decline of the tribal population and the phenomenal increase of the Khandayat caste should be borne in mind while discussing the process of conversions.

Given this scenario, the conversions of the tribals was the result of a very complex, dialectical process, with tribal society itself negotiating the new context as a strategy to cope with changes and the shifts over the nineteenth century. For the affluent tribals it implied getting incorporated as Khandayats/Kshatriyas. This illustrates a level of continuity from the pre-colonial period (Sahu 1985: 180–92). However, from the point of view of the poorer sections it meant getting linked to the agricultural process as agricultural labourers or being classified as 'criminal' tribes or castes. The magnitude of this process is difficult to fathom unless one also keeps in mind the decimation of large sections of the tribal folk—owing to the conflicts with the colonialist and his feudal collaborators—over the nineteenth century. Consequently, the process of Hinduization was far from being a mono-dimensional, non-interactive process. It saw the tribals converting and/or getting incorporated into Hinduism as a survival strategy vis-à-vis their adversaries: the Brahminical order, the internal exploiting classes and colonialism.

A somewhat related feature was the shift to Christianity, although it attracted very few tribals given its close association with colonialism that had spelt doom for them over the first six decades of the nineteenth century. We get references to the curious Sarrea (viz., Sauras/Savaras) tribals of Ganjam asking Amos Sutton in 1826 if adopting Christianity would make any difference vis-à-vis Brahminism (Sutton 1833: 130). In a context of uncertainties and insecurities, some Oraons who converted to Christianity felt that it protected them from the witches and *bhoots*, who were powerless against this system (Dalton 1872: 247). These are metaphors that illustrate the anxieties that Brahminical Hinduism and its allied process of exploitation generated among the tribals, which to a certain extent explain the conversions to Christianity in the latter half of the nineteenth century.

The survival strategies of the tribals also saw the invention of new gods. Thus, the Sauras invented Sahibosum and his consort. Interestingly, Sahibosum, their god who was a touring official, possibly a forest guard or a policeman, carried cholera with him. It is highly possible that it also included the white man. The Sauras carved wooden images in his honour and placed them at the outskirts of their villages to keep him out, or at least divert his attention. Not only was he worshipped but also offered sacrifices since it was considered essential to keep him happy and keep cholera—and metaphorically also Sahibosum—out of their lives (Elwin 1955: 180–1, 490, 510). Most probably Sahibosum also included the white man. Here one cannot miss the association of cholera with the colonial inroads and the fears and insecurities that the latter generated.

Interrogation

At the same time, one does come across serious ways of questioning, interrogating and critiquing the internal order of exploitation. These were not based on direct confrontations and conflicts, but were marked by efforts to delegitimize Brahminical Hinduism and to draw upon features of colonial modernity. Here we can refer to the Mahima movement, the origins of which can be traced to mid-nineteenth century Odisha. Most scholars who have worked on the Mahima movement focus exclusively on its religious angle (Eschmann 1978: 375–410; Banerjee-Dube 1999: 98–125; Banerjee-Dube 2007; and Banerjee-Dube and Beltz 2008) and rarely on its complexities (Pati 2010b: 43–52). The Movement challenged the dominance of caste and the system of inequality it imposed on society and by the 1870s it had assumed the shape of a powerful Movement.

The immediate background of the Mahima movement was provided by the 'Naanka Durbikhya' or the Famine of 1866, which was a major milestone in colonial Odisha's history. On the basis of official reports scholars project that it wiped out between one-fourth and one-third of the population of the coastal tract of Cuttack, Puri and Balasore. Unfortunately, there is no available estimate about the manner in which the Famine affected the western interior, especially the twenty-six princely states. The Famine led to serious dislocations and the rigidifying of caste norms that were reflected in the Movement. It marked a social protest against the order/hierarchy of caste and represented an anti-order that sought to de-legitimize the rajas and the Brahmins. Its contestatory element invoked Mahima and Alekh—which also means unwritten, or oral. While inventing 'His' timeless existence that aimed to de-legitimize Brahminical Hinduism, it negotiated the present with an alternative order that included features which were born out of the interactions with other pre-colonial dissenting traditions and diverse religious systems. Along with these, the imprints of the colonial context, especially the point about colonial modernity, should be borne in mind while discussing the Movement.

The intellectual background of the Mahima movement had wide-ranging features. Thus, it included pre-colonial movements of dissent and protest that were primarily concentrated around the coastal tract. This can be traced back to Sarala Dasa, who lived in the second half of the fifteenth century and the Panchasakhas—'five friends'—the Sudramunis, who became famous in the first quarter of the sixteenth century. The rebellious tradition associated with them had advocated a crusade against the system that created hierarchies of people on the basis of their birth; idolatry; rituals; the mediators between humans and God; and stressed both monotheism and *bhakti* (Mallik 2004). Traces of Buddhism and Islam, as well as Vaishnavism left their imprints on the world-views of this pre-colonial movement of social protest. It is indeed amusing to see scholars almost wishing away the possibilities of any interaction between Brahminical Hinduism and Islam, especially Islam influencing the former. The argument here is that unlike the earlier phase that witnessed assimilation, the fallout in the case of 'Islamized invaders' of the eleventh and twelfth centuries witnessed attempts to codify what is identified as a 'Hindu way of Life' (Pollock 2006: 153–208). The Bhakti, or the Sant movement, with its stress on monotheism, can be cited here to contradict this position (Habib 1993: 77–88; Habib 2007: 133–57). Alongside, efforts to compartmentalize interactional possibilities and syncretism is methodologically unsustainable. Thus, as projected, the fifth and the sixth periods of Hinduism, viz., 1100–1850 and post-1850, respectively—that were characterized by syncretism,viz., Islamic/Hindu and then Christian/ Hindu, respectively (Wessler 2008: 76). Besides being a classic example of looking at history and society 'from above', such a formulation rules out the possibilities for interactions and syncretism between Brahminical Hinduism, Islam and Christianity which, as will be seen, is visible in the case of the Mahima movement in the context of the post-1850s, which as discussed earlier, falls under the so-called 'sixth period' of Hinduism.

One can also mention the way Christianity and missionary activities introduced a discourse of 'equality' and humanism in colonial Odisha. When it comes to the Mahima movement, what normally goes unnoticed is the effort made to draw upon the pre-colonial rebellious tradition and synthesize it with new features that came in with the process of colonialism. In fact, the Mahima movement marked an attempt to invent a discourse of equality—absent in indigenous society and Christianity— and humanism in order to build a rebellion of the poor tribals and outcastes. This was sought to be achieved through an interrogation of exploitation, inequalities and suffering that haunted these marginal sections. The magnitude of the Movement was widely felt in the region. And, unlike the pre-colonial movements of social protest, the impact generated by it was felt both in the coastal tract as well as the western 'interior'. This latter aspect assumes significance since the footprints of regional diversities clearly marked the Movement. The Mahima movement seems to have attracted the attention of the urban world of colonial Odisha as early as 1867. It was shocked by the reports of the Movement having attracted as many as 20,000 to 30,000 followers (*Utkala Dipika*, 1 June 1867). We are told about 'the propagation of a new religion in some of the princely states adjoining Cuttack'. Fears and insecurities expressed were associated about the rapid development of this religious system and it was hoped that the government took the appropriate steps to abolish it or else the people of Odisha would abandon their *gehastha dharma* (*Utkala Dipika*, 20 August 1871). We are told about the response of the Commissioner, Orissa, who took steps to see that the administration was vigilant about these people (*Utkala Dipika*, 26 August 1871) [translations mine].

A very vital component of the Movement included its stress on the 'Creator of the Universe' who was Alekh (which literally means unwritten) or Mahima, viz., glorious which delineate certain characteristics of its rather complex cosmology. Alekh or Mahima was the 'supreme being', who was 'timeless', 'formless', 'omnipresent' and 'omniscient'. The Movement stressed monotheism and clearly rejected caste and idol worship, as well as the rituals associated with Brahminical Hinduism. It also stressed *bhakti* and devotion, and denied the need for any intermediary between the 'supreme being' and human beings in the form of the Brahmins or the priestly section. The primary targets in areas like Jajpur were the kings and Brahmins, viz., priests. This co-existed harmoniously with upper castes like Brahmins and Karanas, along with Hadis (outcastes), joining the Movement (*Utkala Dipika*, 6 September 1873). And, going by a report of the *tahsildar* of Angul, the Movement aided the colonial administration when it came to negotiating with the Panas, who were regarded as 'hard core criminals'. In fact, we are told that the *tahsildar* initiated them into 'Alekhism', after which they gave up their 'criminal' past (*Utkala Dipika*, 19 November 1881). This led to the effort to incorporate Panas as a part of a major drive of the colonial establishment in Angul, a plan to start a Pana settlement at Angul and giving the Panas 'good' lands and loans, which would be written off (Clarke 1907 [1985]). A lot of importance seems to have been attached to common feasting, and the Movement advocated a rather simplified logic of marriage, with the bride garlanding the bridegroom, and the gathering of relatives and friends loudly calling out to 'Alekh' to bless them (Proceedings of the Asiatic Society, January 1882; Laeequddin 1937: 120–1).

What needs emphasis is the importance attached to the oral—not the textual or the scriptural—that transcended the logic of time and space. And, if seen along with the importance attached to some of the attributes of the 'supreme being', viz., especially the 'time-less' and 'form-less' component—one can see this as a strategy aimed to de-legitimize Brahminical Hinduism. The stress on monotheism and *bhakti*, and the emphasis on obliterating any intermediaries between 'Him' and human beings also formed a part of this drive. Similarly a lot of importance was attached to the deletion of memory related to one's past. Thus, the newly initiated were expected to forget their 'past'. This was a strategy that aimed to transcend the *varna* order which had been exposed to extreme dislocations in the context of the Famine, that has been mentioned earlier. Consequently, it created the basis of a new beginning, independent of one's social origins—vital elements that determined one's social position as per the logic of the *varna* system.

What is surprising is the way in which scholars working on this Movement have failed to see its broader linkages and associations. Thus the tribal and outcaste/low caste affinities and linkages get obliterated in attempts that tend to Hinduize colonial movements of dissent and protest. Along with this, the idea of prostrating to Alekh seven times in the morning and five times in the evening probably suggests the influence of and interactions with Islam. It is indeed amazing that most scholars working on colonial Odisha wish away any possibility of interactions between Brahminical Hinduism and Islam. They seem to be particularly amnesic about Salabega (a household name in many parts of coastal Odisha even today) who, we are told, lived in the first half of the seventeenth century and was a 'great devotee' of Jagannatha. Interestingly, the Movement did not prohibit any food except the flesh of domesticated animals. Even the *sanyasis* could take dried fish—a typical plebeian diet in Odisha—as well as meat and wild animals. And, although efforts are made to locate meat-eating as a feature that developed at a later phase, it is most likely that, given its social base, this was a rather normal part of the diet of the followers of the Movement (Kar 2006: 40). Again, coming to the spread of the Movement and the monastic order one observes imprints of Christian missionaries and their activities in colonial Odisha. Here we can cite the missionary zeal through which the Movement was propagated and spread. It included a network of *tungis* (viz., outposts). It also incorporated the concepts of 'sin' and 'confession', with the *sanyasis* confessing to the chief patriarch.

The person who popularized the Movement was Bhima Bhoi. Bhima was a blind Kandha (Adivasi), who was most probably from the princely state of Sonepur. He seems to have been exposed to the Movement in 1862, after which he accepted its principles and became associated with its propagation. His association with the Movement shocked the upper castes, especially since he is reported to have about four or five consorts and two children. A set of counter myths seem to have emerged to counter this image that has been studied by scholars (Beltz and Mishra 2008: 132–57). Of course, it is rather clear that the Movement attracted a large following of women.

Bhima's basic postulates marked a crusade against the *varna* system with the aim of de-legitimizing it. After all, this was the only way of getting some space for the poor tribals and Sudras. Besides, the interaction with bourgeois-humanism and Christianity is visible in a *boli* where he articulates:

Boundless is the anguish and misery of the living,
Who can see and tolerate it
Let my soul be condemned to Hell,
But let the Universe be redeemed.

> (Mahapatra 1983: 1; I have slightly modified the translation).

Nevertheless, the interactions with Brahminical Hinduism, especially after the Movement began to draw upon the support of the princes and tended to get institutionalized, did affect it. One can most certainly highlight features like the 'Otherising' of the Washerfolk (Dhobis) and Barbers (Bhandaris) to prove this point. And, if seen along with its ambiguity vis-à-vis colonialism, one can easily grasp how these together contributed significantly towards compromising its contestatory potentialities.

Contests

The method of resisting their adversaries through direct confrontations was not an easy option for the mass of the tribals, who faced decimation under colonial rule. Besides the differing patterns of resistance, there is an observable shift when it comes to the identification of their enemies. Thus, from confrontations with colonialism in the early years that reached a climax in the hills of western Odisha in the 1850s, one witnesses a shift as one proceeds to the latter half of the nineteenth century. Thus, we observe struggles directed against both colonialism and its associates, viz., the internal exploiters (the princes, *zamindars* and moneylenders). These efforts ranged from those supposedly inspired by insurgents like Chakra Bisoi—that omnipresent rebel, who seems to have been 'present' at most sites of popular rebellions by the colonial establishment during the first half of the nineteenth century and the rebellion in the hills during the turbulent years, 1857–60—to some of the major tribal rebellions like the Kalahandi uprising of the Kandhas (1882) and the Keonjhar *melis* (1868 and 1891–92).

A major point of confrontation was the 'civilising mission's' barbaric assaults that were directed to prevent the so-called the *meriah* (human) sacrifice—a point that has been seriously contested by present-day anthropologists (Pfeffer 2006: 347–64). The discovery of 'anti-British' plots, including one at Patana, that aimed at 'erasing all traces of Europeans in India', led to the terror campaigns of colonialism in the hills of western Odisha (Foreign Department, 28 February 1846, nos. 24–25: National Archives of India, hereafter NAI). These 'plunderings' (as they were described in colonial discourse) saw the 'the terrible power of the Agency under whose direct sanction and direct order numerous villages were burnt, and toddy producing palm trees . . . cut down; heads of cattle were considered public prize; and private property, clothes and ornaments were rudely seized upon and taken away.' As reported, these 'barbarous and savage acts' had 'ruined many tribes'. These ruthless blows (both in the hills and the plains) made the people and the chiefs—whether *zamindars*, rajahs or mullickos, viz., malliks or the propertied sections, loose 'all confidence in the good faith of the servants and agents of [the] Government' (Foreign Department/Political Branch, 31 December 1847, no. 798: NAI; Foreign Department/Political Proceedings, 31 December 1847, nos. 862 and 866: NAI). The available evidence also perhaps indicates the closeness of Chakra and the rebels to some of the princely states like Angul and Sambalpur (Foreign Department/Political Branch, 31 December 1847, no. 799: NAI; Foreign Department/Political Branch, 30 December 1848, no. 251: NAI; Foreign Department/Political Branch, 31 December 1847, no. 799: NAI; and Foreign Department/Political Branch, 30 December 1848, no. 251: NAI).

Colonialism's wars, labelled as 'counter offensive' measures that aimed to justify these brutal actions, saw Chakra's hand behind most of them. One can cite here a typical example. The village Chokapand, in Boad, had seen a raid earlier that had been supposedly led by Chakra. After driving the rebels back into the hills, these 'active operations', were followed up by the destruction of the villages, *pootoos*, and fruit trees at Solagorah and Ghati Khole (two of the 'chief strongholds' of the enemy below the ghats). These were followed by similar 'actions' at Bengrekai that destroyed the Naksar Khonros village and *pootoos* most probably stored stocks of grain (Foreign Department/Political Branch, 31 December 1847, no. 798, NAI).

The anxiety generated by Chakra saw measures being taken for his 'apprehension'. This included a reward of Rs.3,000 that was kept on his head, since it was felt that 'as long as he is at large his name will be used by every plunderer' (Foreign Department/Political Branch, 30 December 1848, no. 251: NAI; Foreign Department/Political Branch, 31 December 1847, no. 799: NAI). In fact, the references to Chakra being behind most acts of tribal insurgency, justify such fears. Equally striking is a reference to Chakra's 'habit of instigating . . . people [especially the Khonds of Daspallah] to rebel by means of letters' which were collected by the colonial administration (Foreign Department/Political Branch, 31 December 1847, no. 799: NAI). This sounds strange if we keep in mind his predominantly tribal following.

The Kandhas had not forgiven the Agent, Macneill, who had arrested Rendo Majhi, the head of the Borikiya Kandhas and kept him at Russelkonda for his so-called complicity in the *mariah* sacrifice. During Macneill's tour of Kalahandi in December 1855, he decided to tie Rendo Majhi and take him around in order to warn the Kandhas. The latter retaliated, and, were joined by the Kuttia Kandhas. The legendary Chakra

Bisoi seems to have become a major symbol of this rebellion. The Agent was cornered by the rebels and had to be rescued by Dinabandhu Patnaik, the Kandha Mahal tahsildar (Mahtab vol. 2, 1957: 59).

These features perhaps explain the development of a broad social base for a major popular struggle against colonial power in the hills of western Odisha during the 1857 Rebellion. Sambalpur, which had been taken over from the Marathas by the British in 1826, was unquestionably the centre of this upsurge. Surendra Sahai, who had been a claimant for the throne of Sambalpur, his brother Udwant Sahai and his uncle Balaram Singh had been removed from Sambalpur by the colonial administration and kept in the Hazaribagh jail since 1840 (Pati 2010a: 46–62).

The English East India Company's direct involvement in Sambalpur can be traced to 1849, when the Political Agent of the Chotanagpur Agency took it over under the provisions of Dalhousie's 'doctrine of Lapse' (Ramusack 2004: 81–4; Bandyopadhyay 2004: 60, 172). The initial policies adopted by the British who took Sambalpur involved a systematic increase in the land revenue demands through two land revenue settlements. Thus, the 1849 Settlement increased the revenue demand by a quarter without taking into account the financial capabilities of the villages and struck off privileged tenures, including religious grants. Those who held rent-free villages were assessed at half rates, without any consideration with regard to the time for which the grant had been held. The 1854 Settlement further raised the revenue demands. This created a great deal of dissatisfaction and anger among a large section of the people—including powerful *zamindars* such as the chief of Kolabira or Jaipur, some tribal chiefs and Brahmins who held privileged tenures—which exploded during 1857 (O'Malley 1932: 34).

The beginnings of the Rebellion in the Sambalpur tract can be traced to a spell of rumours following the news of the Hazaribagh jail break. Some of the Hazaribagh sepoys marched towards Palamau to meet Kuer Singh and their parent body—the Dinapore army. Surendra Sahai decided to march to Sambalpur, and a contingent of 'mutineers' led by him advanced towards Sambalpur amidst rumours of 'insurrectionary' movements (O'Malley 1932: 35–6). Very soon after this there was large-scale guerrilla warfare that saw the participation of the Gond and Binjhal tribals. The tribal folk fought against the colonial forces rather effectively. In fact, this popular struggle attracted rebels from distant parts to join in. What seems significant is the selectivity of the targets of the insurgents which included the colonial troops and even doctors. At the same time, the sepoys captured by the insurgents were released without injury, after being deprived of their horses, arms, accoutrements and baggage.

Colonial power seems to have been thrown out of gear in the tract. In fact, we are told of 'bodies of men' committing excesses in different parts of the district. Alongside, the traffic and postal communication link with Cuttack was left 'suspended'. Besides, a serious effort seems to have been made to prevent the movement of colonial forces by blocking roads with branches of trees.

The anxiety caused by the rebels is indicated by the terror struck through the destruction of villages and the hanging of people suspected to be sympathetic to the rebels. We get references to the organization of 'sorties' to fight the rebel forces. Ironically, counter-insurgency operations such as these further alienated the tribals and outcastes from the colonial order. Interestingly, rumours circulating in the tract reflected efforts by the rebels to demoralize and divert the attention of their adversaries. According to one such rumour, the Raja of Bamra had been made a prisoner by Sahai and his men when he had gone to meet one of his *zamindars*.

In their desperation, the British announced a reward of Rs.1,000 for capturing Surendra Sahai. Some of the chiefs who had remained 'loyal' to the British, like the Rajas of Bamra, Baud, Kalahandi, Keonjhar, Mayurbhanj, Rairakhol, Sareikella, Sonepur, the propertied sections, viz., the *zamindars* of Sambalpur and of Borasambar, and upper castes like Brahmins were rewarded. Besides, the efforts to counter the Rebellion also included getting together and warning the chiefs and *zamindars* to ensure that the rebels did not get any supplies and help in their territories, and capturing and confiscating the estates of 'insurgent zamindars'. Alongside, a series of attacks were made to 'hunt down' rebels, during which a conscious policy was formulated to seize their provisions. Besides requisitioning a sizeable number of troops for the purpose, the British were provided help in the form of contingents of local rajas, who were 'anxious' and willing to support the 'restoration of peace and order'.

The social base of the 1857 Rebellion in Odisha was predominantly tribal—which also explains the presence of women—and included some Ramgurh sepoys, who were with Surendra Sahai. It also included the fisher folk, viz., Keotas and milkmen, viz., Gwalas, along with upper castes like Rajputs. In fact, the involvement of the sepoys with the local tribal population perhaps explains the success of the guerrilla strikes launched by the rebels and why the Rebellion survived in the hills, even after being targeted by major colonial offensives. The 1857 Rebellion continued unabated for a long time but had faded out by the time Sahai was arrested in 1864 (O'Malley 1932: 36–40; Accession no. 1535G: OSA; Foreign Department SC nos. 101–2, 30 October 1857: NAI; Foreign

Department/Political Proceedings, nos. 39–42 FC, 5 November 1858: NAI; Home Department/Public Branch, nos. 105–8, 12 March 1858: NAI; Home Department/Public Branch, nos. 35–37, 9 July 1858: NAI; Judicial Proceedings 298, 17 December 1857: NAI; Judicial Proceedings 147, 11 March 1858; and Judicial Department Proceedings 250–1, 17 June 1858: West Bengal State Archives [hereafter WBSA]; Mutiny Collection 195729 and 197590: India Office Library London; Judicial Department Proceedings 157, 8 April 1858: WBSA; and Home Department/Public A Branch, nos. 24–26, 20 March 1860: NAI).

Moving on, the devastating Famine of 1866 also impacted the princely state of Odisha. This is a theme that is yet to attract serious scholarship. Nevertheless, the available sources indicate that it caused a lot of resentment in two Odishan states—Mayurbhanj and Keonjhar. Thus, the Famine led to a crisis situation among the tribals in the Bamanghati area of Mayurbhanj. The process of displacement that had originated with the 'removal' of the Dharooa tribals, was reinforced through the Deslog, comprising Santals, Bhumijs, Kols and the Hos, being displaced from their villages by the Hatuas, which included the Hindu Goalas, Chasas and Mahantis (Senapati and Sahu 1967: 75). The scanty rainfall in both 1865 and 1866, and the high rates of rent (following the land settlement) caused a lot of hardship to the tribals, including deaths resulting due to the Famine. This led to the tribals 'looting' foodstuff and grain from the well-to-do *hatua* raiyats (*Final Report on the Settlement of the Bamanaghati Subdivision for the Year 1902 to 1906:* ? 62).

It was in this context that Keonjhar witnessed a *meli* in 1868, conventionally referred to as the Ratana *meli*—named after its leader Ratana, a Bhuyan chief, who took up the grievances of the tribals. The uprising seems to be based on palace politics related to the question of succession. However, what needs emphasis is the unbearable exploitative practices that was reinforced by the unresolved popular anger displayed during the 1857 Rebellion, which precipitated the *meli* (Mahtab vol. 2, 1957: 102–5).

The sequence of events outlined in the colonial reports refer to the burning of the Bewurta's, viz., supervisor—a state official's house along with the Santhorapore Sasana, viz., *sasana* = Brahmin settlement on 21 April 1868. This coexisted with 'riotous assemblage' at Fota Tangpur over 21 April and 1 May. The rebels 'plundered' Keonjhargarh and abducted the Bewarta, Chunder Seekar Mahapatur to the hills (1 May). After this we are told about 'dacoities' in Batoong (4 May), Tarah (5 May) and Gorah. Specific targets mentioned included Urjoon Paikra (6 May) and Puthanee Mishra (31 May)—viz., non-tribals; Paikra was most probably a Khandayat (viz., the Odia version of a Kshatriya; his surname was derived from Paika); and Mishra was a Brahmin. In fact, the latter was abducted (31 May) and murdered (1 June). So were Goora Gooalla (Cowherd caste; 15 May) and Nursing Panda (Brahmin) who were abducted and murdered (16 July). Some state officials, like Godei Singh (who was the Raja's *burkandaz*), were 'wrongful[ly] confined' (6 June). Three people including a village headman (Gora Purdhan), a village official (*peada*; Nursing Pattar) and Rudro Pater (details unknown; Chasa caste) were abducted and murdered in July. Besides, 9 constables from the Cuttack Tributary Mahal were kidnapped (9 June), and some 'respectable people'—'baboos'—were carried off and held as captives. The colonial *dak* system was also specifically targeted. Interestingly, we do not hear about attacks on British officials and troops—a feature noticed widely during the 1857 Rebellion—in this phase (Foreign Department/Political A Branch, nos. 43–82, September 1868: NAI; Foreign Department/Political A Branch, nos. 460–5, January 1869: NAI).

The broad social base of the *meli* is visible from the references to the combination of the people in the hills and the plains by those conducting the counter-insurgency operations. Specifically mentioned were the Paori (viz., Pahariah or Hill) Bhuyans, the 'wild Juangs' and the Koles of Hoonda Dundpat and Nowagarh. Alongside, the details of the prisoners who were tried and punished indicates the participation of Ranas and Santals—along with Bhuyans, Juangs, Kols—as well as non-tribals like Khandaits. From among the prisoners 7 of them awarded death sentences and 130 were sentenced to rigorous imprisonment which ranged from 6 months to 12 years, and transportation for life (Foreign Department/Political A Branch, nos. 460–5, January 1869: NAI; Mahtab vol. 2, 1957: 130). The requisitioning of colonial forces from Singhbhum and Calcutta and the Madras Native Army, saw the beginning of efforts to crush the *meli*. These operations were aided by the *paikas* supplied by the durbars of Sareikella, Kharswan, Bonai and Pallalahara and were overseen by Colonel Dalton and Ravenshaw. Needless to say, these resulted in major confrontations between the rebels and the colonial forces. The counter-insurgency operations followed the ruthless pattern of burning down a number of villages and grain. Thus, in rebel strongholds like Kesada about a hundred houses were burnt down and a 'large grain depot' ¾ miles up in the hill was completely destroyed. Similarly Daunlah village along with the property of its residents (except cattle) was destroyed. Searches—perhaps raids would be a better way of defining these—were conducted to seize cattle and locate *poots*, gain and rice. Burkola village was destroyed. Nearly 100 maunds of grain was seized and removed from the hills (Foreign Department/ Political A Branch, nos. 43–82, September 1868: NAI; Mahtab vol. 2, 1957: 104).

After crushing the 1868 *meli* the Keonjhar durbar initiated some reformatory measures inspired by colonialism's 'civilising mission'. Thus, the Raja instituted scholarships to educate the tribals. In fact, the following table provides interesting insights into the social origins of those who studied in the schools of the 19 Odisha states (Foreign Dep./ Internal A Branch, November 1884, nos. 261–3: NAI):

Class	Number of students
Rich	13
Middle	910
Poor	12,744
TOTAL	13,667

Nevertheless, the non-resolution of problems faced by the poor marginal sections re-surfaced during another *meli* very soon. In fact, Dharanidhara, the leader of the 1891–2 *meli*, was patronized by the Raja. Dharanidhara was sent to study at Cuttack where he cleared his school examination (Foreign Dep./B-Political I Branch, September 1882, nos. 9–14: NAI; and Foreign Dep./A-Political I Branch, October 1883, nos. 216–18: NAI). On his return from Cuttack Dharanidhara was appointed as a state surveyor. The shift from a surveyor to a *meli* leader was possible given the interaction with the 'outside' world and more importantly, the oppressive methods associated with the recruitment of forced labourers to build a canal in a rocky portion of the state—a project with which Fakirmohana Senapati (as the state's manager) was connected—and the law on grain sales, which meant that people were forced to sell grain to the state at very low rates.

Fakirmohana Senapati described it as the 'terrible' Keonjhar 'Bhuyan *meli*' which he crushed, aided by the colonial forces. Fakirmohana celebrated victory over this *meli* by writing *Utkala Bhramana* ('Travels in Orissa') during the elephant ride back from Keonjhar (Senapati 1965: chapter 19). Fakirmohana's initial attempt to counter the *meli* proved to be abortive and he was imprisoned by the rebels, who took over the palace. Both he and the Raja were bailed out by the colonial administration (Acc. no. 6125/1891: OSA). The upper-caste tradition has kept memories of this alive as a demonstration of his brain-power, through which he outmanoeuvred the Bhuyans. We are told how 'Senapati ('General') Fakirmohana, true to his family name and tradition, now marched at the head of the militia as its commanding officer'. A coded message sent out by Fakirmohana when he was in the camp of the rebels is cited to illustrate his astuteness (Mansingh 1990: 35, 37). But perhaps more importantly, Fakirmohana's description of the *meli* matches the general upper caste and colonial construction of tribesmen (as well as the low castes and outcastes). Thus, he described the Bhuyans as 'born trouble makers', 'hard drinking', 'ignorant savages', 'cruel', 'vicious' and 'stupid'. However, the available sources indicate quite clearly that the *meli* had rallied the Juangs of Keonjhar. Besides, other non-tribal groups of the state, along with people of Bonai, Singhbhum and Mayurbhanj, viz., neighbouring princely states, were largely sympathetic to it. In fact, this illustrates the ignorance of the upper caste order of coastal Odisha when it comes to the location of the geographical area affected and the intensity of popular anger that had been expressed during the *meli* (Senapati 1965 [1927]: chapter 19; Acc. no. 6125/1891, OSA).

In 1879–80 we witness a popular tribal uprising led by Tomma Dora that swept the eastern Godavari tract (in present-day Andhra Pradesh) and the Malkangiri area of the Jeypur *zamindari* (present-day Odisha). It was much more than a 'Koya (a tribe) rebellion' as described in the colonial records. Dora was hailed as the 'king of Malkangiri' and the rebels took over the police station at Motu (westernmost part of Malkangiri). This was a popular movement that brought together tribals who were affected by issues like the erosion of customary rights over forests and the exploitation of the moneylenders that undermined their very survival. Thus, whereas the colonial government imposed restrictions on customary rights, the dependence on moneylenders for loans saw the tribals losing land. However, the rebellion seems to have ended after Tomma Dora was shot down by the police (Behuria 1966: 68; Arnold 1982: 126–9).

Next, we refer to a major 'Kandha' rebellion in Kalahandi in 1882. Going beyond the palace intrigues following the death of the Raja, we find that by the end of 1882 the 'wild' and 'excitable' Kandhas had petitioned to the Chief Commissioner regarding the enhancement of rent and forest restrictions. The colonial discourse located the problem around the policy of the late Chief and his dewan to oust the Kandhas and settle the Kultas, who were considered to be more 'energetic' and 'skilful cultivators'. Needless to say, the Kultas were preferred to increase the state's revenue. However, nothing was done to look into these problems.

In the events that followed the 'ferocious' and 'cruel' Kandhas collectively plundered many Kulta villages 'unaccompanied by any personal violence'.

The colonial authorities decided to intervene and persuaded the Kandhas to 'return most of the stolen property'. The settlement also saw the colonial administration taking over the management of the state. However, very soon after this we are told of Berry hanging ten Kandha 'ring leaders' since they had indulged in 'large-scale massacres' of Kultas, although the records contain no formal evidence regarding the Kultas killed. Berry's act was defended as 'retributive' and 'preventive'. Most shocking is the reference to this action being prompted by the small contingent of troops at his disposal which made it difficult for him to divert some of them with the prisoners. This act, we are told, was prompted by Berry's desire to 'keep the country in order', 'maintain communications', 'save life' (presumably of the Kultas) and 'guard his prisoners' (Foreign Dep./Political 'A' Branch, July 1882, nos. 396–429 and 523–6, NAI; Mahtab vol. 2, 131–2).

Conclusion

This chapter delineated some of the characteristic features associated with 'tribal movements' in nineteenth-century Odisha. The brutality of the terror strikes that were an integral part of the 'civilising mission' hardly needs any elaboration. In fact, what perhaps needs to be highlighted is the manner in which these devastated agricultural production and the environment which need to be examined separately. Some of the discernible features contradict the stereotyped labels that associate the rebellions with individuals, leaders and elite manipulations, which supposedly precipitated them. Our discussion illustrates that these movements were precipitated by a combination of diverse factors, unlike some scholars who seek to classify different strands (Gough 1974: 1395). They envisaged a just and fair order and drew upon notions of a 'moral economy' that was based on the erosion of customary rights, increasing pressures and exploitation.

A closely related aspect was the search for an alternative order that these struggles sought to actualize. Besides, as seen, these struggles were sustained by rumours and were also associated with messianic traits of the leaders—a phenomenon that we have observed in the case of both Chakra Bisoi and Tomma Dora. The 'presence' of Chakra Bisoi along with his actual absence in many of these uprisings shows how the people in the margins 'incorporated' Chakra and 'armed' themselves with him in order to challenge the might of imperialism. At the same time locating the early pre-1860 rebellions as spontaneous (Singh 1985: 19) would be difficult to sustain as an argument if we keep in mind the organization of the 1857 Rebellion in the hills of western Odisha.

This chapter demonstrates how the rebellions transgressed both the geographical and the social boundaries imposed on them. As seen, the tribals were not bound by what some subaltern historians who invoke 'territoriality' and attempt to surgically isolate rural uprisings to local boundaries (Guha 1983: 308). Nothing illustrates it better than the 1857 Rebellion itself. In fact, most of the movements we have examined transgressed the immediate geographical boundaries. Alongside, one needs to also appreciate their inclusive character. Thus, the Mahima movement which united the tribals and the outcastes, along with upper castes illustrates this quite clearly. A closely related position associated with some subaltern historians refers to the 'hillmen'/'plainsmen' dichotomy (Arnold 1982: 88–142). Thus, the method of dichotomizing the people from the hills and the plains cannot be sustained in the light of our discussion of the movements that we have discussed. In fact, the 1857 Rebellion in the hills of Odisha that saw tribals and outcastes uniting with sepoys can be cited as an example to refute this formulation.

One can also refer to the way in which these rebellions chose their targets. Thus, these ranged from colonialism and the princes (its principal allies) and their symbols, viz., palaces—to other 'internal' exploiters, i.e. exploitative officials, and people from Hindu castes. In fact, these rebellions often oscillated between both the 'external' and the 'internal' exploiters, sometimes targeting both. Thus, the violence associated with the targeting of British officials in the hills of western Odisha during 1857–8 seems to have shifted to targeting people from Hindu castes, viz., Brahmins and Karanas, as in the case of Mayurbhanj and Keonjhar (1866 and 1868, respectively), state officials and the princely rulers, viz., Raja of Keonjhar. These perhaps explain the manner in which these movements perceived the different levels of exploitation on the basis of the inroads of colonialism as well as the consolidation of the process of differentiation. Alongside, the interrogation and contestation of the Brahminical domination, viz., Mahima movement, was also witnessed. Nevertheless, as seen, these attempts were largely unsuccessful since they were (along with other problems) tainted by Brahminical Hinduism, especially its method of 'Otherising' the low/outcastes.

One can end by mentioning that the nature of the problems raised by these movements remained largely unresolved and resurfaced to strengthen and reinforce the Gandhian mass movements. Even if articulated at a different time and in a different context, some of the specificities of these movements as well as features that illustrate possible continuities are discernible.

References

Note: The details of the Archival Sources used are mentioned in the text.

Anon, *The Orissa Tributary States: Their Present Conditions and How to Improve it*, (Report from the *Bengalee* with some additions and alterations), Cuttack: Orissa Patriot Press, India Office Library Collection, British Library, London (hereafter IOL), 1877.

Arnold, D., 'Rebellious Hillmen: The Gudem-Rampa Risings', in *Subaltern Studies I*, ed. R. Guha, New Delhi: Oxford University Press, 1982, pp. 88–142.

Bailey, F.G., *The Civility of Indifference: On Domesticating Ethnicity*, Ithaca and London: Cornell University Press, 1996.

Bandyopadhyay, S., *From Plassey to Partition: A History of Modern India*, New Delhi: Orient Longman, 2004.

Banerjee-Dube, I., 'Taming Traditions: Legalities and Histories in Twentieth-Century Orissa', in *Subaltern Studies X: Writings on South Asian History and Society*, ed. G. Bhadra, G. Prakash and Susie Tharu, New Delhi: Oxford University Press, 1999, pp. 98–125.

———, *Religion, Law and Power: Tales of Time in Eastern India, 1860–2000*, London: Anthem Press, 2007.

Banerjee-Dube, I. and Johannes Beltz, eds., *Popular Religion and Ascetic Practices: New Studies on Mahima Dharma*, New Delhi: Manohar, 2008.

Behuria, N.C., *Final Report on the Major Settlement Operations in Koraput District, 1936–64*, Cuttack: Orissa Government Press, 1966.

Bell, R.C.S., *Census of India, 1941, Vol. XI Orissa Tables*, Delhi: Office of the Commissioner of the Census, 1942.

Beltz, J. and K. Mishra., 'Ascetic, Layman or Rebellious Guru? Bhima Bhoi and His Female Consorts', in *Popular Religion and Ascetic Practices: New Studies on Mahima Dharma*, ed. I. Banerjee-Dube and Johannes Beltz, New Delhi: Manohar, 2008.

Beverley, H., *Report on the Census of Bengal 1872*, Calcutta: Bengal Secretariat Press, 1872.

Brandstadter, E.S., 'Human Sacrifice and British-Kond Relations, 1759–1862', in *Crime and Criminality in British India*, ed. Anand A. Yang, Tucson: University of Arizona Press, 1985, pp. 89–107.

Campbell, J., *Narrative by Major-General John Campbell of his Operations in the Hill Tracts of Orissa, for the Suppression of Human Sacrifices and Female Infanticide*, London: Hurst & Blackett, 1861.

Clarke, R. 'Panas of Orissa', in *The Criminal Classes in India*, ed. M. Kennedy, Delhi: Mittal, 1985 [1907].

Dalton, E.T., *Descriptive Ethnology of Bengal*, Calcutta: Government Press, 1872.

Elwin, V., *The Religion of an Indian Tribe*, Bombay: Oxford University Press, 1955.

Eschmann, A., 'Mahima Dharma: An Autochthonous Hindu Reform Movement', in *The Cult of Jagannatha and the Regional Tradition of Orissa*, ed. A. Eschmann, H. Kulke and G.C. Tripathy, New Delhi: Manohar, 1978, pp. 375–410.

Senapati, F., *Atma Jibana Charita* ('Autobiography'), Cuttack: Jagannath Ratha, 1965 [1927].

Gough, K., 'Indian Peasant Uprisings', *Economic and Political Weekly*, vol. IX, nos. 32–34, 1974, pp. 1391–412.

Guha, R., *Elementary Aspects of Peasant Insurgency*, New Delhi: Oxford University Press, 1983.

Habib, I., 'Medieval Popular Monotheism and Its Humanism: The Historical Setting', in *Social Scientist*, vol. 21, nos. 3–4, 1993, pp. 77–88.

———, 'Kabir: The Historical Setting', in *Religion in Indian History*, ed. Irfan Habib, New Delhi: Tulika Books, 2007, pp. 133–57.

Kar, P., *Against the Tyranny of Society: Reflections on a Protest Movement*, Delhi: Academic Excellence, 2006.

Lacey, W.G., *Census of India, 1931, Vol. VII, Bihar and Orissa Part I: Report*, Patna: Superintendent Government Printing, 1933.

Laeequddin, M., Census Officer, Mayurbhanj State, *Census of Mayurbhanj State 1931, Vol. I*, Report, Calcutta: Calendonian Printing Co., 1937.

Ludden, D., *Agricultural Production and Indian History*, New Delhi: Oxford University Press, 1994.

MacPherson, S.C., *Report upon The Khonds Of The Districts Of Ganjam and Cuttack*, Calcutta: Military Orphan Press, 1842.

Mahapatra, S., *Bhima Bhoi: Makers of Indian Literature*, New Delhi: Sahitya Akademi, 1983.

Mahtab, H.K. et al., eds., *History of the Freedom Movement in Orissa*, vols. 1–2, Cuttack: State Committee for the Compilation of the History of the Freedom Movement in Orissa, 1957.

Mallik, B.K., *Paradigms of Dissent and Protest: Social Movements in Eastern India*, New Delhi: Manohar, 2004.

Mansingh, M., *Fakirmohana Senapati*, New Delhi: Sahitya Akademi, 1990.

Michaels, A., *Der Hinduisms: Geschichte and Gegenwart*, Munich: Beck, 1998.

Mishra, K.C., *Bhuyan Jati*, Cuttack, 1925; Vernacular Tracts, India Office Library London.

O'Malley, L.S.S., *District Gazetteers: Sambalpur*, Patna: Superintendent of Government Press, 1932.

Padel, F., *The Sacrifice of Human Being: British Rule and the Khonds of Orissa*, New Delhi: Oxford University Press, 1995.

Pati, B., 'Report: Perceptions in a Changing Society: A Note on Koraput

(Orissa)', *Economic and the Political Weekly*, vol. XXV, nos. 18–19, 1990, pp. 986–8.

————, 'Beyond Colonial Mapping: Common People, Fuzzy Boundaries and the Rebellion of 1857', in *The Great Rebellion of 1857 in India: Exploring Transgressions, Contests and Diversities*, ed. B. Pati, 2010a, pp. 46–62.

————, 'Religion and Social Subversion: Re-examining Colonial Orissa', *Economic and Political Weekly*, vol. xlv, no. 25, 2010b, pp. 43–52.

————, *Identity, Hegemony, Resistance: Towards a Social History of Conversions in Orissa, 1800–2000*, Delhi: Three Essays, 2003.

————, *Resisting Domination: Peasants, Tribals and the National Movement in Orissa, 1920–1950*, New Delhi: Manohar, 1993.

Pfeffer, G., 'Kondh Classification and Mythology in Macpherson's "Account" ', in *Interrogating History: For Hermann Kulke*, ed. M. Brandtner and S.K. Panda, New Delhi: Manohar, 2006, pp. 347–64.

Pollock, S., 'Ramayana and Political Imagination in India', in *Religious Movements in South Asia 600–1800*, ed. D.N. Lorenzen, New Delhi: Oxford University Press, 2006, pp. 153–208.

Ramdhyani, R.K., *Report on the Land Tenures and the Revenue System of the Orissa and Chhattisgarh States*, vol. III, Berhampur: Indian Law Publication Press, 1942.

Ramusack, B., *The New Cambridge History of India III, 6, The Indian Princes and their States*, Cambridge: Cambridge University Press, 2004.

Sahu, B.P., 'The Brahminical Model Viewed as an Instrument of Socio-Cultural Change: An Autopsy', in *Proceedings of the Indian History Congress*, New Delhi: Indian History Congress, 1985, pp. 180–92.

Senapati, F., *Atma Jibana Charita* [Autobiography—Oriya], Cuttack: Jagannath Ratha, 1965 [1927].

Senapati, N. and B. Mohanty, eds., *Orissa District Gazetteers: Sambalpur*, Cuttack: Orissa Government Press, 1971.

Senapati, N. and D.C. Kuanr, eds., *Orissa District Gazetteers: Kalahandi*, Cuttack: Orissa Government Press, 1980.

Senapati, N. and N.K. Sahu, *Orissa District Gazetteers: Koraput*, Cuttack: Orissa Government Press, 1966.

————, eds., *Orissa District Gazetteers: Mayurbhanj*, Cuttack: Orissa Government Press, 1967.

Singh, G.N., *Final Report on the Original Survey and Settlement Operations of the Ranpur Ex-State Area in the District of Puri*, Berhampur: Sarada Press, 1963.

Singh, K.S., *Tribal Society in India: An Anthro-Historical Perspective*, New Delhi: Manohar, 1985.

Srinivas, M.N., *Religion and Society among the Coorgs of South India*, Oxford: Clarendon Press, 1952.

Sundar, N., 'Adivasi vs. Vanvasi: The Politics of Conversion in Central India', 2005 (http://sites.is.cornell.edu/releco/pdf/nsundar.pdf).

Sutton, A., *A Narrative of the Mission to Orissa*, Boston: David Marks, 1833.

Weber, M., *The Religion of India: The Sociology of Hinduism and Buddhism*, London: Collier-Macmillan, 1967.

Wessler, H.W., 'Idolatry, Syncretism, and Anti-syncretism in Hindu Reform Movements of the Nineteenth Century', in *Colonialism, Modernity and Religious Identity*, ed. G. Beckerlegge, New Delhi: Oxford University Press, 2008.

3 Tribal Social Structure in Odisha

GEORG PFEFFER

The Colonial Legacy

The literature on caste fills libraries with endless facets of ancient and modern social thought, but tribal India, comprising at least 100 million people, is next to unknown. Caste studies occasionally encompass the Nishada as alleged descendants of Brahmin men and Sudra women (Manu X, 8), or a category of fairly impure people of the jungle. However, a historical people appears in an undisputed document when, more than two thousand years ago, Emperor Asoka threatens 'the forest tribes' in his thirteenth Major Rock Inscription. Asoka is not amused, since the jungle folk confront his state and fail to submit. Millennia later the British East India Company invents the policy of patronage. Upon subjugating the forest people the colonial state elates them by a special legal status to be the protégées of the European administration.

The Paharias have but one national hero and he was an Englishman. Producing among themselves no name worth remembrance above its fellows, it was left to another race so to impress them with the genius for administration, his justice, and his sympathy for their needs, that they have ever since regarded him as the greatest benefactor of their race. (Bradley Birt 1905: 78)

The facts: Lord Cornwallis' Permanent Settlement of 1793 entitles a new brand of landlords to pressurize the tribal Santal into paying rent. Many of these hitherto independent cultivators of the present Jharkhand province rather abscond by moving from the plains up into the forested Rajmahal Hills thereby, as a secondary effect, pressurizing the tribal Paharia (lit. 'hill people'). This is the hour of Augustus Cleveland, administrator in the area since 1773. He protects 'his' tribal folk against others by persuading the Governor-General at Fort William to exclude the Hills from ordinary regulation (Dalton 1872: 266).

Subsequently other administrators apply the non-regulation policy in many regions of the subcontinent, whenever they think they find tribal people in distress. Though the colonial state, by the Indian Forest Act of

1878, confiscates the hitherto exclusively tribal terrain (Jewitt 1998) and, since the mid-nineteenth century, invites external industrialists to exploit the rich mineral resources of the highlands on a large scale, the European central power assumes the guise of a grand benefactor and developer by pretending to guard tribal land rights against lowlanders. The latter are sure to follow suit wherever the hills have been opened up by the colonial campaigns. Finally, the legal variations of specific non-regulation, or the different administrative appellations given to legally patronized highlanders, are unified by the Government of India Act of 1935. This outstanding colonial legacy contains 'schedules' of Indian 'castes and tribes' who are formally named as Backward Classes to be advanced by policies of special protection. Ambiguous and unexplained criteria of backwardness let unknown administrators decide which ethnic unit is to belong to the patronized Scheduled Castes (SC), Scheduled Tribes (ST), or Other Backward Classes (OBC).

After independence the new Indian constitution adopts these schedules to reserve governmental jobs and parliamentary seats on a proportional basis for the respective members. As a consequence, socio-cultural anthropology and other disciplines, in due course of time, are also taken in by these administrative measures and confuse the state-defined Scheduled Tribes with academic notions of a tribal society, even though some anthropologists altogether deny the existence of Indian tribes. Such a negation is a reasonable conclusion, whenever these experts come across Scheduled Tribes lacking the anthropological traces of a tribal society. Moreover, given specimen of the latter have altogether lost the attention of the anthropological discipline. The epoch is one of many Westerners touring provincial spots anywhere in the world[1] to find the same kind of hotels, taxis and television shows, familiar food and attractive shopping. Given these general conditions, any specificity of a people's social structure seems to lose significance. Subjects like the Indian celebrations of Valentine's Day[2] or the subcontinental Cricket mania[3] attract far more interest.

Political leaders[4] in India and other countries like slums to be removed from the inner cities. The unbecoming should be kept out of view. Similarly the social sciences and humanities tend to leave the study of Indian tribal cultures to the inconspicuous provincial anthropology departments while the latter, rather than going for tribal ideas and arrangements of social life, engage themselves in the 'uplift' of the ST as found in their respective state, since projects for the development of the Backward Classes are financed generously on all governmental levels. In Odisha anthropologists would study how schools, dispensaries, or irrigation dams are being introduced in the highlands, or how shifting cultivation is abolished. After the many famines in the tribal districts, anthropologists like to investigate how hill people below the state-defined poverty line ('bpl') accept governmental rice rations and state-run cooperative societies. Such an academic agenda of social work is firmly rooted. Some prominent anthropologists of the province have even fought the good fight against tribal beef eating and alcoholism.

Efforts of special governmental officers for 'tribal development' are always addressed to the ST, or units marked as Scheduled Tribes once upon a time by British colonial bureaucrats. On the other hand, empirical research reveals that not all of those who are classified as ST are 'tribal' in the sense of social anthropology. Even more relevant is the fact that not all members of Indian tribal societies—in the academic sense—are defined as ST by the administration. This discrepancy has far-reaching effects upon the given policies of social work and is, at the same time, on a large scale distorting the reality of highland societies as they are presented by the discipline. The discrepancy has also hampered anthropological efforts to understand tribal values.

Fundamental questions of social order are at issue. On the one hand, some undefined Western universalism will assume that Odishan highlanders are to be treated as individuals within the familiar administrative set up, unless a rather different Hindu universalism will treat them as an agglomeration of miscellaneous caste groupings. On the other hand, academic anthropology offers the option of conceiving specific tribal categories that differ from both the Western and the Hindu markers of the socio-cultural universe. Then the highlander's societal whole is a unique classificatory product while, at the same time, referring to the values of the societal design named 'tribal' by anthropological generalization. The latter option is applied here in order to avoid the usual bias of colonial and post-colonial contradictions arising from the state's problematic efforts of undoing, protecting and developing social conditions in Middle India. Arguing in favour of a specific tribal design in highland Odisha will, at the same time, depend upon the general insights of tribal studies.

Generalization and Critique of the Tribal Type of Society

Anarchy is one major criterion marking the tribal type of society. A collective of empirical people is unified as a tribe by several formal and distinct categories, even though it remains without effective leadership. If such an absence of power concentration may impress outsiders as a nightmare, or as paradise, it implies normalcy to insiders. In middle India several tribes have a good number of members who are provided with all sorts of illustrious titles such as *raja*,[5] but they lack central governments with an administrative staff that can expect obedience.

The second central criterion of a tribal society is its members' material provisioning on a long-term basis. Thus middle Indian tribal people are either plough or swidden cultivators. Though lacking leadership, the people anthropology refers to as hunter-gatherers[6] in 'immediate return systems' (Woodburn 1982) are not tribal, because the material provisions of their small and loosely structured bands result from short-term inclinations. Individual members join and leave a band at will, realizing that a 'giving environment' (Bird-David 1998), or what we call nature, is sure to provide for them under all circumstances. Hunter-gatherers conceive themselves as receivers and not as investors like the members of tribal, peasant, or industrial societies.

Attention should also be paid to those people who carry on without domestic plants and animals, in case they construct and utilize weirs, dams, boats, nets, refined weapons, buildings, stores and technical devices of sorts or keep an account of their respective belongings, even if human beings are conceived as such. These 'delayed return systems' (Woodburn 1982) may be run by either tribally organized people or by peasants, depending upon the respective relevance of the state. In short, tribal society is one lacking leadership with members cultivating land, raising animals, or investing in other long-term projects for the material maintenance of their livelihood.

In India, the Scheduled Tribes, having been segregated as such in colonial times,[7] in the southern provinces mostly include, hunter-gatherers of immediate return systems, though the vast majority of ST, living mostly in the middle and the north-east of the subcontinent, is of tribal societies. Thus the colonial invention of a separate status for the Scheduled Tribes is a mixed bag leading some anthropologists—mostly of those working in South India—to deny[8] the very existence of tribal societies in the country. Other members of the discipline altogether reject such a construct for general reasons, or irrespective of things Indian.

Until about 1950 socio-cultural anthropology had been the special discipline for researches in tribal societies as well as those of hunter-gatherers. For another 40 years thereafter, the specific features of peasant society became another major subject until, from about 1990 onwards; any kind of analysis addressed to society with a capital S was rejected in many quarters of the discipline. Considerations of socio-cultural particularities, irrespective of whether these are products of general morphological regularities, have become the post-modern dogma. Conceived as the latest, the trend tends to combine what is understood to be the ethical rigour of enlightenment with Western values one may shortlist as universalism, voluntarism and utilitarianism of various shades, especially those focussing upon individual actors. Unfamiliar relational patterns between and within social collectives or forms of religious classification, hierarchy without power, the formalities and pressures of affinal exchanges and concepts involving a regular transfer of partial personal attributes—to name just a few examples from a multitude—are no longer supposed to enter the realm of anthropological thinking. Postmodernism wants culturally unfamiliar social facts to become plausible within the commonsense of any educated Westerner, rather than feeding these facts into the analytical deliberations of trained specialists. The frequent demand for an interdisciplinary approach is actually intended to remove the accumulated insights of the discipline. Propositions of scholars trained in subjects like literature and art, history, or political science, probably most valuable within their respective fields, imply that technical tools and recorded analyses of anthropological expertise are simply given up without further discussion.

Clifford, as an exemplary case, is content with references to the North American art market, or dispositions and attitudes of those trading objects they define as art, when arguing—over many pages—against the very existence of a tribal society. Only once (1988: 321), when recalling Fried's rejection of this concept, does he touch anthropological researches regarding non-Western cultures. Probably Clifford is unaware of Fried's context, the general dispute over all-embracing evolutionary typologies. For Fried, the tribal type of society is only a secondary phenomenon (1975: 99–105), or the result of given people's confrontation with the state, rather than the latter's predecessor as a separate stage in the socio-cultural evolution of the human species. Instead, Fried (1967) proposes certain other societal types as stages preceding the state. Thus, in view of the post-modern rejection of such typologies, Fried's evolutionism is the diametrical opposite of what Clifford otherwise stands for. Characteristically, his reference to Fried's argument implies that readers are either unfamiliar with Fried's work or fail to understand it; or that it does not matter anyhow. Since the present article altogether leaves aside the idea of evolutionary stages, Fried's proposal of tribal society resulting from contacts with the state—rather than being a pre-state stage—will be neither rejected nor confirmed.

Southall has campaigned with the other general argument against the existence of tribes, stating that '(n)o tribal society which has lost its political autonomy continues to be a tribal society in the full sense. . .' (1970: 29) and he is right. Only in pre-conquest history the given criteria are fully applicable, since, on assuming political leadership, colonial or other external powers have terminated tribal anarchy. Taken in the sense of such meticulous historicism, no anarchic societies continue to exist today, since all territories of the globe have been distributed among states according to documents of international law.

Such a formal assessment, however, will differ from empirical conditions. Thus the Indian government may claim exclusive control over the province of Odisha and such a control is indeed elaborate in the lowlands, and yet it remains highly superficial in the western hills of the province, apart from tiny pockets of concentrated governmental activity. The so-called Naxalites, i.e. the militants of a non-tribal movement against the brief of the state, have their strongholds throughout the tribal zone of Middle India because of the very limited administrative impact upon the people living there. Though governmental agencies may, at times, sell the most valuable highland real estate to powerful multi-national companies, they fail to regulate the daily lives of the indigenous people in the manner they do in the lowlands.

In fact, the paper mills of Rayagada, the aluminium plant of Damanjhodi and other equally ugly and poisonous industrial establishments of the highlands are all staffed by immigrant lowlanders who live in what amounts to gated communities while avoiding all unnecessary contacts with the natives of their neighbourhood. The latter may ride buses and visit the growing number of bazaars, but will stay away from any industrial complex. As indentured labourers some may go to the Assam tea gardens and others downhill as short-time *kulis* in the cities, but all of these intrusions of modernity, like the brutalities of the newly introduced primary schools, imply only very gradual transformations of tribal life. For most, it continues to function without police, businessmen and priests. Like the implanted industrial sites, such individual representatives of another societal order do exist in the highlands but, compared to coastal Odisha, their numbers and activities are insignificant. The immigrant officials, traders and temple servants will be convinced of their respective vocation while, beyond their specific task, they will shun social intercourse with the natives. Obviously they perform as executives of a superior external force.[9]

To conclude: formally the colonial government may have terminated the anarchic societal setup in highland Odisha, but multiple empirical features of tribal society, meaningless in the state context, remain to be observed by anyone willing to admit the existence of such holistic socio-cultural constructs. In fact, the given historical termination of tribal anarchy is the first and most general point in Sahlins' textbook on the tribal people: 'Once discovered, they were rapidly colonized, baptized, and culturally traumatized . . .' (Sahlins 1968: 1).

However, Odisha is different. If Europeans have been guilty of major and minor forms of genocide at the cost of the indigenous peoples of the Americas or Australia, Odishan lowlanders have, until very recently, mostly left alone the hill people. The malaria infested mountain jungles bore little attraction for the peasantry of a country that had been underpopulated some 150 years ago. Similarly, the proselytizing drive to 'recover' the supposedly long-lost Hindu convictions of the tribal people has only gained ground in the last decades as an aspect of the general development policies. In purely economic terms, the latter have proved to be impressive failures. Especially in the central and southern parts of highland Odisha, where industrial ventures are more limited as yet, so far the substance of tribal society has undergone few changes. Nobody must 'conjure up a certain cultural era' (Sahlins 1968: vii), as elsewhere, because tribal formations abound in their live versions.

In order to understand the fundamental idea of the tribal social structure, the Western mind must initially abandon all familiar conceptions of social interaction. No firm and unquestioned framework, like the state's bureaucracy, is assigning operational space, nor is a multitude of fairly undifferentiated individuals engaged in 'the action approach', or performing freedom of decision-making within such an omnipresent and all-inclusive administrative grid. Power is not anonymous. In the singular or the plural version, the neighbour, the fellow across the hill, or the unknown intruder provides head and arm for exercises of power.

The tribal laws of societal statics differ basically: the household is the ground layer of all constructs relating to work, politics and morality. School and army, church and hospital, police and property do not appear on the inventory, unless they have been introduced very recently and very partially. In other words:

The tribe builds itself up from within, the smaller community segments joined in groups of higher order, yet just where it becomes greatest the structure becomes weakest: the tribe as such is the most tenuous of arrangements without even a semblance of collective organization. (Sahlins 1968: viii)

Accordingly, 'the boundaries of the whole' are never 'clearly and politically determined', just as 'institutions in the fields of economics, politics and religion' are designed 'coincidentally by the same kinship and local groups'. The cultural formation is 'at once structurally decentralized and functionally generalized' (ibid.).

The Segments of Odishan Tribes

House and Village

The comprehensive and analytically penetrating monograph on the Dongria Kond (Hardenberg 2006) mentions the reputation of these shifting cultivators in the mountains of Odisha's Rayagada district. Their homicide rate is extremely high and their attitude towards all outsiders very reserved. A decade ago, a team of German architects could, in spite of such impediments, spent a fortnight in such a village, because the foreigners' cash payments crossed all levels of Dongria imagination. Applying their refined electronic equipment, the German specialists measured any construction and space of the settlement only to leave in a highly disappointed mood. In a later lecture[10] the team-leader's detailed pictures and graphs were meant to demonstrate how insignificant—the term primitive was avoided—all of these Dongria mud huts had been. He recalled, as his main point, Nazi praises for comparable settlements in prehistoric Germany, to reject any such romanticism bluntly. Amazingly, he had not seen Niggemeyer's book (1964) of some four decades earlier.

This Frankfurt museum man had studied Kuttia Kond settlements some 50 km. further north in the same Kond mountains of central Odisha. We owe Niggemeyer the detailed blueprint of the standard house and the layout of villages (1994: 30; 34) where, three decades after him, I could stay for altogether four months.

In the Kuttia house (Fig. 7.1), a space of about 3.90 by 4.30 m. is divided between its interior (1) and the roofed veranda (2) facing the village plaza, as well as the closed room on the back (3), consisting of a pig-stall (4) and a menstruation compartment (7). Behind the high threshold (5, 6) the interior central sacrificial spot is marked by a forked pole (11) in front of the shelves carrying stored valuables and grain-baskets (12) opposite the hearth (13). The grinding stone (16) and the pounding hole (17) are the given implements of the women.

Thus the basic cell of tribal society, the household, is juxtaposing the two sides of male sacrificers (west) and female cooks (east), though the separate menstruation compartment is also situated in the east. Niggemeyer's graph (1964: 35) of yet another house turns around the sides, though male youths and outsiders may always sleep on the veranda

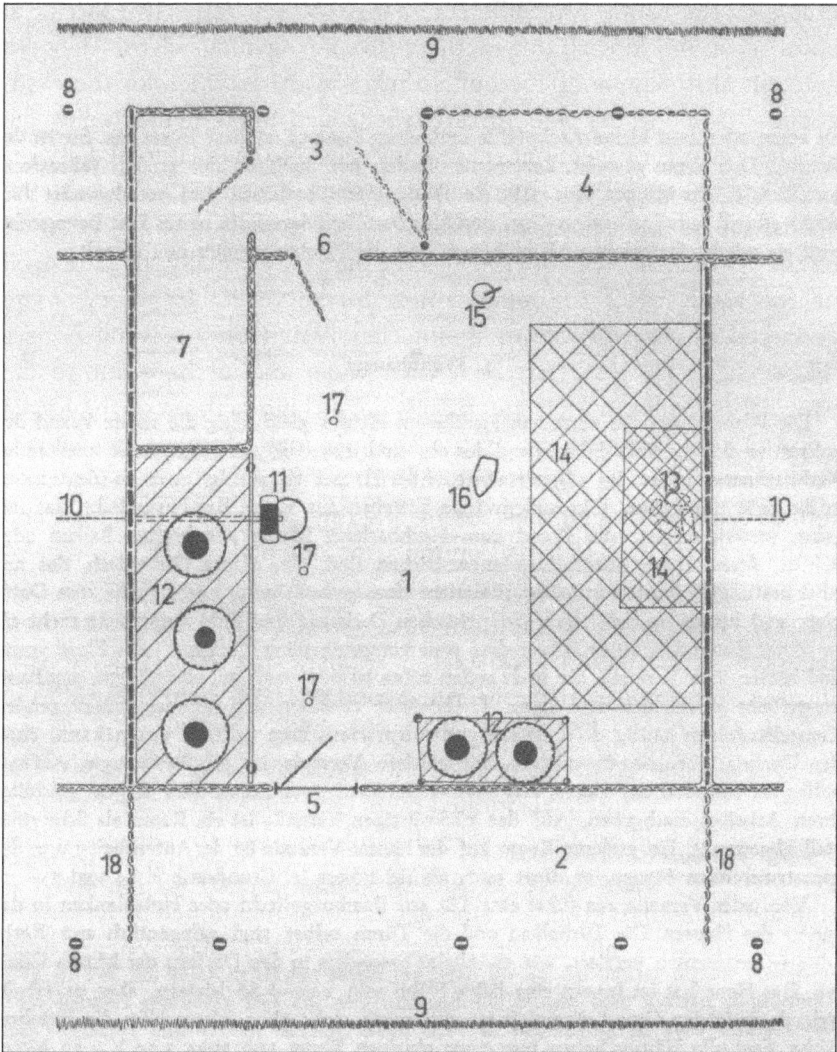

FIG. 7.1: Blueprint of a Kuttia Kond house according to Niggemeyer (1964: 34)

(2) of the plaza side, where all inactive males tend to rest, while females sit on their cots behind the houses on the garden side to peel and dry vegetables, brew beer and raise pigs (4).

Above the hearth, a hanging loft (14) contains all cooking requirements. The forked pole (11) for the household sacrifices is akin to the—much higher—forked pole for the sacrifice on the village plaza, or between the two rows of houses. Niggemeyer never mentions that the particular fork—the long stylized horns of a buffalo found also on the cover of his book—is an emblem restricted to the Saraka territorial clan, whereas others of the Kuttia give different shapes to their respective sacrificial poles according to each one of these seven exogamous clans. They are different abstractions of the buffalo who, at the sacrifice for the earth goddess, is tied to the pole, tortured, beheaded and remembered by the sacrifiers as one of its members that was given to the maternal deity.

If the houses seem to mark a male-female dichotomy, in practise the gender separation is never rigorous. For a short while, a woman may sit on the veranda of the males (2), just as a man may casually stand or stroll on the backyard of the females next to the vegetable gardens. The gendered division of labour is not elaborate. Dongria Kond houses (Hardenberg 2006: 633) are somewhat wider and, perhaps due to the irregular tornados in their mountains, not as high as those of the Kuttia Kond so that within them, even a Dongria man of about 150–60 cm. height must bend his head. The interior room is also subdivided in a refined manner, though the cooking and the worship of the house, and of the ancestors is performed on the same side and opposite to that of the grinding, pounding and resting space.

The Gadaba of Koraput in south-west Odisha bifurcate their separately erected houses into a larger secular and a smaller sacred part. In the latter compartment the ritual food (*tsoru*) is being cooked and the—female—central pillar (on which the—male—crossbeam is resting) is being worshipped as the most sacred representation of the family. The entire order is minutely elaborated by Berger (2007: 66f.). On marriage, a woman should avoid the sacred—and very private—space of her parental home, as she will be initiated into that of her husband's. A similar regulation is observed among the Ho, as mentioned by Reichel in this volume. Generally the blueprints of houses and villages change from tribe to tribe, though 'family resemblances' can be noticed everywhere in tribal Odisha.

A Kuttia Kond settlement may simply appear as an arrangement of mud houses and yet the village territory is sacred to its inhabitants. It contains a fixed number of 'seats' of the earth goddess, permanent stone arrangements around which the two rows of houses may be constructed in east-west direction (Fig. 7.2). One 'seat' will be abandoned for another, if illness and death seem to gain the upper hand so that an entirely new settlement is constructed. Otherwise a house within the row is bound to decay while others are added in due course of time. To this day, many Kuttia buildings remain within gated palisades allowing only limited access (6, 7, 8) as a protection against elephants and bears.

A stone arrangement, the 'seat' of the earth goddess (1), forms the centre of each village and usually the heavy clan pole of up to 2.50 m.'s

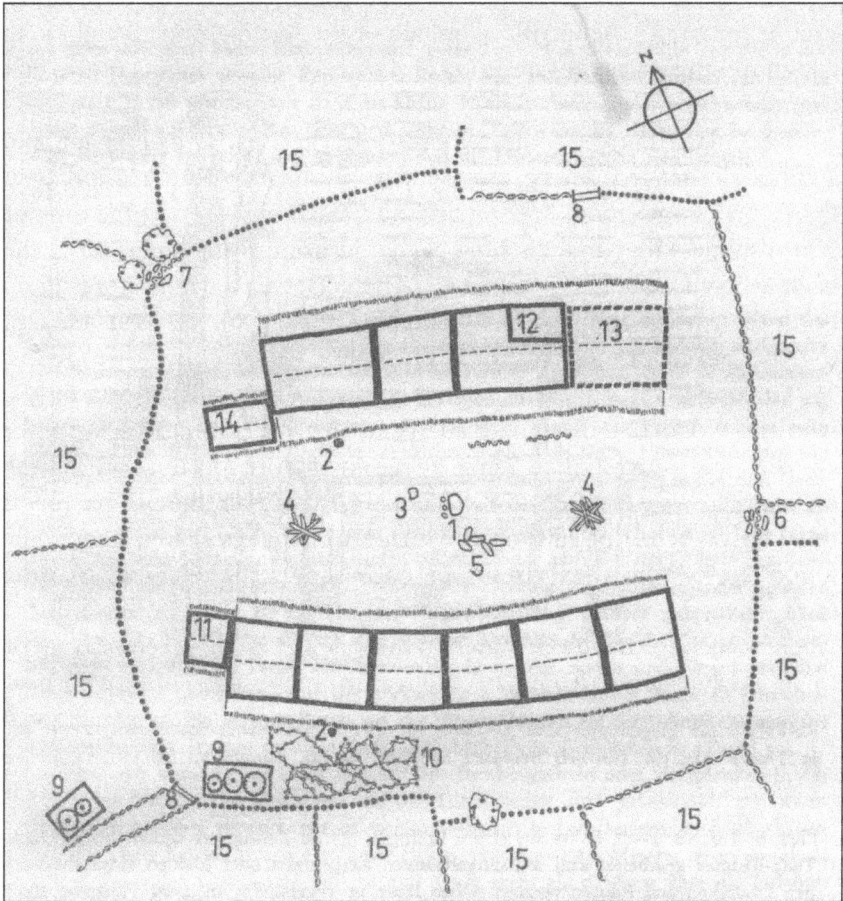

FIG. 7.2: Layout of a Kuttia Kond village (Niggemeyer 1964: 31)

height stands next to it as a reminder of the last buffalo sacrifice when the victim's flesh had been cooked next to it (5). Each village within one of the given sacrificial territories of a clan must take turns in providing the earth goddess with at least one buffalo year after year (Hardenberg 2006: 401f.), or in arranging the many preliminary tasks. On this occasion, the village weaver must invite all inhabitants of the clan's villages as well as those of a limited number of others who give and take brides in marriage as their part of a permanent marriage alliance with the sacrifiers of the village. The males among these latter guests, called affines (i.e. 'those marriageable') in anthropological jargon, act as sacrificers of the buffalo who is said to be a member of the sponsoring village, or its gift to bring fertility to the earth as the return gift of the goddess. The celebration over days involves endless drinking—of the seniors—and dancing—of the juniors. On several occasions, I have personally witnessed how affinal visitors tortured[11] the sacrificial buffalo of the Kuttia Kond all night long and in multiple ways before axing and beheading the animal at the first beam of sunlight.

The plaza between the two rows of houses is male space and additionally fenced during the sacrifice. Ordinarily, Kuttia grind their knives on a large stone (3) or sit around fires at night (4). At the time of a man's illness they may sacrifice a goat in front of his house, or at the back, when a woman is affected (2). The village as a whole stores grain (9) in the garden and next to its pumpkin sticks (10). All cows are kept together in one or more common sheds (11).

Grazing is a major duty assigned to the landless villager weaver (14) who also works as a messenger and generally as a commission agent for all sales and purchases, trading being an inferior occupation for the cultivators. Weavers step in to negotiate, whenever they think this is required, on behalf of cultivators who like to remain reserved. I have only found two or three weavers still practicing the traditional craft and the same have, in recent decades, moved out to become more affluent whereas each Kuttia village retains a menial family that receives a cup of millet every evening from each cultivator household. Those who have moved to their own weaver villages stay in business with their traditional cultivator families for whom they supply the sacrificial buffalo and receive some cooked meat from the sacrifiers, whereas only the raw meat of their own buffaloes, sacrificed annually on the Hindu Divali festival, is taken as return gift by the Kuttia cultivators. Weavers have the same clans as cultivators but follow different affinal rules by allowing the immediate repetition of intermarriage.

The last important marker on Niggemeyer's village plan is the girl's dormitory (12), the extremely small annex of the village elder's house. In 1980/81, when I lived in another Kuttia village, only a boy's dormitory (my quarter) was officially declared as such and it had been formally abolished by 2000. Today male and female youths among the Kuttia and many other tribes are asked to stay away from the paternal sleeping room to spend their nights in quarters that are separate for girls and boys, the village 'siblings'. In all tribal societies of Odisha, these youth dormitories used to be important for the general ceremonial order, but since the lowlanders have maligned the institution as immoral, the arrangements are given little publicity. Psychologists could probably asses the effects of a tribal adult couple's nocturnal privacy as compared to the usual joint family bedroom in the lowlands, and anthropologists, recalling given reports, can mention that the dark, low and narrow girls' dormitories witness female youths in command of their male visitors of other clans and that pregnancies must be avoided (Pfeffer 2010).

The more general issue of the dormitory system is the non-authoritarian type of education in tribal India compared to the highly authoritarian treatment of the young in caste India. Tribal youths are never bossed around. They retain their own sphere of action while the distance towards their parents grows with age to become—as Berger (2007) and others[12] have observed—antagonistic. If the kinship terminology frequently equates members of alternating generations (Pfeffer 2004), this should be understood as an expression of the same ordering principle and not as some 'reflection' of the given behaviour.

The same kind of alternation—highly visible, like the pattern of shifting cultivation—governs the relations with the dead. Whenever I witnessed a death case in a tribal village, relatives and neighbours, though convinced of the physical demise, were equally sure that the dead person had not altogether vanished but would, after an interval in another sphere, return one day within the same tribe, clan and village and, more important, within the same relational pattern of the societal whole.

This other sphere too is divided between the malevolent and dangerous recently deceased and the transformed and benevolent ancestors. Gadaba secondary burial (Pfeffer 2001) marks such a transformation, which is known as a superior type of marriage. Rather than women, the souls of the recently dead are being exchanged between parties that are not mutually marriageable but rather agnatic 'siblings'. Such an incestuous kind of marriage with the dead has a senior status. Rather than a genital unification, the dead—in the temporary shape of buffaloes—are killed to be consumed orally. Their village 'siblings' of the alternate generation will reciprocate when the consumers of the day become the recently deceased of the future to be transformed once again. The local descent groups of a village, as well as their segments, execute the commandments of such 'senior' marriage alliances when exchanging buffaloes—that contain the souls of the recently deceased—for megaliths housing benevolent ancestors. The general issues of death and dying in tribal Odisha have been elaborated by Reichel in this volume and in 2009.

A village blueprint in tribal India is always highly significant even when it differs from tribe to tribe. In the given cases of Kuttia and Dongria Kond, the symbiosis between deities and humans, males and females, cultivators and weavers, or adults and youths is indicated within the layout. When, in 1987, I flew above the treetops of the Kond mountains in a very small aeroplane, the bird's view showed, how one village assemblage, carefully recovered in Niggemeyer's drawing (1964:

28), schematically resembled the next among many hundreds of settlements. I was also wondering whether the arbitrary Western norm of conceiving a vertical north-south direction together with a horizontal east-west dimension would not be instrumental in hiding important cultural messages of the Kond. All of these settlements may have been functional, but they were not constructed in a utilitarian spirit. They were to be representations of the earth goddess as the supreme mother.

Local Descent Groups

Any single Kuttia Kond bears the title of either *Jani* or *Majhi*,[13] sacred or secular leader. These titles are hereditary from father to son. Any village, formally consisting of members of the same clan, always contains these two local descent groups (LDGs). Empirically, some outsiders have always married in to become villagers through time and in spite of their clan difference, but they too are either *Jani* or *Majhi*. The point to be remembered is a difficult one for anthropologists who are trained either to favour or to disfavour the so-called Descent Theory: *Jani* and *Majhi* are not the segments of a clan, they are always segments of a village.

All Kuttia Kond experience this opposition of the binary kind. All Dongria Kond further subdivide each one of the two categories naming sacred and secular leaders into a senior and a junior branch to obtain a tetradic structure of LDGs within each village. Further to the south-west of the province, in the old Koraput district, most tribes share the same four titles referring to four local descent groups that have little to do with either territory or exogamy. Frequently they are further divided into intra-village sub-segments. The Gadaba erect some megalithic arrangements for the ancestors of the inclusive local descent group, others separately for those of its segments, and yet others for those of each extended household. A person may simultaneously reappear as an ancestor in each one of these—major or minor—rock arrangements. In all villages, yet a bigger platform of horizontal and attached vertical slabs is the seat of all village ancestors. The community of the living men—known as the four fellows—assembles on it when discussing serious village matters.

For anthropologists the first difficulty arises from the fact that these Gadaba LDGs, or their segments, are the parties arranging the 'senior', or incestuous, marriage in the shape of the secondary funeral. Members eat the dead—in the shape of buffaloes—of their partner LDG of the same clan. The living marry the dead of their own clan to consume them orally. Thus the 'senior' kind of marriage involving a local descent group implies the very opposite rules compared to a 'junior' one, the only marriage conceivable in Western common sense or textbook exercises. The titles of these tribal LDGs indicate a prestigious status without any reference to either clanship or exogamy.

The second problem arises from the appellations indicating leadership: I have frequently seen, how a person called 'secular leader' was the village expert in performing the complicated rituals of the settlement while another one of the 'sacred' variety would be the one to negotiate with outsiders on behalf of his folk. Probably the Gadaba always let a *Sisa* sacrifice animals as the senior of the sacred branch and a *Kirsani* cook the sacred food as his junior sacred counterpart, but I would not be sure. The sacred/secular dichotomy is formally attached by inheritance but not necessarily reflected by an empirical division of labour.

Finally, all of these titles indicating leadership are imported from the plains. Like the Muslim one of Malik and the Hindu one of Pradhan among the northern Kond, they mark dignitaries, but in reality every man is his own leader and nobody the subject of another. Every cultivator carries such a title of a leader. A village usually has positions of a secular elder and a ritual guide, as well as that of a shaman. Some individuals, performing in any of these three positions, have heard enough of lowland officialdom to pretend to be commanding others. However, the more powerful a person actually is, the less he will claim formal authority. In fact, all villagers will always remain common cultivators or craftsmen. None can expect obedience from another and mere opinion leadership will never be inherited.

A hundred years ago, the distinguished lawyer Sarat Chandra Roy published the first comprehensive ethnography of an Indian tribe, *The Munda and their Country* (1912). Its conjectural history is probably outdated today and its obvious legalism is—as in the works of many luminaries of the discipline—an asset as well as an impediment. Roy cannot think tribal anarchy and yet he mentions the *khunt*, or LDG of the Munda, 'their village organisation with its Munda Khunt and Pahan Khunt' (1912: 69) that was later supposedly 'adopted' (ibid.) by the neighbouring Oraon. The two *khunt* are named, as usual, after the secular and sacred leaders and later 'the Mahto was introduced as a new functionary and gradually a Mahto Khunt evolved in many villages' (1912: 92). Again Roy, like most outsiders, can only associate an officious title with the position of a 'functionary', whereas I would rather recognize a 'petty chief' (Sahlins 1968: 21), or one without the power to give orders and expect compliance.

Roy's is one of the many excellent contributions to Middle Indian ethnography written by non-anthropologists without a training in comparative researches in kinship. Yet another of these authors even mastered the obvious problem of the LDG in a convincing manner. Johannes Gausdal (1953), worked his way through his Norwegian compatriots' outstanding Santal ethnography, dating from the nineteenth century, to differentiate between the 'Paris, or Ancestral clans' (ibid. 16–19) and the 'Khuts or Sacrificial Clans' (ibid. 19–67). The former type, twelve totemic categories that make up the huge Santal tribe, is equivalent to the exogamous patri-clan of anthropological textbooks while the latter type, like the *khunt* of Roy's Munda, refers to the local descent groups in each village. Both are agnatic ascriptions which is one source of the general confusion. The Norwegian missionaries Skrefsrud and Bodding spent their lives in Santal villages to mention, besides innumerable miscellaneous local groups, four 'Sacrificial Clans' to be generally found: those of *Naeke* (priest) and *Manjhi* (chief), as well as those of *Nij* (genuine, pure) and *Sada* (common). Like the LDGs elsewhere in tribal Middle India, these are the agnatically assigned operational units for the ritual give and take within and beyond the village, while the Munda *kili* and the Santal *paris* are the agnatic units determining exogamy, or the give and take of brides. A Western observer would probably remark that ritual exchanges have been shaped according to the marriage model, whereas an insider might comment that the sacrificial exchanges, compared to those of marriage, are of a 'senior' status that is of different and of the same kind. Both units of reference imply agnatic ancestors, and Reichel (in this volume) has even developed the important category of 'migrating ancestors'.

Two empirical facts apparently rule out the unexceptional presence of LDGs in tribal Odisha. The first refers to the major social changes in the northern tribal area, though not among the Bhuiya and Juang of the Keonjhar district, on account of conversions to Christianity, i.e. the ritual factor, and due to the many modern migrations in the wake of industrial ventures carried out in Chotanagpur and the Sundargarh district. The second factor is leading to a structural specificity of many millions of Gond and Gondide tribes figuring under different administrative appellations. All of these *Koitor*—the Gondi term for humans as such and members of the own tribe—assemble a specific number of clans within one of four or five exogamous phratries named after tortoise (of a 'senior' and a 'junior' variety) and cuckoo, cobra (sometimes substituted by porcupine) and leopard. The point is that, irrespective of the clans that each phratry encompasses, these four or five larger units will be equally represented in most villages. As such, they are responsible for the ritual as well as affinal exchanges, though the included clans practically regulate the intricacies of each marriage. Accordingly, rituals unite the earth-bound kind (cobra, porcupine) with the sky-bound (cuckoo), and the land-bound category (leopard) with the water-bound one (tortoise). The meat eaters (cobra/porcupine, leopard) unite with the others (cuckoo, tortoise).

Tribal Clanship

The Kond who are dominating the hills of central Odisha are perhaps the only remaining tribe to retain territorial patri-clans. Bailey (1960: 47f.) has described them initially and Hardenberg (2006: 188f.) offers the most intricate descriptive analysis of Dongria Kond clanship. Elsewhere, Berger's penetrating fieldwork of about two years among the Gadaba has led to clan categories with a territorial reference that must have been of greater importance in earlier times (2007: 104f.). Had there been more empirical research of the required anthropological standards, probably more reports on territorial clanship would have come in.

The Kond territorial reckoning is obviously based upon the central sacrifice for the earth goddess. Territory is not a given piece of real estate but—for any village unit—a very minutely delimited part of the maternal deity to be fertilized annually. Six among the seven Kuttia Kond clans left their mother through a hole in the sacred grove right in the middle of Kuttia territory. The seventh and junior most is of lower status for having reached the upper world elsewhere through a disreputable exit of his mother. Because of this difference, these junior most Timaka belong to the only clan that is allowed to enter the sacred grove. All others must stay away from the spot of earth they assume to be their original place of birth. Consequently, the Timaka are the executioners of the grand buffalo sacrifice for the goddess once in every seven years at the common sacred grove of *Saphangara* when the Kuttia as a whole must fertilize the earth in this manner.

Among the northern Kond of the Phiringia Block, two patri-clans, one senior and one junior, jointly control a piece of territory which implies that they must not intermarry. They marry members of their permanent enemy clans. In 2004 my informants there were sure to have given up the buffalo sacrifice since thirty years, just as Bailey's Kond informants of 1955, also in the northern areas, thought that the ceremony had ceased since decades and yet the territorial boundaries (Bailey 1960: 54) of mutually antagonistic clans and clan federations were clearly marked and contested.

All over tribal Middle India, only the two Paharia tribes (Vidyarthi 1963) of the Rajmahal Hills in Jharkhand and the Sora of southern Odisha

(Elwin 1955, Vitebsky 1993) are definitely without exogamous patri-clans though all three certainly operate with LDGs. The excellent ethnographer McDougal does mention such clans among the Juang (1963: 65f.) of Keonjhar but, judging from the details of his account, they rather seem to be equivalents of the by-now familiar LDGs. In any case, the four given territorial units, or *pirh*, and the alternating generation-sets of the Juang seem to carry a much greater structural importance. Similarly, the 'senior siblings' of the Juang, their neighbouring Bhuiya, organize themselves territorially in several *bar*, with each containing three or more villages (Roy 1935: 93). But Roy does not mention any exogamous patri-clans and I have only heard of their LDGs from my own Bhuiya informants.

The Sora I have visited in the southern Gunupur district, as well as the Juang and the Bhuiya of the northern Keonjhar district, are all known to regulate their marriages on an egocentric basis involving positive affinal alliances. Egocentrically all Bhuiya (Roy 1935: 134f.) and all Juang (McDougal 1963: 155f.) bifurcate the entire tribe into non-marriageable 'own' (i.e. *kutumb* or agnates) and marriageable 'other' (i.e. *bondhu* or affines). Accordingly, such a particular moiety structure can do without exogamous clans. Since the Western mind is simply unaware of positive marriage concepts, this point has received next to no attention in the literature.

Middle Indian clanship has otherwise evolved in different lines. In the north, Ho and Munda as well as their 'juniors', Oraon and Kisan, are known to have an infinite number of totemic patri-clans, each with a local centre of gravity, while their related Kharia neighbours have only eight in the 'senior' and nine in the 'junior' Kharia segment of the whole. In the Mayurbhanj district the affluent Bhumij are usually thought to be Munda and yet my informants were sure to exchange brides only within the ranks of eight totemic patri-clans, whereas their neighbours, the Santal, everywhere conceive twelve of such categories to form the tribal whole, the last one being of a hybrid kind and consequently of lower status.

The old Koraput district of south-west Odisha is dominated by numerous tribal societies with most of them sharing the same of eight exogamous patri-clans assigned to different totemic emblems of animals, plants and celestial bodies. All Bondo as well as all Bhumia and all Matia assemble within two exogamous moieties only: cobra and leopard, whereas the 'senior' Gadaba branch, like the neighbouring Didaye, contains four clans. The 'junior' Gadaba branch, like most other tribes of Koraput, is a combination of eight mutually intermarrying clans named fish, cobra, cow, bear, leopard, monkey, vulture and sun. All of these depend upon one another like the biospheres of water (fish) and soil (cobra), grazing ground (cow) and lower branches with honey combs (bear), upper branches to rest (leopard) and tree-tops (monkey), or the sky (vulture) and the atmosphere (sun). Half of these eight (cobra, bear, leopard, vulture) are conceived as meat-eaters.

Marriage is everywhere practically organized by a given LDC of a village that is, thus, allied to several external ones through time. Where clans exist, the rule of exogamy is definitely respected, even though inter-tribal marriages may occur as long as the clan membership differs. This is worth mentioning, because not just in Koraput, but to an equal extent in the northern block of tribal Odisha, the same clan emblems reappear in different tribes.

Marriage is a holistic clan concept and, at the same time, very much a personal decision, though all people must be married. A woman or a man would normally become accustomed to flirting from the days of the youth dormitory onwards and experience regular romantic adventures in the course of regular youthful dancing and singing events. Parents may arrange marriages between infants and yet, once the principals have become adults, the latter must consent or cancel the planning. A man would very frequently abduct and marry his lady-love who would consent in spite of demonstrative resistance in public. The resulting concubinage would perhaps only much later, be sanctioned by the sacred ceremony when the bride-wealth payments are completed and children may have grown. Over the years, a man may abduct more than one woman to support several wives who may quarrel and leave with other men. The latter in turn must compensate past bride-wealth payments so that multiple chains of indebtedness are a regular feature. I have never heard of a woman leaving her husband after having had a child, but before such a crucial event, individual decisions rule the day even if societal bars of a general kind, like the positive and negative marriage rules, are duly respected. Once in a while, however, a woman runs away with one of the 'wrong' category, or even with a low status weaver. Such breaches of conventions may be healed by sympathetic relatives after years of exile.

Conclusion

The modern state is known for efforts to develop tribal Indians into people, like those found in the lowlands. Wherever such efforts have been successful, these tribal converts have moved into urban slums to be associated with assemblages of low castes of their rather different neighbourhood. At the same time, many millions of people continue to live within their given tribal natural and socio-cultural environment that is far from idyllic. Lives are short, consumer goods limited. But the setup remains without officialdom. External power holders remain external. In some tribal cultures laughter and a generally relaxed mood is apparent, while in others brooding and violence meet the visitor, though more often intermediary moods seem to persist. All of these communities continue on their own, or without what is known as the office.

Notes

1. On tourism in tribal Middle India see Pfeffer (2008a: 83–5)
2. Brosius 2011.
3. Appadurai 1996; Pfeffer 2008a.
4. Sanjay Gandhi's actions of this kind during 1975–7 have probably received the most attention.
5. Among the Kharia, for example, I was told that units of villages were always 'ruled' by a 'king', and I personally met several such 'kings' who happened to be respected elders of their local communities. Generally, external observers from Western countries tend to confuse status and power differences.
6. Because gathering is always in female hands and much more important for survival than hunting, the order of the two terms has been switched on occasions.
7. 'The genesis of the Fifth and Sixth Schedules of the Constitution can be traced to certain provisions of the Government of India Act 1935 . . .' (see page, National Commission of Scheduled Tribes; Special Report, May 2012).
8. Such denials are registered in the course of personal communication rather than in publications.
9. Strümpell (2006) describes how immigrant mechanics and petty business people continue for decades in the hills away from 'home'.
10. I attended the memorable presentation at Bad Salzau/Germany in May 2003.
11. I mention this part of very lengthy and meaningful ceremonies, because British officers reported such torture of the human victims, before the colonial power prohibited Kond human sacrifice in the middle of the nineteenth century. In view of the Hindu or the European style of working and keeping cows, I see no reason to moralize with regard to Kond torture practices.
12. Of the German anthropological research team in Orissa during 1999–2005.
13. These are Sanskritic terms within the Dravidian language of the Kond, as others are within the Munda tribal languages.

References

Appadurai, A., *Modernity at Large: Cultural Dimensions of Globalization*, Minneapolis: University of Minnesota Press, 1996.

Bailey, F.G., *Tribe, Caste, and Nation: A Study of Political Activity and Political Change in Highland Orissa*, Manchester: Manchester University Press, 1960.

Berger, P., *Füttern, Speisen und Verschlingen. Speise, Ritual und Gesellschaft im Hochland von Orissa, Indien*, Berlin: LIT, 2007.

Bradley-Birt, F.B., *The Story of an Indian Upland*, Whitefish: Kessinger Publishings Legacy Reprint Series, 1905.

Brosius, C., 'Love is in the Air. Der indische Valentinstag', *Frankfurter Allgemeine Zeitung*, vol. 9, no. 2, 2011.

Clifford, J., *The Predicament of Culture: Twentieth Century Ethnography, Literature, and Art*, Cambridge, Mass.: Harvard University Press, 1988.

Dalton, E.T., *Descriptive Ethnology of Bengal*, Calcutta: Government Printing, 1872.

Elwin, V., *The Religion of an Indian Tribe*, Bombay: Oxford University Press, 1955.

Fried, M.H., *The Evolution of Political Society: An Essay in Political Anthropology*, New York: Random House, 1967.

———, *The Notion of Tribe*, Menlo Park: Cummings, 1975.

Gausdal, J., 'Ancestral and Sacrificial Clans among the Santals', *Journal of the Asiatic Society*, vol. XIX, no. 1, 1953, pp. 1–97.

Hardenberg, R., 'Children of the Earth Goddess: Society, Marriage, and Sacrifice in the Highlands of Orissa (India)', Unpublished Habilitation-Thesis, University of Münster/Germany: Faculty of History/Philosophy, 2006.

Jewitt, S., 'Autonomous and Joint Forest Management in India's Jharkhand: Lessons for the Future?', in *The Social Construction of Indian Forests*, ed. Jeffery Roger, New Delhi: Manohar, 1998, pp. 145–68.

McDougal, C., *The Social Structure of the Hill Juang*, Ann Arbor: University Microfilms, 1963.

Manu, *The Laws of Manu*, tr. Georg Bühler, Oxford: Oxford University Press, 1886.

National Commission For Scheduled Tribes; Special Report Good Governance for Tribal Development and Administration, New Delhi, 2012.

Niggemeyer, H., *Kuttia Kond: Dschungel-Bauern in Orissa*, Munich: Renner, 1964.

Pfeffer, G., 'A Ritual of Revival among the Gadaba of Koraput', in *Jagannath Revisited: Studying Society, Religion and the State in Orissa*, ed. Herrmann Kulke und Burkhard Schnepel, New Delhi: Manohar, 2001, pp. 123–48.

———, 'Order in Tribal Middle Indian "Kinship"', *Anthropos*, vol. 99, 2004, pp. 381–409.

———, 'Bondo Violence', in *People of the Jungle: Reformulating Identities and Adaptations in Crisis*, ed. M. Carrin and Harald Tambs-Lyche, Delhi: Manohar, 2008a, pp. 69–92.

————, 'Versuch über Cricket', *Zeitschrift für Ethnologie*, vol. 133, 2008b, pp. 193–212.

————, 'Jugend und Gender: Schlafhäuser der mittelindischen Stammesgesellschaften', in *Spiegel und Prisma. Ethnologie zwischen postkolonialer Kritik und Deutung der eigenen Gesellschaft*, ed. D.E. Schulz and Jochen Seebode, Hamburg: Argument, 2010, pp. 242–60.

Reichel, E., *Notions of Life in Death and Dying: The Dead in Middle India*, New Delhi: Manohar, 2009.

Roy, S.C., *The Mundas and their Country*, Calcutta: Government Printing, 1912.

————, *The Hill Bhuiyas of Orissa*, Ranchi: Man in India Office, 1935.

Sahlins, M.D., *Tribesmen*, Englewood Cliffs: Prentice Hall, 1968.

Southall, A., 'The Illusion of the Tribe', in *The Passing of Tribal Man in Africa*, ed. P.C.W. Gutkind, Leiden: E.J. Brill, 1970, pp. 28–50.

Strümpell, C.,'*Wir arbeiten zusammen, wir essen zusammen*', Konvivium und soziale Peripherie in einer indischen Werkssiedlung, Münster: LIT, 2006.

Vidyarthi, L.P., *The Maler: A Study in Nature-Man-Spirit Complex of a Hill Tribe in Bihar*, Calcutta: Bookland, 1963.

Vitebsky, P., *Dialogues with the Dead: The Discussion of Mortality among the Sora of Eastern India*, Cambridge: Cambridge University Press, 1993.

Woodburn, J., 'Egalitarian Societies', *Man*, n.s., vol. 17, 1982, pp. 431–51.

4 Feeding, Sharing and Devouring
Alimentary Rituals and Cosmology in Highland Odisha, India

PETER BERGER

Like many other highland communities in middle India, the senior or Boro Gadaba of Koraput District in southern Odisha mainly structure their society along horizontal lines; in other words, they prefer oppositional to genealogical reckoning (Pfeffer 1997: 14). The ancestor category is not genealogically segmented and does not serve as a reference point for structuring relationships among the living. Instead, ancestors oppose the living *en bloc* and are not differentiated internally. Among the living, groups of different segmentary orders are related by transactions, and it is the repetition of such transactions that provides the diachronic element. The relationships of this kind are embedded in ritual processes, and because deities, demons and spirits of the dead are involved as agents we may speak of a cosmology. Such a cosmology also entails a moral aspect inasmuch as particular relationships demand or display certain types of approved or despised behaviour. Hence, the relationships that make up this social and cosmological system are hierarchically related; in other words, they are differently valued. Perhaps the most conspicuous feature of this system of relationships is the alimentary idiom. Food and feeding are not merely matters of the domestic sphere, but nearly all types of relationships are conceptualized as alimentary processes. Although food may serve only as a metaphor at times, it usually involves the physical actions of cooking, distribution, feeding and consumption. Feeding, sharing and devouring, then, are the fundamental relationships that constitute this cosmology. The terms simultaneously embody practices, attitudes, social relationships and values; moreover, despite some overlap, they categorize in significant ways ritual domains in Gadaba society.

My aim here is to present a synopsis of this cosmology and describe its most salient features in order to facilitate comparison with other highland communities in the region. Although in its stress on alimentary processes this particular cultural manifestation is specific to the Gadaba, family resemblances are evident throughout central India, for example, with the Sora, the Dongria Kond, the Bondo or the Juang, to name only some communities (Elwin 1950; Hardenberg 2005; McDougal 1963; Vitebsky 1993). As I am going to present this cosmology in a relatively abstract form, there is little room here for the variations and nuances that do of course exist. I have dealt with many of the issues mentioned here separately and in more detail elsewhere (Berger 2007, 2009, 2010, 2011, 2015a). Furthermore, processes of cultural change, which are a focus of my more recent research (Berger 2014), do not concern me here.

I will first present some general features of Gadaba society and then try to outline some aspects of the indigenous notion of cosmology or divine social order known as *niam*. In the following, I will deal with relationships of feeding/eating, sharing and devouring respectively.

The Boro Gadaba[1]

As is common throughout central India, tribal communities in Koraput are divided into elder (*boro*) and younger (*sano*) segments (Pfeffer 1997).[2] The Gutob[3]-speaking Gadaba are thus classified as senior in relation to the Ollari-speaking Gadaba who are their neighbours to the north and east. Although I will speak simply of the Gadaba from now on, the following will be restricted to the Gutob Gadaba. However, many aspects of ritual and religion mentioned here hold true for the Ollar Gadaba as well (see Thusu and Jha 1972). The Gadaba populate parts of the Koraput plateau, some 900 m. above sea level, alongside several other communities, some of which are cultivators like themselves (such as Bondo, Parenga, Joria) while others follow particular vocations such as gardening (Mali), smithery (Kamar), pottery (Kumar) or petty trade (Dombo) (see Berger 2002; with reference to the Dombo see Hardenberg in this volume). Together they consider themselves 'indigenous' or Desia, a term which also refers to the name of the language all of them speak as *lingua franca* (see Gustafsson 1989; Mahapatra 1985). The Gadaba number perhaps some 15,000, and they cultivate rice in terraced riverbeds and millet on the dry fields as their staple crops. 'Gutob' probably means 'earth creature' (Griffiths 2008: 675), signifying the crucial relationship to the territory, which is connected to original villages (Berger 2009). In the cosmology to be described, villages are crucial sacrificial entities and units of exchange. Below I will repeatedly refer to the village of my research using the pseudonym Gudapada.

Approaching *niam*

When the Gadaba speak of how things should be done, particularly regarding the sphere of ritual and religion, they refer to *niam* (or *niomo*). This could be glossed as 'divine order', 'tradition', 'law' or just as the 'right way of doing things'. It is an order that has been instituted by gods (*maphru*) but that is conceived of as functioning quite independently. *Niam* clearly is normative, and transgressions (*dos, umrang*[*4]) are automatically followed by sanctions, without the intervention of any particular deity. It is said that *dos* 'attaches' to the action (*dos lagiba*); in fact, one could say that the transgression and the reaction are two sides of the same coin and *dos* actually refers to both. *Niam* is a cosmic order that should be harmonic, 'good and even' (*bol soman*), in contrast to suffering and calamities (*bipod*). What keeps things 'good and even' is the proper execution of actions in diverse contexts and along the lines of different relationships. The most common consequences of transgressions are blindness, madness, vomiting and vomiting blood.

The most basic ontological assumption, which is also at the heart of *niam*, is the division of the Gadaba, in fact of all humanity, into agnates or 'brothers' (*bai*) and potential affines or 'others' (*bondu*), literally 'those connected'. A person acquires that status at birth from his or her father and it is unchangeable through life, and thus women retain the status of their *bonso* or clan after marriage. From a set of eight categories current in the region, the Gadaba employ four clan categories (cobra, tiger, sun and monkey), while the Bondo only distinguish between two (cobra and tiger), and some other communities on the plateau, such as the Ollar Gadaba, employ all eight (in addition bear, hawk, cow and fish). A myth that is common in variations throughout central India relates that incest is at the beginning of humanity, so intermarriage and exogamy is a crucial aspect of this classification (Berger 2015a: 194f, see below). However, as with the opposition of senior/junior, the distinction of, in Christ Gregory's (2009) apt phrasing, brotherhood/otherhood structures all kinds of relationships among the Gadaba and in central India in general. As we will see, the kinds of exchanges and actions of sharing that are allowed in any particular context are predicated on this primordial distinction.

It may perhaps come as a surprise to hear that although *niam* would appear to be so fundamental to Gadaba society, it is nevertheless vaguely defined. The Gadaba hardly feel a need to define it in abstract terms or to summarize its main points. As until today many Gadaba are illiterate, *niam* is only codified in actual practice and public local knowledge and is consequently a matter of negotiation and modification. To jump to the conclusion that *niam* is constantly changing, however, would be to underestimate the resilience of such cultural patterns. I would say instead that, as a system of relationships, *niam* has the potential to accommodate new elements while remaining distinctive.[5] However, it may also be that *niam* has changed quite dramatically over the course of history, but neither we nor the Gadaba know much about the time before 1940, which is the time ethnographic research in the area began. From the Gadaba perspective, either despite or because of its vagueness, *niam* has the aura of continuity. If pressed as to what is at the heart of *niam*, the Gadaba refer to a particular type of sacrificial food called *tsoru* or *go'yang*.* Such a type of food may appear at first to be an element of *niam*, yet its main quality is relational again. As I will show, *tsoru* constitutes relationships between groups and makes persons grow ritually when fed with it. It is to these feeding relationships I want to turn first.

Feeding/Eating Relationships

The Gadaba distinguish between a number of prescribed, collective and enduring relationships that connect local groups at various levels of the social structure. Generally, all these relationships are what Sahlins (1965: 141) called 'between' relationships and they usually connect local groups from different villages. Those relationships that connect higher-order units are considered 'senior' to those involving lower-order units. For example, a relationship between two villages is senior to a relationship of the same type between merely one local line of each village, units that are called *kuda*. Although in principle such 'between' relationships connect units from different villages, for practical purposes relationships of the same type may also be maintained between different local groups in one village. Such intra-village relationships are considered 'junior' to inter-village relationships. All types of relationships are balanced in the sense that they are mutual: one group feeds another one in some way, the latter thus being the eaters—and this relationship of feeder/eater is reversed on some other occasion. In fact, this mutuality of feeding/eating is a crucial value within *niam* and contrasts with the aspect of unilateral or negative reciprocity perceived as devouring that will be described later.

Despite this common feature of mutuality, the feeding/eating relationships are quite different on several accounts. First, they are different with respect to the brotherhood/otherhood classification; second, the objects transacted and the type of flow between the partners differ; third, the relationships therefore perform very different functions;

fourth, the actual actions carried out and attitudes displayed are quite unlike in moral terms (see also Pfeffer 2001).

Tsoru and tsorubai

The first relationship to be described is that of the 'sacrificial food brothers' or *tsorubai*. Before the ritual processes particular to this type of relationship are described, the main features of the sacrificial food called *tsoru* in general need to be outlined. *Tsoru* is not only prepared by *tsorubai* but by a number of people in a variety of contexts that will be dealt with in various sections of this contribution. However, it is not offered or consumed as part of devouring relationships.

Tsoru or *go'yang**—consisting of rice and meat—is always part of a sacrificial process that produces a hierarchy of food and eaters. *Tsoru* refers to the superior type of food consumed by an in-group, and *lakka'** signifies the subordinate type of food eaten by contextually defined relative 'outsiders'. If the sacrificial animals are small, as in the case of a chicken, the whole animal is prepared as *tsoru*, whereas in the case of pigs, goats, sheep, cows and buffaloes *tsoru* is prepared from the head, while *lakka'** is prepared from the rest of the animal. As this kind of division is considered to be paradigmatic, 'head-meat' (*mundo manso, bob cheli**) is synonymous with *tsoru*, while 'body meat' (*gondi manso, gondi cheli**) is identical to *lakka'.** In addition to the head, *tsoru* should contain the liver and blood of the victim. These parts of the body are associated with life-force (*jibon*), and I would argue that much of the efficacy of *tsoru* at transforming and regenerating relationships is due to this aspect. Blood is said to 'enliven' (*bonchiba*) ritual objects if sprinkled on them after a sacrifice, and the liver especially is the target of sorcery. The word *go'yang** may indicate this vital feature, since the Gutob syllable *g'* often signifies living entities (such as *gu'bon,** bear; *gi'sing,** chicken; *gu'tob,** earth creatures).

The hierarchical aspect of the sacrificial process, the *tsoru/lakka'** distinction, may be more or less pronounced. It can generally be said that it is less in evidence when *tsoru* is fed, as in the cases discussed in this section. Hierarchical opposition—in Dumont's sense (e.g. 1986), i.e. as part-whole relationship—is emphasized in those situations in which *tsoru* is shared, as in collective sacrificial communions of village agnates during the annual ritual cycle. However, the hierarchical dimension may also be more or less marked in cases of *tsoru* sharing, which points to a hierarchy of ritual contexts. At the most senior shrines, hierarchical distinctions are sharp and certainly not a matter of negotiation, so more rules will apply to *tsoru* consumption here than in less valued contexts. Thus, while *tsoru* should always be cooked in a new earthenware pot and consumed on the spot of the sacrifice, participants at the most senior shrines need to be ritually married and to have refrained from any food on the day of the sacrifice (preceding the ritual).

The *tsorubai* epitomize *tsoru* preparation, although in principle all the Gadaba (men and women) are eligible to cook *tsoru* in certain contexts, and it is this activity that is most directly related to *niam*. In sacrificing, cooking and feeding the *tsorubai*, the Gadaba say, 'restore' or 'make' *niam* (*niam korbar*).

Together with the affinal category of the mother's brother (*mamu*) that I will introduce below, the *tsorubai* are crucial for the transformation of the person in life-cycle rituals. While early life-cycle rituals are left to healers (*gunia* or *dissari*) and the local group itself, at wedding and death rituals the actions of the *tsorubai* are decisive (see Berger 2007). If a person dies, his or her local agnatic group or *kuda* will inform their *tsorubai*, another local group of the same descent category (*bonso*) and usually from another village. Although it is a collective relationship, generally only one male member will come to the village of the deceased to perform the ritual tasks. The *tsorubai* is provided with a sacrificial animal by the hosts, which he sacrifices and from which he prepares *tsoru* afterwards. In some cases, feeding is followed by sharing. During death rituals, for example, the *tsorubai* first feed *tsoru* placed on leaves to the spirit of the deceased (*duma*) and then join the group that actually shares the dead person's food, which has been prepared by the *mamu*. During a wedding ceremony the *tsorubai* also mouth-feed the bridal couple and then share the same food with them.

The fact that the *tsorubai* 'make' *niam* is most evident in cases when *niam* has been violated or social relationships have been broken off. I will only give the example of excommunication here. In this case—as in others, e.g. a break-up of a relationship due to an oath (*porman*) (see Berger 2015a: 486f)—the status quo of the relationship contradicts *niam* and is a hindrance to the smooth execution of ritual activities that concern the village as a whole. Also in this context feeding and sharing are separate but connected activities.

The Gadaba use the terms *kul* or *jati* when they refer to the different communities of the plateau, as well as to their own group as Gadaba. If a Gadaba man or woman transgresses *niam*, he or she can lose his or her membership of the group and has to 'buy' (*kiniba*) back this status in the form of a feast; hence this ritual is called *jati kiniba*. If the daughter of the house runs away to live with a member of a low-status community—such as the petty traders or Dombo—the rest of the house will have to buy back their status, whereas the daughter will henceforth be considered Dombo in ritual and commensal terms. In order to buy their status back, the *tsorubai* of her father's house are called and they sacrifice a pig in the inner, sacred part of the house, in front of the central pillar representing the house deity. As with all the other requirements, the pig has to be bought by the daughter's low-status husband. While the *tsorubai* are preparing the pig's head as *tsoru* in the house, the pig's body is cooked as *lakka'** in the yard. The members of the house whose status is to be redeemed sit in a row in the yard and are mouth-fed by the *tsorubai* from one plate. Each of them then receives a plate of his or her own and the *tsorubai* walk past putting a bit from their own plate on to each of theirs in turn, while the members of the house give back a handful of their own *tsoru* by placing it on the plates of the *tsorubai*. Such mixing (*bata, tero'be**) can be done with beer, liquor or food and is frequently performed when social proximity is stressed. While only those Gadaba in the village who have been ritually married may engage in *tsoru* commensality, on this occasion, *lakka'** food may be shared by all the Gadaba of the village plus the *barik*, the village herald who always belongs to the Dombo community. Only after the *tsorubai* have thus 'restored' *niam* do the members of the house resume their ritual rights, in particular with regard to *tsoru* consumption during village festivals.

Panjabai

Like *tsorubai*, the term *panjabai*—the meaning of *panja* is unclear—refers to a relationship that permanently connects local groups of the same descent category (hence brothers) through exchanges. However, while *tsorubai* cook for and feed one another, *panjabai* reciprocally eat their liminal dead. This is done during a ritual called *go'ter,** which has received considerable attention through the decades (Fürer-Haimendorf 1943; Izikowitz 1969; Pfeffer 1991, 2001; Berger 2010, 2015b). This complex ritual is performed by a local agnatic group roughly once a generation. The spirit of a deceased person (*duma*) is fed *tsoru* by the *tsorubai* and his or her mother's brother on various occasions after death. This has the effect of transforming him or her from a member of the local community to a member of the *duma kul*, the community of the liminal dead. Although thus transformed, the dead remain close to the village and it is the *go'ter** that brings about the final transformation. All the spirits of those persons who have died since the last such occasion are 'awakened' and each one is transferred into the body of a living water buffalo.

Literally as the 'living dead' the animals—ranging from two or three to more than a hundred—are fed for days, before being dressed according to sex and age and led outside the village where they are tied up and mourned by the women for the last time. They are finally untied and taken away by external brothers of the hosts to be killed and eaten in the weeks to come. Although other 'brothers' such as the *tsorubai* are also involved in this 'intra-agnatic exchange of souls', as Pfeffer calls it (1991), the paradigmatic buffalo-takers are the *panjabai* and they usually receive more than half of the buffaloes. While the *tsorubai* are called upon on many occasions as described above, *panjabai* only perform in the context of the *go'ter.**

Not only are the liminal dead consumed by the *panjabai*, they are also replaced by stone slabs that represent all ancestors (*anibai*) of that generation. On the occasion of a *go'ter**, each buffalo-taking group (there may be several) brings stone slabs that are erected in pairs—one upright, one flat—in different places. The most conspicuous of these locations is the stone platform (*sadar*) in the village centre—opposite the shrine of the local earth deity—that serves as an assembly place for the village. When the most 'senior' group of the village, the *sisa* or sacrificers, perform the *go'ter** their *tsorubai* bring and erect two stones at the central platform. As such, the *sadar* is an abstract representation of all generations of village ancestors since the foundation of the village. These stones are not the object of worship itself; except during the sacrifices for the village deity (*hundi*), whose shrine is always located in the village centre opposite the *sadar*. Only then do the two oldest stones, representing the founding generation, receive some drops of blood and liquor.

Tsorubai go about their task of sacrificing, preparing and feeding *tsoru* in a concentrated and calm way. Certainly, quarrels are quite common among the Gadaba and when alcohol has been drunk, as it surely is at wedding and death rituals, arguments between hosts and *tsorubai* may occur. However, the standardized relationship between *tsorubai* is polite and friendly. The *panjabai*, on the other hand, play a greedy, aggressive and effervescent role during the *go'ter** (see Berger 2015c). They arrive in the village like combatants and demand more of everything, particularly more buffaloes to take home.

Affines

While *tsorubai* exchange services surrounding *tsoru* feeding and *panjabai* mutually perform the consumption of the liminal dead and their replacement by ancestors, affines exchange 'milk' (*kir, da'tor**). 'Milk' is the idiom for symmetric exchanges of brides between *bondu*, those of a different descent category. 'We drink their milk' (*ame tar kir kaibu*) is a common expression indicating a *somdi* relationship, i.e. a de facto alliance in contrast to potential affinity as the term *bondu* indicates. The mother's brother (and his local sub-line or *kutum*) is conceived of as the donor of this milk-gift and this entails certain enduring rights and duties. Although lower-level groups in the social structure—the local groups of a village and their sub-groups—are involved in marriage negotiations, affinal relationships are generally associated with relationships between villages. Considered empirically, at least in the case of Gudapada, matrimonial exchange is only relatively balanced at the village level. Reciprocity in the exchange of brides is not enforced and the only explicit marriage rule is the prohibition of intra-clan (*bonso*) marriage, which is strictly followed. So-called cross-cousin marriage, however, is common, preferred and terminologically prescribed (Pfeffer 1999). Considered ritually, inter-village reciprocity is enacted in the bride-wealth transactions, which, however, are only made when requested. Part of the bride-wealth is a female calf (*bachuri*) that is given 'for drinking milk' (*kir kaiba pai*); that is, it is not supposed to be sacrificed as gifts of cattle among affines usually are, but is the symbolic equivalent of the bride and thus an immediate return of the gift. If and when a 'real' bride is reciprocated is another matter.

Affinal relationships are strikingly ambivalent. A myth, widespread in various versions in tribal Middle India, narrates how primordial siblings are turned into spouses by the Great God, from 'own' into 'others'. A brother and a sister are the only survivors of a flood. God encounters them and strikes them with smallpox, so they no longer recognize each other. After this transformation they become husband and wife and live together in a house. From their union all tribes came forth (Berger 2015a: 194f). The ambivalence of 'own' and 'otherness', a classic anthropological theme, reverberates in many ways in Gadaba society: status is opposed to equality, distinction to unity.

On the one hand, equivalence between affines is stressed and established; on the other hand, this equivalence is challenged. Equivalence is ritually achieved in various ways; I have already mentioned the immediate symbolic reciprocation of the bride with a calf. Furthermore, cattle are evenly exchanged whenever affines visit in the context of life-cycle rituals. The guests then bring the hosts a cow or an ox and receive a leg in return to take home. Especially pronounced is the equivalence in the exchanges of husked rice that belong to the reciprocal visits in the marriage process. The rice exchanged is measured exactly by the receiving group and excess rice is returned. A few days later, an *almost* identical transaction occurs in the opposite direction. In any particular marriage context the seniority of the bride-givers is acknowledged, hence the wife-givers, in addition to the exactly equivalent amount of husked rice, are also provided with a miniature pot containing liquor and a coin for their group's midwife (see Berger 2011). The seniority of the wife-givers is only of a temporary nature, though, and Andrew Strathern's term 'alternating disequilibrium' (Strathern 1971: 11) may be appropriate here.

Even in the contexts where equivalence is ritually expressed, such as in wedding rituals, challenge, competition, and at times, latent aggression can also be part of the proceedings. Hospitality is the arena for this side of affinal relationships. As part of the wedding process, both the local groups involved visit each other, and in these contexts the guests are alimentary victims and force fed by the hosts. In a sequence called 'feeding the affines' (*somdi kuaibar*) that is scheduled in the groom's village on the second day of the wedding, the guests are seated in rows and are fed hand-to-mouth by the hosts—the temporarily junior wife-takers—with beer and food; 'beating the mouth' (*tond maribar, rik tom**) is the name of this practice. Such scenes may involve many variations of resistance, flight and surrender.

Another wedding sequence that immediately follows the 'feeding of the affines' is called 'mud joking' (*kado kiali*)—joking being an activity especially associated with particular kinds of affinal relations. It too is a display of competition and rivalry, but ends up stressing unity rather than distinction. The affinal groups meet on a dung heap and first start washing themselves but then begin throwing mud and dung at each other. This can become quite boisterous. However, no matter how badly one is hit, or how often, feelings of resentment or anger are out of place and should not be displayed. At one point, the fight or 'joking' turns into a dance. All actors involved, men and women from both sides, now soaked in water and mud, dance a circular dance on the dung heap to the music of the Dombo musicians. At this stage, all differentiations seem to have dissolved as the people have literally become unrecognizable, covered as they are in mud. This scene could be reminiscent of the mythical state of undifferentiated brother-sisterhood mentioned above, but regardless of whether the Gadaba would directly connect 'mud joking' in any way to the myth, the relationship of 'own' and 'otherness' certainly is at stake here. Both ritual sequences—the force feeding and the mud joking—testify to the ambivalences that characterize affinal relationships.[6]

In sum, the affinal relationship is more complex than the *tsorubai* and *panjabai* relationships. It is a balanced relationship that pivots around the exchange of 'milk'. However, the ritual efforts to produce and communicate equivalence conflict with alternating status differences and competitive feeding.

*Moitor or dissel**

Compared to relationships between affinal groups, the *moitor* or *dissel** relationship[7] is not only ambivalent but may even seem paradoxical. As with the foregoing between-relationships, local groups are connected through the generations as *moitor*, but there the similarity ends. In terms of clan status, *moitor* would be classified as affines, because they belong to different clan categories. However, the idea that *moitor* would marry provokes outrage and is considered a breach of *niam*. Accordingly, *moitor* do not exchange cattle during live-cycle rituals as affines do; neither are they agnates and the idea that they would eat each other's buffaloes (i.e. the dead) as agnates do is also regarded as a severe transgression of *niam*. The statement I heard often that *moitor* are 'the most senior of all' (*sobutu boro*) thus oddly seems to contradict the fact that they do not appear to be involved in any kind of ritual work or exchange. Since I have described the different 'between' relationships in this section as balanced and based on reciprocity, the question arises as to what *moitor* actually do exchange. In short, one could say that they worship each other and that as a consequence their relationship can be described, using Fortes' term, as reciprocal 'prescriptive altruism' (Fortes 1969: 251).

The Gadaba say that the *moitor* relationship, like *niam* itself, was instituted by the gods. This could be one explanation for why *moitor* are also called *takurani moitor* or *mahaprasad moitor* to distinguish this relationship from other much less relevant *moitor* relationships. *Takur* is a word that generally refers to deities (though *maphru* is the more common term) and *mahaprasad* refers to the sacred food (*prasad*) that is provided by the Jagannath temple in Puri, and hence the 'great' *prasad*.[8] Another plausible explanation for the name would be that they treat each other like gods.

Alongside these terms, the *moitor* relationship is also characterized by the reference to the liver. As mentioned above, this organ is an obligatory ingredient of sacrificial food or *tsoru* and is particularly associated with the vitality of a being. The term 'liver *moitor*' (*koloj moitor*) could thus indicate the fact that *moitor* share this essential aspect of personhood (or, more generally, being) or that their relationship is literally vital. A story (*katani*) I was told about how a *moitor* relationship originated proves this point. In mythical times, when the two local groups concerned—one from the cobra category from the village of Gudapada, the other from the tiger clan of Tukum—still existed as these animals, the cobra drank up all the water from a river. The tiger came to the same place and found the river dried up. He called on the great god (*maphru*) to help him and the latter arranged for the tiger to meet the cobra. Seeing the tiger's distress and in order to prevent him from dying of thirst, the cobra vomited up the water again for the tiger to drink and thus saved his life (see Berger 2015a: 182). Besides the fact that the relationship proves vital for the tiger, the story reveals other features as well. First, the relationship is based on divine intervention; second, the tiger did not ask the cobra to do anything but the cobra acted on his own account; third, the tiger drank the snake's vomit. The second feature relates to the strict code of prescriptive altruism between *moitor* and the third to their identity in particular. Eating someone else's vomit, I would argue, is an extreme form of 'mixing' that signifies proximity, as mentioned above.

None of the relationships described so far maintain such a strict code of conduct as the *moitor* relationship. *Moitor* are not supposed to mention each other's names, and I have seen two women within this relationship who live next door to each other calling each other by teknonyms in their everyday life. When *moitor* meet they stop and bow humbly towards each other even if this is in the midst of a crowded weekly market. Deference is the appropriate attitude and rude behaviour as witnessed among *panjabai* or joking as witnessed between affines is out of the question. As idealized in the myth, *moitor* should give freely to each other, explicitly without the thought of any return. As in the myth, transactions are unilateral in theory, but in practice, as both sides maintain this attitude, they prove to be balanced and reciprocal. Once, a dance troupe was visiting a number of villages in the region to perform. The troupe's *moitor* lived in Gudapada and not only did the dancers receive due hospitality but in addition Rs.100 notes were attached to their costumes, whereas under normal circumstances they would have received Rs.10 notes.

Because of the strict code of conduct and the prescribed altruism, *moitor* in fact rarely meet. They would be welcomed at all life-cycle rituals and would even be allowed to share each other's *tsoru* (yet another indication of their identity) but they rarely show up. One reason is because they do not have any ritual role to perform, but I have also been told that *moitor* avoid visiting each other too often so as not cause too much embarrassment on the side of the hosts. This is because the hosts would have to comply with the altruistic regime, whereas the guests—conforming to the rule—could come 'empty handed' (*kali hate, dio titi**) and would have to be given everything without being allowed to ask for something themselves. However, even if they do not attend they are never forgotten but receive 'memory meat' (*china manso*) from the cows or oxen killed at marriages or death rituals. Not a leg, as is the case with *tsorubai* or affines, but the chest or the neck of the animal is brought to their village.

If the *moitor* do not drink 'milk', do not consume the 'dead' and do not cook *tsoru*, what type of alimentary relationship, one wonders, does exist between them then? Although I never actually witnessed it, I have been told many times that *moitor* 'eat from one plate' reciprocally hand-feeding each other. This again stresses the identity that is at stake. As in the myth, a distinction is not made between 'my food' and 'your food'. This type of consumption is different from the feeding/eating relationships described above in that affines or agnates usually feed in one direction only in any specific context. It contrasts with sharing because in such contexts, which I will describe in more detail in the following section, each person involved receives a plate of his or her own. As in the case of clan status, *moitor* thus also transcend the common alimentary processes.

Let me sum up some of the main aspects discussed in this section on feeding/eating relationships. The balanced exchanges of feeding/eating relationships that I have described so far permanently connect local groups. These exchanges bring about transformations through the alimentary processes involving milk, the dead and *tsoru*. Despite these similarities, as indicated at the beginning of this section, the relationships are not of the same type. *Tsorubai* reconstitute *niam* and transform the person undergoing life-cycle rituals, while *panjabai* consume and assimilate the dead and replace them with memorial stones. Affinal milk circulates between local groups and through the generations. Only the affinal relationship is truly productive since milk engenders milk to be exchanged again. The *moitor* do not seem to fit in anywhere here but appear to transcend the basic distinction between agnates and affines and associated transactions. Their exchange of honour, devotion and altruism brings about none of the above results. The next mode of alimentary process—*tsoru* sharing—depends to a significant extent on the effects of feeding by *tsorubai* and affines. Only complete ritual persons—those having undergone the full wedding ritual—are allowed to join those contexts of *tsoru* commensality that are ascribed the highest value.

Relationships of Sharing

Relationships of sharing relate to the structure of a local group in connection to the deities of the territory. At various shrines and sacred places in and around a village, sacrificial food or *tsoru* is shared between deities and 'their' people. While the ritual order as a spatial feature thus covers the whole village territory, it also temporally embraces the annual cycle and structures the activities around the cultivation of crops. In each of the seasons that the Gadaba distinguish—the hot, wet and cold seasons—one of the three major festivals is scheduled, each of which lasts for some three weeks. During these festivals the social structure of the village unfolds as different contexts of *tsoru* sharing emerge, at one time highlighting the parts of the village—the houses, the local sub-lines, the local lines—, at another the 'village as a whole' (*ga matam*). This whole is also referred to as the 'four brothers' or *chari bai*.[9] This term emphasizes that such rituals of sharing generally have an agnatic focus; it is 'us' from a certain place who share food with 'our' deity, the 'us' being variously defined depending on the segmentary level concerned. As mentioned before, the hierarchical aspect is much more pronounced in such contexts of sharing. Moreover, it is not the oscillating or alternating kind of status distinction as in reciprocal marriage transactions. The alimentary processes of sharing produce permanent, in theory unalterable, hierarchies of *tsoru* and *lakka'** consumers. In certain contexts this distinction is expressed in the opposition of 'earth people' (*matia*) and 'latecomers' (*upria*), which stresses the superiority of the autochthonous village population. Thus, it is 'us being the creatures of this earth/locality sharing sacrificial food with our deity' versus all others.

Processes of sharing *tsoru* occur at all levels of the village structure and vary according to who is included or excluded, the type of animal sacrificed and the specific patterns of distribution. However, the following aspects generally remain constant: first, the sacrifice is financed by those who are part of the commensal group; second, the animal is sacrificed by a male and the food is usually cooked by a female, or someone classified as such in the context of the ritual; third, the food is cooked on one fireplace in a new earthenware pot; fourth, *tsoru* is put onto plates and each member receives his or her own plate from which to eat; fifth, *tsoru* is consumed first, in the vicinity of the shrine, and *lakka'** food or body meat is distributed and consumed later by 'others'; and sixth, the idiom of sharing is 'to mix and eat' (*misai kori kaiba*). It is this mixing among 'ourselves' with 'our' deity that is crucial; therefore, finally, it is the maintenance of relationships rather than aspects of transformation, assimilation or reproduction as in 'between' relationships of feeding and eating that is the main intention of sharing.

In the Gadaba ritual system the annual festivals and ritual contexts throughout the year are connected and refer to each other in various ways. The ritual movement goes back and forth between the village as a whole and its constitutive parts, thus reiterating the integration of the village and the dynamics between part and whole, and expresses the superiority of the whole through ritual precedence; i.e. collective sacrifices always precede sacrifices at the level of the house. For every Gadaba *tsoru* commensality within his house—here understood as a social unit usually comprising a married couple, their unmarried children and perhaps a widowed parent of the man—is of utmost importance. Of the various annual village sacrifices three are of particular significance, one in each season: in the cold season for the village deity (*hundi*, also 'village mother-father'; pig sacrifice), in the rainy season for a hill deity (*jakor*; annually alternating pig and cow sacrifice) and in the hot season a sacrifice of the 'senior house' (*boro gor*; goat sacrifice) or *pat kanda*, associated with *dorom* or the sun-moon deity. The latter is the most 'senior' sacrificial context of the whole annual cycle. Women are excluded from collective village sacrifices and *tsoru* commensality. However, they participate in these activities at the level of the house, to which I will now turn.

'House people' sharing tsoru

The house is the most important place for any Gadaba. Here humans are protected by the house deity represented by the central pillar known as *doron deli*, which is a representation of the earth deity at the level of the house and stands in a metonymic relationship to the shrine of the village deity (*hundi*) mentioned above. All house people (*gor lok*) engage in *tsoru* commensality with the house deity a couple of times per year. However, the house is not the only place where the people of a house share *tsoru*: the other important place, with which I want to start here, is the threshing ground adjacent to the wet-rice fields.

In the Koraput highlands, two crops are the most important: wet-rice (*dan, kerong**) and millet (*mundia, sa'mel**). The cultivation cycles of these two staple crops have an immense impact on the ritual order, not only among the Gadaba but on every cultivating community in the region. Among the Gadaba, the dry fields on which millet grows (alongside rice and oil-seed) are conceptualized as pertaining to the village and thus as vaguely agnatic, belonging to 'us'. This becomes evident, for example, when the village sacrificer distributes only dry-field seeds from the shrine of the village deity (*hundi*). The wet-rice fields, by contrast, are conceptualized as affinal. They lie 'outside' the village and are also 'low', since they are directly constructed in the riverbeds and, possibly over many centuries, the water has cut deep and wide trenches into the earth; one has to climb down to the wet-rice field. Although rice is also grown on the dry fields on the hill slopes, the wet-fields produce the paradigmatic rice that is most highly valued.

The affinal character of the wet-rice fields in relation to the village becomes especially apparent during harvest (November/December), when the rice is brought as a 'bride' into the village by each house. Before this the 'parents' of the bride, the dual river deities—*jal* (water) *kamni*, *patal* (earth) *kamni*—receive a sacrifice once the paddy has been piled up on the threshing ground. Following a sacrifice for *kamni* and the new paddy *tsoru* is cooked and shared by the 'people of the house' (*gor lok*) only. With great ritual care, i.e. in precisely prescribed ways, one small basket is filled with rice and first placed on the ground outside the threshing ground. This basket of paddy is called *joni tifni*—*tifni* referring to the basket, *joni* meaning 'harvest' as well as 'vagina' (see Gustafsson 1989). The *tifni* is sent first to the house and welcomed there before it is placed next to *doron deli*, the house deity. About five months later, this rice is cooked as *tsoru* at the very same place, during the festival of the hot season or *chait porbo* (April Festival). This connection between the harvest of the 'bride' in November and 'her' consumption as *tsoru* by the 'house people' illustrates two things: first, the interconnections between the different ritual practices—syntagmatically (November > April) and paradigmatically (harvest = marriage)—and, second, although *tsoru* may only be shared among agnates it always contains an affinal element, the rice itself. Ideally, the rice is always wet-rice and for *tsoru* preparation this most highly valued paddy is certainly used. In the context of *tsoru* commensality at the level of the house, when the 'bride' is consumed, this aspect is even more obvious than usual.

The consumption of *tsoru* at the level of the house during the April Festival occurs after the collective sacrifice for the village deity (*hundi*) in the morning of the same day, indicating the seniority of the latter. At the house level the man of the house sacrifices two cocks in front of the wooden pillar, a red one for the house deity and a black one for the seeds of the dry fields. His wife prepares *tsoru* next to the sacred pillar (*doron deli*) in the sacred room of the house. This room (the 'inner house', *gondi dien**) is painted in the same red earth colour as the above mentioned post itself and is only a little wider than one meter. It only serves sacrificial purposes and has access to the attic where the crops are stored. The black cock is prepared as *lakka'** food in the big room (the only other room of a house). One enters this room first and it serves all purposes except sacrifice and *tsoru* preparation. When the *tsoru* is prepared the house people sit down for their first meal of the day.[10] The house people usually, i.e. in everyday contexts, take their daily meals in the big room and often do not eat all at the same time. Old people and children may take their plates out onto the veranda or eat next to a fire, and the woman of the house eats only after having served the others. However, the synchronicity of consumption is important when sharing *tsoru*, as is proximity to the deity. After the deity has been offered food, all house people squeeze into the inner room and jointly commence eating. Following the sacrificial communion of the house people, each house distributes *lakka'** food throughout the village. The women and children of a house carry baskets to those other houses they exchange *lakka'** food with and one bowl is given to each house involved. The whole village seems to be on its feet distributing *lakka'**, so this food is appropriately described as 'walking rice' (*bulani bat, alal lai**).

'Four brothers' sharing tsoru

The 'four brothers' share *tsoru* at different times of the year at various village shrines. These agnates are conceived of as descendants of the original settlers and are also called 'earth people' (*matia*) in opposition to those inhabitants that later settled in the village, the 'latecomers' (*upria*). In the case of Gudapada several groups count as latecomers: Gadaba from other villages who settled as internal affines of the earth people generations ago, families of weavers, musicians and petty traders (Dombo), the blacksmiths (Kamar) and the herders (Goudo). All Gadaba villages—in any case all original villages that are not only a settlement but the specific named unit of Gadaba society I call 'village clan', which defines the identity of men and women even if they were born elsewhere (see Berger 2009)—consist of an agnatic core that owns the land, is numerically dominant, performs the sacrifices and shares *tsoru*. This unit is called the 'four brothers' because the agnatic group in every village ideally segments into four different status groups: Sisa, Kirsani, Boronaik and Munduli.[11] Because of the ritual functions associated with these categories, the Sisa and Kirsani are senior to Boronaik and Munduli. The sacrificer, known as the *pujari* (the one who performs the sacrifice or *puja*) is selected from a village's Sisa group, while the Kirsani group provides the person who cooks the *tsoru* on all collective occasions, the *randari* (the one who cooks, *randiba*). Although the *randari* is always male, his task is conceptualized as female in opposition to that of the sacrificer. Throughout the year this ritual duo not only sacrifices and cooks but also initiates agricultural activities for the village as a whole (*ga matam*), such as the first transplanting of the wet-rice, the first ploughing, etc., that are followed by all individual houses or 'all of the village' (*gulai ga*).

I have mentioned the sacrificial proceedings at the most senior shrine of the village—the *pat kanda* deity—in earlier publications (Berger 2002, 2011), so here I will briefly summarize another sacrificial context in order to illustrate *tsoru* sharing among the four brothers: the sacrifice for the village deity (*hundi*) during the November Festival (*diali porbo*). Before sunrise, in the chill of the winter morning, sacrificer and cook proceed to the centre of the village where the shrine of the village deity is located opposite the assembly place of the four brothers, the *sadar*. The *hundi* shrine is a heap of stones little more than a meter in height. It has a stone plate as a 'door' in front, which is only opened three times a year. Inside is a small hollow with two small erected stones representing the deity. The shrine as a whole is surrounded by a low stone wall that separates the inside from the outside. While the sacrifice proper is taking place, only the sacrificer and cook are allowed to be inside whilst others watch or assist from the other side of the stone wall. After the sacrificer has opened the stone door of the shrine he draws a pattern (*bana*) with rice powder in front of it and around the stones inside, which is crucial for communication with the deity. Offerings are always placed here. Another small pattern is drawn at the far end of the walled space, in the direction of the *pat kanda* shrine. Here, the sacrificer first kills a white chicken for this superior deity, whose shrine lies outside the village proper. Then a black cock and a piglet are sacrificed for *hundi*.[12] As usual, the heads of the victims are immediately placed on the sacrificial patterns so that their life departs there. Blood is sprinkled on the patterns and the stones representing the deity as well as on the founding stones of the assembly platform opposite the shrine. Some blood is also allowed to drip on husked rice and this 'blood rice' (*rokto chaul*) is the first offering for the deities. The cook then cuts out the pig's liver and uses it together with a piece of its gullet and some rice to prepare a small amount of cooked food (*tsoru*), which is a second offering to the deity, along with some drops of liquor. Then the door is closed and the sacrificer and cook eat a little of the deity's *tsoru* and drink liquor. As both of them represent the village as a whole, this action would be sufficient in terms of commensality with the deity and on other occasions at less important shrines this is all that happens. However, here the cook then begins to prepare, next to the shrine, the pig's head, liver and blood, parts of the cock and, separately, the rice as *tsoru*, while the body of the pig is cut up outside the confines of the wall.

Ultimately, the married men belonging to the 'four brothers' sit down next to the shrine, inside the walled space, and each one is presented with a bowl of rice and meat for himself. The sacrificer and cook sit closest to the shrine. The sacrificer starts eating first and is also the first to get up when all have finished their *tsoru*. Again, the sequence of action is important when it comes to highlighting and confirming relationships of seniority. Only after the 'four brothers' have commenced eating *tsoru* may the consumers of *lakka'** food (body meat of the pig) begin eating. The unmarried Gadaba men of the agnatic group sit just on the other side of the low stone wall, the affines of the earth people sit a bit further away and the *barik*—the village herald—receives food from their pot. The Dombo also sit in one corner, having cooked their share of the pig's body on one fire. The blacksmiths take away raw body meat from the pig and the herdsmen raw meat from the cock to cook for themselves next to their houses. Neither the blacksmiths nor the herdsmen accept cooked food from the hands of the Gadaba. The general status ranking of *jatis* of the region cuts across the locally defined high status of the earth people as sacrificers here (Berger 2002).

Such sacrificial contexts thus serve to maintain the relationship between earth people and their deities, a pivotal relationship all village inhabitants depend on for protection, well-being and fertility. Moreover, the alimentary process reinforces and perpetuates the 'eternal' hierarchy of the earth people and all the rest, a hierarchy based on a combination of territory, descent and commensality. Not only members of other communities but also Gadaba from other original villages, no matter how many generations they have lived in the village, remain latecomers and are thus excluded from *tsoru* commensality (except, in theory, the *moitor*). Sharing food not only signifies status but actually reproduces the group in opposition to others. The efficacy of *tsoru* sharing is highlighted by stories that narrate the accidental consumption of another group's *tsoru*, which is a breach of *niam*. One local Gadaba group called Murjia originally belonged to the cobra category and the 'twelve brothers' (see below) did not take brides from this group. Due to the accidental consumption of the *tsoru* of a tiger group the status of the whole Murjia group changed. In Gudapada, their status is now regarded as ambivalent. The village cook's blindness in one eye is said to be the result of marrying a woman from this group with its unclear clan status. Another example of this might be a statement by a Dombo whose house I visited frequently. At times, I have been pressed by members of this group to take some food, a request that put me in a dilemma, because the Gadaba do not accept cooked food from the Dombo. This man, now the *barik* or herald of the village, however, just served me some liquor and said, 'I know you cannot take our food; you share their [the Gadaba's] *tsoru*.' For him the fact that I shared *tsoru* with the Gadaba made me in some respects a member of that community.[13]

'Twelve brothers' sharing food

Beyond the village, there is no social or political unit in Gadaba society. The status categories (*sisa*, etc.) cut across Gadaba society as do the clan categories the Gadaba share with other highland communities. As such, the Gadaba social structure is part of a general pattern of the encompassing Desia society, which Pfeffer calls 'Koraput Complex' (1997: 16). But neither the Gadaba nor the Desia appear as units of action. On certain occasions, such as on the main day of a large scale *go'ter** ritual, the final death ritual mentioned above, thousands of people may gather, but never does the Gadaba act as a single community similar to, for example, a gathering of a certain caste in the plains. This complies with the well-known fact that in 'tribal societies' in general, the tribe as a whole is not a very coherent or relevant social unit (Sahlins 1968:16). However, the Gadaba certainly have an idea of their society as a totality, a notion that again is based on *tsoru* sharing and the distinction between brotherhood and otherhood. *Baro bai tero gadi* is a notion that literally translates as 'twelve brothers, thirteen seats/thrones'. As I eventually came to understand it, the twelve brothers are complemented by 'one' seat pertaining to the affines. The number of brothers is thus specified and fixed, with twelve representing a totality[14] and the affinal part remaining numerically unspecified.

As a category of reference *baro bai tero gadi* is frequently mentioned whenever matters of general relevance or *niam* are at stake, as, for example, when the gods are invoked. However, as an empirical phenomenon *baro bai tero gadi* hardly ever materializes. A story told by a Gadaba from Gudapada narrates the formation of the 'twelve brothers' in mythical times. As will become evident, the twelve brothers are represented nowadays by twelve original cobra villages. The story is as follows:

On arrival from the Godavari River the Gadaba assembled and cooked sacrificial food. When it was ready they distributed it but it was not sufficient and only twelve of the brothers ate, thereby becoming the 'twelve brothers' [all from the cobra category] who still share sacrificial food today. Among them are [the following are all village names] Alangpada, Totapada, Guneipada, Deulpada, Gudapada, Soilpada, Poibada, Auripada, Bondpada and Potenda. For the Oleibir, Osol [titles of original villages present in the villages Orna and Deptahanjar], Guga [in Kalapada] and Kupa [in Ponjol] the food was not sufficient so they had to associate among themselves. Among the tiger [descent category] the food was likewise not sufficient, but among the monkey and sun it was plenty, because they are so few.

As I mentioned at the end of the last section, this story testifies to the efficacy of *tsoru* sharing: it produced the group of 'twelve brothers' and, in contrast, those excluded became 'others'. The Gadaba also mentioned that the same was true for the tiger category, who are as numerous as the cobra, and that for the remaining two categories the food was sufficient, because there are only a few monkey and sun villages. In fact, every group—whether belonging to the cobra, tiger, sun or monkey category and no matter how many villages exist pertaining to this category—refers to the idea of *baro bai tero gadi* and thus refers to Gadaba society as a totality. For some other central Indian tribal communities such 'village confederations', as they are called by Robert Parkin (1992: 74f, 90f), act as 'clan councils' (ibid.: 95). Among the Bondo, who are culturally very close to the Gadaba, Elwin also described the *bara-jangar* group as a ritual unit of the twelve original Bondo villages, representatives of which gather at the annual *pat kanda* sacrifice (1950: 6f). However, I never heard of such a regular gathering and, unlike the Bondo, the Gadaba do not have one village that is regarded as their 'capital' (ibid.: 6).

During my research only once did the *baro bai tero gadi* become a matter of direct ritual action. The village headman—headmen always belong to the dominant group of earth people—had died as a consequence of a severe beating at the hands of his son during the April Festival, a time at which fighting is explicitly prohibited. To make matters worse, the son did not consider sacrificing a cow for the deceased as should have been done according to *niam*. The death rituals were conducted in a condensed form so as to be through with them before the main festival day. However, on the day after the main day of the festival, the brother of the deceased became possessed by the enraged liminal spirit of the headman. To appease the spirit a cow was brought and a cow sacrifice was indicated that would be later performed in full. A piece of the cow's ear was cut off and together with some husked rice, like an offering, fed to the possessed man on behalf of the spirit. But to no avail. The brother died too and his cremation also did not proceed as it should. Even before the festival was over it was decided to sacrifice in the name of *baro bai tero gadi* in order to prevent the issue getting further out of hand.

A member of the senior *tsorubai*, not the local *tsorubai*, from a neighbouring village was called and 'twelve heads' were sacrificed for the deceased headman, as should be done in the case of a 'bad death'.[15] In addition to a number of animals to make up the twelve, such as a cockroach and a mouse, a pig and a cow were sacrificed. The pig was given to the internal affines of the earth people of Gudapada. They sacrificed the pig and prepared *tsoru* from its meat in a new earthen pot, and consumed it among themselves. In parallel and completely separately from this, the headman's agnates—under the leadership of the *tsorubai*—sacrificed the cow and shared *tsoru* whilst their women and children ate *lakka'** food.

Even in this context, representatives of all twelve villages were not actually called to share the *tsoru* directly. Twelve raw portions of cow meat were spread on leaves on the ground and the twelve villages were named. As this is not an everyday affair, it took a moment before everyone settled on which twelve cobra villages should receive a share as part of the 'twelve brothers'. One share remained in the village—as the village was part of the 'twelve brothers'—and was given to the local *tsorubai* of the deceased's group; i.e. by the Sisa (group of deceased) to the Kirsani (their local *tsorubai*). At a different place, the affines of the headman's group laid out nineteen portions of raw pig meat to be distributed to the affines of the headman's local subline (*kutum*). Thus, for the agnatic component of the sacrificial context the number twelve was crucial, whereas the number of shares for the affines was purely accidental, depending on the number of local groups to which the headman's local subline happened to have sent 'daughter-sisters' (*ji bouni*) for marriage. The agnatic whole represented by the number twelve is thus complemented by a numerically unspecified affinal category. Both made up the totality of Gadaba society.

Devouring

Relationships of feeding/eating and sharing constitute the benevolent, balanced and predictable socio-cosmic order based on sacrifice and *tsoru*. The rituals in which these relationships and practices are embedded are public, definite in number, internally coherent and interdependent; one could thus speak of a ritual system. Among the key values expressed in the alimentary processes are brotherhood (agnatic continuity) and otherhood (affinal reproduction). Relationships of devouring contrast in all of these aspects. They are violent, one-sided, unpredictable and based on the meanest aspects of humans, namely greed (greedy, *lobra*) and envy (*ongkar*), which lead to destruction (*nosto*). However, these relationships too are ritualized and occur in ritual contexts. These rituals lack the systemic aspect mentioned above since they are performed on demand, as disaster strikes.[16] They are performed secretly, after dark and partly at places humans would normally avoid. In short, these relationships are not *niam* and the alimentary mode of violent, one-sided consumption or devouring in contrast to feeding/eating and sharing epitomizes this fact.

Disorder results in illness. Put the other way around, illness and healing are about precarious relationships. They include relationships between all agents of the cosmos—humans, animals, gods and the dead—and as such healing cannot be narrowly defined. The body, the house, the village, the crops, domestic animals or children: all may fall prey to illness due to relationships that have gone wrong or been neglected or violated. Nevertheless, the Gadaba do distinguish between different kinds of calamity, although not always very clearly. The notions of *bipod* or *bada* refer to disaster on a broad scale, *jor duka* 'fever-sorrow' signifies a broad range of physical and mental problems and *bota* simply means pain. Yet, even a 'simple' stomach ache can be the sign of a precarious relationship with a liminal spirit of the dead and ultimately fatal in its consequences, if ignored. Specialists are consulted to diagnose the cause or causes of an illness and perform rituals to counter such attacks as are generally considered to have caused the disease. A person's life force, blood or liver—all three closely connected as I pointed out earlier—may be devoured (*kai debar*) by aggressive agents, who are rarely gods, frequently humans, at times the dead and most often the demons *soni* and *rau*. I call the latter 'demons' because—in contrast to gods, humans and the dead—they never act in any other way than attempting to feed on the life of humans. They represent the relationship of devouring par excellence. In most cases, however, it is a combination of forces, for example, a spirit of the liminal dead (*duma*) sent by a sorcerer (*pangon lok*), and the rituals countering such attacks of aggressive consumption mostly deal with a whole range of possible agents. Identifying a single cause of an illness is ultimately not particularly relevant to the Gadaba because their focus is on ritually providing a counter-force.[17]

As the rituals related to devouring relationships are various and idiosyncratic it is difficult to provide a generalized description as in the case of village sacrifices that always adhere to the same pattern. I will therefore briefly describe three cases of *nosto* or acts of destruction that involve bodies, houses and crops. A range of other practices—possession and exorcism, evil eye, witchcraft and oaths—will be left out here. I will also not deal with three other causes of disaster, because they lack the agency characteristic of relationships of devouring: first, illnesses that arise 'by themselves' (*nije*); second, transgressions (*dos*) of *niam* that involve an immediate and automatic response; third, the destiny that has been 'written' (*leka*) at the birth of a person. In all severe cases of illness I encountered, agency was assumed and references to destiny or illnesses that arise by themselves were not made, partly, I assume, because it allows humans to take action themselves. Essentially, there are two ways humans react to attempts of aggressive consumption: they try to compensate the assailant with blood and food to persuade it to let go of the victim, or, if this does not work, they try to turn the hunter into prey. Thus, one line of the spells (*montor*) against aggressive spirits of the dead runs *tui cheli mui bag*, 'you are the goat; I am the tiger'. It therefore is a question of the power to reverse the direction of predation. This is done with the help of the gods and the saying accordingly goes: 'call for the gods; defeat the demon' (*maphru mangibo, rau bandibo*).

Before I describe the three cases of *nosto* I shall briefly introduce the main specialists and their techniques. There are three specialists in these rituals: first, the healer (*gunia*); second, the diviner (*dissari*); and third, the ritual medium (*gurumai*). The first two are often jointly referred to by the term *dissari*, and both tasks may be performed by a single individual. I will henceforth use the term *dissari* in this comprehensive sense. Like the village sacrificer and cook, these specialists are normal cultivators like anyone else rather than full-time specialists. Unlike the former, however, they perform their tasks for individual clients on demand. The healer does most of the dangerous work, such as chasing the liminal dead on the cremation ground, and also mixes and administers medicine, while the diviner uses a rice oracle or, if he is able to read, an almanac. Whereas the healers and diviners are usually male, the ritual mediums are often female and the term *gurumai* refers to femininity (*mai*). The *gurumai* becomes possessed by deities and thus communicates with the divine. In many rituals of healing, *dissari* and *gurumai* work together.

The techniques of a *dissari* can be described as a triangle of features that reinforce each other and centre on sacrifice. It is blood that enlivens his tools and renders them effective. The first tool is a *jupan* and consists of two rings of twisted black iron, perhaps 10 cm. in diameter, to one of which an iron chain with sharp ends like barbed wire is attached. This tool is used as a weapon when thrown, but can be used to search for otherwise invisible objects as well. The second important aspect of defence and attack are spells (*montor*), which are combined with the third, 'medicine' (*oso, sindrong**). Medicine, usually different kinds of plants, takes many forms. For example, it can be placed in a kind of pointed iron cartridge (*kuti*) that is beaten into the ground to protect an area, immobilize an aggressive force or prevent an assailant from crossing it.

The family resemblances between the different healing rituals will become evident from the brief description of the cases that follows. Case one describes a ritual dealing with the identification and destruction of magical objects sent into the house of the afflicted person; in case two objects of the same kind have been sent to diminish the harvest; in case three objects have been sent into the body of a young man causing illness.

Case 1: Sadep, a teenager of about fifteen, died of high fever within a matter of days and his sister also developed a fever soon afterwards. A *gurumai* from a different village divined that Sadep had been attacked by the *rau* demon in the form of a wind. The *gurumai* also claimed that *rau* had been sent by someone and that the same sorcerer was now causing the girl's illness. Mangla Kirsani, the children's father, contacted the *gurumai* of his own village who further divined that his house had been attacked with *jontor*. These are little parcels, smaller than a thumb, that are sent with the help of *montor* by a sorcerer into the house or fields of a person, to harm their bodies or reduce their crops. Some remnants of the ritual that supposedly caused the destruction are usually wrapped up in a small piece of cloth. In this case, a ritual was scheduled in which the *gurumai* and a *dissari* from Gudapada should dispose of these objects and the threat in general.

After dark, the two specialists commenced the ritual in Mangla's house. They drew a sacrificial pattern on the floor of the big room and made the girl sit behind it. Making invocations (calling the gods for help) they held the sacrificial animals in their hands: a crab (for the *duma*), a white chick (for the *rau* demon) and a black chick (probably again for the *duma*). During the invocations the power of the specialists was asserted when they laid the animals on their backs on the sacrificial pattern and the animals remained there as if paralysed. The animals were then taken up again and made to eat some grains of rice, which they did immediately and thus signalled the acceptance of the offerings by the recipients. They were then killed and some blood was poured over the *jupan*, the iron cartridges (*kuti*) and the medicine. The specialists then drank liquor, which helps fight demons (see Berger 2002). Then the *dissari* tried to locate the *jontor* by searching the room indirectly with a mirror. He spotted one in the inner room of the house, jumped into the respective corner and grasped it. This apparently caused him pain and people rushed up to pour medicine over his clenched fist. He dropped the small packet into a container of medicine, which rendered the *jontor* harmless. It was opened outside the house and contained some pieces of an eggshell and other ingredients no one could identify. All of this was burned and the men then beat iron *kuti* filled with medicine into the floor of the house, all around it and at all thresholds and crossings on the way to the cremation ground. At the ritual border (*bejorna*) especially associated with the spirits of the liminal dead the *gurumai* (in this case a male) urinated across the path and remained there while the *dissari* proceeded a hundred metres farther to the cremation ground. The *dissari* threw himself onto the ashes of Sadep's cremation pyre and rolled wildly around before lying still. Helpers beat *kuti* into the ground between his toes and fingers and close to his head before helping him up again. Then they all returned to Mangla's house taking further ritual precautions to prevent any evil force from following. There Mangla's wife had prepared the meat of the sacrificial animals and along with further liquor the specialists—but no member of the family—dined on them.

Case 2: Like many Gadaba Biju Challan was afraid his harvest might be diminished due to rituals of *nosto* or destruction. A *dissari* divined that indeed such actions had taken place and predicted that *jontor* had been sent to his millet harvest, which at that time had already been piled up on a scaffold next to the threshing floor. The ritual commenced after nightfall. In the house the dissari drew a sacrificial pattern and began the invocation with the victims as usual. However, a complication occurred. The white chicken did not eat any rice grains. It often takes a while before a chicken starts to peck at the grains, and the *dissari* know various ways to motivate the animal to eat. However, nothing worked and after about twenty minutes it seemed evident that this offering had been rejected or that somebody had interfered. Ultimately, the *dissari* placed the chicken on its side in the middle of the sacrificial pattern and with a stone drove an iron *kuti* through one eye of the animal into the ground, thereby completely smashing its head, before throwing it through the open door into the yard. Then a group of men accompanied the *dissari* as he proceeded to the threshing floor in search of the *jontor*. Using his *jupan* like a night vision device the *dissari* spotted two *jontor*, caught them and put them in a bowl of medicine, as described above. The *dissari* then drew a diagram of a human figure with a bow and arrow in the middle of the threshing ground, where he made a number of sacrifices including an egg and a crab before inspecting the contents of the *jontor* (a piece of charcoal, ash, a tooth and some grains of millet). The *jontor* was burned and everyone returned to the house where the specialist and his helpers consumed the meat of the sacrificial animals.

Case 3: Bogu Sisa, a young man of about 25 at the time, was suddenly unable to walk or move his legs and all movement was very painful for him. A *dissari* diagnosed that someone had probably harmed him with a *kudal*, i.e. objects had been sent into his body. *Kudal* thus resemble *jontor*, except that their destination differs: the body in the former and the house or fields in the latter case. After sunset, the *dissari* commenced the ritual by drawing a pattern on the floor of the big room of Bogu's house and constructing a clay figure, which he put in its centre. He also made a small bow and arrows with tiny pieces of cloth tied to their ends. After sacrificing various animals, the *dissari* lit the ends of the arrows and shot them in all directions, the last one into the clay figure. Bogu was then asked to cut the figure with a knife, and all remains of the ritual were then put on a leaf plate onto which Bogu was asked to spit. Another person was then sent to dump all of this in the river. The *dissari* then began the extraction of the *kudal*. He placed the rings of his *jupan* on Bogu's body, put a small pipe in the middle and started to suck the *kudal* out of his body. Eventually, a piece of charcoal and a splinter of a bone appeared, which were put into a bowl of medicine. Afterwards the *dissari* found and neutralized a *jontor* in the house (containing ash and a pig's tooth). Later, food was prepared from the sacrificial animals and offerings made to the house god and the fireplace before the specialist began to eat.

Many details have been left out in the brief descriptions of these cases. I have presented them briefly here to draw particular attention to three related aspects, the first of which is the feature of violence. Violence is experienced in terms of the harm done to a person's body, children, animals or crops. However, violence is also committed when burning arrows are shot and the *jupan* is thrown. Furthermore, in the second case, the chicken's refusal to eat the grains was perceived as a direct confrontation. Originally a sacrifice to the demon, the animal, I would argue, came, in the course of the proceedings, to represent the demon itself, and by driving a *kuti* through its eye the *dissari* was trying to turn the aggressor into the prey, the tiger into the goat. This leads to the second feature, the demonstration of power by the specialists. Such demonstrations of power do not always entail violence, but they often do. That sacrificial victims dedicated to *rau* or a *duma* do exactly what the *dissari* wants, e.g. lying still as if paralysed, is one expression of his control. At times, this control is tested even further. On one occasion, the *dissari* cut off a chicken's beak and one of its wings commanding it to continue pecking the grains offered, which it did. He then broke the animal's other wing and legs, cut its belly open while it was still alive and took out its liver. He buried half of it in the sacrificial platform and ate the other half raw himself. With such behaviour the *dissari* show that they are as truculent as the demons themselves or that they also devour. Finally, all examples show that these devouring agents such as *duma* or demons are given their share to leave the living alone, and their share is mostly raw 'food' such as crabs or blood, or food that has been 'cooked' in a leaf over a small fire. However, there is no commensality with the agents of disaster and they are not offered anything after the sacrifice itself. Only the gods who assist in fighting the aggressors are provided properly cooked food offerings. Moreover, because of the association of the sacrificial animals with the agents of black magic, those affected by the attack generally do not consume any of the food, which is reserved for the specialists and their helpers.

Conclusion

Feeding, sharing and devouring are the main parameters of Gadaba cosmology. In this contribution I have tried to outline this world view and related rituals in an abstraction of the indigenous model the Gadaba enact in ritual practice rather than verbalize explicitly. The alimentary modes of feeding, sharing and devouring have multiple dimensions: they signify ritual domains (life cycle, annual cycle and rituals of healing respectively), social relations, ritual actions and values. The most basic conceptual distinction made with all relationships is the distinction between brotherhood (*bai*) and affinity (*bondu*). This distinction is a crucial element of the social structure. Each local group—at various levels of the social order—defines its own identity on the basis of agnation and affinity vis-à-vis other groups. However, brotherhood and affinity are much more than merely a socio-structural feature. They are the principle that structures much of the reality as the Gadaba perceive it and materialize most prominently as values in the sacrificial process.

   This sacrificial process results in a hierarchy of food and people. The superior alimentary category of *tsoru* encompasses the subordinate *lakka'** food and the consumers are united and differentiated by the hierarchical opposition in the same way. Although *tsoru* can be shared between affines on certain occasions—as is the case during death rituals— the primary and most common referent of *tsoru* is the agnatic unit or brotherhood and the main signified or referent of *lakka'** are affines. In rituals of sharing during the annual cycle the *tsoru/lakka'** opposition again and again distinguishes earth people (the agnates) from latecomers (most prominently among them, the affines). In the case of the sacrifice on behalf of the slain headman the ritual process separated the cow sacrifice of the twelve brothers from the pig sacrifice of the affines, the latter clearly being an encompassed element. The brothers represented the whole signified by the number 'twelve', whereas the affines, being numerically unspecified, merely complemented the brotherhood. In the story that narrates the establishment of the twelve brothers when they came from the Godavari River, it was *tsoru* commensality that actually produced this unit and transformed the rest from brothers into excluded others. Brotherhood, then, representing the whole is a value superior to affinity. Brotherhood represents agnatic continuity that is made possible through *tsoru* commensality between local deities and their people. It is that relationship to the local gods that provides any particular group of people with the status of earth people, and it is through *tsoru* sharing that it is sustained.

Although encompassed in contexts of *tsoru* sharing, affines too represent a key value, that of procreation. It was the primordial divine transformation of brother and sister into husband and wife that brought the Gadaba community into existence and ever since it has been the flow of 'milk' that guarantees human reproduction. It is the mother's brother (*mamu*) who is regarded as milk-giver and hence rewarded with a high (temporal) status. He plays a major role in transforming the fruits of his milk-gift—his sister's children—during rituals of the life cycle: the wedding rituals that produce ritually complete persons that feed into the annual ritual cycle, and at death transforming them into members of the 'community of the dead'. In each of these cases, the mother's brother cooks and feeds affinal[18] *tsoru* to his sister's children and in the course of their death rituals he—or usually his descendants—receives and can claim brass objects in return (Berger 2010, 2015a). Affinal procreative powers are needed in spheres other than the strictly human ones too. I have argued elsewhere that the affinal contribution to the final phase of death rituals or *go'ter** can be interpreted in these terms (Berger 2010). Moreover, the most precious crop—the wet-rice—is classified as affinal and this affinal element is part of each *tsoru*. This feature is most conspicuous during the April Festival, when the rice-bride of the previous harvest is consumed by the house-people as *tsoru*. In itself, then, *tsoru* always combines affinal and agnatic elements: with their sacrificial killing agnates—who are both sacrificer as well as sacrifier—providing the life-enhancing blood (and liver) that is separately cooked but then jointly consumed with the affinal rice.

The hierarchical opposition of agnates and affines as consumers of *tsoru* and *lakka'** respectively is permanent and uncontested in the contexts of *tsoru* sharing among the four brothers during annual festivals. Beyond these most formal contexts, however, there is plenty of room for the claims, challenges and competition that the dependence on affinal procreative exchange engenders. As such, affinal guests are turned into alimentary victims, and a mother's brother may prove demanding after the death of one of his sister's children or may even decide to challenge his affines by bringing a buffalo to their final death ritual or *go'ter**, an aspect I have not elaborated upon here (see Berger 2010). These ambivalences that are played out in at times dramatic but generally choreographed ways, however, do not question the values of agnatic continuity and affinal procreation but bring them into the dialogue, making them objects of social and ritual discourse.

Predicated on the distinction between agnates and affines, all relationships of feeding/eating and sharing are part of the socio-cosmic order or *niam*. In reciprocally exchanging milk, feeding *tsoru* and eating the dead things are kept 'good and even'. *Tsoru* sharing reproduces local hierarchies and the sacrificial processes always index the 'twelve brothers, thirteen seats', the notion of Gadaba society as a totality. Actions of the *tsorubai*—the paradigmatic *tsoru* cooks and feeders—are generally related to the *niam* that these actions are said to restore.

Obviously, not everything in life is 'good and even'. The Gadaba conceptualizes the dark side of human existence, especially illness and death, in terms of devouring. In contrast to feeding and sharing, relationships of devouring are violent and unilateral. Although there are a number of causes that frequently combine to produce an illness, the demons *soni* and *rau* epitomize this domain. Unlike humans, gods or the dead they never reciprocate anything but always take life and feed on humans. However, the Gadaba do recognize immorality in humans too. The vices of greed and envy are the basis of human agency that leads to 'destruction' or *nosto*. Through rituals of black magic, calamities are inflicted mostly on brothers, their bodies, their families, their houses and their crops. Because greed and envy pivot around issues of land that is kept within the agnatic local group there would be little reason, the Gadaba say, to inflict such harm on affines. Brothers, not affines, may try to 'eat your land', i.e. take it away. However, in general the Gadaba are content to fight the causes of aggression in rituals of healing but are not interested in identifying, let alone punishing, the offender. Although there are rumours about sorcerers, I never encountered actual accusations or even trials. The agency behind acts of destruction—whether it stems from humans, spirits or demons—enables the afflicted to act and counteract, to defend themselves, to reconcile, to appease or to turn the 'goat into the tiger'.

The socio-cosmological order of *niam*, constituted by acts, relationships and values of feeding and sharing, thus also integrates morality,[19] which is what the claim that relationships should be 'good and even' clearly points to. The devouring relationships contradict and negate *niam* but this domain of devouring is, I would argue, itself opposed by an institutionalized relationship that is considered 'most senior' and thus most highly valued. It is here that the *moitor* relationship comes into play. Transcending the relational logic of agnates and affines and the associated exchange relationships, the *moitor* represent a mirror image of the agents of devouring. Like the latter, the *moitor* relationship is unilateral in principle, but in an inverse way. *Moitor* always give without asking anything themselves. The *moitor* relationship represents deference and altruism in opposition to violence and greed.

The Gadaba do not bother much about individual sin, which is certainly also related to the fact that their cosmology does not entail a soteriology. Sinfulness is not regarded as an inherent characteristic of humans and overcoming sin does not lead to salvation or the accumulation of merit (see von Fürer-Haimendorf 1974). Transgressions of *niam* (*dos*) have an immediate and automatic effect such as madness or the described changed clan status as a consequence of eating the 'wrong' sacrificial food, and neglecting ritual practices may result in the anger of gods and spirits, who may consequently cause illness. There is very little in Gadaba religion that regulates quotidian social life in any ethical way, and to a large extent behaviour that is regarded as immoral is accepted if not approved. After the former headman of Gudapada died as a consequence of his son's beating, the latter was publicly humiliated in a village gathering. However, soon afterwards the son was chosen as the new village headman. Most of the villagers regard him as the opposite of a 'righteous person' (*dorom lok*), considering him to be a drunkard, greedy and violent, all reasons, the villagers say, why all of the women he married or lived with subsequently ran away. However, this has not made him ineligible for the role as headman. Yet despite the relative indifference towards individual vice or virtue in everyday affairs, the Gadaba have—in the form of the *moitor*—institutionalized deference and altruism as a collective relationship opposing the greedy violence of the demons.

Notes

1. The ethnography of the Gadaba began with a contribution by von Fürer-Haimendorf (1943) on 'megalithic rituals'. The few ethnographers after him were also mainly interested in the 'secondary burial' of the Gadaba called *go'ter* (Izikowitz 1969; Pfeffer 1991, 2001). Among the ethnographers of the region, only Pfeffer had a sustained interest in the Gadaba and also published an article on their relationship terminology (Pfeffer 1999). Noteworthy is also a contribution by Mohanti (1973–4) on 'bond-friendship'. Some useful information can also be found in a contribution by the Anthropological Survey of India on the Ollar Gadaba (Thusu and Jha 1972), a development 'handbook' (Nayak et al. 1996) and an account by a trained biologist (Kornel 1999).

2. Research was conducted in southern Orissa for 22 months between 1999 and 2003 and was funded by the German Research Foundation (*Deutsche Forschungsgemeinschaft*; DFG) and the Fazit Foundation. Recent research was conducted for two months in 2010 and supported by the University of Groningen.

3. See Griffiths (2008) and Ranjan and Ranjan (2001a, 2001b, 2001c) on the Gutob language.

4. Gutob words like *umrang* will be marked with an '*'; all remaining indigenous terms are Desia.

5. One could, thus, state that the cosmology described here is close to what Sahlins (1985: xii) called a 'prescriptive structure', an ideal-type in which a culture assimilates the circumstances and represents events as fitting into the already constituted scheme. This contrasts with 'performative structures', which are more open to history and realize themselves by acknowledging and valuing the potential of events to lead to transformations and change.

6. The topic of own and otherness is also very pronounced in *go'ter,** the ultimate Gadaba death ritual mentioned before. Certain affinal categories, questioning the common transactional logic that defines cattle exchanges as affinal and buffalo exchanges as agnatic, donate buffaloes and, thus, challenge the hosts of the ritual (Berger 2010; Pfeffer 1991, 2001).

7. The Gadaba distinguish between three very different *moitor* relationships (Berger 2007: 173f). Here I am concerned only with the most sacred and collective of these, which is the only *moitor* relationship referred to with a Gutob term (*dissel**), the meaning of which is however unclear. On ritual friendship in middle India see further Desai (2010), Hardenberg (2003), Mohanti (1973–4), Pfeffer (2001) and Skoda (2005: 147–65).

8. This term (as many others) was probably adopted from other lowland

communities. The Jagannath cult is of no relevance for the Gadaba and nobody of my acquaintance ever bothered to visit the temple.

9. The Gadaba also speak of 'four people' or *chari jono* (Pfeffer 1991).

10. Following the collective sacrifice for the village deity earlier that day, only the unmarried boys of the dominant agnatic group have shared *tsoru*, not the other adult male members. This is done, it is said, so that the boys 'have seen the four brothers'. For everyone else the house *tsoru* is the first meal of the day.

11. The Sisa of different villages have nothing in common except this status and no particular relationships exist between the Sisa of different localities. This status division is only of relevance for the village. A capital letter is used and the word is not italicized when local groups are concerned (e.g. Sisa); lower case letter and italics indicate that the term is used as a category of reference (e.g. *kirsani*). The Gadaba use the term *kuda* to refer to both.

12. As I have described elsewhere (2002: 75), the sacrifice for the village deity during the November Festival is organized differently with regard to who is financing the ritual. Usually, money and rice are collected from each household. Sacrificial animals are bought with the former and *tsoru* rice is prepared from the latter. However, the *hundi* sacrifice in November, which is called *hundi sitlani* or 'cooling of hundi', is especially connected to the harvest, which it precedes. Therefore, all clients of the village who receive a share of the harvest (*pholoi*) have to pay 'respect' (*manti*) to the earth people—the landowning agnatic core—and their deities. Accordingly, in Gudapada, the *barik* must contribute the liquor for the sacrifice, the herdsmen the cock and the blacksmiths the pig every alternating year. Although not a client like the others, the village headman (*naik*), a member of the four brothers, provides around 12.5 kg. (5 measures or *man*) of husked rice for the *tsoru*. His ancestors were given a small wet-rice field in order to provide this rice for the occasion.

13. In fact, my status in terms of *tsoru* sharing remained ambivalent throughout my stay. Although I shared the *tsoru* at the house level with my cobra hosts, the earth people of the village, I was not allowed to share *tsoru* with them on the collective occasions described here but was seated next to their affines, sharing their food (see Berger 2015a: 531–53).

14. For example, a Gadaba once told me that there are 1,012 Gadaba villages (which, if taken literally, would be a wild exaggeration). I understood it to mean 'many', indicated by the number 1000 and the 12 indicating a 'totality'.

15. Being killed is not necessarily considered as a 'bad death', and originally the headman's death was not classified as such. However, the events that followed made it seem wise to offer 'twelve heads' anyway.

16. That is to say, healing rituals are not sequentially connected as rituals of the life cycle or annual cycle. However, healing rituals too are systematic in the sense that they have recognizable structures of action. They are also

connected in important ways to the life cycle and the annual cycle, because certain elements of these domains can be considered as healing rituals.

17. With reference to the region under discussion, the complex of illness has been described in great detail by Tina Otten (2006) and Piers Vitebsky (1993) with reference to the Rona and Sora respectively.

18. This food the mother's brother cooks and feeds is, of course, 'affinal' from the perspective of the recipients but not from his own perspective.

19. Joel Robbins describes such an integrated morality that is part of the cultural value system as a 'morality of reproduction' and contrasts it to 'moralities of choice' (2007: 296). Especially where conflicts between value spheres arise, such as in instances of rapid cultural change, as is the focus of his research, actors consciously reflect and choose to act according to certain moral standards and values (2007: 300).

References

Berger, P., *Feeding, Sharing, and Devouring: Ritual and Society in Highland Odisha, India*, Boston and Berlin: De Gruyter, 2015a.

———, 'Death, Ritual, and Effervescence', in *Ultimate Ambiguities: Investigating Death and Liminality*, ed. P. Berger and J. Kroesen, New York: Berghahn Books, 2015b, pp. 147–83.

———, 'Liminal Bodies, Liminal Food: Hindu and Tribal Death Rituals Compared', in *Ultimate Ambiguities: Investigating Death and Liminality*, ed. P. Berger and J. Kroesen, New York: Berghahn Books, 2015c, pp. 57–77.

———, 'Dimensions of Indigeneity in Highland Odisha, India', *Asian Ethnology*, vol. 73, nos. 1–2, 2014, pp. 19–37.

———, 'Feeding Gods, Feeding Guests: Sacrifice and Hospitality among the Gadaba of Highland Orissa (India)', *Anthropos*, vol. 106, no. 1, 2011, pp. 31–47.

———, '"Who Are You, Brother and Sister?" The Theme of "Own" and "Other" in the *Go'ter* Ritual of the Gadaba', in *The Anthropology of Values. Essays in Honour of Georg Pfeffer*, ed. P. Berger, R. Hardenberg, E. Kattner and M. Prager, New Delhi: Pearson, 2010, pp. 260–87.

———, 'Conceptualizing and Creating Society in Highland Orissa: Descent, Territory and Sacrificial Communion', in *Contemporary Society. Tribal Studies, Vol. VIII: Structure and Exchange in Tribal India and Beyond*, ed. G. Pfeffer and D.K. Behera, New Delhi: Concept Publishing, 2009, pp. 119–34.

———, 'Sacrificial Food, the Person and the Gadaba Ritual System', in *Periphery and Centre: Studies in Orissan History, Religion and Anthropology*, ed. G. Pfeffer, New Delhi: Manohar, 2007, pp. 199–221.

———, 'The Gadaba and the 'non-ST' Desia of Koraput', in *Contemporary Society: Tribal Studies, Vol. 5. The Concept of Tribal Society*, ed. G. Pfeffer and D.K. Behera, New Delhi: Concept Publishing, 2002, pp. 57–90.

Desai, A., 'A Matter of Affection: Ritual Friendship in Central India', in *The Ways of Friendship: Anthropological Perspectives*, ed. A. Desai and E. Killick, New York: Berghahn Books, 2010, pp. 114–31.

Elwin, V., *Bondo Highlander*, Bombay: Oxford University Press, 1950.

Fortes, M., *Kinship and the Social Order: The Legacy of Lewis Henry Morgan*, London: Routledge, 1969.

Fürer-Haimendorf, C.V., 'The Sense of Sin in Cross-Cultural Perspective', *Man*, vol. 9, no. 4, 1974, pp. 539–56.

———, 'Megalithic Ritual among the Gadabas and Bondos of Orissa', *Journal and Proceedings of the Royal Anthropological Society of Bengal*, vol. 9, 1943, pp. 149–78.

Gregory, C.A., 'Brotherhood and Otherhood in Bastar: On the Social Specificity of "Dual Organisation" in Aboriginal India', in *Contemporary Society. Tribal Studies, Vol. VIII: Structure and Exchange in Tribal India and Beyond*, ed. G. Pfeffer and D.K. Behera, New Delhi: Concept Publishing, 2009, pp. 67–82.

Griffiths, A., 'Gutob', in *The Munda Languages*, ed. G.D.H. Anderson, London: Routledge, 2008, pp. 633–81.

Gustafsson, U., *An Adiwasi Oriya-Telegu-English Dictionary, Mysore*, Mysore: Central Institute of Indian Languages, 1989.

Hardenberg, R., 'Children of the Earth Goddess: Society, Marriage, and Sacrifice in the Highlands of Orissa (India)', post-doctoral thesis edn., Westfälische Wilhelms-Universität Münster, 2005.

———, 'Friendship and Violence among the Dongria Kond', *Baessler Archiv*, vol. 51, 2003, pp. 45–57.

Izikowitz, K.G., 'The Gotr Ceremony of the Boro Gadaba', in *Primitive Views of the World*, ed. S. Diamond, New York: Columbia University Press, 1969, pp. 129–50.

Kornel, D., *Tribal Cultural Heritage and Cult: The Gutob Gadaba Tribe of Orissa*, Bhubanseswar: Modern Book Depot, 1999.

Mahapatra, K., 'Desia: A Tribal Oriya Dialect of Koraput Orissa', *Adivasi*, vol. 25, 1985, pp. 1–304.

McDougal, C.W., *Social Structure of the Hill Juang*, Alberqueque: The University of New Mexico, 1963.

Mohanti, U.C., 'Bond-Friendship among the Gadaba', *Man in Society*, vol. 1, 1973–4, pp. 130–55.

Nayak, R.K., B. Boal and N. Soreng, *The Gadabas: A Handbook for Development*, New Delhi: Indian Social Institute, 1996.

Otten, T., *Heilung durch Rituale. Vom Umgang mit Krankheit bei den Rona im Hochland Orissas, Indien*, Berlin: Lit, 2006.

Parkin, Robert, *The Munda of Central India: An Account of their Social Organization*, New Delhi: Oxford University Press, 1992.

Pfeffer, G., 'A Ritual of Revival among the Gadaba of Koraput', in *Jagannath Revisited: Studying Society, Religion and the State in Orissa*, ed. H. Kulke and B. Schnepel, New Delhi: Manohar, 2001, pp. 99–123.

————, 'Gadaba and the Bondo Kinship Vocabularies versus Marriage, Descent and Production', in *Contemporary Society. Tribal Studies IV: Social Realities*, ed. D.K. Behera and G. Pfeffer, New Delhi: Concept Publishing, 1999, pp. 17–46.

————, 'The Scheduled Tribes of Middle India as a Unit: Problems of Internal and External Comparison', in *Contemporary Society. Tribal Studies I: Structure and Process*, ed. G. Pfeffer and D.K. Behera, New Delhi: Concept Publishing, 1997, pp. 3–27.

————, 'Der intra-agnatische "Seelentausch" der Gadaba beim großen Lineageritual', in *Beiträge zur Ethnologie Mittel-und Süd-Indiens*, ed. M.S. Laubscher, München: Anacon, 1991, pp. 59–92.

Ranjan, F.H. and J. Ranjan, *Grammar Write-Up of Gutob-Gadaba*, Lamtaput: Asha Kiran Society, 2001a.

————, *Gutob-Gadaba Language Learner's Guide*, Lamtaput: Asha Kiran Society, 2001b.

————, *Gutob-Gadaba Phonemic Summary*, Lamtaput: Asha Kiran Society, 2001c.

Robbins, Joel, 'Between Reproduction and Freedom: Morality, Value, and Radical Cultural Change', *Ethnos*, vol. 72, no. 3, 2007, pp. 293–314.

Sahlins, M., *Tribesmen*, Englewood Cliffs: Prentice-Hall, 1968.

————, 'On the Sociology of Primitive Exchange', in *The Relevance of Models for Social Anthropology*, ed. M. Banton, London: Tavistock, 1965, pp. 139–236.

————, *Islands of History*, Chicago: University of Chicago Press, 1985.

Skoda, U., *The Aghria: A Peasant Caste on a Tribal Frontier*, New Delhi: Manohar, 2005.

Strathern, A., *The Rope of Moka: Big-men and Ceremonial Exchange in Mount Hagen, New Guinea*, Cambridge: Cambridge University Press, 1971.

Thusu, K.N. and M. Jha, *Ollar Gadba of Koraput*, Calcutta: Anthropological Survey of India, 1972.

Vitebsky, Piers, *Dialogues with the Dead: The Discussion of Mortality among the Sora of Eastern India*, Cambridge: Cambridge University Press, 1993.

5 On Death and Ho's Relationship with their Dead

EVA REICHEL

Introduction

This chapter is about the Ho, one of almost 100 ethnic categories living in the middle Indian states of Jharkhand and Odisha. The ethnographic observations presented here are the result of fieldtrips between 2006 and 2012. Fieldwork was mainly done in and around the Chaibasa area of Singhbhum/Jharkhand and in the north-western tip of Mayurbhanj/Odisha near Rairanpur.

Right from the beginning of my fieldwork when I entered a Ho house for the first time I immediately became aware of the continued presence of the dead in the everyday lives of the living. Ho ancestors in their pure essence are spatially really close to the living—sheltered literally under the same roof where they are routinely and ritually treated on a daily basis. Also, in participating in several first and secondary funerals I was in the midst of Ho mourning their dead and coping with the universal bio-physiological phenomenon of death in their culture-specific ways. The field trips included participation in several first and secondary funerals, where the Ho mourning their dead and coping with the universal bio-physiological phenomenon of death in their culture-specific ways were observed.

In this respect the issue of death itself becomes a topic of discussion. Anthropology as the study of Man in a Lévi-Straussian sense has been identified as Entropology, the study of processes of disintegration, of transformation, of death (Lévi-Strauss 1970: 367). In fact, an 'Anthropology of Death' (Fabian 1973) has evolved with its comparative approaches and cross-cultural analysis (Hertz 1907, Bloch 1982 and 1988, Parry 1986, Alex 2008) that will be referred to in this chapter, as 'death throws into relief the most important cultural values by which people live their lives' (Huntington and Metcalf 1979: 5). The chapter ethnographically focusses on these cultural values as they come to the fore in the Ho's relationship with their dead.

Embedded anthropologically, the argument will run as follows: Ho society is a specific type of a 'holistic society' (Dumont 1986: 279) assuming the unity of the cosmos and a universal order permeating the entire cosmos. The dead in Ho society remain included in this universal order and continue to be ritually treated as constitutive elements of this cosmic unity. Ho death rituals illustrate the social character of death that is indigenously conceived of as a process of transformation of those affected by it and an initiation of the dead into a social (after-)life as ancestors. Ancestors are vested with authority, agency and powers. Ho mortuary rites construe relations of dependence, interdependence and solidarity. They contribute to the collective making of meaning by creating and reproducing a dynamic web of collaboration among the living and between the living and the dead. Death related issues in Ho society thus reveal quintessential insights into core values touching upon and informing the Ho concept of the person and Ho understandings of what (death as constituent component of) life is about.

The chapter consists of six sections. The following section introduces the Ho as a distinct category within the socio-cultural setting of tribal middle India. The next section gives the ethnographic description of a casualty in my immediate vicinity revealing the choreography of the living mourning their dead in the course of a first burial. The chapter then examines the concept of the relations between the living and the dead and the transformation of a dead Ho into a protective ancestor—person followed by a discussion of the notions of death and the dead in broader anthropological terms and contrasting understandings of death 'here' and elsewhere in cross-cultural perspective. The chapter will be rounded off by ethnographic notes on what Ho call an 'untimely, sudden death' and the consequences for a deceased person's soul resulting from this diagnosis.

The Ho: a distinct category in central-eastern India

The majority of the more than one million Ho[1] live in the Kolhan, a region on the Chotanagpur Plateau reaching south-easterly into the southern parts of Jharkhand, Singhbhum and Dhalbhum areas, into adjacent parts of northern Odisha and also into West Bengal.[2]

Ho see themselves as Adivasi or first settlers who in the course of their history have migrated into this region coming from the north and north-west. Their understanding and evaluation of historical facts is based in mythology, and the cultural memory of the history of Ho settlement is recreated in yearly rituals.[3] 'Ho' carries the meaning 'man, husband' and quite generally 'a Ho person' (Deeney 2005: 154). Identification of 'Ho' and 'man' contrasts with the term *diku* which sums up everything that is classified as the outside, the other and which comprises all notions and concepts foreign and alien to the Ho cosmos.

Ho in their self-perception are a tribal category. However, this is a term and a concept that seems and has seemed more relevant for social anthropologists attempting at constituting a meaningful difference between the category of tribe and the category of caste. It also seems to be a meaningful category for the Indian administration trying to have all Indian tribes listed, uplifted, modernized, and civilized.[4] Somehow for the Ho that I have met the category of 'tribe' was relevant only insofar as it would aptly and concisely underpin their insistence on their being different from everything and everybody they consider *diku*, especially Hindus from the plains, more generally and as a matter of principle and definition everybody who is a non-Ho (like myself, for example[5]). The dichotomy Ho-*diku* is a cultural distinction reflecting a graded concept of inclusion and exclusion. 'A *diku* is an outsider, someone who does not belong to the "land of the forest" (*buru disum*), who does not speak a tribal language, and does not have a clan graveyard' (Verardo 2003: 26). For the very same reasons Santal, often neighbours of the Ho and sometimes more numerous than the Ho population in this area, are by definition clearly considered non-Ho and a separate tribal category, but not *diku*. Likewise, there are members of non-tribal categories who have been living together with the tribal Ho for ages and who are also not considered *diku*. They are usually landless and of inferior status. By being functionally distinctive and professionally specific these service groups are conceptually part of the indigenous communities and physically part of Ho villages. They share cultural norms with the Ho and they speak Ho. When referring to their conceptual opposite '*diku*', Ho would proudly claim to be members of the Ho tribe. Otherwise they relate to themselves as Ho and speak their mother tongue Ho, although many of them have a good command over languages like Odia, Hindi or Santali.[6]

Many Ho make their physical and spiritual living within the framework of settled agriculture and the collecting of forest produce from the jungle. Dry rice is cultivated as the main crop. Regular attention and irrigation is given to gardening. As landowners the Ho's status is high. The complex of central ideas and values is different from that of the Hindus of the plains in fundamental ways. For example, even though both categories adhere to ideas of the transmigration of the soul and to notions of ritual purity and impurity, the underlying concepts are semantically non-identical. The tribal concept of reincarnation differs from that of Brahmanic Hinduism, which is tied to individual *karma* and consequently allows for individual mobility after death. Also, the *varna* model as frame of reference is absent. The tribal construction of the soul differs qualitatively from both Christian notions about it as well as those alive in 'mainstream' Hindu caste society.[7]

An individual Ho finds himself in a social web of relations of which the membership of one of by now more than 132 *kilis* or clans is of paramount importance. Exogamous patrilateral Ho clans—and also those of the Santal with whom they co-reside and interact in their villages for that matter—are socially organized beyond the Hindu system of castes, temples, gods and goddesses. However, the Ho do have their own spirit world to which also *Sinbonga*, their creator god as well as their ancestors belong. With all of these, Ho are interrelated in a system of reciprocal exchanges. In ritual offerings at the household and village level their protection is being demanded and guaranteed; in this process their very existence is publicly constituted, symbolically institutionalized and materially integrated into the sphere of the living. It is shocking to the *diku* or Hindus *of the plains* that Ho tend to eat any kind of meat, drink a lot of alcohol and do so publicly—seemingly without any self-consciousness about it. They avoid milk, they marry *outside* their clans, and they bury their dead instead of burning them and perform a second burial—to mention just a few differences.

Statistics

The overall number of all tribal people living in South Asia may be 80–100 million. No other country in the world is home to tribal communities as large as those in India.[8] They have been listed in a schedule of the Indian Constitution as Scheduled Tribes (ST). According to the Census of India 2001 they constitute 8.2 per cent of the Indian population. In these schedules more artificial categories such as Scheduled Castes (SC), Other Backward Classes (OBC) have been invented in a formal politico-administrative procedure separating what has been interpreted as a kind of symbiosis elsewhere[9] cross-cutting those jural frontiers. The official label is one of 'protective discrimination' accompanied by financial subsidies and benefits for those so classified—and an issue of public discourse for that matter. Those Ho and Santal that have been scheduled by the government as being ethnically or culturally different for reasons that are not given or known live in the same villages as those that have been 'neglected' or forgotten by the (scheduling) system. Among those that have been omitted are members of castes who refer to themselves and who are referred to by others as 'General' which means that they have *not* been pigeonholed into the categories ST, SC, or OBC. In Manbir, during the fieldwork in 2006, these 'General' constituted 32 per cent of the village population. Their title was Mahakud in most cases. They were not considered Ho by the Ho community and did not consider themselves Ho, 'yet' they spoke Ho as their mother tongue or used it as a *lingua franca* (they easily switched to Hindi when they had visitors from Jharkhand). They performed rituals very much in the Ho way as the section titled 'Death in Manbir' will show. Their houses inside were structured very much like Ho houses consisting of one large room and, separated from it by a wall, a smaller portion: the *adin* or kitchen. Like Ho people they produced and loved to drink and share their rice-beer, they ate meat, though not beef.

Tribal society and status

The symbiosis of tribal and non-tribal categories in middle India does not aim at assimilation and creating a society of equals. Members of different categories conceive of themselves as separate, yet involved and interrelated in many ways and as such not excluded from the societal pattern of the hills and plateaux. Hierarchical status distinctions are kept alive within a practised, accepted, transparent and known social division of labour between these different categories according to principles and criteria of purity and pollution. This division of labour is characterized by the members of the ST and the OBC functioning as patrons and the members of the SC functioning as their clients, i.e. specialists at village level such as petty traders, cattle herders, blacksmiths, musicians, and craftsmen. Ho people say that since times immemorial they have been jointly migrating: 'we have asked them to come with us and to work for us. In former times they were poor. Now they are often richer than we are.' These differences or inequalities—according to the Western understanding of personal freedom and unlimited possibilities of the individual—are considered a given to be continued, a given that is based in history and sanctioned by their ancestors' demands. For this reason, the Ho and the other inhabitants of the hilly regions and plateaux of central-eastern India as a *tribal society* along with Pfeffer (1997). In mixed villages they live side by side in ordered, well-structured conviviality that does not ask for, but does not exclude intermarriage as a matter of principle either. Of this tribal society, this is the argument, also *caste* members—sometimes compared to *Sudras*—are a constitutive and inclusive part. Despite their being Hindus they are and conceive of themselves as being different from the Hindus of the plains as indicated above. The whole set up in this region is perhaps held together by Ho (and Santal) values and ideas constituting the overall *tribal* world. These function as the dominant model and are expressed in a number of ways. So, for instance, death rituals are performed in ways that are informed by—yet not identical with—the familiar Ho choreography of treating their dead.

The last argument shall be proved in the next paragraph which is about a case of death in very close vicinity. A woman of the category 'General' had died in the middle of the night. Her title was Mahakud. Although as 'General' the members of the household were not Ho, the dead woman's son had become the son-in-law to Giridari Bage, the Ho *munda* or village head of Manbir, who is in charge of everything of a secular nature and whose daughter had married into the category 'General'.[10] This was an accepted and public thing to do, obviously, or so I thought. I had been informed about the fact of the marriage in quite a matter-of-fact way by both G. Bage and his wife. Whenever they went to see their daughter they ordered an Ambassador, a rare sight in the village and a big thing. Also, I saw him turn up regularly at our neighbour's to have a cup or two of rice-beer and a little chat. However, the couple did not live patrivirilocally, but in Bhubaneswar, and one day when I enquired into the pedigree of G. Bage and asked about the names of his grandchildren, I was told that as the children were not Ho, he would not know their names. So although the marriage was a well-known fact in Manbir and there was no awkwardness whatsoever about the fact as such, there were probably consequences for behaving beyond the pale.

Death in Manbir: from my field notes[11]

Manbir, Mayurbhanj, Northern Odisha, India. 22 February 2006, 3:30 a.m.: *Death at our neighbour's house: nana buri[12] dies.*

Death has come close. At about 3.30 a.m. we hear the sudden and loud wailing of our neighbours.[13] She is a widow living next door together with her four children. Her husband died last year. Now her mother-in-law, her *hanar* or husband's mother has died.[14] It is the same kind of wailing that by now is familiar to me from the Ho way of mourning their dead: a standardized arrangement of minims, crotchets, and quavers within the range of a fourth, a set intonation and rhythm repeated time and again. A small kerosene lamp is lit. It is dark—seven nights after full moon. Within minutes villagers arrive: men, women, and children. As soon as they set foot inside the courtyard only the women—in the blink of an eye—start their ritual wailing holding their arms crossed behind their heads. Instantaneous, excessive and deafening. After paying a brief visit to the dead inside her room the male villagers squat down along the *pindigi*[15] talking to each other or just watching. After having left the room of the deceased the women stop wailing—as sudden as they started it. They assemble in a corner of the courtyard, separate from the men, with our neighbour being one among many involved and concerned. Children are running around, playing, and laughing. Nobody seems to mind. Whenever a female newcomer arrives the wailing starts afresh and is immediately answered by the wailing of our neighbours. Of the entire Ho community of Manbir, an elderly Ho widow and her son standing and watching, eyewitnesses to the scene, but not participating actively, also not in the ritual wailing. There seems to be a familiar script, and everybody seems to know their roles and acts accordingly.

At 11 a.m. the cot with *nana buri* on it is carried outside her room and put inside the courtyard, the body completely covered by some cloth, her head pointing southwards, and her feet northwards. Ho usually sleep their heads pointing eastwards. As soon as someone has died, however, the cot is moved around, so the head will be in a southward direction, the feet in a northward position. This will also be the position of the body inside the grave. The same has been done here. By now the yard is quite crowded—roughly 60 people have turned up. The villagers gather around the cot at once. The wailing is resumed, this time very loud, almost fiercely, and including the children, girls and boys alike; again arms are crossed behind their necks, again tears roll down their cheeks. . . . It took several hours and elaborate procedures until the body was buried the very same day in the late afternoon. Of many more important details only a few more shall be mentioned. The cloth is pulled back from the body, the blouse is torn open and the body lies naked. The bottom part of the corpse remains covered throughout the purification procedures that follow. All the bangles are broken and fall to the ground; the necklace is torn and left on the cot. The body is rubbed with turmeric and oil.[16] This is done expertly, routinely, and publicly by a male person[17] accompanied by continuous and urgent comments of those observing thus ensuring that everything is done just exactly right—at least this impression is conveyed to me. Coins are put on the dead person's forehead, her eyes, cheeks, throat and lips. Her belongings, a blanket, two blouses, a white saree, are wrapped up in a bundle and put on the cot, her head is bedded on rice. Rice is put into her right hand and passes several times through the open palms of those family members who squat close to each other next to the cot and who hold up their hands. A child of the category grandchild or *jaitadi*, is lifted across the cot and the body seven times.

More oil, rice, leaves of the sal tree,[18] *karkad* or toothbrushes which are tender twigs from the saltree, vermillion powder or *sinduri*[19] are offered and left with the dead; her body is covered with a number of used and newly bought sarees. Eventually the cot is carried by six male persons towards the burial site of the 'General' accompanied by everybody present; however, women and girls—apart from the anthropologist—will soon stay back and return at the boundary of the village, a materially unmarked and to me invisible line. The burial party does not follow the shortest path. They walk towards the nearby river Balisudra instead and criss-cross it seven times on their way to the burial ground which is quite apart from the Muslim as well as the Ho burial sites. Vivid discussions are being led throughout the process. Having arrived at the site the men will work hard for another three hours to dig the grave, while young boys of the category *jaitadi* or grandchild take turns in fanning the body with a twig from a mango tree from below the cot. Finally the body is taken off the cot and lowered into the grave. It will rest there, the head turned towards west. The bed is broken and left inside the grave which is finally being covered by earth. There is no burial stone[20] as is the Ho tradition, and there will be no burial stone later.

That day the community well is only randomly used. Usually it is a very busy place. Coincidence? A number of obligatory death rituals and ceremonies will follow in the days, weeks and months to come. *Diri dulsunum*[21] is fixed for 3 March, day 9 after (the physical) death.

Diri Dulsunum is part of the Ho mortuary rites and constitutes what has been called the second burial since Hertz (1907). This is an obligatory institution which takes place weeks, months or sometimes years later and which may last up to three days. On the occasion of this secondary burial *bala* or affines 'who are generically referred to by this term' (Yorke 1976: 88) and *haga* (agnatic category) 'meet, celebrate (*jomnu*: eat and drink), dance, and pour oil on the burial stone' (Reichel 2009: 95). This is an ordered, structured, and ritual performance, however, and not a 'creatively' morbid get-together of equally affected mourning individuals. For the affines temporary huts will be erected where these will stay, sleep, cook and perform food exchanges with other affines. These huts are built apart and at some distance from the dwelling site of the members of the agnatic category. This may be interpreted as a clear demonstration of how *bala* and *haga* are interrelated in a kind of complementary opposition.[22] The liminal phase of the participants' social pollution due to their having materially or notionally been in touch with death comes to an end and 'normal' life is resumed—for the living and the dead. The deceased has been transformed into a marriageable person yet again participating in affinal exchanges, however in a new mode after death. In this context it is interesting to realize that at least in this region members of the category 'General' relate as non-tribal non-Ho to this part of their death rituals by the identical Ho term *diri dulsunum*, although clearly no flat slab of stone is used. By oil and turmeric being applied in the rituals a deceased and a marriageable person are treated equally. As such she conceptually belongs and remains part of a collective or socio-cultural system. By being dead she is not just gone, she has not simply ceased to exist. She was a socio-cultural being before death; she remains a socio-cultural being after death. A familiar, well-known change from one phase into another one, both implying sociality, has been performed.

The metaphor of marriage hints at a transition. This transition which consists in the participants' reintegration into society in the course of the second burial is also communicated in the language of marriage. United by their identical language of ritual it may be argued that Ho and 'General' share central value—ideas about life and death—despite distinctions at the empirical level. It may also be argued that in this region where 'General' individuals keep narrating histories of their migration into this area, they became Ho-ized in a number of ways.

Relations between the living and the dead: The Ho and their ancestors

Every Ho is assumed to eventually transform into an ancestor of her or his living descendants after death unless in the case of a 'sudden' or 'violent' death as shown in the section titled 'Sunai Kondangkel'. Ancestors will remain members of their *miyad mandi chaturenko*[23] or 'people of one rice pot', including those 'descended patrilineally from a known or putative common male ancestor [which] is reckoned as far back as people can remember, e.g. 4 or 5 generations' (Deeney 2005: 242) and in-marrying wives, but excluding out-marrying daughters and sisters. *Miyad mandi chaturenko* represents a distinct socio-ritual Ho unit. It is a culture-specific consanguine Ho kin construct that expresses the unity and oneness (*miyad*) of its living and dead members (*-renko*) in a metaphor of commensality (*mandi chatu*: the earthen pot in which rice—and rice-beer—is prepared). *Miyad* carries the meanings 'to be one with; to become one with; to be united with; to have sexual intercourse' (Deeney 2005: 250). This concept of oneness keeps being regenerated at different levels. By daily feeding the collectivity of their ancestors before starting to eat themselves Ho people reciprocate and re-enact this oneness in intimate communion. Commensality and the exchange of food is 'us-centric', because eating together demonstrates that people 'are one' or 'become one' in the process as the status and symbolic transition of in-marrying wives will show. By initiating and continuing commensality relatedness and social cohesion—among the living and among the living and the dead—is lived out and continued. The ritual and structural unity of *miyad mandi chaturenko* is documented and becomes publicly visible at the death of one of its members. Then the 'people of one rice-pot', however locally dispersed they may live and irrespective of whether the funerary ceremonies have been attended or not, transform into 'those who reciprocally throw out their rice-pots' (*mandi chatu epera:ko*).

Membership of this institution is not a formal, but an active one—for both, the living and the dead.

Ancestors remain obliged towards the living. In addition, there are extra duties waiting for them, such as being in charge of the ritual purity of the household(s). They are supposed to continually interact with the spirit world in a more direct way than was possible before, because having died they have become spirits themselves. They are also assumed to be able to interact with Sinbonga, their God who has created the world and the Ho. Ancestors are said to be able to communicate with the living, and they are attributed a certain agency. Ancestors constitute an active, omnipresent, basically positive, and constructive category in a Ho life. This is balanced by the living knowing that ancestors will most certainly have built the houses which the living inhabit and which may be 100 years old and older; these have cleared the jungle and then cultivated the (ancestral) land that the living nowadays use and pass on to later generations within the *miyad mandi chaturenko*. Rice is notionally related to ancestors in manifold ways (cf. Vitebsky 1993). Ho personify rice as *baba enga* or, literally, rice mother when referring to its original source Mother Earth. By non-vegetarian sacrifices ancestors will also have appeased those gods, goddesses and spirits who are believed to have resided in the trees that needed to be cut in the process of clearing. The living will continue to regularly sacrifice in the fields on their behalf. Although the newly 'acquired' gods and goddesses have been invited to migrate together with the Ho, some are assumed to still linger around their former dwelling sites and thus need to be attended to, addressed, and fed as an obligation within a system of divine gift exchange.

The bodies of the dead are buried near the houses of the living: inside the courtyard, behind the houses, often close to the threshing ground, in the shade below the tamarind trees and within the village boundary.[24] Graves are covered by a *sasan diri* or large slab of stone[25] that needs to be chosen and carried along from the jungle. This can be an affair of a complete day, and as a norm each household should be represented by one male in this stone-getting party, all males representing the whole village. 'I can punish any household in case they fail to turn up', the *munda* or head of the village told. On these stones—after the burial rites have been performed—people will sit and talk, drink rice-beer, laugh, whisper, and gossip, kill and debone animals for meals and sacrifices, make rice-flour; children will play on them, the anthropologist and her assistant will sit there working on translations, rice is being husked. It seems that these stones turn into a locus of the social, of life and are no more associated with death, grief, and ancestors. These are being treated with the utmost respect—within the *adin* which is the specific separate kitchen of the Ho inside their houses. The *adin* is the sacred compartment, somewhat hidden behind a wall and to be entered through a rather narrow opening. Here surplus rice is stored and sometimes eggs are kept, on the occasion of the annual festivals meals are also cooked here. It is that part of the house that I was strictly prohibited to enter—in order not to pollute it. Only members of the *miyad chaturenko* are allowed there—male and female. A daughter, when visiting after marriage, is still welcome to enter, but not her husband.

Ancestral bodies are left to decay inside the grave and will remain there for good. While the overall physical body including flesh and bones is treated as immobile matter, the soul or *rowa* (also carrying the meaning of 'shade') is conceived as mobile and immortal. In the phase of a lengthy and troublesome transition the souls are expected to transform by working themselves through necessary and complex purification rituals. This is assumed to be accomplished in cooperation with as well as separate from the living. During the first burial there is a ritual called *umbul ader* or *keya ader* in the course of which the souls are being accompanied towards the *adin* where they are invited to dwell with their fellow soul-shades or ancestors. It happens, though, that souls sometimes tend to cling to the physical body and find it hard or impossible to join the party trying to guide them in a procession from the grave to their final abode. In these cases the souls are spoken to, argued with, implored, pushed, screamed at, intimidated, and also softly seduced by the living, and all this is done in intense, familiar utterances and actions. The language of mourning is standardized and yet[26] highly emotional. While observing and participating in a number of such rituals I gained the idea that a Ho *rowa* or soul is attributed all the resources, competences, and qualities of a living human—apart from its material physical being. The concept of an immaterial non-physical existence seems to be constructed in analogy to that of the living. When eventually the soul of a dead person has stood the test and arrived at the *adin* they will be attended to, they will be nourished and talked to, and they enjoy a high status.

There are ritual phases in the Hos' lives in which ancestors are particularly closely related to the living. A newly born baby, for example, will not only need to establish a relationship to the living, but also to its ancestors. It is from an ancestor that a child will receive its name. Only after the naming ceremony children will acquire their social identity. Before that they are considered incomplete[27] and do not count as a person in the Maussian sense. Another example are Ho women who grow up with their father's or patrilineal ancestors and who after marriage will adopt their husband's *kili's* or clan's name and ancestors. It is only after a specific ritual in the course of which they are being introduced to their husband's ancestors, that they are given permission to enter their husband's *adin* and touch the *mandi chatu* or rice pot, in which the common meal is cooked. Also in the case of migrating somewhere else the living will see to it that their ancestors accompany them and do not feel neglected by performing special *bongas* or rituals for them on the way. Due to these rituals the living become socially and permanently merged with the dead, and it is in these rituals that the ancestors' purity is brought about. Impurity is conceived of as contagious and thus dangerous—for the living and the dead.

Any death is considered polluting for everybody involved in it.[28] And, there are ways of dying that are considered polluting to the effect that the souls of those concerned will be permanently denied access to the respective *adin* and their ancestors. Ho diagnose the death of a person as particularly 'violent', 'sudden', or 'bewildering' in the cases that a woman dies during delivery, that a child dies before the naming ceremony has been completed, in the case of an infectious disease, of murder and suicide, and in the case that someone has been killed by an animal (snake or leopard). Unlike Parry (1994) suggests for northern India, Ho do not make a principled distinction between what he calls a 'good' and a 'bad' death, since the Ho consider any kind of death as 'bad', i.e. violent, untimely, or unnatural. What they do distinguish, however, are specific manners of dying such as those mentioned above that to them reflect a diagnostic quality bearing on the ritual treatment of the deceased person's soul and future fate. This distinction is a matter of classification, not a moral statement or negative assessment. Just as the various ways of dying are differentiated, so are the ways in which the respective bodies plus the separation of the souls from the physical bodies are ritually differentiated. All those considered to have suffered a 'deviating' death, will be categorized and addressed as *bongas* or spirits, since they do not qualify to turn into an ancestor and to be reborn in their descendants.

In Ho there is no term denoting ancestors. Instead, they are addressed and referred to as *ham hoko, dum hoko* or old men, sleeping men. Hence they are conceptualized in analogy to human beings: they are hungry and thirsty and require proper ritual treatment. This is considered the duty as well as the responsibility of the living. If these duties are performed adequately—one never knows, so it is a constant topic of discussion to ensure nothing has been forgotten—ancestors are expected to reciprocally protect the living in every respect in a kind of gift exchange: from diseases, death, and other kinds of discomfort. Due to this notional interdependence ancestors are habitually included in everyday life right 'down' to the sphere of commensality—on the level of the homestead and that of the village as well. When it comes to having a meal everybody, young and old, will offer a few grains of the cooked rice or *mandi*, a few drops of whatever is there to be drunk, rice-beer, or water, onto the floor. This gift is meant for the ancestors. Blood sacrifices in the fields, in the course of which different kinds of animals are ritually slaughtered in the midst of their rice-fields, are offered to the ancestors[29] and meant to guarantee the fertility of the crops and a good harvest.[30] These gifts on the village level are also part of the ritual-symbolic food. According to the cultural logic of (divine) gift exchange as practised by the Ho the *burying* of the dead in the land that was cleared by their ancestors may be interpreted as a sacrifice directed to their ancestors in a reciprocal circle of *'do ut des'*. Yorke writes: 'Kinship, ancestors and land may be considered separate analytical categories, but for the Ho they are different aspects of the same reality' (1976: 126).

The Ho that I met are convinced that their ancestors will turn angry and dangerous in case they are neglected, ignored or not treated adequately. It is assumed that ancestors may effect diseases, epidemics, and even death when angry, hungry, or thirsty. Linguistically the process of 'falling ill', 'becoming ill' or 'dying' in Ho is expressed in the passive voice by an intransitive verb. This implies that the specific condition of a *patiens* is being caused by an *agens* acting or taking effect from outside. The meaning or more correct translation would come fairly close to 'I am died', 'somebody (else) dies me', or also 'I am being killed, eaten, seized, grabbed, etc.' In our (Indo-European) language the process of dying cannot be expressed in the passive voice, whereas in Ho it can only be expressed in the passive voice, i.e. on the part of those dying. The Ho say that—after death—ancestors do transform into a grammatically active, causal agent: by help of transitive verbs they are conceived as 'eating' the living, as 'drinking their blood', as 'grabbing them', etc.[31] This is particularly true for the souls in the case of a 'bad' death. The logic is as follows. In all walks of Ho life a clear relation between cause and effect is taken for granted. No effect without cause. So if someone falls ill or dies, illness and death are understood as effects to which the causes should, need and can be traced. Often the cause is assumed in the 'wrong' human behaviour of actors who themselves need not necessarily be aware of the consequences of their doings. For this reason in lengthy, painful and sometimes unsuccessful consultations people try to remember and understand what it was that went wrong. In many, not only in difficult cases, Ho seek the services of those ritual specialists or shamans that in Ho are called *dewa*. They will perform a ritual or *bonga* in order to find out and pacify those spirits that may have caused the harm. However, in this process the living are no passive victims of the negative agency of spirits or their ancestors. They are active and pragmatic, they test what is suggested to them by the shaman or *dewa*, dispense with what does not work out, discuss publicly and negotiate what best to be done, try another *dewa*, etc.

On death and the dead in anthropological perspective

It will have become obvious by now that the concept of death and the ontological state of the dead in Ho society is fundamentally different from our Western ideas about it. What may be similar in a case of death—perhaps, if at all—is that the very responses are 'felt' by those affected to be unquestionably 'normal', 'natural', 'authentic', 'rational', 'making sense', and 'taken for granted'. If, however, fundamentally *different patterns* of responses are seen as fundamentally natural ('such is our culture', my Ho informants said), this so-called 'naturalness' will not convey insights into the character of what actually is going on, but rather socio-cultural specifics constituting and shaping the base of the diversity of people's behaviour.

The study of the nature of death within a given social context has played a prominent role in the field of anthropology since its beginning as an academic discipline. It seems established by now that death and people's relations with their dead reveal deep-rooted convictions about the concept of a person, of society, of what life is about. Within an 'Anthropology of Death' substantial literature has been produced on this topic set in its historical and social context and perspective. Among many others due ancestral and anthropological reverence should be paid to Frazer (1890), Hertz (1907/1960), van Gennep (1909/1960), M. Bloch (1988), Parry (1986), and Fabian (1973). Although these authors' loci of interest may differ, the following statement may hold true for all of them: responses toward the 'organic event' (Hertz 1960: 27) are not identical worldwide, they are universally not the same. At the same time they are never arbitrary or accidental. They are loaded with meaning, and symbolic. Just as the participants' individual behaviour, so the emotions involved in the process of mourning differ tremendously. The thesis of 'inner states as universals' has already been counter-argued by R. Needham in 1981. So, I argue, that if in my culture someone cries at a relative's funeral, that person's behaviour, tears, and emotions will neither be 'naturally' informed nor identical with the behaviour, tears, and emotions of, let's say, a Ho. Why? Weeping is always a weeping about something, and this 'about' is something culturally translated and because of this culture-specifically different.

Death—'here' and elsewhere

Our language betrays our basic notions and us: we talk about the *moment* of death, the h*our* of death, and generally of death happening in an *instant*. Scientific encyclopaedias offer as the lexical denotation below the entry 'death': 'the end of life'. Conceptually death signifies the negation of life, its final point as it were. So life and death are considered opposites, two fundamentally different categories separated by an obvious and clear-cut boundary. Despite the pitfalls of unjustified generalizations one might argue that for western minds death occurs within an instant. It is seen as a natural, i.e. a biological event; the point of time in which it happens can be objectively traced by objective instruments and scientific methods. Legal, medical, and neurological givens are to be paid attention to, and accordingly professional specialists are involved in the process of dying, either taking on full responsibility or sharing it with relatives. Thus death and dying remain within the realm of the intrafamilial or individual context. The Christian concept of death will likewise offer a reward for good deeds or punishment for sins committed in a life time to the souls who after one's last breath are supposed to immediately appear before their judge. However, also within the frame of this Christian concept there is no structure providing for a meaningful period of transition. Anyway, within the shortest possible period of time the corpse is being withdrawn from its social context—for hygienic reasons. The process of mourning and grieving becomes individualized, intrapersonal and intrafamilial. In particular there are Bloch and Parry (1982), who highlight the relation between the Western concept of the person, the in-dividuum, the in-divisible, and our concept of death as well as our ways of dealing with the dead. In our kind of society an individual is considered to be the smallest, complete unit implying soul, body, bones, flesh, and blood. Clear, well-defined and sharp boundaries between this individual and any other individual are assumed as a matter-of-fact. This individual commands respect and status. Bloch says: 'In our logic, when an in-dividuum dies, the whole person dies' (1988: 3). I argue that in Western individualized societies a linear worldview and view of linear progress prevails. This linearity of 'our' rational reasoning is also reflected in a deep seated conviction of the irreversibility of the chronological order of birth–life–death. So, as a clearly fixed boundary is conceptualized around the 'elementary man: both a biological being and a thinking subject' (Dumont 1970: 9), *one* burial will finalize things of a very final nature. According to this cultural logic *one* burial will do.[32]

Distinguishing between the notions of *in-dividual* and *dividual* is important for our topic insofar as this concept refers to the empirical single being as embedded in a web of a social whole, to which in so-called holistic societies the highest social esteem is attributed. In dying it is not exclusively and not even primarily the body of an empirical being that is affected, but the body of the social whole, if the metaphor be allowed, or the category to which this being was attached and an integral constituent of. It is this social whole that is affected in the case of death and will respond and interact as a whole. Hertz (1960) interprets death explicitly as an attack on the social order of the social whole. It would be the idea behind elaborate burial rituals to restore this social order. In the case of the Ho the second burial or *diri dulsunum* is supposed to accomplish and complete this process. In societies with a cyclical worldview, and there is reason to assume that the Ho tribal society belongs here, too, death itself becomes part of a cyclical process, more specifically a cyclical process of renewal.[33] It was Hertz who in his study about death has focussed on the concept of a structured transition, of the transformation(s) of corpse, soul and mourners and the meaning of the second burial. And it was van Gennep's contribution, based on the findings of Hertz, to work out a tripartite structure of all rituals of transition including death rituals. These consist of a number of semantically related, structurally separate phases which I was able to observe among the Ho when participating in several death rituals—first burials as well as second burials.[34] I could also observe that each phase is, again, subdivided into several rituals of different duration of several days. The choreography of the first two phases aims at reinstalling the state of social purity of all those involved and defiled—of the soul or shade of the deceased and of relatives and ancestors, and this is reflected in the one term comprising all the different rituals of these two phases, which is *sabsi*.[35] The third phase relates to Hertz's second burial or van Gennep's postliminal phase, in which 'the soul is integrated into the world of the dead, and the mourners are re-integrated into society'. All in all, very short and contrary to our Western notions of death, but true for a great many cultures and also that of the Ho: death is no final point in time, but a transition or a birth into a new phase, in the course of which all actors involved will acquire a new social identity. Death is considered a transition from the visible, real world into an invisible, equally real world. Death does not occur in one instant, but is a process, a process of renewal. The after-death world is modelled on the social world of the living and is differentiated as such. Death is neither conceived as a negation nor as an end of life; it is its continuity in a different shape. The symbolism of death rituals for those eligible for transforming into ancestors is expressed in metaphors of biological and spiritual fertility, of sexuality and growth.

However, in the case of a 'sudden, violent' death the souls of the dead have to do without the sociality of their ancestors, without the protection of and inside the *adin* and the communicative care—to avoid terms such as veneration or worship—of the living. It is by their particular way of dying that the souls are conceptualized as individual and unpredictably harmful in differently diverse ways. Simultaneously those souls remain in a state of need and dependant on the living. That way they also remain part of the same cultural system. This is what the next paragraph is about.

Sunai Kondangkel: ethnography of a 'bad' death

During my fieldwork 2009/2010 I stayed in the Jamda area of Mayurbhanj near Rairanpur. With respect to the tribal population this area is mainly inhabited by Ho and Santal, and very few Munda live also there. In order to improve my language performance in Ho I luckily succeeded towards the end of 2009 in moving to Boja Sai, which is a pure Ho hamlet in the very same area. All its inhabitants are members of the Kondangkel *kili* or clan, but they do not belong to one and the same *miyad chaturenko* or people of the same rice-pot. My younger classificatory brother there was Sadurgon Kondangkel, the *munda* or village elder living in an adjacent hamlet, Gara Sai.[36] He had helped me find this place to stay with his classificatory mother who had become my mother that way. It took me quite some time and was a real strain on my hosts' nerves until it was confirmed that she was the FFBySyW[37] to my younger brother who addressed her as *kaki* or father's younger brother's wife[38] just as I was supposed to do being his elder sister. On the other hand I was not only addressed by my mother as *mai* or 'young girl', but also treated as such.[39] Of her five children Sunai was the eldest of her four daughters. In 2006 she was bitten in a toe by a snake and died a few days later. At that time the girl was 16 years old.

Shortly after I had moved in the big metal box that contained all the family valuables and that was kept inside the *adin* was opened by my *kaki* and its contents presented to me. Of this daughter there were a few photographs inside—a portrait, photos showing her in school uniform, together with her sisters, and together with her school mates. There were also her earrings which my *kaki* put into my palms and made me admire them. Weren't they the most beautiful earrings? She was very wordy about these earrings, and she used to wear them on special occasions, when she was singing and dancing herself. It was for the first time then that my *kaki* informed me about her daughter and her death. In the course of my stay I was told this story time and again—and always in an almost identical, clear, matter-of-fact way, non-sentimental and emotional at the same time. Two photos showing the daughter hung on the outside wall of the house above the entrance. Two teachers had been present for the funeral—this piece of information was also conveyed to me several times.

That Sunai's death had been classified as a 'bad' death[40] and what the consequences of this were, I realized only in the morning of 14 January and coincidentally. It was the time of new moon, the rice harvest and necessary follow-up work had been completed, and huge lumps of brown sugar cane were sold in the streets and bazaars. On the occasion of *Mokor Porob*, the '*Makar Sankranti* feast of the Hindus held about January 14th [see also *diku porob*]' (Deeney 2005: 253) popped rice or *ata* and *lad* or sweet bread are homemade. This was done at night in the cowshed half of which had been whitened for this purpose, and the fireplace there was used for the first time. The food was prepared solely by the 13-year-old daughter and the 10-year-old son, no adults were around (apart from me) or assisting. And they had finished their work before dawn.[41] While busy with the usual daily chores in the kitchen after that, I coincidentally overheard my *kaki* address her ancestors[42] in the *adin*:

'I am offering/giving to you[43] *lad* of Mokor Porob. Today is Mokor Porob. I am giving you all *lad* of *Mokor Porob*. Today is *Mokor Porob. Ham hoko, dum hoko,* I have not seen all of you. I do not know how many you are. This *lad* here, divide it and give each his share. This is how I am performing the *bonga*.'[44]

Having said that she disappeared outside. As I saw in each of her hands a portion of *ata* and *lad* filled into a leaf cup I followed her and observed this: behind the house there were about ten tall tamarind and mango trees below which, in the shade, a number of burial stones of enormous size lay. Right next to these stones was the *kolom* or threshing ground behind which, further away from the house, there was a tall bamboo tree. Houses, trees, gravestones, and threshing ground were surrounded by a fence running around most of Boja Sai and beyond which were the rice-fields. Now my *kaki* stood below this bamboo tree and addressed that very daughter who had been bitten by a snake. She did not address her as ancestress (*ham ho-dum ho*),[45] she did not call her by name either, but referred to her as *beti*, which is Hindi for 'daughter'.[46] This is what she said:

My daughter's soul has been called to this site and is still lingering around. That daughter's soul has been called to this site. I am offering/giving *ata* and *lad* on behalf of that daughter on the occasion of *Mokor Sankranti*. This is what I am giving her. That soul has not been called inside the house. It has been called to this site.

Next to the bamboo tree there was another burial stone separated from the other stones by the threshing ground and very near the enclosing fence, but still inside of it. Eventually I realized that this was my *kaki's* deceased daughter's grave. Contrary to the other graves covered by those massive slabs of stone or *sasan diri* lying flat on the ground, this grave was lavishly maintained. Instead of a flat *sasan diri* covering the body there was a terraced cement construction sealing ground and body below. And, additionally, it had an upright burial stone informing about the girl's data (name, year of birth and death) in Oriya and English chiselled into the surface of the stone. I have never seen a double construction like this anywhere else in the area. My *kaki* had also planted a tree next to the grave which she would also regularly water to make sure that her daughter be comfortable in the shade. Concerning her daughter's soul, however, my *kaki* was convinced that it was floating and dwelling among the branches of the bamboo tree. I was also told with an air of pride that her daughter's cloths had neither been burned nor left inside the grave to cover the body (as would be the usual Ho way). They had been handed over to a river instead. This was expressed by the term *atu* meaning 'to place something in flowing water so that it is carried away' (Deeney 2005: 18). Many people had participated in this ritual, she added, among whom were two of her teachers.[47] Inside the courtyard a ceremony had been performed. The daughter's body had been covered by a great many *sarees*, also newly bought ones. 'She will not be cold,' my *kaki* informed me. On the occasion of the following two seasonal feasts *Mage Porob*[48] and *Ba Porob*[49] the offerings were repeated in the same order and the same way.

By having been bitten by a snake my *kaki's* daughter's death was classified as a 'bad' death. Her on-going dependence on the living was revealed in the ritual and gustatory treatment by my *kaki*. She and the ancestors were materially given identical offerings; however, the ancestors were addressed differently, they were being served first and at a different location. Due to the identical gift in the course of the ritual, I argue, Sunai remains conceptually related to her ancestors. She is ceremoniously and materially taken care of, yet simultaneously a symbolic difference is established and made visible. The classification of a particular kind of death as a 'bad' death is a mental assessment, a matter of evaluation. It is not a moral statement. It is not a matter of devaluation. It is an instance calling for action.

Conclusion

The focus of the essay was on death related matters as they unfolded before the authoress in the course of her fieldwork among the Ho of Odisha and Jharkhand between 2006 and 2012. The field of death was singled out for a number of reasons. First, there are earlier and highly informative publications on the Ho. Most of these are concentrating on legal, historical, demographic, administrative, economic, ecological, religious, linguistic, or sociological aspects. None of these was written, however, from and in an anthropological perspective. Second, apart from J. Deeney who had lived among the Ho for more than 60 years since 1949, who had been a keen observer of Ho culture and a scholar of the Ho language, two more contemporary monographs on the Ho were accessible that were based on long-term participant observation. One deals primarily with the politico-economic domain (Yorke 1976), the other one with processes of Sanskritization and de-Sanskritization, of transforming Ho tribal identity into one of caste membership and instances of a reversal of this process (Verardo 2003). In both *individual behaviour* in its social context figures as the central category to be observed, described, discussed, and analysed. Third, for the reason that both monographs have not been published, the descriptive ethnographic parts in this paper have attempted at conveying in greater detail a kind of graphic introduction into the world(view) of the Ho centring and revolving around themselves. For this purpose death and mourning have been a most apt focus for this paper as in this central notions and values of Ho cosmology are condensed as well as expressed and as such to be observed. There is a clearly structured multifaceted convivium of Ho, Santal and Munda, of patrons and clients, of the living and the dead, of the sacred and the secular, of equals and non-equals. In Ho death rituals anthropological issues come to the fore such as the concept of the person lending itself to reveal that dying in Ho country is considered a cultural affair and burying and mourning a social, non-individual matter beyond biological givens. It has also been touched upon in this article how the Ho by sub-classifying death[50] are able to keep those who have suffered a 'deviant' death at a distance and apart from the living, but to keep them for the time being—empirically, visibly, publicly, materially, and notionally.

Notes

1. Lewis speaks of a Ho population of 15,00,000 in 2003 (2009: 377–93). Anderson, Head of the Living Tongues Institute for Endangered Languages in Salem/Oregon/USA, points out that the Munda group of languages of the Austroasiatic family of which Ho is one language is spoken by almost 10 million people within central and eastern India (2007: 7; 2008: 2–3).
2. Of course, there are Ho outside the three states of Jharkhand, Odisha and West Bengal. Individual Ho keep working in the tea plantations in Assam, go to Gujarat and as far as Kashmir for the sake of wage labour or to Jharkhand to work there in the mines. According to my informants, they do not constitute any kind of organized diaspora in these regions. Coming back, however, is not always an easy job since they will have to undergo a number of severe purification rituals in order to get rid of the pollution acquired outside their Ho villages.
3. The proper Ho term of this ritual is '*disum amin—disum nam*' (*disum*: country, territory; *amin*: to acquire by clearing, [e.g. to acquire a piece of cultivable land by cutting all trees, etc.]; *nam*: to get, receive): to acquire the right of land and cultivating it by clearing the jungle. This right of cultivating is reciprocally linked with the obligation to keep worshipping the autochthonous gods related to this territory, since local and territorial deities are considered to be and remain highly influential by the Ho.
   All matters of vocabulary in this chapter have been checked with Deeney 2005.
4. Ratha (2009: 314) points to the fact that '[I]n the Census of India of 1872 and later the regular decennial Census initiated in 1881, the Indian population was divided into two "social types", tribes and castes, by which time the

term "tribe" was already in vogue in Europe to designate non-European communities of Africa, Asia, Australia and the Americas.' For this reason Ratha also says that a nasty air of evolutionism lingers around the term 'tribe', for which 'no Indian language had a word in its vocabulary synonymous with the English word "tribe"' (2009: 318). In his dictionary of 2005 Deeney gives—below the entry jati—the following denotations: 'race; tribe; caste; type, kind' (Deeney 2005: 177). Surely, the term 'tribe' is of Latin origin. Nowadays it seems that jati functions as a generic term instead for all the implied connotations (historical, colonial, post-colonial, evolutionary, etc.) and, thus, has probably become an even more sensitive issue.

5. It was quite a process and a matter of public Ho commitment to assist me in turning into a social being, i.e. into a Ho. This involved my becoming a member of the Purty *kili* or clan and *saki* or namesake of the local *munda's* wife or secular village head. The *saki* relationship is a ritual friendship. In my case it contributed to the Ho making cultural sense of an anthropologist of sorts determined to stay among them by including her into their social web of relations and transforming her initial state of *diku*. In fact, quite of their own accord, they constructed me into a Ho whose ancestors had left Ho *disum* long ago, who had forgotten about her own culture and who had finally returned to learn from scratch. This example is given as it reveals that the social scenario is characterized by different degrees of 'other-ness'.

6. 'Ho is used vigorously in the Ho communities and there is a positive attitude towards its use, despite the use of Oriya, Hindi, or even Santali by the Ho in a limited set of appropriate domains' (Anderson 2007: 7–8).

7. For differences between Ho notions of rebirth and Christian concepts of the soul see chapter 5. For details concerning the after-death fate of a tribal soul see Pfeffer (2009: 242).

8. Cf. Pfeffer (2009: 263).

9. For this patchwork kind of society Pfeffer (1997) has coined the term tribal society with its focus well beyond an individual tribe. For a description and an assessment of the tribal issue in middle India in more detail see Areeparampil 2002, Das Gupta 2011, Reichel (2009: 17–26; 72 f.), Skoda 2006.

10. This marriage arrangement may reflect the following cultural twist: the status of the wife-givers ranks higher than that of the wife-receivers in the tribal value system of middle India, whereas in north India, for example, wife-receivers are in a permanent state of superiority over wife-givers. Accordingly, each of the two parties might consider themselves to rank higher in *this* case—that is if future field work can prove that daughters of the category 'General' are supposed to be married hypergamously in an otherwise dominant tribal context.

11. The major part of this paragraph is based on my fieldwork among the Ho and has partly been published in Reichel (2009: 8f).

12. '*nana:* grandmother (paternal or maternal, sometimes used as vocative, also *jiyan*)'; '*buri:* old' in Deeney (2005: 54, 261).

13. Houses are usually quite close to each other. Between our house and that of our neighbour there was a distance of about 25 m.

14. The information given to me in Ho was that 'our grandmother (has died) [*sic*]': *abuwa:* (our; the colon here is phonemic) *nana buri* (address and reference term for grandmother, cf. above).

    If in a conversation three and more people are involved there are ways in Ho to indicate whether the person that one talks to is meant to be included in what is said or not. This is done by two different possessive pronouns to express 'our': (1) *aleya:* is the first person plural excluding the person addressed, (2) *abuwa:* is the first person plural including the person addressed. So in this case I was included in the web of social relations.

15. *pindigi:* a Ho word to denote a small veranda-type elevation built around or in front of a Ho house.

16. *sasan sunum:* turmeric and oil mixed for this purpose

17. At that time, six weeks after the beginning of my fieldwork, I was too shy to enquire into the relationship between this man and the dead.

18. *sarjom daru* (shorea robusta). This tree is considered a holy tree. From its leaves cups and plates are made during rituals, and *ba porob* or the flower festival, one of the major annual festivals, takes place when its flowers blossom. Each *desauli*, the sacred grove, is supposed to have at least one sal-tree.

19. *sinduri:* 'vermillion, red lead; to apply the same (e.g. in some action of divining or at time of marriage)' (Deeney 2005: 344). See later for turmeric, oil, and *sinduri* as symbols of marriage within the context of death.

20. *sasan diri:* 'a large stone put flat over a grave (as distinct from bid-diri, a standing memorial stone)' (Deeney 2005: 331).

21. 'Pouring oil on the (burial) stone'. Actually, quite towards the beginning of the second burial, oil and turmeric rice is poured on the burial stone slabs. This is done by women only.

22. I was once invited to a second burial and given a temporary hut in the area allocated to the *bala*, although beforehand I had been told that I would belong to the agnatic category by my being related to my *saki* due to our ritual kinship. In fact, every hut displayed in Odia on a piece of cardboard the kinship relationship (term) to the deceased, e.g. *mamun* or Mother's Brother, and the village that the visiting party came from. In my hut the sign read *haga* and Borlin as my natal village. Positioning a *haga* on a site reserved for *bala* indicated to me that for the Ho kinship is a process rather than a state, an affair of degrees rather than something essentially fixed, a matter of becoming rather than being (for good).

23. This term is a specific Ho concept or category of some consequences which has been discussed in Deeney 2008, Pfeffer 1997: 24, Reichel 2009: 72f, 108f, Yorke 1976.

24. It may and will be a different story in the case of a 'bad' death. Interestingly,

the case of the 'General' above has revealed that they bury their dead outside the village boundary as a rule.

25. The setting of the stone is being done on an uneven day as counted from the day of (physical) death. It takes place as one ritual among many, all displaying a necessary element within the tripartite structure of death rituals which have been described in more detail in Reichel (2009: 95f).

26. Of course, this contrast indicated by 'yet' is the contrast 'felt' by the authoress coming from a Western individualized background. Cf. Vitebsky (1993) on the difference between emotions as interior versus exterior social qualities.

27. Cf. Sahlins (2008: 101).

28. This may take drastic forms: my assistant, a Santal, for example, had accompanied me to a neighbouring village to participate in the burial procedures of the Ho *diuri* or village priest there. I had taken the obligatory bath in the *banda* or tank together with the whole female party. This purification ritual or *sabsi* is being performed after the deceased's widow had fixed her dead husband's soul tied to his hoe in the ground of the tank. My assistant never joined in this public activity when it was the males' turn to have their bath. They did that locally separate from the women, but still at the same tank. So when we came home his wife enquired if he had had a proper bath, and when he denied she insisted on his getting rid of his death pollution first before she was prepared to have him enter the courtyard of her—and his—house. At that time it was winter, it was pitch dark, it was quite cold, and the next tank was far away. So my assistant implored me to fetch a bucket of (cold) water. I had to douse him several times, until he was utterly soaking wet and allowed inside.

29. These sacrifices in the field are different from those addressed to the 'autochthonous' gods and goddesses and discussed in Chapter 1.

30. Mary Douglas is quoted as relating bloodshed and life-giving in Berger (2007: 13).

31. Cf. Vitebsky (1993: 14, 214) makes a very similar grammatical and semantic point as concerns the Sora, another ethnic category of Middle Eastern India, and their language which is a language of the Munda branch of the Austroasiatic language family such as Ho and Santali.

32. For differences between Hindu, Ho and Christian concepts of death and reincarnation see Chapter 1, fn. 7.

33. Of course, this is a gross generalization, as in such societies there are linear elements, too. However, the focus here is on the cyclical quality as people in such societies, this is the argument, are exposed to and rooted in recurring cyclical continuities of processes of renewal in their specific ecosystems, kinship classifications, marriage patterns, life-cycle rituals, and their social interactions in general.

34. Cf. chapter 3.

35. *sabsi:* consists of two words: *sab* (v.) denotes 'to catch, to seize', *si:* denotes

'the foul smell of, e.g. rotten fish or meat; foul, offensive (e.g. of language)' (Deeney 2005: 340). The colon at the end of 'si:' is phonemic. Its pronunciation is a glottal stop. Interestingly, the terms of rituals often reflect what people are *doing* in the course of these rituals: here they will *catch* impurity, there—in the case of the second burial called *diri dulsunum*—they will *pour* oil on the burial stone. This comes close to Trawick's remarks on 'culture . . . as an activity. . . done among people, leaving its traces in memory' (Trawick 1990: 89–90).

36. *gara*: small river; *sai*: hamlet.

37. She was the wife of my (younger) brother's paternal grandfather's younger brother's younger son who became my *kaka* and father.

38. As a relationship term *kaki* refers to FByW (the wife of a father's younger brother) *and* to MZy (a mother's younger sister).

39. It did not matter much in this respect, when I told my *kaki* that at home, in my culture, I would be mother of two daughters and grandmother of two grandchildren. First, they said that as the elder sister of the *munda*, who was their classificatory son, I would become their daughter and *mai* as a matter of cultural fact. Second, as I knew so very little or almost nothing of almost everything this would even more turn me into their *mai*. In fact, my *kaki* was a brilliant and patient teacher, and a lot of what I have learnt, I owe to her.

40. The different ritual treatment of the *rowa* or soul is something that can be empirically witnessed in participant observation. For analytical reasons I make use here of Parry's (anthropological) construct of a 'bad' death, although I have tried to show above that it is a simplifying classification when it comes to illustrating the Ho's understandings of death. In their language they speak about the different ways of dying, the various kinds of death in quite concrete and descriptive terms, e.g. of a death due to being bitten by a snake, to being burnt, by having fallen into the fire, etc. In another case when it was not clear whether a woman had been murdered or committed suicide, they called the death *tataka* ('stupefaction; amazement; to be stupefied, amazed', Deeney 2005: 371) or *roka* ('suddenly; sudden, fresh, for the first time', 2005: 313).

41. There are a number of ritually important elements involved in this process which cannot be enlarged upon within the scope of this chapter. They concern questions of who prepares the food, who does not, what kinds of vessel are being used, where and how the food is kept, what kinds of ingredients are being used, what kind of firewood, etc.

42. A Ho woman will gradually adopt her husband's ancestors after marriage.

43. She addressed her ancestors in the second person plural.

44. In terms of readability this is an approximate English version: 'I am offering to you, our ancestors, sweet bread prepared on the occasion of today's festival, *Mokor Porob*. Today is *Mokor Porob*. I am giving to you all sweet bread of today's festival. Today is *Mokor Porob*. Old men, sleeping men, you, who are my ancestors, I have not seen all of you. I do not know how many you

are. This sweet bread here, divide it and give each his share. This is how I am performing the ritual'.

45. In Ho gender is linguistically not differentiated.

46. It may be interesting in this context that in the area of my fieldwork a comparatively pure Ho was spoken with rather little Hindi mixed into it. It was, however, quite common in Boja Sai and the surrounding hamlets and villages to use *beti* and *beta* (son) as reference terms to their living children— alongside *kui hon* and *kowa hon* which are the equivalents in Ho.

47. Teachers in the Jamda area were usually people from the plains speaking Oriya as their mother tongue and teaching the children in Oriya. There was no school in the vicinity in which Ho or Santali were spoken or taught. Similarly, in Jharkhand alphabetization was done in Hindi or in English, where parents could afford the school fees.

48. *Mage Porob* is the Ho feast observed in each village after the harvest work is done; in the course of this feast obscene language is used.

49. *ba*: flower. *Ba Porob* is the annual flower feast celebrated at the time when the flowers of the sal tree (*sarjom daru*) blossom.

50. There is by now an impressive body of scholarly literature not only on the dilemmas of death in secular settings and beyond, but also on such culture-specific classifications of death as dealt with in this essay (Parry 1994, Schömbucher and Zoller 1999, Alex 2008). Within the scope of this chapter it has not been possible to discuss and compare different mourning rituals and cults of remembering. It might be especially rewarding to explore and compare notions of death in Brahmanical Hinduism with those of specific Ho concepts.

References

Alex, G. and Suzette Heald, eds., 'Good Deaths/Bad Deaths: Dilemmas of Death in Comparative Perspective', *Curare: Journal of Medical Anthropology*, vol. 31, no. 1, Berlin: Verlag für Wissenschaft und Bildung, 2008.

Anderson, G.D.S., ed., *The Munda Languages*, London, New York: Routledge, 2008.

———, *The Munda Verb: Typological Perspectives*, in *Trends in Linguistics: Studies and Monographs 174*, ed. Hock Walter Bisang, Hans Heinrich and Werner Winter, Berlin and New York: Mouton de Gruyter, 2007.

Areeparampil, Mathew, *Struggle for Swaraj: A History of Adivasi Movements in Jharkhand (from the Earliest Times to the Present Day)*, Lupungutu: Tribal Research and Training Centre, 2002.

Berger, P., *Füttern, Speisen und Verschlingen. Ritual und Gesellschaft im Hochland von Orissa, Indien*, Berlin: Lit Verlag, 2007.

Bloch, M., 'Introduction: Death and the Concept of a Person', in *On the meaning of Death. Essays on Mortuary Rituals and Eschatological Beliefs*, ed. S. Cederroth, C. Corlin and J. Lindström, Uppsala, 1988, pp. 11–30.

Bloch, M. and Jonathan P. Parry, 'Introduction: Death and the Regeneration of Life', in *Death and the Regeneration of Life*, Cambridge: Cambridge University Press, 1982, pp. 1–44.

Das Gupta, S., *Adivasi and the Raj: Socio-economic Transition of the Hos, 1820–1932*, New Delhi: Orient BlackSwan, 2011.

Deeney, J.S.J., *The Spirit World of the Ho Tribals: And Other Glimpses into the Ho World*, Ranchi: Xavier Publications, 2008.

———, *Ho⊠English Dictionary*, New Edition, Revised and Enlarged, Ranchi: Xavier Publications, Catholic Press, 2005 [1978].

Douglas, M., 'Introduction', in *The Anthropologists' Cookbook*, ed. J. Kuper, London: Routledge and Kegan Paul, 1977.

Dumont, L., *Homo Hierarchicus: The Caste System and its Implications*, London: Weidenfeld and Nicolson, 1970 [1966].

Fabian, J., 'How Others Die: Reflections on the Anthropology of Death', in *Death in American Experience*, ed. Arien Mack, New York: Schocken, 1973, pp. 177–201.

Frazer, J., *The Golden Bough, A Study in Comparative Religion*, London, 1890.

Hertz, R., 'A Contribution to the Study of the Collective Representation of Death', in *Death and the Right Hand*, tr. Rodney and Claudia Needham, with an Introduction by E.E. Evans⊠Pritchard, Aberdeen: Cohen & West, 1960 [1907 in French], pp. 27–86.

Huntington, R. and Peter Metcalf, *Celebrations of Death: The Anthropology of Mortuary Ritual*, Cambridge, London, New York and Melbourne: Cambridge University Press, 1979.

Lévi-Strauss, C., *Traurige Tropen. Indianer in Brasilien*, Köln: Kiepenheuer & Witsch, 1977 [1955].

Lewis, M.P., ed., *Ethnologue: Languages of the World*, 16th edn., Dallas, Texas: SIL, International—The web edition of the *Ethnologue* is supposed to contain all the content of the print version: http://www.ethnologue.com/,2009.

Needham, R., 'Inner States as Universals: Sceptical Reflections on Human Nature', in *Indigenous Psychologies: The Anthropology of the Self*, ed. Paul Heelas and Andrew Lock, London: Academic Press, 1981, pp. 65–78.

Parry, J., 'Death and Digestion: The Symbolism of Food and Eating in North Indian Mortuary Rites', in *Man*, n.s., vol. 20, 1986, pp. 612–30.

———, *Death in Banaras*, Cambridge: Cambridge University Press, 1994.

Pfeffer, G., 'The Scheduled Tribes of Middle India as a Unit: Problems of Internal and External Comparison', in *Contemporary Society: Tribal Studies, vol. I, Structure and Process*, ed. G. Pfeffer and D.K. Behera, Delhi: Concept, 1997, pp. 3–27.

———, 'Social Evolution: History or Ideal Types?', in *Contemporary Society: Tribal Studies. vol. 8: Structure and Exchange in Tribal India and Beyond*, ed. Georg Pfeffer, Deepak Kumar Behera, New Delhi: Concept Publishing Co., 2009, pp. 257–65.

Ratha, S.N., 'Beyond the Tribal Society: To be or Not to be a Tribe in India', in *Contemporary Society: Tribal Studies. vol. 8: Structure and Exchange in Tribal India and Beyond*, ed. Georg Pfeffer, Deepak Kumar Behera, New Delhi: Concept Publishing Company, 2009, pp. 314–21.

Reichel, E., *Notions of Life in Death and Dying: The Dead in Tribal Middle India*, New Delhi: Manohar, 2009.

Sahlins, M., *The Western Illusion of Human Nature*, Chicago: Prickly Paradigm Press, 2008.

Schömbucher, E. and Claus Peter Zoller, eds., *Ways of Dying: Death and its Meanings in South Asia*, New Delhi: Manohar, 1999.

Skoda, U., *The Aghria: A peasant Caste on a Tribal Frontier*, New Delhi: Manohar, 2006.

Trawick, M., *Notes on Love in a Tamil Family*, Berkeley: University of California Press, 1990.

van Gennep, A., *The Rites of Passage*, London: Routledge, 1960[1909].

Verardo, B., 'Rebels and Devotees of Jharkhand: Social, Religious and Political Transformations among the Adivasis of Northern India', unpublished Ph.D. thesis submitted to the London School of Economics and Political Science, University of London, 2003.

Vitebsky, P., *Dialogues with the Dead: The discussion of Mortality among the Sora of Eastern India*, Cambridge: Cambridge University Press, 1993.

Yorke, M.P., 'Decisions and Analogy. Political Structure and Discourse among the Ho Tribals of India', unpublished Ph.D. thesis submitted to the School of Oriental and African Studies, University of London, 1976.

6 'Juniors', 'Exploiters', 'Brokers' and 'Shamans'

A Holistic View on the Dombo Community in the Highlands of Odisha

ROLAND HARDENBERG

Introduction: Kond and Dombo— tribals and untouchables?[1]

The land south of the river Mahanadi in Odisha is populated by people called Kond who are considered to be the original inhabitants (Adivasi) of this mountainous area. In the terminology of the government, these people are referred to as members of a 'Scheduled Tribe' (ST) as the constitution guarantees them certain rights and privileges in order to improve their living conditions and their social standing. The Kond are divided into a number of categories such as Malliah Kond, Dongria Kond, Kuttia Kond or Kuvi Kond who settle in different regions (see Padel 2000: 12–14). Together they form a population of at least one million people (ibid.: 12) who largely subsist on wet rice cultivation, horticulture and/or shifting cultivation.

A visitor to the Kond area will, however, most probably not meet with the Kond first but be welcomed by people from a different social category. Depending on the region, these people are called Domb(o) or Pan(o) and are referred to in governmental terms as members of a 'Scheduled Caste' (SC). To a caste Hindu these people fall into the category of 'untouchables' (achua) even if this term is not used in public any more.[2] The Dombo/Pano often live in the same or neighbouring villages as the Kond. They are involved in different occupations and usually function as mediators between the Kond and the outside world. Many of them have some education, speak various languages and some have even acquired substantial wealth. Many visitors to the Kond areas will experience them as industrious, open and curious people. However, Western and Indian anthropologists (as well as 'agents of development') sometimes portray them as astute or at worst dishonest people who use the resources of the 'innocent' tribals for their personal benefits. Thus Pfeffer states that

(S)ome prominent ethnographers, e.g. Elwin (1955), do mention them off and on in a derogatory manner as the cause of most aspects they consider as negative in the tribal world. They wrongly characterize them as Hindu immigrants from the plains who give a bad name to their faith. In fact, this is one of the most obvious cases of academic discrimination in Indian anthropology. (1997: 7)

The co-existence between Kond and the above mentioned groups is not a new phenomenon, whereas the distinction between 'Scheduled Castes' and 'Scheduled Tribes' is. In the mid-nineteenth century, Major Samuel Charters Macpherson (1806–60), a colonial officer responsible for the suppression of human sacrifice and female infanticide in the Kond areas, still considered the 'Panwa' (Pano), 'Dombango' (Dombo), and 'Gahinga' (Ghasi) to be 'aborigines' like the Kond themselves (Macpherson 1865: 115).[3] Modern sociological writers are divided in their opinion, some stressing the social and cultural unity of Kond and their clients, others describing the latter as representatives of Hindu caste society essentially different from the tribal Kond.

The relations between Kond and Dombo/Pano have been discussed by a number of ethnographers working in Odisha, especially by Bailey (1960, 1961), Niggemeyer (1964a, 1964b), Pfeffer (1982, 1997), Berger (2002) and by a group of Indian social anthropologists and ethno-botanists under the guidance of Klaus Seeland (Jena et al. 2002).

Niggemeyer points to the fact that Kond and Pano—as the Dombo are called in the Kuttia Kond area (Kandhamal District)—form a community (1964b: 407). The Kond are land owners and cultivators while the Scheduled Caste people work as traders and supply the Kond with items ranging from alcohol to sacrificial animals and clothes. The Pano are considered by the Kond to be socially inferior but this does not hinder them from entering into ritualized bonds of friendship (ibid.: 411). From an economical point of view the Pano range from poor village servants to rich bankers to whom the tribals are indebted (ibid.: 411).

In comparison to Niggemeyer, Bailey presents a slightly different social situation for the Kond of Phulbani. In this area, the Pano are distinguished into Kond Pano and Oriya Pano, the latter regarded as having a higher status than their 'tribal' caste fellows (Bailey 1960: 121). Furthermore, Bailey reports that the Pano actually work as agricultural labourers on the fields of their Kond masters (ibid.: 140), who regard them as their subjects (*praja*) (ibid.: 133).

Pfeffer based his analysis on Niggemeyer's findings and his own fieldwork among the Kuttia Kond. He again stresses the role of the Pano/Dombo as 'intermediaries' or 'culture brokers' (1997: 11, 13), the latter preserving the purity of the former since they allow the Kond to avoid contact with the supposedly polluted outside world. Pfeffer regards the Dombo/Pano as part of the tribal world of ideas and comes to the conclusion that tribals may be seen as 'communicators with the divine' in contrast to the clients who are 'communicators with human beings' (ibid.: 13). He only shortly mentions the ritual duties of the clients and describes them as 'indispensable', especially their musical performances (ibid.: 10).

Berger in his article describes the position of the Dombo in the Koraput District, where they live together with a number of different communities such as Gadaba, Rona, Kumar, Sunda and Gouda. In official language these communities are classified as either Scheduled Tribes (ST), Scheduled Castes (SC) or Other Backward Classes (OBC), yet from local perspective they all belong to one category named Desia and often share the same totemic clan categories (Berger 2002: 58; Pfeffer 1997: 17). According to Berger, the Dombo of Koraput do not fit into the standard stereotypes: 'They are neither economically better off than the Adibasi, nor do they exploit the cultivators' (2002: 61). In the past, the Dombo worked as weavers, but discontinued this profession due to competition from modern manufacturers. Like Pfeffer, Berger emphasizes the important role of the Dombo as musicians at *rites de passage* as well as local festivals (ibid.: 61–2). He briefly describes the role of the Dombo as middlemen, who sell the cash crops produced by the Adivasi, their engagement in the trade with cattle and their important role as *barik*, i.e. messenger and intermediary, who closely cooperates with the head of the village and usually has quite some influence over local affairs (ibid.: 62–3). In summary, there is some agreement that the Dombo or Pano play an important economic and political role through their access to the market and that they participate in local rituals. Individually, they may become rich and even more powerful than their Kond neighbours, yet ethnography shows that even these people cannot escape the low status ascribed to them in many contexts.

A book on the Dongria Kond of Rayagada District written by Indian authors in cooperation with Klaus Seeland (Jena et al. 2002) completely ignores the work of Pfeffer and Berger. They state that Dombo are regarded as 'untouchables' by the Dongria who do not allow them to enter their houses. However, the authors also see an economic and political interdependency between the communities and describe in relative detail the functions of the *barik* (Jena et al. 2002: 71–2). In contrast to Pfeffer, who sees the function of the 'communicators with the divine' restricted to the tribal patrons, the authors report about the Dombo's participation in festivals and about the Dombo adopting shamanic practices. Yet they also reproduce the standard stereotypes when writing: 'Since time immemorial, the Dongaria Kondh are being exploited by the Domb, who are more clever than the former' (Jena et al. 2002: 76).

In this chapter I follow Niggemeyer, Pfeffer and Berger in questioning the distinction between the Adivasis as 'Scheduled Tribes' (ST) and the Dombo as 'untouchables' or 'Scheduled Caste' (SC). This classification appears to be based on official categories highly influenced by colonial ethnography.[4] Modern ethnography shows that in different regions of Odisha, the Dombo/Pano are part and parcel of the local social systems. My own ethnographic data refers to a special group of Kond, the Dongria Kond, who reside together with the Dombo in the Niamgiri Hills of Rayagada District.[5] By inquiring into local value-ideas[6] and forms of interaction between Dongria and Dombo, I can show that both communities form one society based on hierarchy,[7] separation and interdependency. These are the same features that according to Dumont (1998 [1966]: 43) also characterize caste society. As will become apparent in my description of the relations between Dongria and Dombo, the cultural elaboration of this hierarchy, i.e. the value-ideas and forms of interaction, differ from those of caste society in the plains.[8]

I begin my account of the society in the Niamgiri Hills by describing how this hierarchy is conceptualized. For this purpose I give a summary of the metaphors and analogies used to express the superiority of the Dongria and the inferiority of the Dombo. In the next part I exemplify these value-ideas by discussing rules and practices meant to separate Dongria from Dombo. Then I draw attention to concepts of interdependency, which stress social proximity, if not unity between Dongria and Dombo, and to the numerous ways in which both communities interact as members of one society. By describing in detail the social, economic and religious ties between both communities I can show that the Dombo are an inseparable part of tribal life in the highlands. They may even rise to powerful and respected village leaders as I illustrate with reference to Dombo holding the title *barika*. In my view they are not simply 'economic' or 'culture' brokers but vital agents in the renewal of the socio-cosmological order. The argument is that their 'economic' and 'political' functions[9] are a prerequisite for sacrifices in the performance of which they are often included as important religious actors. At the end of this essay I will therefore especially focus on the ritual activities of the Dombo which have been recognized, but has been rather neglected in the literature on these clients.[10] In contrast to Pfeffer I will not draw a radical distinction between the Kond as 'communicators with the divine' and Dombo as 'communicators with human beings'. My ethnographic data show that although Dombo are excluded from some forms of communication with the divine they are strongly included in others. This becomes clear when we consider the roles of Dombo ritual specialist in the Niamgiri Hills.

Value-ideas: Hierarchical relations between Dombo and Dongria

Dongria and Dombo populate a hill territory with peaks of almost 1,600 m.[11] In about half of all villages one finds a majority of Dongria houses, usually not more than 20–30, and a few Dombo households, usually only one to ten houses. According to a study undertaken in 1975, the 110 villages in the Niamgiri Hills were populated by 5,618 Dongria and 1,173 Dombo (Das Patnaik 1984: 23).[12] In the 1980s, the number of people and villages increased. According to statistical data published by Nayak in 1989, the number of villages increased to 116 which were inhabited by 7,858 Dongria and a total number of 1,365 Dombo. However, only in 52 out of the 116 villages, Dongria and Dombo lived together (Nayak 1989: pp. 221–6). Apart from the Dombo, one sometimes comes across a few households of blacksmiths (Lohar), sweepers (Leli) and brass workers (Ghasi). While the Dombo are usually present in every larger village, members of these three groups settle in very few villages and often do not exceed one or two households. My own research took place in a village named Gumma, which consisted of 31 houses of the Dongria and four houses of the Dombo at the time of my fieldwork (2001–3).

The lower status of the Dombo is expressed in different ways. Thus, Dombo must live outside or in the 'backside' (akagiri) of the village in order to be kept away from the earth goddess. They are considered 'junior' or 'smaller' (icha) brothers of the Dongria and they are treated as dependent 'clients' (praja) who emerged out of the earth last and who perform different services in order to make a living. Dombo are also associated with ancestors and in particular with evil ghosts (marha). In the following sections I will elaborate these value-ideas which establish a hierarchy between Dongria and Dombo.

Kond 'on the front path' *(*rechagiri*),*
Dombo 'on the back path' (akagiri)

A typical Dongria village[13] consists of two rows of houses facing each other and forming a circle that is interrupted at the eastern and western entrance to the village. The place in the centre, in between the two rows, is called *rechagiri*, the backyard as *akagiri*.[14] The houses of the Dombo are normally found behind the village, and even if their houses are located at one end of the village rather than behind a row of houses, the Dombo are always said to live *akagiri*.

The area behind the houses is the daily meeting place of the village women, whereas men assemble on the main road (*rechagiri*) in front of both rows of houses. The stones representing the earth goddess (*dharni*) and her husband (*koteiwali*) are located on this main road, while the area behind the houses is associated with ghosts (*bhut*) and ancestors (*mahane*). For example, when somebody dies, the dead body will be carried via the backside of the village to the cremation ground and the dead persons' souls are said to return to the houses by the same way.

As the pigs of the Dongria stay in the backside of the house and as Dongria throw away their dirt into these backyards, the place behind the row of Dongria houses is always a very filthy and muddy place, in particular during the rainy season. Thus, the Dombo somehow live on the rubbish heap of the Dongria and their houses are out of sight of the gods and the male members of the village.

Why? The idea is that the Dombo must not come near the place of the earth goddess in the centre of the village (Jena et al. 2002: 25).[15] In a way they are treated like menstruating women. During her menses, a Dongria woman has to stay in a room of her house that opens towards the backside (*akagiri*) of the village. As an explanation for this seclusion, people will refer to the possible wrath of the gods, in particular of the earth goddess (*dharni penu*), if a menstruating woman approaches her site of worship. As the sacrificial place for the earth goddess is present in the centre of the village, a menstruating woman must stay away from her by remaining in the backside of the house, farthest removed from her shrine-stones. If she does not obey this rule, she commits a *dosa*, a serious mistake or offence, and the goddess will punish her, her family or even the whole village by withdrawing her protection against diseases and various calamities. Whenever women move around in the Niamgiri Hills, they normally do not enter a village by the main road, but use a road at the back of both rows of houses to avoid any accusations of arousing the wrath of the earth goddess. I witnessed the same practice followed by

Dombo traders moving to the markets and avoiding trespassing the inner village boundaries. As Jena et al. write: '. . . *dharani penu* did not like the presence of the dombs [*sic*] in the place she had given only to Dongaria. She did not like the Domb people passing by her altar' (2002: 25).

Kond as 'kings' (raja), Dombo as 'subjects' (praja)

An idiom that is sometimes used by members of Dongria and Dombo communities to describe their relationship is that of ruler/patron (*raja*) and subject/client (*praja*) (see also Jena et al. 2002: 72). When angry, the Dongria shout that they are not 'small people' (*ichun loku*), but children of the king (*raja mila*). They consider themselves the legitimate owners of the land given to them by the gods. In myths pertaining to the first phase of creation, their father is the sun god, *dharmuraja* or 'king of order'; in those relating to the time after a great flood their culture hero is *niamraja*, literally meaning 'king of rules' or 'king of tradition'. The relation to the king, the mythological as well as the former kings living in Bissamcuttack or Jeypore,[16] defines their status as subjects (*praja*), a status they are very proud of. In relation to the Dombo, they consider themselves kings or patrons and regard the Dombo as their subjects, their clients.

The higher status of the Dongria as 'kings' is clearly expressed at the time of the festival of *dipawali* (in October-November), when they are honoured by the Dombo living in their village. On the third day of this festival the Dombo slaughter a buffalo and sell the meat to the Dongria. However, one portion of the meat, the loin (*bema*), will be kept separate and divided into four parts. In the afternoon the Dombo will carry each portion on a stick to four different Dongria houses, where they sing a song, present the meat as a gift and receive some rice and money from the head of the household in return. Some hours later the Dongria who were given the meat will one after the other pay a visit to the street where the Dombo live. The Dombo will keep a cot in front of their house and ask their Dongria patron to sit down. Then they pour water on their patron's head, hands and feet and give him alcohol to drink. The patron is only allowed to get up when he has given money to the Dombo.[17] In Gumma, the meat was given to the four leaders of the village, two traditional (*jani* and *bismajhi*) and two modern (senior *member* and junior *member*), who all belonged to the dominant clan of the village named Sikoka.[18] The meat is kept on the roof or in front of the house as a sign of their superior status, but in the evening it is taken away by some villagers who cook it on the village plaza and share it with everybody who comes to attend this small feast.

Kond as 'senior' (kaja), *Dombo as* 'junior' (icha)

Another idiom used to define the relations between both communities is that of seniority. As described by Pfeffer (1982: 29; 1997: 13–14) and Berger (2000: 19; 2002: 69; 2007) for other communities in the highlands of Odisha, the opposition between 'big' or 'senior' (*kaja*) and 'small' or 'junior' (*icha*) is one of the main value-ideas that structures social relations in this region. The implications of this opposition will be clarified by the following elaboration of relations between Dombo and Dongria.

In the context of village relations, members of the Dombo community often address Dongria as elders. This is linked to the idea that the Dongria were the first who appeared on earth and all people descended from their ancestors.

This is clearly expressed in Dongria myths about the origin of human kind (Hardenberg 2005a: 81, 635–6; Jena et al. 2002: 133–63). According to these myths, which differ in detail, first the Kond and then all other people were created by goddess *jamarani* inside the earth, where they stayed in darkness. The goddess then created the sun god (*dharmuraja*) to rule the people and when his rays pierced the earth through a small hole, the people saw the light and came out, first the Kond, then the higher castes and finally the lowest like the Dombo. The Kond divided themselves into several groups and established the first villages with sites of worship for the earth goddess (*dharni penu*), their mother. Later the sun god punished the human beings by sending a great flood and all of them were killed except a brother (Duku) and a sister (Dumbe). *Dharmuraja* disfigured the face of the sister with smallpox so that the brother could no longer recognize her and agreed to take her as his wife. With the help of the sun god the soil became firm and life on earth again became possible. The Kond began to populate the land which the gods divided among them. They were distinguished into different castes, all castes being considered descendants of 12 brothers born of Dumbe.

The origin of human beings is represented as an act of creation by the goddess in the earth, the role of the father being limited to 'opening' the earth and showing the way out of her.[19] He is a king who punishes, destroys and restores order, but who is not a creator. After flooding the earth and killing most of his children, the sun god helps to make life on earth possible again by joining brother and sister in marriage and by re-establishing order. Hierarchy is expressed in terms of the order of creation and the order of coming out of the earth. In the context of the original creation, the Kond are the first to be created and the first who come out of the earth followed by the different castes from high status to low status. In the second phase, they become the ancestors of all human beings, who are divided according to territory and service. The Kond are generally known as hunters and agriculturalists, whereas people from other castes perform services such as cooking (Brahman), brewing alcohol (Sundi), making iron tools (Lohar) or sweeping the streets (Dombo). Thus, what Berger writes for the Desia, also holds true for the Dongria: 'When Desia talk about their communities (jati) . . . they generally do not mention "purity" and "impurity" (sud, asud), but again employ the "big-small" dichotomy' (Berger 2002: 69).

Kond as 'humans' (kuang), Dombo as 'ghosts' (marha)

Dongria refer to themselves as *kuang*, a word literally meaning 'men' or in the extended sense 'human being'. Dongria call their own language *kuang kata* and all Kond people are said to be *kuang* in contrast to the Oriya people, *kaska loku*, from the plains. The word *kuang* is often used to distinguish themselves from the Dombo whom they equate with ghosts or with dead people. Dongria and Dombo distinguish two types of death: a good and a bad death.[20] A bad death results in the transformation of the living person into a violent soul (*marha*) that wanders around and is capable of inflicting its own death experience on others. When a Dongria dies of such a death, for example by falling from a tree, he is considered to lose his caste and become a Dombo. Such a violent soul is not considered a 'proper ancestor' (*mahane*) and will not, therefore, be called into the house. In other words, like a Dombo such a ghost is restricted from entering the house. Because these violent souls do not belong to the Dongria community any more, they receive offerings in a space separate from the place where the proper ancestors are fed. When such a violent soul gets reincarnated in a Dongria child, a ritual must be performed to reintroduce the ghost into the community of the Dongria.

Dongria say that Dombo worship these ghosts on Dipawali. On this day, Dombo first offer cooked rice along with different curries and cow meat to their ancestors inside the house. Then they go outside, take some rice in their right hand, throw it on the roof and call the different types of ghosts. Finally they place the rice plates with curry and meat on the roof while shouting *pau*, which means the ghosts 'received' their share, should take it and go. The offering remains on the roof throughout the night, and on the next day the Dombo children will take the food and go to the small stream that marks the border of the village. There they drop some food into the water, cross the stream and eat the offerings. The Dongria call the ritual *pau kina* meaning 'to make receive' and point to the fact that the Dombo feed the ghosts with cooked food like they do with their own ancestors. In other words, the Dongria who have lost their right of belonging to their community by dying a bad death turn into Dombo who accept cooked food from them. Not only that, the Dombo themselves exhibit their close relations with these ghosts when they send their children to eat their left-overs.

Not only these ghosts, but sometimes even the pacified souls who died a good death are compared with Dombo. When no Dombo is around, Dongria jokingly call the Dombo *dhumba*, the Oriya word for ancestor, obviously playing with the phonetic similarities. It is said that the *dhumba*, like the Dombo, belong to a 'smaller' community (*jati*). The *dhumba* live on the cremation ground which like the settlement of the Dombo is always outside and to the west of the village. This stands in contrast to the Dongria, whose settlements are located to the east of the houses of the Dombo and the cremation ground, the east being associated with life in many contexts (Hardenberg 2009a). The idea behind this association of the Dombo with the ancestors seems to be that the dead are inferior to the living just like the Dombo are inferior to the Dongria.

Rules of Separation:
Space, Food and Marriage

The lower status of the Dombo is made apparent in daily life in a set of prohibitions which regulate the interaction between Dongria and Dombo with regard to (1) space, (2) food and (3) marriage.

Spatial segregation

A first restriction applies to spatial boundaries. Dongria will not enter the inner part of the house of a Dombo because this will make them 'small persons'. This avoidance becomes a rule when applied to the Dombo. Dombo should not enter the inner part of a Dongria house because that will make the goddess of wealth and rice, *sita penu-lahi penu*, leave the house. This goddess is worshipped at a wall called *handani kuda*. The room behind the *handani kuda* is usually empty and only used for ritual purposes, especially for invocations to the ancestors. The grain is stored in the attic, where Dongria also preserve sacred pots (*bohandi*) and bamboo baskets (*buldang*) containing paddy (*kulinga*) and rice (*manjinga*) and gourds (*kaktedia*) filled with rice and millet (*hiko*), which represent different forms of the goddess. Myth and rituals relate to the coming and going of this goddess: her presence brings wealth, her absence leads to poverty. When Dombo started offering me cooked food, I was warned by one of the local development officers that I should not accept it because the Dongria will then prohibit me from entering their houses, in particular at the time of rituals when the gods are called. If a member of either community enters the house of the other, he or she will commit a 'mistake' (*dosa*) that will disturb relations with the gods. This is expressed in the following short myth told to me by a Dongria:

In the past, *niamraja* used to walk around a lot. But one day he came into one of our villages where somebody with the name 'Dombo' lived. He was a Kond, but his name was 'Dombo'. When *niamraja* heard others calling this man 'Dombo', he thought that these people are not Kond but Dombo and he went into hiding. Since that time *niamraja* cannot be seen any more.

What this myth expresses is the general idea that the gods fear having contact with Dombo. If a Dongria transgresses the rules restricting the contact with the Dombo, he disturbs the proper order of relations and risks the withdrawal and even punishment of the gods, in particular of his own house. As described above, this spatial separation between Dongria and Dombo also governs the layout of the village as a whole.

The rules against building a house inside the village or entering a Dongria's inner house are obeyed by every Dombo. A Dombo may be allowed to sleep on the inner veranda of a Dongria's house at night but under no circumstances will he dare to step inside the main house. In the same way, I often saw Dongria sitting on the veranda of a Dombo's house chatting and drinking alcohol, but never saw a Dongria entering the inner part of the house.

Food prohibitions

A second restriction concerns the sharing of food. According to the following myth which I heard from a Dongria ritual specialist (*gurumeni*), the gods once wanted to attend a feast in the house of a Dombo family, but god *bima* prevented this by destroying everything:

In the old days a group of hunters went around to hunt a mouse deer (*gensi*). They reached a place with a big flat rock. They were tired and sat down and because they wanted to smoke they lit a fire. They took a stick and started chafing it between their hands in a hole of the big rock. From the dust of the wooden stick arose the gods followed by the different castes, like Ghasi, Dombo, Kumti, and Lohar. After *lahi penu* came out of the hole, she went around looking for grain. She went to the house of a Dombo, because once a year the Dombo receive grain from the Kond for herding the cows. When she arrived at the house of a Dombo, she asked for grain, but while the Dombo man was willing to give her something, his wife refused. Because her wish had been declined, *lahi penu* told the gods accompanying her to transform their hair into rats. They did as requested and the rats ran into the Dombo's house, took away all the grain and carried it into heaven. When the Dombo women saw that all her grain had disappeared she thought: 'Oh, these people asking for grain were not humans but gods. Had I given one *ada* [approximately 1 kg], they would have returned two *ada*. Had I given two *ada*, they would have returned one *mana* [approximately 4 kg]. Now we have nothing.' They recognized their fault and, therefore, wished to give a feast to the gods. They slaughtered a goat, cooked rice and distributed everything on leaf plates. Then they called the gods but the moment the gods arrived a huge storm broke out and everything became dusty. *Lahi penu* took cover in a piece of bamboo. When the storm died the gods saw that everything was gone and disappointed they went back into heaven. There *lahi penu* realized that they had no food. Therefore she returned to earth. Half way she met *bima penu*, her mother's brother. He talked to her and tried to prevent her from going back to earth, but *lahi penu* responded: I go back to the humans and will settle down near the *dharni* [earth goddess]. I will request feasts for you and the other gods. Nowadays, for this reason, we bring *akat manjing* [sacred rice representing *lahi penu*] to the *dharni*.

   This myth deals with several aspects important for the discussion of the Dombo's status. First, the Dombo refused to give grain when asked and now they are punished for this by having all the grain they possess taken away. When the Dombo woman regrets her behaviour she expresses a basic Kond paradigm: when asked by a higher person one should give because one can expect greater gifts in return. This is the basic logic in all Kond rituals, and because the Dombo did not act accordingly, they are of a lower status, deprived of *lahi penu*, who is represented by grain in many rituals. Second, when the Dombo want to present the gods with cooked food, the gods are ready to attend the feast, but they are taught a lesson by *bima penu*, who destroys everything. The message is that people of higher status can demand raw rice from Dombo but not cooked food.[21] Third, when *lahi penu* returns to earth, she settles near the *dharni*, i.e. in a Kond village. From them she can demand grain, because she can be certain that it will be given to her. It is implied that the Kond understand the essential norm of reciprocity: *lahi penu* has given a part of herself, the grain, to the Kond, and when she demands it at the time of sacrifice, they will return it to her and the other gods.

It is also with reference to food and the idea of an original sin that Dombo explain their present low status. Thus, I recorded the following story from a Dombo woman:

We are not a small caste, we are Brahmins. Once there was a Brahmin who had seven sons. One day one of his cows died and the father sent away his sons to cremate the cow. They carried the cow to a river, hung up their sacred threads on a tree and placed the cow on a fire. Then they took a bath in the river, put on their sacred threads and went away. On the way the oldest brother told the youngest to return and to see if the cow had properly burnt up. When he arrived at the place of cremation, he smelled the meat and since the cow had been very fatty, the smell was very good. He took off his sacred thread, placed it in the tree and began to eat the meat. His middle brother had followed him, and when he saw that his younger brother ate the meat he quickly informed his other brothers. They came and scolded the youngest brother, took away his sacred thread and reported everything to the father. The father repudiated his son. He told him that he is no longer a Brahmin and that no one [from another caste] will ever eat with him again.

Very similar myths are told by 'untouchables' all over India (e.g. Kolenda 1981: 175–6; Moffatt 1979: 120-1; Randeria 1992: 132, App. 213–9). The common topic of all these narrations is the fall of one's caste from high status due to a very grave sin, proven or alleged, like in this case eating the meat of the sacred cow. The main plot of the myth refers to popular Hindu ideology and not to ideas expressed by the Dongria. Eating cow meat is not considered a sin according to Kond values. Cows are being sacrificed by Dongria Kond at certain ritual occasions and only medicine men sometimes take a vow to avoid cow meat because they are assisted in their work by very powerful gods who would refuse their help. However, whenever discussing the status of the Dombo, Kond people will hurry to explain that they do not eat with them, nor with the Ghasi or the Leli, the two other castes considered being of low status. When asked why, Dongria will reply that all these people are *icha* (small or junior), while they are *kaja* (big or senior).

Dombo often claim that the Dongria do not strictly obey their own food restrictions. In public I never saw a Dongria eating in the house of a Dombo but the latter often assured me that Dongria sometimes come at night and eat their meat. They also claim that in other villages at the time of Dipawali Dongria and Dombo nowadays sit together and attend the feast given by the Dombo. When I once refused to eat in the house of a local home guard belonging to the Dombo community by saying that the Dongria of my village would otherwise prohibit me from entering their houses he assured me that even the chief of the village I was staying in had eaten cooked food in his house.

Dongria's reaction to the suggestion that they may take food from the Dombo depends completely on the context. When, for example, explaining the status differences between communities they will say that the difference between them and the Dombo is that the latter will accept cooked food from them but not vice versa. To prove this claim of a higher status they will point to the fact that Dongria give *gandi kahpe* to the Dombo. This word refers to cooked food, in particular boiled rice and gruel, that is given to the Dombo as a remuneration for services offered by them. Thus the Dombo (often children) who look after the Dongria's livestock receive *gandi kahpe* twice a day, in the morning and the evening. It is given to them either in leaf plates or in aluminium pots the Dombo themselves bring to the veranda of the Dongria's house. This offering is one of the most explicit markers of the status difference between members of both communities, not because of any impurity involved, but because of the dependency of the clients on their patrons.

When, however, sitting along with other Dombo around the *salap* tree drinking and chatting, Dongria will publicly deny that these restrictions carry any relevance. The above quoted myth collected by Jena et al. (see footnote 19) ends with the god advising the hunters to pretend they accepted the Dombo's food even if they have not. This reflects the general diplomatic attitude of the Dongria who will not insist on status differences when Dombo are around. For example, when a Dombo from another place once came to visit our village he told the Dongria with whom he was drinking that nowadays there are only two castes, the caste of men and the caste of women and nothing else. The Dongria happily agreed. This was certainly due to their idea of polite behaviour but equally due to the context of drinking. Drinking wine from a *salap* tree is an occasion where status differences are denied, except those between men and women, the latter never attending these drinking sessions. Dongria will not drink from the cup or gourd touched by the lips of a Dombo but since everybody avoids drinking in this way, this status marker does not count.

When discussing the topic of eating the food of Dombo in an interview situation, one receives different responses from the Dongria. One of my best friends, who also had a ritual friendship with a Dombo of his village, told me that he does not care about any restrictions but will eat food from everybody. Others declined to take food from the Dombo inside their village, but expressed their readiness to accept food from everybody in the 'plains' (*panga raji*). However, when Dongria move to the smaller towns or to market places in the valley, they always take cooked food with them which they eat somewhere on the way, never in the vicinity of any settlement or market.[22]

At the village feasts, Dombo and Dongria always eat together, but everybody considers the Dongria to be the sponsors and cooks, even if the Dombo help by cutting the meat. If the location allows it, all men will sit more or less in a circle with the fire and the cooking pots in the centre. However, despite the circular form of the sitting arrangement, I often had the impression that Dombo and Dongria behave like two groups facing each other, because the Dombo always sit together in one part of the circle. The Dombo will never serve the Dongria, rather the young Dongria boys will go around and divide the cooked meat and boiled rice or millet between everybody including the Dombo. The idea is, of course, that the Dongria give 'their' cooked food to the Dombo, not the other way round.

Forbidden women

A third restriction applies to marriage relations. Dongria boys and Dombo girls often joke with one another using language with a clearly sexual content. According to one of my informants at least half of the Dongria boys have slept with a Dombo girl, an estimation which I think is exaggerated. However, such casual sexual relations certainly do occur, but are not openly talked about. A Dombo girl that has sexual relations with Dongria men is called Minkawani, 'wife of the fishes', a derogative term that implies that she is promiscuous.[23] Such women sometimes dress like Dongria girls, dance and sing with them.[24] However, if a Dongria falls in love with a Dombo woman and takes her permanently as his consort, he commits a great 'mistake' (*dosa*) which will lead to his expulsion from society. In the area of my stay I heard about two cases, where Dongria entered into a permanent liaison with Leli women, who are regarded as even more inferior than the Dombo. In one case, the Dongria committed suicide due to the rejection by his family members; in the other case the man had to leave his village and settle some hundred metres away from the main settlement of another village. If a Dongria takes a woman from a 'smaller' caste as his wife, the members of his village will call the *bismajhi* or, according to others, the *mondal*, i.e. local leaders who watch over the abidance of the social rules. According to Nayak, the *mondal* can reintroduce the Kond marrying outside the community by touching his tongue with heated gold. The *mondal* keeps the gold and the Kond thus reintegrated has to give a feast (Nayak 1989: 181). I have also been told that the *mondal* can expel the Kond taking a Dombo girl as his wife, probably in case he is not willing to give up this relationship. He will perform a ritual to reintroduce the outcaste's house into the clan community. The members of the house then have to provide the village community with a feast. The culprit himself will lose his status as a Dongria and will become a member of the 'smaller' community just like the children born of this union. I have never heard of any case of a Dombo man taking a Dongria woman as his wife,[25] but I recorded cases among the Kond in the plains, of marriages of Kond women with men from higher castes like Gauda and Brahmin. Again, joking with a Dombo man is allowed for a Dongria woman. I watched for several weeks as Dongria girls tried all their charm on a handsome Leli boy and nobody talked badly about them or prohibited them from visiting his house.

Concepts of Interrelations

In the above sections I illustrated local ideas about status differences and described in detail the prohibitions which separate members of both communities. This separation is, however, only part of the total picture. One also comes across certain concepts of interrelations which stress social proximity and even unity between Dongria and Dombo.

Dombo and Dongria as one clan (ra kuda)

The two communities, Dongria and Dombo, are organized in clans (*kuda*) which are named and spread over the whole territory (Hardenberg 2009b). These named categories are important in several ways, but especially for marriages because one may not marry a person from the same clan category. Dongria clans have a clear territorial reference even if, due to migrations and land purchases, the members of a clan do not occupy a discrete territory with fixed boundaries. Interestingly, these Dongria clans are linked to Dombo clans in a system of analogies.[26] For example, the dominant clan of the village where I stayed was called Sikoka. Sikoka (or Hikoka[27]) is a Kuvi[28] terms for a special kind of millet (*hiko*) cultivated in the hills. The corresponding Dombo clan is named Kausilya, derived from another term for this kind of millet which is called 'Kosala' in Oriya. When asking about such correspondences for a variety of clans I often got quite different information from various informants[29] but everybody equated certain Dongria clans with specific Dombo clans.

An explanation for this association of clans was once given to me by a Dombo. He insisted that the correspondence was based on marriage between the two communities. According to him, his forefathers were originally Dongria belonging to the Sikoka clan. One of his forefathers then married a Dombo girl and they all became Dombo and accepted the corresponding Dombo clan title, Kausilya. This may indeed have been the case, because the Dongria husband as well as the children born to this union will belong to the Dombo caste and can no longer bear the original Dongria clan name. But the theme of this 'personal history' is also similar to the theme of other myths told by low caste people about the fall from high status that one wonders if it is not only repetition of the idea of the original sin, in this case of the marriage with a low caste woman.

If one asks the Dongria about the existence of such clan analogies, one gets a range of answers. Some consider this to be a matter of translation as in the case of Sikoka and Kausilya mentioned above, while others see it as a result of the work of the government officials who wrote down clan analogies. Some Dongria distinguish between the fact that both communities have the same clan and the status differences deriving from belonging to 'different castes'.[30] A Dongria is always aware of his higher status but at the same time considers a Dombo to be either a member of his own clan and addresses him like an agnate or a member of a non-related clan and addresses him like an affine. For example, Dongria often address Dombo of the associated clan as 'brother' or 'father's brother' and are addressed with the reciprocal terms in return. In other words, people belonging to associated clans fall into a category of 'brothers' (*bai*). If, however, they know each other well but do not belong to associated clans, one often hears them addressing each other as 'sister's son' or 'mother's brother' if belonging to different generations or as 'wife's brother' and 'sister's husband' if belonging to the same generation. In this case the non-associated Dombo and Dongria clans classify each other as 'affines' (*bondu*). The clan system thus serves as classification which divides the whole society, i.e. Dongria and Dombo, into either 'brothers' (*bai*) or 'affines' (*bondu*).

Dombo and Dongria as 'friends' (tone/ade)

The above described association of clans creates a relationship between Dongria and Dombo on a group level. The institution of friendship,[31] on the other hand, establishes long lasting bonds of an egalitarian character between individuals of the same sex. Within the village where I conducted my research, most Dombo children had ritual friends (male: *tone*, female:

ade) among the Dongria, often since childhood. A Dombo in the village where I stayed had for example started such a bond with two slightly younger Dongria men in his childhood. To initiate the bond they had eaten together from the same plate, something Dongria refrain from in other contexts. This commensality has the effect of creating a new bond, but the breaking of the commensal rules itself is not continued. Thus, his Dongria friends do not eat in his house, although they partake in mutual visits. At the time of Dipawali, the two Dongria men will come to his house, drink some liquor and will accept uncooked rice and some lentils as a gift from him. On the day of the Dasera festival, the Dombo will pay a visit to the house of his ritual friends, eat boiled rice and curry before he is sent away with some bananas or other gifts.

Forms of Interaction

In the previous section I dealt with ideas about the interrelations of Dongria and Dombo on the level of groups or individuals. I will now turn to concrete forms of interaction, especially to collective forms of agriculture and trade. In this context I also describe the functions of the *barika*, a local Dombo who performs various functions for the community and may in fact become a relatively rich and powerful leader. It will then be argued that the 'economic' and 'political' functions of the Dombo are closely linked to the performance of rituals which are conducted by members of both communities.

Collective Work (buti kam)

The Dongria Kond are shifting cultivators who use the forest land on the hill slopes for agriculture. They produce a variety of crops such as various types of millet, beans, peas, lentils, chillies and roots. The Dombo sometimes have their own swiddens which they receive from the Dongria land owners as members of a specific village community. The Dombo also cultivate wet rice in the few places where the natural conditions are favourable for this type of agriculture. The Dombo help the Dongria on their swidden in the context of a particular institution for mutual help called *buti kam*. For very time-consuming work like cutting the forest or weeding the fields, each household can ask the village community for help. For a whole day, either the boys or the girls or at least one person from each household works on the swidden of a particular family. Assistance from the boys (*dangananga buti*) will be demanded for cutting trees, removing bushes or setting fire to the dry wood, while women and girls (*daaska buti*) will be engaged in weeding. Sometimes all households may form one collective work group (*kutumba buti*) representing the whole village, for example when preparing the swidden for the shaman of the village. A further type is the collective work of a group formed on the basis of agreement. Such a group (*punda buti*) will consist of a number of households (including those of the Dombo) who agreed to help somebody on a given task. For other types of *buti* work, the person will not make the arrangement himself but will approach the chief of the village and ask him to assemble the boys or the girls on a specific day on his swidden. On this day, his wife will cook enough food to feed the helpers at midday and additionally the family will pay a nominal amount of money, normally Rs.20, for a whole day of work. This amount is very small considering the payment for contract work which is about Rs.40 per person per day, an indication that the work is not performed in order to earn money. On the other hand, it is also not a free service. When several households have made use of this institution and enough money has accumulated, a buffalo will be bought, slaughtered and shared by the whole village in a feast. The Dombo are included because they earned a right in the share by participating in the collective work. If somebody assembles a particular work group (*punda buti*) he will either pay the nominal amount of Rs.20 to them or, if the work extends over a long time, he will agree to buy a buffalo and hand it over to this group at the end of their work. A Dombo may also make use of this collective help from his co-villagers. For example, one Dombo from Gumma gave a buffalo to 17 households for preparing his swidden for cultivation. The possibility to ask for collective help is not restricted to agriculture. The village leader of Gumma once needed rice for his big-man feast (*ghanta parba*) and he asked the girls of the village, including the Dombo, to help him carry the rice he bought in the plains to his house. For this *buti kam* he paid Rs.20 to the girl's fund. When Dongria started building new houses with the help of development funds, one of them asked a group of co-villagers to assist him making the bricks, a work which took several weeks. When the work was finished he remunerated them with a buffalo.

Selling products

Dombo not only help producing agricultural products but also play a vital role in selling them.[32] This trade with the products of the Dongria ideally involves two different communities. In the villages, the Dombo buy the products of the land from the Dongria and carry these to the next town. In the town, the village Dombo will sometimes sell the products to another Dombo but more often to a Komti. The Komti (or Kumti) are a Telugu caste renowned for their trading skills are considered to be of a status lower than the Dombo. They do not live in the mountains, but reside in small cities in the foothills like Bissamcuttack, Chatikona or Kalyansingpur where they have their own shops or act as moneylenders (Sahukar).[33]

Which products do these traders deal with? The major cash crop in this area is turmeric (*hinga/merka*) which is nowadays provided in great amounts by the government. Some years ago, the government started a programme through their development agency (DKDA) supplying each household with 200 kg. of turmeric free of cost.[34] The Dongria plant the turmeric rhizomes into small fields on their hill slopes and dig them out after a period of two years.[35] Turmeric cultivation is not very intensive work except for the fact that the fields must be cleared of all roots— something the Dongria do not do on their regular fields.[36] When a Dongria is in urgent need of cash, he will sell the whole field to a Dombo for a price lower than what the Dombo will receive when he later sells the crop back to the government. In addition to the amount given for the crop, the Dombo will have to pay the Dongria for digging out the turmeric. If a large part of or even the whole village is involved in digging out the turmeric, the Dombo will give them one or two buffaloes as a compensation (*kuli kodru* or 'labour buffalo'). The Dombo will boil and dry the fresh rhizomes and carry them to the town to sell them.

Dombo living in Dongria villages further trade bananas, oranges, pineapples, and castor seeds. Most Dongria keep only those bananas for consumption that can be cooked while they give the rest to the Dombo, who carry the shrubs to the local shop owners. The lowest segment of each shrub is given to the Dombo as their profit (*laba*). They calculate Re.1 for four bananas, while the Dombo will receive Re.1 for two or three bananas. Normally the Dongria selling his bananas will not accept money but ask the Dombo for alcohol, which he then shares with everybody present. In this way, the Dombo makes a double profit and the Dongria raises his status as a generous man.

Oranges and pineapples, which are not eaten by Dongria, were introduced in large amounts by the DKDA, but in contrast to banana plantations these plantations are less successful and profitable. In some areas, Dongria have given up pineapple cultivation completely because the plants are all eaten by porcupines. If the harvest is successful, the Dongria carry the fruit to the town themselves because they will make higher profits when selling the fruit on their own instead of giving it to the local Dombo. The Dombo from the plains will wait on the way to the town in order to buy the pineapples for a slightly lower price and sometimes Dongria agree because they need cash for buying alcohol in a nearby Dombo house. The same happens with oranges, but because Dongria leave the trees almost unattended, the harvest is usually so small that trading with oranges has almost no economic importance. Castor seeds are grown by Dongria in great amounts on their swiddens and are then carried to local markets where they are either sold (*prana*) or exchanged (*patela kina*) for rice.

While formerly the local Dombo acted as middle men in this trade, the Dongria nowadays carry the product to the markets and towns themselves, where they sell their products to businessmen, mostly Komti. The same happens with brooms (*bedunika*) made by the Dongria from grass. Either the grass itself, which Dongria collect on their hill slopes, or the readymade brooms are exchanged for money or alcohol with the local Dombo, but the majority of the brooms will be bought by a trader from the plains, usually a Dombo or a Komti. A village will often collectively sell its brooms to one trader—a Dombo but more often a Komti—from the nearest market town for a fixed price. Other crops like pigeon-peas, arrowroot or chilies are always sold directly or exchanged for rice by the Dongria without the help of the local Dombo. This means that those making the highest profit from trading with the Dongria are living in the market places in the plains, which are mostly the Komti, and not the Dombo staying in the Niamgiri Hills.

Sharing and Selling of Alcohol

Dongria and Dombo are often intimately connected in the production and sometimes also consumption of various kinds of alcohol. The main type of alcohol is made from the fruits of the *mohula* tree that ripen between March and May. The trees grow everywhere in the mountains but usually not in large numbers. Early in the morning, Dombo and Dongria go to these trees, which are not owned by anybody in particular, to pick the fruits from the ground, take them home and dry them in baskets placed on their roof. Once dried, the Dongria sell the fruits to the local Dombo, who store them in their houses. If they run out of fruits they can buy them in the towns where they are heavily mixed with chemicals for preservation and sold for comparatively high prices. From time to time, the Dombo ferment the fruits with water and a local fertilizer (*kara*) and carry the mixture to a stream for distillation which takes about two hours. This work is usually done by men, but if no men are available in the household, a woman is allowed to do the task. After distillation he sells the alcohol per bottle (*kanch*) at his home to the Dongria, while the Dombo themselves usually abstain from drinking distilled alcohol. A second type of alcohol made in this way is produced from sugarcane molasses (*gudu*) bought by the Dombo per kilogram in the market. The amount of alcohol produced varies from village to village. Some of the more highly-populated Dombo villages are renowned as places where every day alcohol can be bought. Dongria will come to these places to buy alcohol for ceremonial occasions or when 'thirsty' following a trip to the market or a distant village. Dombo in less accessible villages, like the one in which I stayed, usually make alcohol only on the eve of a village feast or when they have no other source of income.

The status difference between both communities is made very explicit with reference to alcohol. A Dongria who distils alcohol shares a part of the product with the people present at the place of distillation in the forest, and then carries the rest to his house where he drinks it together with family members or close friends. This is done more or less secretly because everyone who enters the house at the time of drinking can expect a share. A Dombo, on the other hand, also shares part of the product at the place in the forest, but then takes it home for selling to others. Dongria often say that they will never sell the fruit alcohol; otherwise they would be like Dombo. What they mean is that they will never sell it to other Dongria, but they may sell their share to the Dombo if they are in urgent need of money.

The same idea exists about sharing and selling palm wine (*mada kalu*). Palm wine trees are owned by Dongria and Dombo. While the Dongria inherit these trees from their parents who planted the seed, the Dombo buy the trees from those Dongria who already possess many.[37] A Dongria owning a tree will always share the alcoholic sap with everybody present. A Dombo owning a tree will also be obliged to share some of it with the people who come and wait under the tree while he or a Dongria authorized by him cuts the inflorescence. But if the flow of sap from the tree is strong, he can retain a portion for himself which he may sell or share with others in his village. In certain months, when palm juice is available in great amounts, Dombo sometimes make an agreement with one or two Dongria from a certain village. The Dongria sells a certain amount of juice either every day or on the eve of certain festivals to the Dombo, who comes in the morning with a canister to collect it. The Dombo then carries the juice to his own village or to a village where a festival takes place and sells it to the Dongria. I once witnessed a young Dongria from a village selling the juice to an old Dombo woman, who then re-sold it to other Dongria boys in the presence of the original owner. The Dombo woman earned approximately double the amount she paid to the Dongria boy, but this boy would never have sold the alcohol to the other Dongria himself.

Selling and Sacrificing Animals

For various festivals and ceremonies, Dongria need animals as sacrificial victims. These are bought by Dombo from local markets (*hat*) in the plains. In such places people from all castes assemble to trade various things, but the animal market is always dominated by Dombo who come to sell buffaloes, cattle and goats. A Dombo from a Dongria village will mostly be interested in buying old buffaloes that can no longer be used for ploughing and are, therefore, relatively cheap, in the range of Rs.900 to Rs.1,300. These are sought by Dongria as animals for village feasts and as gifts to one's affines. He rarely buys a goat and never a chicken, because these are also available in the hills where he can often buy them at cheaper rates and with less effort than in the market which may be several hours walking distance from his village.

A Dombo usually goes to the market where he is well-known and, therefore, will not be bothered by the police. Once a Dombo from Gumma went to a market different from the one he usually visited for buying animals. There he faced problems with the police because he had no bill (*rasida*). When dealing with cattle and buffaloes the dealers need to issue bills listing the names of buyer and seller as well as the price, sex, colour, and appearance of the animal, and the purchaser must carry this bill with him. Normally, neither buyer nor seller can read or write, and since they usually want to save the costs of hiring a professional writer who offers his services in the market, they mostly settle the deal without any paper work. In this case, the Dombo was not well-known in the market place and the police stopped him, asked for the bills and, since he had none, put him in jail under the suspicion of theft. It took him several hours and a bribe of Rs.1,000 before he was released.

On the eve of a feast or marriage ceremony, the Dongria asks the Dombo to buy a buffalo who then goes to the market to try and find a bargain. A Dombo who regularly trades in animals usually has a fixed number of villages as his clientele and if any other Dombo tries to sell animals in his area, a serious quarrel or even a fight may ensue between them. In the market, he usually buys more buffaloes than required if they are available at a cheaper rate; since there is a constant need for these animals, he can be certain of selling them in the near future. However, if he buys too many, he may be faced with two problems—first that of taking them into the hills and second of herding and looking after them once they are in the village.

On the day of the feast or before leaving the village for visiting the affines, the Dongria calls the Dombo to the village plaza. The Dombo brings the buffalo with him and the Dongria starts inspecting it, commenting on how thin and weak he looks. One of the influential Dongria of the village, usually a village elder, asks the Dombo to make an offer and the bargaining starts. The Dombo does not reveal the price at which he bought the animal, but Dongria are experienced enough to estimate it correctly. The Dombo then appeals to the Dongria's generosity by saying that he has to feed his children or that he has no rice of his own but has to buy it with money. He becomes less demanding if he has two or three buffaloes to sell in other villages, knowing that his efforts will yield enough profit. Because the Dombo can sell the skin of the buffalo to Muslim traders (called 'Pathan') in the city, he may reduce the price if the Dongria promises not to mutilate the skin when killing the buffalo. A reduction of about Rs.200 will be calculated for the skin, but often the Dongria boys cannot resist slaughtering the buffalo by hacking him into pieces—a way of killing which is considered particularly joyful. The horns of the buffalo are not calculated into the price; they belong to the Dombo who will sell them for Rs.5 a piece in the town. From what I witnessed, they finally agree on an amount that is between Rs.150 and Rs.300 above the price for which the Dombo bought the animal. An elder Dongria gives Rs.10 or a stone to the Dombo as a sign that the deal is settled and nobody else can buy the buffalo.

The money is collected by the Dombo himself. If the buffalo has been bought for a village feast, the Dombo calculates the number of participating households and divides the amount accordingly. Every morning after sunrise he stands on the village plaza and demands the outstanding debts, but it often takes weeks before he is able to collect the money from everybody. In case a single person bought the buffalo as an affinal gift or for a death ceremony, the Dombo will from time to time visit his house and demand the money. Often, the person does not pay up all at once but gives small amounts each time the Dombo makes a demand. A Dombo of the village in which I stayed, once explained to me that the Dongria owe him an amount of money totaling Rs.32,000. Since he is illiterate, he has to keep all the sums in his mind and must be an expert in mental arithmetic. He stressed the reliability of the Dongria who may pay with delay but will eventually always clear their debts. He contrasted this with the attitude of people from his own community, who in case of his death would not pay their debts to his wife, whereas the Dongria would honour their obligations.

The demand for cattle is lower than the demand for buffaloes, because they are not given as gifts to affines[38] and are sacrificed only on rare occasions. Dongria buy cattle for varying reasons. If they buy the animal collectively, they intend to sacrifice it to the goddess protecting the village (*yatra kudi*). If they buy it individually, they may use it for a sacrifice to a violent ghost (*marha*), keep it as a kind of security, sell it in times of need, or use it for ploughing and threshing. When Dongria use their cattle as a kind of financial security it may happen that one animal is sold back and forth between the same two owners. Whenever the Dongria needs cash, he sells the animal to the Dombo, only to buy it again when he has enough money. In the area of my stay, only few Dongria owned wet rice and dry fields, but a couple of families kept cattle for ploughing and threshing on the fields of their affines in another village. Such cattle cost between Rs.1,000 and Rs.2,000 and are often bought in pairs. Possessing cattle is a status marker and sometimes the wealth of a person is expressed with reference to the number of cattle he owns. Dombo also keep cattle, sometimes even buffaloes, for ploughing and threshing on fields located in the valleys which either belong to them or to close consanguine kin. At the time of ploughing and again at the time of harvest they take their cattle to the village and stay until the work is over. They also sacrifice cattle at the time of their major festival, the Dipawali ceremony in the month of Kartika (October–November). While Dombo milk the cows for their own consumption, Dongria do not because they do not drink milk. In comparison to the Kond in the valleys, Dongria appear to be rather inexperienced in keeping cattle and they do not feel a particular affection for their animals. They are not experienced in breeding and I had the impression that many cows died due to lack of proper care. Dombo, on the other hand, know how to keep and treat cattle. If for example an animal is injured or has to be castrated, Dongria will bring it to the local Dombo for treatment.

Apart from buffaloes and cattle, Dombo also deal with goats, which are kept by Dongria for financial security and for ritual purposes, in particular for sacrifices to the house gods. Since the amount of meat is small in relation to the high price of a goat, goats are never slaughtered for village feasts. The demand for goats is therefore limited and they are sold only if one is in need of urgent cash. Cattle as well as goats are looked after by the young boys of the village, Dongria and Dombo alike. Each boy is assigned to care for animals belonging to one or two households and, in case he is a Dombo, the household will provide him with cooked food (*gandi kahpe*) twice a day, in the morning and in the evening. When the seeds are sown in the fields and on the hills slopes, the boys take the animals into the forest and keep them away from the areas of cultivation. When the harvest is over, they stop herding the animals and let them roam freely.

Trading with animals is one of the main sources of income of the *barika*, the most respected Dombo at the village level.

Barika: Trader, Arbitrator, Messenger and Politician of the Village

The term *barika* means 'barber' in Oriya, but the person carrying this title is not at all associated with the functions of a barber. He always belongs to the Dombo caste. In case the village is very big and factions between the Dombo exist, the duties of a *barika* may also be shared by two persons.[39] If the villages are small or if the *barika* is very influential, one Dombo may be responsible for three or four villages. For example, in the village I stayed in, one Dombo was officially recognized as the *barika* for three villages with 79 Dongria households (34 + 26 + 19) altogether, and, additionally, he provided sacrificial animals for a fourth village without being acknowledged as its *barika*.

The position of a *barika* is not hereditary[40] and must be confirmed once a year. In the month of Phalgun (February–March), at the time of the *ambadadi* festival, a Dombo is acknowledged as the *barika* of the villages for which he works. He has to give a buffalo to each village as well as one *mana* (around 4 kg.) of rice for cooking the sacrificial food (*bana paga*) offered to the gods. If he neglects this duty or if the Dongria accept the buffalo from somebody else, he loses his position as a *barika*. The Dongria consider this festival and the giving of the buffalo by the *barika* as the beginning of the New Year. A second obligation of the *barika* is to give one buffalo to the villages he is responsible for at the time of Dipawali, when the Dombo worship the ancestors. The buffalo is slaughtered outside the village where the *barika* resides and representatives of all the villages he works for come and take away their respective share. On the day of the Dasera festival in the month of Ashvina (September–October), the *barika* will go together with his wife and children carrying big baskets to each house in the villages he works for and ask for his share (*gandi*). He will be given bananas and cooked rice. Each day he will send his children to the house of the local chief to ask for gruel (*dare kahpe*).

After harvest, he has the right to demand a share of the harvest, usually one basket (*mana*) from each house.[41]

A *barika* has the following functions:[42]

1. In case a meeting (*bereni kina*) has to take place because of a dispute or an urgent collective work, he wakes up the important Dongria men and asks them to assemble at the village plaza. He leads the discussion and announces the decisions. When it is considered necessary to summon a person not present at the meeting, the *barika* goes and calls him or her.
2. He buys everything necessary for the performance of collective festivals, in particular the sacrificial animals, but in some villages he also buys other items like alcohol, pots or baskets. He decides where to store the items and what to do with them. He collects the money for all expenditures related to the festivals.
3. He settles disputes within a village and between members of different villages by holding meetings and giving or accepting fines. The *barika* is sent by the bride's or the groom's party to discuss anything concerning marriage payments and gifts and to settle disputes between affines.
4. He is a messenger in the event of death. When somebody dies, the *barika* will go and call the relatives and members of neighbouring villages to attend the funeral ceremonies.
5. He represents the village in all matters relating to the 'outside world'. If visitors come, he will receive them, and if somebody is killed or dies under unnatural circumstances, he has to inform the police.

The *barika*'s main duty is to acquire the sacrificial animals just as in the past the Dombo or Pano according to colonial officers (Macpherson 1863 [1842]: 64; 1865: 114; Campbell 1864: 52–7) used to sell the human victims[43] that were sacrificed to the earth goddess at the time of *kodru parbu* (buffalo sacrifice).[44] The *barika* of Gumma explained to me that nowadays, when he sells a buffalo to the Dongria for the purpose of performing the *kodru parbu*, he receives one *ada* (one kilogram) rice and Rs.10 from the village as a kind of compensation for the sin he commits by providing the *meria*, the word referring to the sacrificial victim. He himself attributes the sin to the purchase of a young buffalo who will be killed brutally by the crowd (*dunia loku* or 'people of the world', i.e. people who come from far away places) instead of the old and 'useless' buffaloes who will be slaughtered at other festivals by one or more people from the village.

The trade of sacrificial animals is a very lucrative business for a *barika*, in particular if he is a good bargainer and supplies several villages. He can achieve considerable influence due to the fact that a vast number of people become indebted to him, and he may even rise to the status of a small village 'banker' in the sense that people will come and ask him for money at the time of need. My experience in Gumma was that many festivals could be held only because the *barika* did not insist on an immediate payment but was able to advance the money on loan.

The second major function of the *barika* is that of a mediator and arbitrator, in particular in matters concerning marriages. For example, if the people of his village abducted a woman, her relatives and village people would come, sometimes taking their *barika* along, and start demanding either the return of their daughter or a considerable amount of money. This usually leads to open quarrels and the *barika* is called to intervene and discuss the matter with the family members and the *barika* of the bride. In case a daughter of the village runs away with somebody other than her fiancé, the fiancé's *barika* comes to the woman's and her new husband's village to demand a fine. In such cases he often comes alone and discusses the matter with the whole village, including the *barika*. When demanding money for giving one's daughter to another village, the *barika* of both parties will be present. During such negotiations, the *barika* puts forth the demands of his party, while his opponent of the rival party argues against these demands and tries to reduce them. Normally, such disputes are not settled in a few hours or a single day; the *barika* comes and goes, informing his party and getting new instructions from them. The *barika* is also responsible for handing over money to another party or, if he belongs to the receiving party, for counting it. In the same way he is sometimes summoned as an arbitrator if a fight erupts. In such cases he goes back and forth between the conflicting parties until a settlement is reached. He assembles the conflicting parties in one place and makes sure that fines are paid. A ritual is then performed to guarantee peace for the future.[45]

The *barika* also performs the function of a messenger for both Dombo and Dongria, particularly at the time of death of someone in the village. If somebody dies, he has to inform the villagers and the relatives of the dead person staying in other villages to come to the funeral ceremonies (*dosa karma*). This is particularly required if somebody dies unexpectedly, for example, when a young boy suddenly fell ill and died the same day. In such instances, witchcraft or poisoning is suspected as the cause of death. The relatives must be given an opportunity to inquire into the death before the body is cremated. If somebody dies an unnatural death like falling from a tree, the *barika* goes to the next town and informs the police. The police along with the *barika* comes and examines the possible causes of death.

As the last example illustrates, the *barika* represents the village to the outside world. According to Nayak (1989: 178), a *barika* used to accompany a Dongria with the title *mondal* on his way to give a gift of honour called *bheti* to the kings of Jeypore and Bissamcuttack. The *barika* had a variety of contacts with people of the plains and with the police officers to whom he reported events that took place in the village. In Nayak's opinion, 'the role of the *barik* has been minimized so far as interconnections of regional polity with village polity is concerned' (ibid.). My own experiences lead me to be of an opposite opinion. With the increasing number of people coming as representatives of the state or of non-governmental organizations into the Dongria Hills, the *barika*'s functions are becoming increasingly important.

The *barika* thus plays a major political and economic role in the society despite being of a lower status. Depending on his personal abilities, he may rise to become a kind of village 'banker' or a 'judge' and extend his influence from one to several villages in the region. He influences decisions at the village level and beyond and mediates between the political forces from outside the village and the local village leaders. A *barika* will often pay deference to local Dongria leaders due to his status as a Dombo, but most Dongria consider him to be among the 'important people' of the village. A good *barika* is respected for his wealth, his experience and his influence outside the village even if the Dongria does not eat his food or allow him to enter their houses. While the Dombo as a whole can be seen as clients in relation to the landlords, the situation is somehow reversed when we consider the relation between the *barika* and the Dongria. The latter are his clients in the sense that they have become dependent on him.

Communication with the Divine

At the beginning of my fieldwork in Gumma I attended a festival for the goddess of smallpox (*aji budi*). The festival began with the local female Dongria shaman (*bejuni*)[46] bringing small pots filled with grain from each Dongria house to the centre of the village, where a small baldachin was built. Some Dombo women were also around, but I did not expect them to participate. As my following field notes show, my expectations were proved wrong:

After some time, the [Dongria] *bejuni* woman stood up, the others [Dongria boys] started drumming and she began to dance. The *member* and one female assistant [*gurumeni*]⁴⁷ vividly spoke to the [main] *bejuni* and she answered them. The *bejuni* opened her hair. In the meantime, the old Dombo woman from Lamba [adjacent village] had arrived, the one who is building a house in Gumma. She sat on the ground with open hair and swung her head back and forth. Suddenly she fell into trance, tried to get up, but needed the help of two Dombo girls. Like all other *bejuni*, the Dombo *bejuni* started rubbing the rice [in the winnowing fan] with her hand, recited and danced. There was no difference between her and the other [Dongria] *bejuni*.

This last statement was made too rashly because in the course of further events, certain differences became apparent. For example, shortly after the dance finished the Dongria and Dombo called the children to sit down on the village plaza for receiving a protective mark (*linga*) on the forehead. The *bejuni* divided this task among them according to the children's status: the female Dongria shaman touched the Dongria children, the female Dombo shaman the Dombo children.

In the remainder of my stay in the village I learned that one of the major duties of a Dongria shaman is to heal by falling into a trance, communicating with the gods and inquiring into why a particular person was struck by symptoms of disease.⁴⁸ Again I was astonished when one day I visited the house of a Dombo where such a healing session was taking place and instead of a Dongria *bejuni*, the old Dombo woman performed the inquiry in a state of trance. When asked, people confirmed that the shamans will only perform the healing ceremony for members of their own community. The conclusion I drew from these instances was that both communities have a similar shamanic tradition, and that they celebrate independently in the context of their house affairs but jointly in the framework of village festivals. I understood the separation as an expression of the hierarchy between the two communities, the Dongria expressing their higher status by not touching the Dombo *bejuni* and her children. Indeed, in the context of festivals I experienced many other markers of the Dombo inferiority. For example, a village festival can take place without the participation of the Dombo *bejuni*, but not without the Dongria religious specialists.

In the plains, Harijan often perform the function of musicians, especially of drummers and flutists. According to Pfeffer, clients work as 'master musicians' on all festive occasions. 'Tribal youths sometimes beat the drums for the dances, but none of them is allowed to touch the oboe, or the leading melody maker' (1997: 10). When Dongria celebrate a village festival, the oboe is rarely used, while the drums will be played by the Dongria. These drums are kept by the Dongria in their houses and they are worshipped like gods at the time of festivals, receiving small chicken and rice as offerings. Without the drums, the gods cannot dance. Only in the context of the *kodru parbu* (buffalo sacrifice) did I witness the participation of Dombo musicians, who played the oboe (*mohuri*). An indication that making music is an inferior ritual activity became apparent only at the time of the big-man festival, the *ghanta parba*. At the end of this festival, the Dongria drummers are called to the house of the big-man (*kaja loku*) and sprinkled with turmeric water by the female shaman. When asked why, they responded that for the time of the festival the Dongria have become Dombo and Ghasi. For this reason they are prohibited from entering the house of the big-man for the time of the festival. The turmeric water is used as a substance of purification, this being one of the few occasions when Dongria show concern about ritual pollution. The reason, I think, was that the Dongria performed music for somebody else in return for payment in rice and meat. They behaved like Dombo who work for a patron in order to receive something for a living.

Assuming that Dombo can participate in festivals only in an inferior position, I was astonished to find out at a *kodru parbu* (buffalo sacrifice) that many of the major rituals were performed by a Dombo from the plains, who looked like a *sadhu* (Hindu ascetic) with his matted hair and was addressed as *dissari*[49] or *beju*[50] by the Dongria. First, I thought this may have been an exception but a year later I attended another buffalo sacrifice in a completely different area and witnessed the worship of one of the highest deities of the Dongria, god *niamraja*, and again the main shaman was a Dombo from the village of the organizers. He performed the ritual alongside three or four female Dongria shamans, but he was clearly the head of these ritual specialists. The reason why in both cases a Dombo could perform these rituals must be sought in the special relations of shamans, who derive their powers from the gods. If a Dombo has enough experience and has a reputation as a powerful shaman, he is selected as the chief ritual specialist, whatever his social status outside the ritual sphere may be.

Dombo may perform various ritual activities, yet they are not addressed as *jani*[51] and *pujari*.[52] These are titles linked to Dongria status categories (*punja*) and certain functions connected with these status categories are reserved only for Dongria. Apart from this exception,

Dombo clearly are 'communicators with the divine' when performing the functions of *dissari*, *beju*, or *bejuni*. They perform these functions often in an inferior position when compared to Dongria ritual specialists, yet they may become very powerful and are then asked to conduct the most important rites for their patrons.

Conclusion

This chapter confirms Niggemeyer's and Pfeffer's view that Kond and Dombo clearly form one society even if nowadays they are treated as belonging to different 'social types' when they are classified as 'Scheduled Tribes' and 'Scheduled Castes' in the official language of the state. The question, however, remains how exactly this society is structured: what is its ideology and how are value-ideas acted out in practice? To give an answer to this question I concentrated on a specific region, the Niamgiri Hills of Rayagada district, where the Dongria Kond live together with the Dombo, often in the same village. My ethnographic data show that the Dongria majority considers the Dombo majority as being of lower status. The Dongria think of themselves as the children of the earth goddess and to be 'senior', because they came out of the earth first; they claim to be the land owners and 'kings', who reside in the centre of the village. In contrast, the Dombo are portrayed as 'junior', who came out of the earth last, as dependent people who must make a living by engaging in trade and as clients who reside on the land of their lords, the Dongria. They are equated with ghosts and must live in the backyard of the village. There are a number of rules which confirm these status differences by prohibiting the Dombo to enter the houses of the Dongria, to give food to them or to enter into mutual marriage relations. The low status of the Dombo is also attributed to their ways of making a living. Thus, Dombo buy and sell products and depend on the profit they make, while Dongria proudly claim to subsist on the cultivation of their own land. However, with regard to ideology and practice, this picture needs to be elaborated by looking at the forms of interdependency and association between the communities. Thus Dombo and Dongria clans are united in a single classification system that is based on the association between clans. A Dongria clan is equated with a Dombo clan and they address each other as agnates. Similarly, the status difference is partly denied in individual forms of friendship which are created by explicitly breaking the rule of communal commensality. In practice, the Dombo fulfil a number of essential functions for the Dongria and may even acquire a dominant position in the village. Despite their lower status, they may become rich and powerful and turn the Dongria into their clients. From the perspective of the Dongria, such individual achievements do not change the lower status of the Dombo as a whole. Yet they consider these functions as important, not only for their individual interests, but for society as a whole. The Dongria need the Dombo for the organization and performance of rituals, i.e. for the creation and renewal of relations with various cosmic forces. They form one society, in which people of both communities have to contribute their share and abilities to hold up the socio-cosmic order. While the Dombo as a group perform functions considered to be of lower value in relation to the work of the Dongria, some outstanding individuals may act as ritual experts or as powerful brokers for the whole society.

Notes

1. This chapter is a heavily abridged and revised version of the second chapter of my unpublished post-doctoral thesis (Hardenberg 2005a: 52–137).
2. Expressions such as Harijan or Dalits are used instead, sometimes also in self-reference.
3. For an overview of how the categories 'Scheduled Castes' and 'Scheduled Tribes' came into being see Béteille 1991: 77–8; 150–6. According to Béteille, '[T]he process of designating or "scheduling" tribes in India began during British rule and acquired a systematic character from the time of the 1931 census. It became involved in political controversy almost from the very beginning. On the one side were the official anthropologists, mostly British members of the Indian Civil Service, who argued that the aboriginal tribes had a distinct identity that marked them out from the rest of Indian society. On the other hand were the nationalist anthropologists who argued that they were part and parcel of Hindu society' (1991: 77).
4. This is only an assumption and there is certainly a need for more historical research on the question of how exactly this distinction between the tribal Kond and the untouchable Dom/Dombo came into being. For example, it would be worth studying the history of this categorization on the basis of colonial ethnographic accounts and Census reports from the region. In this chapter, however, I use ethnographic data in order to analyse ideas and practices related to these categories today.
5. My research took place from 2001 to 2003 and lasted altogether 16 months. I mostly stayed in a village of the Dongria Kond in the Niamgiri Hills of Rayagada district, Odisha. The research was generously sponsored by the German Research Foundation (DFG) as part of the Orissa Research Project. Previous long term research among the Dongria was conducted mainly by Nayak (1989) and Jena et al. (2002).
6. This expression was coined by Louis Dumont and Daniel de Coppet.

According to Dumont, modern ideology separates values and facts (or science), while non-modern ideologies embed values in their world view. Since values express the order of the whole cosmos in the later type of ideology, these values are often linked to ideas about the world, and Dumont, therefore, speaks of 'value-ideas' (Dumont 1986: 252).

7. The term hierarchy as used by Dumont (Dumont 1998 [1966]: 240) is unrelated to social stratification, military ranking, or power inequalities, and instead refers to a special configuration of values. Hierarchy does not derive from empirical relations but rather provides the form according to which these relations are ordered in a specific ideology.

8. For an elaboration of this argument see Pfeffer 1997: 11, Berger 2002: 69 and Hardenberg 2010.

9. I write the words 'economic' and 'political' with inverted commas because according to local ideas there is no separate economic or political domain.

10. In recent years Lidia Guzy has increased our knowledge about the ritual importance of Scheduled Caste people in western Odisha. Her research focuses on the musical traditions of the Ganda in the Bora Sombar region. See Guzy 2008a, 2008b.

11. The hill range occupied by the Dongria derives its name from its highest peak, the Niamgiri, locally also called Nebaharu. It is considered to be the seat of their divine king, Niamraja, who according to myths was selected by the sun god, Dharam Devata, to rule over the people (Jena et al. 2002: 159–63). The word *niam* means 'moral law' and describes actions considered to be in accordance with the rules and traditions laid down by the gods.

12. For a small demographic study comparing Dombo and Dongria in the village Kambesi see Panda 1969–70.

13. See also Jena et al. 2002: 27–36.

14. *Giri* means literally 'path'. For more details see Hardenberg 2009a.

15. In practice, however, I have often seen the Dombo men of Gumma meeting with the Dongria in the centre of the village. Dombo from outside the village indeed avoid entering the central plaza.

16. When talking about the *raja* Dongria are never quite specific whether they mean the gods who are represented as kings or the kings living in the palaces in the plains.

17. The amount of money expresses the status of the patron. For example, in Gumma the man who at that time was respected as the main leader of the village, explained to me that he is expected to give more money than the others.

18. The senior *member* (*kaja member*) is authorized by the development agency (DKDA), the junior *member* (*icha member*) by the educational department (DPEP).

19. For a discussion of concepts of sexuality and gender see Hardenberg 2005b.

20. For a discussion of the concepts of 'good' and 'bad' death, see Bloch and Parry 1982.

21. The same idea is expressed in the following part of a myth collected by another research team: 'Having cleared the hill slopes, the men turned to *dharam devata* to inquire about when the slashes should be burned. After some thought, he advised them not to light a fire without the permission of *bima penu*, who, if irked, would become wrathful. He told them to appease *bima penu* on a Sunday and also to worship the hill god (*danda penu-horu penu*) on the same day; the slashes were to be burned on Monday. After this, the men asked *dharam devata* for seed to sow. He gave them some which he had taken from the demon's tongue. Since they did not suffice, they went in search for more seeds, and hoped to acquire them in a distant village from a Domb boy who sold clothes and had large amounts of seed. They offered to pay three times the price, but the boy was only willing to part with the seed on condition that the men ate at his house. The men were in a quandary as they had vowed never to accept food in a Domb's house. Thus, they went to *dharam devata* for a solution. He told them to agree to a meal at his home, provided the seed were delivered beforehand; but, upon getting the seed they were to rush back, thus avoiding the meal. The Dombo boy promptly delivered the seed, then he began to prepare the meal, killed a goat for this purpose. While he was doing so, *dharam devata* created wind and rain in a ruse, so that the men could flee. Then he asked them whether they had eaten at the Domb boy's house, and hearing that they had not, told them to claim that they had indeed eaten there' (Jena et al. 2002: 152–3).

22. But when I invited some Dongria friends to eat with me in the local restaurants, they agreed happily as long as I paid the bill.

23. Jena et al. also point to the sexual connotation of the word *minka* 'fishes'. See Jena et al. 2002: 84.

24. I am not certain if these Dombo women also sleep in the girl's dormitory, which is usually not entered by Dombo women.

25. Nayak only states in brackets that sometimes 'Domb also took away Dongria Kond girls' (Nayak 1989: 181).

26. In Koraput district, the Dombo even have the same clans as the tribal landowners and other communities of this region, which are collectively referred to as Desia. See Pfeffer (1997: 17) and Berger (2002: 58; footnote 3).

27. The consonants 's' and 'h' are not clearly distinguished by local people.

28. Linguists distinguish between the Kui language spoken by inhabitants of the Kondmals (see Winfield 1928, 1929) and the Kuvi (or Kuwi) language of the less numerous southern branch of the Kond (see Israel 1979) such as the Dongria Kond. Both languages belong to the Dravidian linguistic family.

29. For example one old Dombo women mentioned the following clan analogies (Dongria = Dombo): Wengesika = Benia; Mandika = Barasagudia; Wadaka = Gurida; Himberika = Manandia; Kurtruka = Dongri; Pusika = Takri, Huika = Mongri. A young Dongria man gave me the following equivalences: Wengesika = Benia, Karchika = Kurkuria, Palaka = Palkia, Jakesika = Batria, Kundika = Mandika. A Dombo informant mentioned again slightly different

analogies: Kadraka = Bagha, Palaka = Hial, Wadaka = Kakaria, Jakesika = Kondapani, Mandika (here considered a Dongria clan) = Batara, Pusika = Takri. Further equivalences were collected from different informants throughout the period of research like for example: Praska = Chati, Saraka = Kataria, Perisika = Ganta.

30. Dongria and Dombo use the word jati for what I translate as 'caste'.

31. For more details on the different types of friendship in the Niamgiri Hills see Hardenberg 2003.

32. Also see Jena et al. 2002: 70.

33. This system of transaction between Kond, Dombo and Komti has earlier been described by the Orissa District Gazetteers: 'During hard months, the tribal people particularly the Soaras and the Khonds get loans from the Sahukars who are mostly the Kumuti businessmen or the Sundhi [wine sellers] through the Dombs. The moneylenders who are but casual visitors to tribal villages come in direct contact with the Dombs and transact through them' (Senapati and Sahu 1966: 203).

34. The DKDA provides 200 kg. for free and after cultivation buys it back for fixed rates. These rates went down, in the period of my stay from Rs.5 to Rs.4 per kg.

35. It is generally believed that the amount will increase by seven times.

36. It is my impression that in the long run, intensive turmeric cultivation will destroy the forest much faster than the local practice of shifting cultivation because once the roots are taken out, the forest will not recover. In the Kambesi area I already saw wide stretches of land without forest, overgrown by a particular grass.

37. A tree is sold for about Rs.50 to Rs.100.

38. Desia Kond, i.e. the Kond inhabiting the valleys, give cattle as part of the gifts to the bride's kin.

39. Like for example in the village Phakeri with its 60 households where two *barika* divide their responsibilities among the two rows of houses.

40. According to Jena et al., it is hereditary, yet they write that 'it may change on certain conditions. If a person expresses his unwillingness to work as *barika* after his father, then the Dongria look for a new *barika* from a different family' (2002: 72).

41. Banerjee reports that in the Kuvi Kond village he studied near Rayagada the *barika* is given an earthen pot by the village headmen when he first joins the post. With this pot he goes to every house in the village to ask for gruel which is given in return for his services. Further, the *barika* has a right in 'one full measure of a winnowing fan, of all the articles grown by them, namely, paddy, mandia, *kandala* and kassala which is sufficient for him and his family to pull on for a year apart from the paddy fields he had on his own possession' (Banerjee 1969: 104).

42. For a similar enumeration of his functions see Jena et al. 2002: 71–2.

43. Local people in the hills and the valleys even nowadays speak about this former practice of buying the human victims from the Dombo.
44. For a detailed analysis of this festival, see Hardenberg 2005a, 2008, 2009c, 2009d.
45. For an analysis of these fines, see Hardenberg 2004.
46. A *bejuni* is a female village shaman. She is said to have a sign (*linga*) on her forehead through which the deities enter her body in dreams and trance sessions and she uses ritual language when performing rituals. A *bejuni* can speak with the voice of gods after falling in trance (*banga ate*) and can identify the causes of sickness. She worships house deities (*ijo kama*) and performs village festivals (*yatra*).
47. A *gurumeni* is the assistant of a *bejuni* and does not fall into trance but functions as interpreter because she understands what the gods through the *bejuni* are saying and is able to respond in the metaphorical language used by the *bejuni*.
48. On untouchables acting as shamans see Berreman 1963, Moffatt 1979, Kolenda 1981.
49. A *dissari* can be a Kond, a Dombo or a member of a Hindu caste. He usually knows how to read the local astrological almanac (*panji*) and is familiar with certain rituals linked to astrological constellations. Dongria are usually not acquainted with astrology.
50. A *beju* is male village shaman. He has a higher status than the female village shaman (*bejuni*) and is called to perform the more important rituals (*kaja kama*), for example at the time of death or during clan festivals; some *beju* are cross-dressers, remain unmarried and adopt female behaviour.
51. A member of the *jani* status category (*jani punja*) and/or a ritual specialist responsible for the buffalo sacrifice (*kodru parbu*).
52. A member of the *pujari* status category or a ritual specialist. As a ritual specialist the *pujari* performs the worship of the god of fire (*bera penu*) during a festival called *bali yatra*.

References

Bailey, F.G., *Tribe, Caste and Nation: A Study of Political Activity and Political Change in Highland Orissa*, Manchester: Manchester University Press, 1960.

———, ' "Tribe" and "Caste" in India', *Contributions to Indian Sociology*, vol. 5, 1961, pp. 7–19.

Banerjee, S., *Ethnographic Study of the Kuvi-Kandha*, Calcutta: Anthropological Survey of India, 1969.

Berger, P., 'Gesellschaft, Ritual und Ideologie. Eine relationale Betrachtung der Gadaba des Koraput Distriktes, Odisha', *Mitteilungen der Berliner Gesellschaft für Anthropologie, Ethnologie und Urgeschichte*, vol. 21, 2000, pp. 15–38.

———, 'The Gadaba and the "Non-ST" Desia of Koraput, Odisha, (pp. 57–90)' in *Concept of Tribal Society (Contemporary Tribal Studies, vol. 5)*, ed. G. Pfeffer and D.K. Behera, New Delhi: Concept Publishing Co., 2002.

———, *Füttern, Speisen und Verschlingen: Ritual und Gesellschaft im Hochland von Odisha, Indien*, Münster: LIT Verlag, 2007.

Berreman, G.D., *Hindus of the Himalayas*, Bombay: Oxford University Press, 1963.

Bloch, M. and J. Parry, eds., *Death and the Regeneration of Life*, Cambridge: Cambridge University Press, 1982.

Campbell, J., *A Personal Narrative of Thirteen Years Service amongst the Wild Tribes of Khondistan for the Suppression of Human Sacrifice*, London: Hurst and Blackett Publishers, 1864.

Das Patnaik, P.S., 'Ownership Pattern, Land Survey and Settlement and its Impact on the Dongaria Kondhs of Orissa', *Adibasi*, vol. 23, no. 4, 1984, pp. 23–32.

Dumont, L., *Essays on Individualism: Modern Ideology in Anthropological Perspective*, Chicago and London: The University of Chicago Press, 1986.

———, *Homo Hierarchicus: The Caste System and its Implications*, Complete Revised English Edition, Delhi: Oxford University Press, 1998 [1966].

Elwin, V., *The Religion of an Indian Tribe*, Bombay: Oxford University Press, 1955.

Guzy, L., 'Music, Musicians and Non Brahmin Priests in Western Odisha', in *Tribal Studies VII*, ed. D.K. Behera and G. Pfeffer, New Delhi: Concept Publishing Press, 2008a, pp. 369–80.

———, *Par e Sur: Sounds of the Goddess from the Boro Sombar Region of Eastern India*, Berlin Museum Collection, ed. Lars-Christian Koch, Mainz: Wergo Schott Verlag, 2008b.

Hardenberg, R., 'Friendship and Violence among the Dongria Kond (Odisha/ India)', *Baessler Archiv*, vol. 51, 2003, pp. 45–57.

———, 'Vitalität und Tausch: Heirat und Opfer bei den Dongria Kond (Odisha, Indien)', *Mitteilungen der Berliner Gesellschaft für Anthropologie, Ethnologie und Urgeschichte*, vol. 25, 2004, pp. 31–46.

———, 'Children of the Earth Goddess: Society, Marriage, and Sacrifice in the Highlands of Odisha (India)', Unpublished Post-doctoral thesis (Habilitation), Münster: Westfälische Wilhelms-Universität, 2005a.

———, 'Mädchenhäuser, Schöpfung und Empfängnis: Kulturelle Konstruktion der Geschlechter bei den Dongria Kond (Odisha/Indien)', *Zeitschrift für Ethnologie*, vol. 130, 2005b, pp. 69–98.

———, 'Sacrificing in Highland Odisha: Self-Reproduction and Dependency', in *Transformations in Sacrificial Practices. From Antiquity to Modern Times* (Proceedings of an International Colloquium, 10–12 July 2007), ed. E. Stavrianopoulou, A. Michaels and C. Ambos, Heidelberg: LIT Verlag— Reihe: Performances: Intercultural Studies on Ritual, Play and Theatre, 2008, pp. 113–34.

———, '"Village Relations": Exchange and Territory in the Highlands of

Odisha', in *Tribal Society: Category and Ritual Exchange (Contemporary Society: Tribal Studies, vol. 8)*, ed. G. Pfeffer, New Delhi: Concept, 2009a, pp. 135–58.

———, 'Reconsidering 'tribe', 'clan' and 'relatedness': A comparison of social categorization in Central and South Asia', *Scrutiny: A Journal of International and Pakistan Studies*, vol. 1, no. 1, 2009b, pp. 37–62.

———, 'Categories of Relatedness: Rituals as a Form of Classification in a Middle Indian Society', *Contributions to Indian Sociology*, vol. 43, no. 1, 2009c, pp. 61–87.

———, 'The Buffalo Sacrifice of the Kond and the Creation of Society', in *Tribal Society: Category and Ritual Exchange (Contemporary Society: Tribal Studies Vol. 8)*, ed. G. Pfeffer, New Delhi: Concept, 2009d, pp. 52–66.

———, 'A Reconsideration of Hinduization and the Caste-Tribe Continuum Model', in *An Anthropology of Values. Essays in Honour of Georg Pfeffer*, ed. P. Perger, R. Hardenberg, E. Kattner and M. Prager, New Delhi: Pearson/ Longman, 2010, pp. 89–103.

Israel, M., *A Grammar of the Kuvi Language*, Trivandrum: Dravidian Linguistics Association, 1979.

Jena, M.K., P. Pathi, J. Dash, K. Patnaik and K. Seeland, *Forest Tribes of Odisha: Lifestyle and Social Conditions of Selected Odishan Tribes, vol. 1 The Dongaria Kondh* (Man and Forest Series 2), New Delhi: D.K. Printworld, 2002.

Kolenda, P., 'Religious Anxiety and Hindu Fate', in *Caste, Cult and Hierarchy: Essays on the Culture of India*, ed. P. Kolenda, Meerut: Folklore Institute, 1981, pp. 169–84.

Macpherson, S.C., Lieut. *Macpherson's Report upon the Khonds of the Districts of Ganjam and Cuttack*, Madras: Graves, Cookson & Co., 1863 [1842].

———, *Memorials of Service in India: from the Correspondence of the late Major Samuel Charteris Macpherson, C.B., political agent at Gwalior during the Mutiny, formerly employed in the Suppression of Human Sacrifice in Orissa, edited by his brother*, London: John Murray, 1865.

Moffatt, M., *An Untouchable Community in South India: Structure and Consensus*, Princeton: Princeton University Press, 1979.

Nayak, P.K., *Blood, Women and Territory: An Analysis of Clan Feuds of the Dongria Kondhs*, Delhi: Reliance Publishing House, 1989.

Niggemeyer, H., *Kuttia Kond: Dschungel-Bauern in Orissa*, Frankfurt am Main: Klaus Renner Verlag, 1964a.

———, 'Kuttia Kond und Pano: Zur Stellung der verachteten Klassen in Indien', in *Festschrift für Ad. E. Jensen (Teil 2)*, ed. E. Haberland, M. Schuster and H. Straube: München: Renner, 1964b, pp. 407–12.

Padel, F., *The Sacrifice of a Human Being: British Rule and the Konds of Odisha*, New Delhi: Oxford University Press, 2000.

Panda, S., 'Demography of a Kond Village', *Adibasi*, vol. XI, 1969–70, pp. 27–35.

Pfeffer, G., *Status and Affinity in Middle India*. (Beiträge zur Südasienforschung Bd. 76) Wiesbaden: Franz Steiner Verlag, 1982.

————, 'The Scheduled Tribes of Middle India as a Unit: Problems of Internal and External Comparison', in *Contemporary Society: Tribal Studies, Vol. 1: Structure and Process*, ed. G. Pfeffer and D.K. Behera, New Delhi: Concept Publishers, 1997, pp. 3–27.

Senapati, N. and N.K. Sahu, eds., *Orissa District Gazetteers. Koraput*, Cuttack: Odisha Government Press, 1966.

Winfield, W.W., *A Grammar of the Kui Language*, Calcutta: Baptist Mission Press, 1928; repr. 1929.

7   *Thea-phony* in Western Odisha

LIDIA GUZY

Introduction

This essay analyses the crucial role of music for a local society of the Bora Sambar region of western Odisha. The data for the present study has been collected during a long term ethno-musicological fieldwork in rural and urban western Odisha, undertaken from 2002 to 2005 in the context of the Orissa Research Project.[1] From 2006 to 2009 this research was followed by a project on local museums and music documentation (Guzy, Hatoum and Kamel 2009; 2010).[2] The aim of my investigations was to document and analyse the unknown and vulnerable musical and artistic traditions of marginalized musicians of the Bora Sambar region of western Odisha, especially of subaltern Ganda village musicians and of various non-Brahmin priest-musicians of ambivalent social status.

In western Odisha, discourses on the divine are enshrined in particular concepts of sacred sounds. My research on the immaterial side of culture of western Odisha showed that ritual music transports an indigenous knowledge, value and belief system. Music of marginalized musicians, the music of the non-Brahmin priest-musicians and the dance of the ecstatic ritual priest-dancer of the goddess discloses a *thea-phony*, a local theory of the goddess (*thea*) resonating in a system of sounds (*phony*) and mediated through the human body.

Manifold correspondences can be traced between the thea-phonic structures in the Bora Sambar region and pan-Indian phenomena of goddess worship in rural contexts. Besides the powerful male gods of the Indian religious traditions—for example Vishnu or Shiva—multiple local goddesses are worshipped all over India.[3] They are generally called *Devi* (goddess) or *Ma* (mother). The *devi* or *ma* is considered to be the creator as well as the destroyer of the world and the cosmos. She is omnipotent and associated with the idea of *shakti*.[4] This Indian concept of religious power has an extremely ambivalent character, as the goddess at the same time embodies a creative and destructive power: She can kill and she can create.

In rural as well as in urban regions of India, cults of goddesses are often powerful. The worship of the goddess has an important impact on the life of her believers, manifest for instance in pilgrimages, although personal devotion levels differ between rural and urban contexts.[5] Altars of local goddesses are scattered everywhere—at crossroads, under trees or in plain fields. To her believers, the local goddesses manifest themselves in an iconic form—as stones, as quarries, as eruptions of the earth, as waterfalls, rivers or other natural phenomena (Stietencron 1972). Goddesses are often worshipped under a number of different names. Frequently, local cults of goddesses are integrated into the pan-Indian worship of goddesses like Kali or Durga (Mallebrein 2004: 273–99).

The goddess is held to exert an enormous influence on the life of her believers: In her manifold manifestations she is responsible for one's fate—she gives and takes life; she can change its course benevolently through advices given in dreams or she can change it through destructive intrusions in the form of dangerous illness, as for example chicken pox. The life-giving and life-taking power and energy of the goddess is conceived as an uncontrollable, wild force but it can nonetheless be appeased and positively influenced by means of the correct worship.

In India, the agency of human trance mediums, as I will describe it in the *boil* ritual of the Bora Sambar region, is a widespread mode of communication with a goddess (Assayag and Tarabout 1999). Ritual goddess embodiment is generally characterized by trance, ritual language, often ecstatic forms of expression like dance or other ritual performances and the existence of a specialized male or female priesthood.[6] Enactments of goddess-embodiment or goddess-spirit possession are regularly accompanied by music, performed exclusively by initiated male musicians on highly symbolic instruments which at the same time provokes and indicates spiritual transformation. Goddess-spirit possession is specific to non-Brahmin social groups and mostly found in rural regions of India (Roche 2000: 288–95).

The essay argues that diverse subaltern musicians and non-Brahmin priest-musicians play a crucial role in the socio-religious life of the region. Marginalized musicians happen to be mediators between diverse social groups as well as the clients of today's peasant tribal categories such as the Binjhal, the Gond, the Khand, the Sahara and the Gour. As musicians and clients they can be compared with the Dombo musicians of the tribal Koraput-complex of southern Odisha (Pfeffer 1994: 14–20). These two features—the musicians' vital mediator-client role and the socio-cultural and emotional importance of music in the region seem to represent the cultural pattern of an indigenous tribal (Adivasi) complex of Bora

Sambar. It is argued that the specific cultural identity and memory of the region are transmitted and preserved through specific local musical traditions. These can be understood as shards of sounds, vessels of an immaterial cultural memory. My hypothesis is that one crucial way in grasping the local knowledge, value and belief-system of the Bora Sambar region is the analysis of its ritual music.

The Region

The Bora Sambar region lies in the Bargarh district of western Odisha. It is the region around the town of Padampur, surrounded by the highlands of the 90 km. long Gandha Mardhan. According to the Sambalpur Gazetteers of 1971 (Senapati and Mahanti 1971) the territory of Bora Sambar (Raj Bora Sambar) is estimated to be 2,178 sq. km. and to have 476 villages. The Bora Sambar region is located in the area bordering Chhattisgarh and literally means 'the region of the deer swallowed up by the cobra'. The language spoken in this region is *Sambalpuri*.

The Bora Sambar region is blessed with a rich musical heritage and a sacred landscape formed by the Gandha Mardhan Mountains. The feeling of a regional and cultural distinctiveness is expressed and transmitted through its indigenous music. This music is an expression of a specific cultural memory transmitted through the re-enactment of local vocal, instrumental and orchestral musical traditions and religious rituals reflecting local theological (*thea-phonic*) concepts about the goddess.

The Population

The population of the Bora Sambar region lives in small rural communities of semi-tribal and caste groups of Binjhal, Gond, Dumal, Khand, Mali, Telli, Kulta, Brahmin, Gour and Ganda (Harijan) origin. Today the communities live mostly as peasants with a very distinctive cultural self-esteem that belongs to the Bora Sambar region.

Bora Sambar: A name and a legend

Mythologically, the name Bora Sambar can be traced back to Bora Sambar, a small Binjhal village. The legend relates how the Bora Sambar kingdom (Raj Bora Sambar) originated in this very village 150 to 200 years ago. Strictly speaking, in this case we rather should speak of the local chiefdom of the Binjhal. Later, the centre of the chiefdom or local kingdom shifted to the small town of Padampur.

The name of the village recalls the mythical place where a deer was swallowed up by a cobra. The following story about the village and the region is told: '*Once upon a time a cobra (bora) attacked a deer (sombar). At the moment when the big snake opened its jaws and tried to kill the deer, the Binjhal saved it.*'[7] Ever since that time the Binjhal became the guardians and representatives of this region.

The Binjhal

The local Binjhal community claims to have mythological roots in the Bora Sambar region. They are an Adivasi Scheduled Tribe (SC) (the Indian administration has listed them under 'Tribes'). Binjhal means 'without sweat' and locally the Binjhal are known as tough fighters and hardworking labourers. The Binjhal consider themselves to be descendants of the most ancient people in the region, the *purkha lok,* who cleared the jungle (*safa koriba*) and then introduced agriculture (*chas bas*), which means they created culture by taming nature. Even today, although the Binjhal may be day labourers (*bhuti*) besides following their traditional occupation as agriculturalists they still have the proud self-perception of being peasants who own their land. The Binjhal once had their own language—called Binjhal *bhasa*—which is no longer spoken even by the oldest members of the community. Only some fragments of this tongue are remembered by the old people in the form of songs. Binjhal music, thus, can be interpreted as representative of a kind of cultural archaeological find, audible as shards of sound vessels of the cultural memory.

The most important deity of the Binjhal is the goddess Bindyabasani. Yearly, during the summer month of *choit* (April/May) religious services and big festivals take place in her honour. In addition, the god Dongra Bura and the goddesses Bhima Buri, Patneshwari, Samley, and Buri Ma are venerated.

A boil ritual in Sargival village

In Sargival, one of the villages of the Bora Sambar region, the Goddess Durga is worshipped weekly in a spirit possession ritual—*boil*. But during *sula puja*, the 16 days worship of the goddess Durga taking place before the tenth day of *dusshara*, *boil* performances take on a particular intensity, and are ascribed a special efficacy to cure the ailments of attending patients.

To start the *boil* ritual during *Dusshara*, the *dhunkel* instrument, an earthen pot (*handi matire*), is played by the *dhunkel*-player (*dhunkelya*) at the altar of the *dhunkel*, called the *dunkhel kutti*, *Durga kutti* or *sula kutti*. The altar is a separate square room with mud walls, located inside the house of the village priest (*pujari*). Here, the *dhunkel* instrument is kept, and the local gods and goddesses are venerated. The *dhunkelya* begins the ritual with a sung meditation, accompanied by the *dhunkel* to call the goddesses and gods into the altar. The *dhunkel* is placed on a straw crown (*dhora/oira*) and topped by a straw mat (*kula*). It is rubbed with an iron rod (*jumka bari*) fixed on a bamboo bow (*dhun*). A straw string, which is fixed on the bow, is simultaneously plucked in order to create a dull, low sound. The sounds of the *dhunkel* are considered to be the sounds of the goddesses Durga and Lakshmi. They are also held to attract or call all other gods and goddesses into the place of the ritual, and thus, to prepare the following manifestation of the goddesses. The *dhunkel* player, who is also called *dhunkel gayako* ('the singer of the *dhunkel* instrument'), sings mythical stories (*katani*) about the seven sisters (*sato bhani*) Rohela, Tulsa, Krishtei, Subokeshi, Nila Rani, Onjona Rani, Dohona Rani. The names of the mythical sisters may vary from village to village, but they are mostly known under the names given here.

During this ritual prelude for the *boil* ritual, the *dhunkel* player sings the story of the origin of the *dhunkel* instrument. With this song, together with the sound of the *dhunkel* instrument, the microcosmic character of the instrument is put in relation with the macrocosm of the local worldview, as the following narrative fragment illustrates:

When the 7 sisters did the puja for Shiva, Shiva told them: If you want to satisfy me, you should meditate. You should meditate with the dhunkel.

The 7 sisters got the dhunkel from the Adi Khond village. There lived a female singer (gauni) who played the dhunkel.

The 7 sisters took the Khond gauni to their kingdom. Brahma then told the 7 sisters about the making and playing of the dhunkel.

Brahma told the 7 sisters to take a straw mat (kula) from the Mahar (bamboo maker) and then he told them to take a pot (handi) from the khumbar (potter).

Brahma himself gave a bamboo, for the bow (dhun) to the 7 sisters. For the bow, the 7 sisters made the string (sitalpot) and the straw crown (oira) by themselves.

From the blacksmiths (luhar) the 7 sisters took the iron for making the iron rod (dhunbari).

According to the accounts of *dhunkel* artists, the *dhunkel* is made for meditation as well as for the worship of all gods and goddesses. No kind of trance or goddess spirit possession occurs during the *dhunkel* performance (*'boil ne ase'*). Singing accompanied by the *dhunkel* (*dhunkel gana*) has merely the function of narrative story telling, ritual preparation and ritual accompaniment. The sound of the *dhunkel* only calls and attracts the goddesses and gods, but it does not transform the musician itself.

When the persistent, monotonous sound of the *dhunkel* is heard by the villagers, people start to gather in the *dhunkel kutti*. The local priest (*pujari*), who some moments later will transform to *boil*, the trance medium of the local goddesses, is a middle aged man with long hair who belongs to the Mali community. Some years ago, after an apparition of the Goddess Durga in a dream, he became her priest.

While the *dhunkel* is played, he performs the worship (*puja*) for the goddess Durga. Coconuts, flowers, and incense-sticks (*agerbati*) are sacrificed in the *sula* or *Durga kutti* to please the goddess. Finally, the priest meditates without moving. For this part of the ceremony, he is wearing white clothes. After the end of his 'white *puja*' (*dhola puja*) and his meditation, the music of the *ganda baja* village orchestra starts outside the *Durga/dhunkel kutti* but it can clearly be heard inside.

While the monotonous sounds of the *dhunkel* instrument are held to recall the divine local narratives, the wild sound of the *borua par*, the holy rhythms of *ganda baja,* leads to an escalation of the ritual atmosphere and incites the following eruption of the divine power embodied by *boil*, the trance-medium.

Inside the small and crowded altar the tension rises. The rhythm and the volume of the *ganda baja* orchestra rise and fuel the nervousness and excitement of the crowd.

A villager acting as assistant priest (*pujari*) helps the main priest to change from his white clothes into a red female sari skirt. Slowly, the main priest (*pujari*) starts to lose control over his body. His eyes close and his limbs become heavy and powerless. Finally, the assistant priest touches his head with a small lamp of melted butter (*ghee*). Touched by the light, the almost unconscious priest starts to tremble. He is moving his head as if he is weeping. '*Boil asila!*' ('*Boil* has come'), the people whisper. '*Ma asila*' ['the mother (goddess) has come'], they tell each other. Now the mother goddess has taken possession of her priest, and the priest himself has become '*boil*'. *Boil,* the priest turned trance medium, then takes an iron chain—a symbol of the local goddess—from the ground with his right hand. He grunts and falls into a wild ecstatic dance. During the dance, *boil*—the possessed priest—silently starts to sing a melody.

Immediately after the priest has transformed himself into *boil*, the trance medium, physically and psychologically suffering patients (*kosti*) approach him from out of the crowd and wind garlands of flowers around his neck. The trance medium *boil* trembles and starts to utter predictions and incantations. In a repetitive tune he is chanting different names of goddesses:

Mother is with you–Mother is with you–Mother will save you–Mother will save you– Durga Ma (mother)–Durga Ma–Maha Kali Ma–Maha Kali Ma–Mangala Ma–Mangala Ma–Tarini Ma–Tarini Ma–Oila Ma–Oila Ma–Subakesi Ma–Subakesi Ma–Tulsa Ma– Tulsa Ma–Bontei Ma–Bontei Ma–Chandraseni Ma–Chandraseni Ma–Ganga Ma–Ganga Ma–Parvati Ma–Parvati Ma–Lakshmi Ma–Lakshmi Ma–Buri Ma–Buri Ma–Patneshwari Ma–Patneshwari Ma–Samleshwari Ma–Samleshwari Ma–Mother is with you–Mother is with you–Mother will save you–Mother will save you–Mother will save you.

While *boil* chants to the patients, the music from outside, which up to now has driven on the ceremony, stops. For a time, the tension level of the priest's ecstasy is moderated. But as the *ganda baja* music sets in anew, the *boil's* body starts to tremble again and he commences to move in a circular movement. After moving around for some time with closed eyes, *boil* steps outside the altar. Here, he meets the *ganda baja* musicians who are playing their instruments: *dhol, nissan, tassa, mohuri,* and *jumka*. The *dhol* player (*dholya*) takes a leading function in the following trance performance. He visibly interacts with *boil* and drives forward an ecstatic communication process. A provocative dialogue between the sound, beat and rhythm and the dance of the trance medium sets in. The *dhol* seems to offend *boil*. The *baja* which means 'music', but also signifies 'bite', literally 'bites' (*baja*) the goddess. An aggressive communication unfolds between the beats of the *dhol* and the dance of the trance medium, who expresses the answers and reactions of the goddess through his wild ecstatic movements, which are derived from the *dalkhai* folkdance.[8]

The music, the rhythms, the dance and the cries of the crowd touch everyone gathered around the sacred space of the dancing *boil*. There is a thrill about the ritual escalation, about the sudden appearance of *boil*, the goddess embodied in her trance medium. But the crowd is also excited about the power and effectiveness of the ritual performance. The *boil* ritual and the consultation of the *boil* trance medium are particularly believed to make fertile those who attend the performance—both men and women. The dance and the wild music are held to manifest a curative and procreative energy which flows from the goddess personalized in *boil*, to the participants of the ritual. The iron chain and the iron sword that *boil*, the trance medium, carries, are symbols of the power of the goddess. In *boil's* body the goddess dances for her believers. She is wild and she can give fertility. But it is also the feminized male priest transformed into a divine woman, who is held to have obtained healing and transformative powers. The creative and procreative power of the goddess, according to the belief of her worshippers, is not only manifested in *boil* as a medium, but transferred from the Goddess to the possessed priest.

Thea-phony—Music and the Goddess

The *boil* ritual reveals an indigenous multi sensory and intermedial theory of the sacred and of healing transmitted through the cultural idiom of trance and possession of the trance medium *boil*. In cross-cultural perspective, music is often a crucial medium which accompanies, enables and guides trance mediumship in trance and possession cults (Rouget 1990: 87–91; 134–238). Trance mediumship implies a specific relationship between a ritual agent and his or her deity, overreaching the boundaries between the individual and the environment (Boddy 1994: 407–34). It is in most cases expressed through embodiment, understood as a non-dualistic perception and lived experience (Csordas 1990: 5–47). While possession refers rather to external influences in terms of the notion of a subject being possessed by something exterior to her or him, trance according to Gilbert Rouget, denotes a sounding, agitated, unusual state of transitory consciousness in a social context (ibid.: 47, 55), induced through music. However, in academic discussion, the concepts of trance, possession or ecstasy (Lewis 1971) are often used arbitrarily and interchangeably to describe various kinds of ritual techniques which are connected to an 'altered state of consciousness' (Bourguignon 1973).[9]

It is also a common feature that trance and possession are acted out in a performance which may be termed 'theatrical' (Leiris 1958). Trans-culturally, trance and possession performances seem to be intrinsically related to ritual efficacy and healing (Laderman and Roseman 1996; Csordas and Lewton 1998: 435–512) and are central elements of initiations.[10] In South Asia, possession and trance are generally widespread as idioms for ritual communication and expression.[11]

During the trance mediumship ritual *boil*, a central indigenous meaning and belief system of the Bora Sambar region becomes visible, which I have tentatively termed *thea-phony*. The term *thea-phony* is intended to express the idea that a local goddess (*thea*) is manifested in a system of sounds (*phony*) related to ecstatic body expressions. In the Bora Sambar region, social values, ideas and morals are associated with the idea of a feminine sacred power personified by diverse local goddesses and ritually mediated through musical and trance performances. The belief in local goddesses, such as the *sato bhani* (the seven sister goddesses),

Durga, Maha Kali, Mangala, Tarani, Nissani Oila Devi, Subakesi, Tulsa Devi, Bontei Devi, Parvati, Lakshmi, Boiravi, Burhi Ma, Patneshwari and Samleshwari/Samley Ma is predominant throughout the region. This belief must be seen in the larger context of the widespread religious notion of the feminine sacred (Tambs-Lyche 2004), which can be traced all over India, manifesting itself in local cults of diverse goddesses.[12] The pan-Indian idea of the feminine sacred embraces manifold indigenous notions of power which are often referred to as *shakti* (ibid.: 15–16; Wadley 1975). In the Bora Sambar region, these indigenous conceptions of divine powers are particularly associated with the sound of the *ganda baja* music and the concept of *par*, the rhythm. Ritual polyrhythmic music is believed to effect transformation, consolation and healing. Local goddesses are assumed to manifest themselves in the sounds and rhythms of the village orchestra *ganda baja* as well as in a variety of drums played in various contexts, such as *nissan*, symbolizing the goddess Nissani and *sarmangalia* symbolizing the Goddess Mangala. The local goddesses are venerated through the sound and rhythms of these drums, while at the same time being identified with them. Sounds, rhythms and instruments are simultaneously the medium and message (see McLuhan 1964) of a goddess.

The village orchestra—ganda baja

Ganda Baja is perhaps the most prominent musical and ritual feature of the Bora Sambar region. It is an instrumental orchestral[13] music, performed exclusively by musicians originating from the marginalized Harijan caste Ganda (also called Pano). The instruments forming the *ganda baja* village orchestra can be divided into three categories: membranophones (*dhol, nissan, tasa,* also called *timkiri*), an aerophone (*mohuri*) and idiophones (*kastal/jhang* or *jumka*).[14]

Dhol

The *dhol*, which is the village orchestra's leading instrument, is a large membranophone. This large, long drum (90 cm. to 1.5 m. in length) is made from the trunk of a tree and strung with cowhide (*gai chomora*) on two sides. Along the length of the *dhol* run strips of cowhide (*badi*) which are attached to the instrument by rings (*kol kola*). The skin of the right-hand side, named *tali,* is made from calf's skin; the left-hand skin *dhaaya* is made from cowhide. The *tali* is slightly smaller (37 cm. in diameter) than the *dhaaya* (38 cm. in diameter). The *dhaaya* is beaten with a rubber stick (*khanda/nara*) of about 40 cm. in length; the *tali* side is played with the right hand. The *dhol* player, known as the *dholya*, directs the changes of the rhythms of the *ganda baja* orchestra. Rhythms usually emerge spontaneously with the *dholya* giving the lead. Musicians gain knowledge of the rhythmic and melodic patterns by listening to various rhythms from early childhood on. It is said that the voices of the goddesses appear first in the *dhol* drum and express their moods by changing the rhythms.

Nissan

The *nissan* drum, another membranophone, has a tapered form, resembling a melon cut in half. It is reported to be the most ancient instrument of the village orchestra. A *nissan* is made of wooden and iron sheets and is played with two rubber sticks (*chimta*). The leather (*chipra*) of the drumhead is made of cowhide or goatskin and often covered with colourful paintings. In the Bora Sambar region and Sambalpur area, *nissan* drums were traditionally decorated with deer antlers, but as hunting deer has been forbidden, today this form of embellishment has nearly disappeared.

The *nissan* is always played with maximum strength, thus producing a deep and penetrating sound which is compared to the '*sound of the thunderstorm*' and identified with the horrifying strength of Goddess Nissani.

Tasa

The *tasa* (also called *timkri*), a small membranophone, is a drum made from clay (*matul*) and strung with cowhide (*gai chomra*). The drumhead is attached with leather strips to the tapered body of the instrument (*mola*). It is played with two thin bamboo sticks. The *tasa* produces a high and thin sound. Even if the sound of the *tasa* drum is not associated with a specific goddess, it contributes to the divine drum chorus.

Mohuri

The *mohuri* is an oboe-like instrument. According to the Ganda musicians, its sound plays a crucial role in changing the character of the music and rhythm. It is often compared to the '*seductive voice of a capricious woman*', as the musicians explain, but can also be associated with the '*desperate wailing of a mother crying for her dead son*'. Those poetic descriptions refer to the arbitrary character of the mohuri's sound, which is considered the most difficult instrument to play in the orchestra. The sound of the *mohuri* is identified with the expression of the specific goddess which enters the musical scene during a *ganda baja* performance.

Kastal

The *kastal* or *jhang* are iron cymbals; they may be replaced by a kind of rattle called the *jumka*. Their sound is associated with the goddess Gantheshwari ('the goddess of bells'—*gantha*, which means bell).

Ideally, an orchestra consists of five instruments and might include five to seven players. Sometimes, it is also called *panchabadya* referring to the five instruments assembled. Similarities can be traced between *ganda baja* and other orchestral traditions like those of Chhattisgarh (Prévôt 2008: 75–88) or Nepal (Helffer 1969a/b, Tingey 1994, Wegner 1988).

All *ganda baja* instruments play together in tune and rhythm. It is central for the formation of a Ganda musician to listen to the play of other musicians and to learn to play together with them. Besides the command of one's instrument, playing *ganda baja* thus implies a sophisticated culture of listening. The beat of the right-hand *tali* side of the *dhol* provides orientation for the *tasa*, which in response beats a double rhythm. The beat of the left-hand *dhaaya* side of the *dhol* provides orientation for the *nissan*, which answers with a counter-rhythm to the beat of the *dhaaya*. As the sound of the *mohuri* is intended to resemble the flirting of a women's voice, it is played in an extremely alluring way. All the instruments in the inter-village orchestra are worshipped before being played. Notably, they are used for the worship of gods and goddesses, but at the same time require worship themselves. The instruments are usually only touched by the musicians, but there is no ritual prohibition to touch the instruments. However, no one should step over them as this is considered disrespectful and is supposed to cause a curse by the goddesses. The instruments are stored in a secular context: they are kept by the particular musician who plays an instrument. The sacredness of the instruments evolves mainly through the ritual context and the sound vibrations transforming the instrument to the mediator as well as to the corpus of a particular goddess.

In the performances of *ganda baja*, notions of an identity between music and goddesses come to light. Various goddesses are assumed to appear through the sound of specific instruments and their rhythms (*par*), while the polyrhythmic structure of the orchestra is understood as the manifestation of their voices.[15] In the rural regions of Bora Sambar no socio-religious ceremony, such as marriage or *puja*, the ritual service for gods and goddesses, may be celebrated without *ganda baja* music, played exclusively by the Ganda musicians. A village orchestra, usually formed by inhabitants of one and the same village, is called to the neighbouring villages for the celebration of such musical-religious events. The musicians are invited through turmeric powder by the different local communities of Binjhal, Gouro, Dhol Khond, Mali or Kulta in order to perform in their villages. Thus, the music of the Ganda musicians connects local communities, places and religious concepts. The *ganda baja* can be considered as an inter-village orchestra, representing a force of relatedness, connection and communication between different villages and communities. The Ganda musicians play the role of ritual and social mediators,[16] linking tribal and semi-tribal local groups and mediating local values as well as local power configurations. The *ganda baja* orchestra thus plays a double role. On the one hand, the *baja* transcends local communities in its function as a ritual inter-village orchestra. On the other hand, through its musical expression of transcendence, the *baja* creates a sensual experience of the local community in terms of communication with a holy sphere and the manifestation of the powers of local goddesses.

In former times, musicians were engaged and patronized by local *rajas* or landowners (*zamindar*) of the Raj Bora Sambar kingdom (later Padampur). Local power holders employed village musicians for the performance of politico-religious rituals, legitimating their social and symbolic power during events such as *dusshara*, the festival of the goddess Durga, and of the clan goddess Patneshwari.

A proverb describes the ritual relationship between musicians and the local king: '*ager baja, poche raja*'—in front of the local king, there should always march the village orchestra. While performing in front of the *raja* or the *zamindar*, the musicians had to wear colourful and extravagant clothes, a tradition that can still be traced today in the multi-coloured clothes and longer than usual hair of village musicians. The performance of the politico-symbolic powers of the power holder was designed to be a cheerful event, associated with public entertainment and joyful festivities.

Marginalized musicians

The *ganda baja* musicians who are orchestrating the *boil* performances are without exception male and originate from a subaltern impoverished

Harijan caste, called Ganda or Pano. Besides their activity as musicians, the traditional trade of the landless Ganda was the weaving of simple cotton clothes used as underwear. With the emergence of a cotton industry in Odisha over the last 50 years, this trade went into a decline and today many Ganda earn their living as agricultural day-labourers.

The indigenous term '*Ganda*' which literally means '*the bad smelling*' refers to the activity of tanning the leather for drums but also expresses the socio-cultural concept of 'untouchability' or 'pollution' of the Ganda musicians. From the perspective of the local culture, Ganda musicians are considered to be 'untouchable' (*achua*) for two reasons. First, because their drums are made from cowhide and second, because by playing the oboe *mohuri*, they touch their own saliva while creating sounds. The direct physical contact with cowhide and saliva classifies them as extremely impure and thus 'untouchable'. But it is exactly this 'untouchability' that qualifies the *ganda baja* musicians for contact and communication with the divine sphere of the local goddesses. Here, the paradoxical character of the Indian category of 'untouchability' or 'pollution' becomes visible in the shape of a ritual inversion. In the ritual performance, the socially marginalized become spiritually powerful by communicating with the sacred powers of the goddesses. The ideological notion of being 'untouchable' is, so to say, prerequisite for successful contact with the 'untouchable'—the intangible, immaterial, prohibited sphere of the sacred. The power of performance of the goddess is thus transferred to the socially most powerless performers who, during the ritual performance, take in and transmit the divine powers of the goddesses. That the socially powerless have physical and spiritual power inverse to their social status is a widespread notion all over India. Thus, by their marginal status they are qualified for ritual specialization and the handling of strong, uncontrolled, divine powers feared by others.[17]

In the *boil*-performances of the Bora Sambar region, the symbolic and musical powers of the orchestral instruments, their sounds and rhythms, unite with the ritual strength of the socially marginalized musicians. Thus an indigenous theory of power takes shape, based on the empowering effects of music in a ritual context. The ritual effectiveness of music furthermore hints to an indigenous media theory where polyrhythmic music is socially and culturally considered as a crucial vehicle and message of the otherword.

The marginalized status of the musicians directing the *boil* performance plays a substantial role in the inner logic of the ritual. The polyrhythmic music of the village orchestra musicians is generally understood as an 'untouchable' sacred entity, expressing notions of the divine as a wild, uncontrolled power, manifesting itself in the rhythms of the instruments and in the dance of the possessed priest. The instruments mediate and manifest the other world of the goddesses, while the subaltern social status of the musicians, as we have seen, paradoxically qualifies them for communication with the divine world. But although it is the musician alone, who has the capacity to control the goddess, he remains socially marginalized even while interacting with her: in contrast to the ritual priest and trance medium, Ganda musicians are not allowed to enter the inner sanctum of the *dhunkel kutti* altar, where the goddess embodiment takes place.

Ganda Baja Music and Goddess Embodiment

The instrumental orchestras of the Ganda musicians play a central role in the *boil* rituals of goddess embodiment and ritual healing. Every Monday during the worship of the Goddess Durga, the Goddess appears in the body of her priest: '*boil*' comes upon the *pujari*. The *ganda baja* orchestrates the act of possession with specific rhythms. The goddess manifests herself in the dance and speech of the priest. This weekly *boil* tradition is an artistic ritual healing performance which integrates dance, music, and ritual speech in order to heal patients (*kosti*). Once a year, during the festival of *dusshara* or Durga *puja* in honour of the goddess Durga, which takes place during the month of *dusshara* (October), *boil* rituals gain a special intensity.

Goddess Embodiment and the sixteen Rhythms

The goddess spirit possession *boil* is musically symbolized by a specific sequence of rhythms, the *sulapar*, or 16 holy rhythms. These rhythms are named after 16 different goddesses and are said to express their speeches and characters. As different rhythms (*par*) are beaten, different goddesses manifest themselves in the body of the possessed trance medium. The concept of *bol*, the rhythm, plays a crucial role both in structuring the ritual performance of the trance medium *boil*, as in the healing of patients (*kosti*). *Sulapar*, the sixteen possession rhythms, represent the polyrhythmic and polyglot interacting of the different goddesses with each other. The musicians aurally recognize the identity of the specific goddesses and rhythms.[18] As the structure of 16 rhythms is a core element in all *boil* rituals, I would tentatively describe it as a rhythmic sound liturgy within the ritual of goddess embodiment.

Drums and the Goddess

Rodney Needham has pointed out that 'there is a connection between percussion and transition' (Needham 1967: 613) and that 'practically everywhere it is found that percussion is resorted to in order to communicate with the other world . . .' (ibid.: 610). In the Bora Sambar region, the drums, *dhol*, *nissan*, and *tasa* are primordial for inducing trance. These membranophones are identified with local goddesses and they are simultaneously equated with goddess embodiment. The *dhol* drum plays a crucial role in communicating with the goddess. By means of the *dhol*, a musician proves his strength (*shakti*) in order to detract the goddess' power of embodiment from himself and to direct it towards the priest. On multiple layers of meaning the drum is instrumental for mediating and transferring and directing the power of the goddess as well as itself identified with the divine entity.

Boil and dance

Like the percussion centred sound of the *ganda baja* orchestra, the dance of the trance medium *boil* signifies the appearance of the goddess. She dances in the body of the possessed priest, who hence becomes a dancing goddess himself. In the dance patterns of the *boil* ritual the traditional elements of *dalkhai*, the most popular folk dance style in the Sambalpur district of western Odisha, are integrated into the performance of goddess worship. The *dalkhai* dance is traditionally associated with puberty rituals for unmarried girls, preparing young girls for their social and biological maturity. It is generally conceived as an expression of sensuality and a symbol of erotic attraction. Integrated into *boil* performances, *dalkhai* patterns indicate the intimate dialogue of the trance medium and the goddess. The trance medium *boil* is conceived as the 'divine dancer' the sacred dancer of the goddess Durga—referring both to his ritual activity and power. The erotic power of the dance symbolizes the power of fertility ascribed to all *boil* rituals and its trance mediums.

Boil and ritual speech

A third element of the *boil* ritual besides the rhythms of *ganda baja* and the priest's dance is the ritual speech of *boil*. For the most part, it consists of spontaneously created poetries sung by the trance medium. The rhythmic and repetitive uttering of the names of gods and goddesses intertwines with a specific melody only known to the trance medium *boil*. The melody of the ritual speech whispered by *boil* is a personal characteristic of the trance medium. It may express the affiliation to his guru or *boil*'s own personal note. Here, the medium of dance interconnects with the medium of music and rhythmic speech to form an intermedial ritual.

The ritual incantations of *boil* show a repetitive linguistic and melodic structure that can be described as a balancing of pairs of successive syntactic unities. This is the kind of 'parallelism' highlighted in the ethno-linguistic discussion about *'talking in pairs'* (Fox 1988). A parallelism, according to Roman Jakobson, is an elementary operation of oral communication that consists of a 'coming together of two elements. . . . By this definition, parallelism is an extension of the binary principle of opposition to the phonetic, syntactic, and semantic levels of expression' (Jakobson, cited by Fox 1988: 3). For Jakobson, even the rhetoric figures of comparison and metaphor were semantic variations of parallelism. Fox collects observations attesting to the dual structure of ritual language in many cultures, which he calls 'dyadic language'. The parallelism of sentences is considered by Fox to be a characteristic of poetic language, understood as a special vocabulary that is rarely used in other contexts. Parallel sentences and word constructions, the ordering of words and sentences in an alternating, repetitive form are characteristic for the ritual language of oral societies (Fox: 1–3; 6–11).[19] *Boil*'s trance son[20] with its parallelism of sentences and alternating repetitions seems thus a pertinent example of ritual poetry.

Practices of asceticism

Boil rituals are embedded in cycles of interconnected micro-rituals including temporal ascetic practices. The boil ritual on *dusshara/durga puja* is preceded by a preparatory phase of sixteen days. During the *sula puja* which starts from the celebration of *puojuntya*—the festival of mothers who celebrate their sons, the local priest (*pujari*) fasts for 16 days until the day of *nowomi*, the ninth day and the day before the day of *dusshara*. During this time the priest may not rest on any wooden bed (*kotha*) but has to sleep on the ground. He is supposed to take a bath three times a day as well as to perform the worship of the sixteen goddesses three times daily: in the morning hours (*sokale*), at 12 O'clock (*bar baje*) and in the evening (*sondhya bele*) hours. With these ascetic practices of cleansing and control of body and mind, the priest prepares himself for the contact with the goddesses during the *boil* performance on *durga puja*.

Boil as a healing performance

A central aspect of the *boil* ritual is that of a multi-sensory and inter-medial healing performance. The ritual dynamism of goddess embodiment in *boil*-ritual reveals a strong healing power of music for the ritual participants and patients who seek spiritual cure for a psychological ailment. Music induces an enormous sensorial experience with a strong affective and psychological effectiveness. 'For healing to take place in this manner, aesthetic distance must be achieved. . . . The healing effects of performance are on one level caused by the catharsis that can occur when a patient's unresolved emotional distress is reawakened and confronted in a dramatic context', Laderman and Roseman (1996: 7) point out. This aesthetic distance occurs in *boil* performances through the dramatically ecstatic rhythms which change a priest into a dancing goddess, embodied by her trance medium *boil*. The loud sound vibrations of the *ganda baja* drums create an exceptional atmosphere and tension perceived by all participants. The dynamic and dominant sounds incite the pulsating healing powers of the ritual (Stoller 1996: 165–84).

The movements of *boil*, the trance medium, combine artistic patterns with an immediate physical, muscular presence. The *boil* ritual as a whole follows a dramaturgy of preparation, escalation and relief. The performance starts with a worship (*puja*) continued by the meditation and narrative accompanied by the *dhunkel* instrument. The music of *ganda baja* then incites a phase of escalation during which the goddess takes possession of her priest. A tensed atmosphere of hope, fear and common excitement is evoked by the orchestra's play. This escalation culminates in the ecstatic dance of the priest interacting with the beat of the *dhol* drum. Finally, the voice of *boil* whispering in the ears of the participants brings consolation and relief.

In the course of the ritual, the visual experience of the trembling, rhythmic body movements of the trance medium blends with the sensual experience of the touch of *boil* and of his body covered with sweat, while the aural experience of the escalating music of *ganda baja* reinforces these impressions. This multi-sensual perception, in terms of Howes' 'intersensorality' as the 'multi-directional interaction of the senses and of sensory ideologies' (2005: 9), seems to bring about psychological relief for the patients.

The ecstatic *boil* performance provides a possibility to touch the wilderness, which is considered to be the goddess. Everyone who has touched or was touched by the wild goddess returns consoled to his or her local and social context. Satisfied about the concrete, sensual communication with the goddess, participants return re-integrated into their community. Many of those who attended *boil* rituals confirmed that questioning the embodied goddess gave them psychological comfort. They considered the words of the trance medium as a consolation and as expressions of a divine truth: '*Be quiet, Ma is with you*', thus *boil* spoke to them. With these simple words the suffering and the barren were assured and strengthened in their hope and belief that their afflictions will be cured, that the children they desire, will soon be born.

While the ecstasy of the trance medium boil and the collective excitement during the ritual of goddess spirit possession can be conceived as the manifestation of a wild and to a certain extent uncontrolled power both without and within the community, the *boil* ritual as a whole has a reconfirming, integrative function. This becomes especially visible in the role of the *dhunkel* instrument and the narrative songs performed to its sounds. The *dhunkel* singer remembers and repeats collective metaphors, values, ideas and stories.[21] The meditative recollection of the local world view reconfirms the collective ideas and values of the local community, thus ensuring a cultural continuity.

Conclusion

In the *boil* performance it can be observed that the media music, dance, and language interweave effectively for healing. This intermediality illustrates how music opens a human for transformation into a divine being. The ritual music which is embodied in the playing of the *dhunkel* and in the music of the *ganda baja* orchestra touches the priest and his body. While dancing, the priest becomes *boil*, the manifestation of the Goddess. Finally, *boil* touches the suffering patients whose hope will be strengthened and whose pain will be eased.

Performing arts in rituals operate as media of transformation on a theological, psychological and sociological level. They integrate a distraught member of a local community and console him or her through sensuality. It may be assumed that the healing power of *boil* rituals lies in the sensual and transformational power of the aesthetics of ritual music, dance, and speech.

I would like to argue that the *thea-phony* of *boil* can not only be described as a ritual performance but in the same right as an indigenous theory of the Sacred or Sublime. An oral/aural culture as that of the local population of the Bora Sambar region, implies that local value and meaning systems are enshrined and transmitted in acoustic or visual media as speech, song, music, dance or acting. The *boil* tradition of the

Bora Sambar region shows a local meaning and belief system which is based upon the central idea that the goddess *is* the system of sounds mediated through music and embodiment. A sonic, sensual and intersensorial approach to sacrality thus shapes cultural ideas and mediates them in a specific way. The musically conceptualized sacred is on the one hand intangible as manifested in the sounds of *ganda baja*, on the other hand embodied in the trance medium *boil*, sacralizing, thus, the message and the medium itself.

Notes

1. The project was overseen by the German Science Foundation. I would like to thank the German Research Council (Deutsche Forschungsgemeinschaft) for the generous grant without which the research could not have been undertaken. I would also like to express my gratitude to Professor Dr Georg Pfeffer who assigned me the academic task to do research into Indian folk music and Professor Dr Deepak Kumar Behera for his constant and unfailing practical help and intellectual guidance.

2. The research was funded by the Volkswagen Foundation (Volkswagenstiftung), which I would like to thank for the generous grant without which the research could not have been undertaken. I would also like to express my gratitude to Professor Dr Hartmut Zinser, who hosted the research project at the Institute for Scientific Studies of Religions (Institut für Religionswissenschaft) at the Freie Universität Berlin, for his constant and unfailing support and his thoroughgoing and challenging intellectual advice.

3. See Kinsley 1985; Wilke, Michaels and Vogelsanger 1994; Fischer, Goswamy and Pathy 2005.

4. For the concept of Shakti, see especially Wadley 1975.

5. On the differences between urban and rural goddess worship see Bakker and Entwistle 1983.

6. For an impressive example of a female priesthood in spirit goddess embodiment, see Carrin 1997.

7. Translation from an interview with Binjhal elders in 2008.

8. Dalkhai *is* the most popular folk dance style in the Sambalpur district of western Odisha, for details see later in text.

9. For a discussion of the definition of concepts such as trance, ecstasy or possession and the problem of their exchangeability, see Zinser 1990: 253–58. For a comparison with ecstatic cults of classical antiquity, see Schlesier and Schwarzmaier 2008. For a comparison with ecstatic and possession cults in contemporary Southern Europe, see Hauschild 2002. For a general discussion on the performative turn in anthropology and ritual studies, see Köpping and Rao 2000.

10. Especially the studies on Korean shamanism by Laurel Kendall reveal the

crucial role of initiations for effective and successful ritual specialization and healing (Kendall 1988; 1996: 17–59).

11. For an overview on studies on possession cults and trance see Assayag/ Tarabout 1999 and Schoembucher 1999: 239–67; 2006; for an example of female possessions see Obeysekere 1981. In contrast to the mentioned broad ethnographic literature on lived traditions of religious possession in South Asia, Frederick M. Smith (2006) explores diachronically the multifaceted and multi-vocal forms of possession from ancient Sanskrit literature to vernacular living traditions, giving an exhaustive overview of the cultural and religious phenomena of deity and spirit possession in South Asia.

12. For extensive studies of goddess worship in India, see Kinsley 1985; Wilke, Michaels and Vogelsanger 1994; Fischer, Goswamy and Pathy 2005.

13. An instrumental orchestra is understood as an ensemble of instruments, where the interplay of the diverse instruments has a choral character but which does not contain any form of human vocals. The instrumental orchestral tradition of South Asia differs fundamentally from the traditional (classical) form of Indian modal music. The classical Indian modal music is characterized by individual solo performers and solo compositions (Daniélou 2004: 10–11). It lacks the choral character of instruments playing together as 'voices'. The South Asian orchestral tradition could rather be compared to the tradition of European orchestral performance (chamber orchestra, opera orchestra, etc.), except for the facts (a) that musicians belong to special social groups or ethnic categories, (b) that the music is restricted to special occasions (Sachs 1923: 2–3) and (c) that it represents specific regional traditions of ensembles of regional instruments (see Sachs 1923: 3–11), as for example the *Naykhibaja* of the Newar (Wegner 1988) or the *Damai baja* (Helffer 1969a/b), also known as *Pancai baja* of the Damai (Tingey 1994), in Nepal.

14. Membranophones are musical instruments that produce sound by a stretched membrane (animal skin). Aerophones are musical instruments which produce sound only by using air without any string or membrane and idiophones are musical instruments which resound in themselves, without any strings, air or membranes. The classification refers to the Hornbostel-Sachs scheme of a universal fourfold division of musical instruments: membranophones, aerophones, idiophones and chordophones (strings) (Hornbostel and Sachs 1914: 553–90).

15. Rhythms are recognized as the specific language of a goddess and accordingly named: Durga Par (the rhythm of Durga); Maha Kali Par (the rhythm of Maha Kali); Ma Mangala Par (the rhythm of Mother Mangala); Ma Tarani Par (the rhythm of Mother Tarani); Oila Devi Par (the rhythm of goddess Oila); Subakesi Par (the rhythm of Subakesi); Tulsa Devi Par (the rhythm of goddess Tulsa); Bontei Devi Par (the rhythm of goddess Bontei); Chandraseni Par (the rhythm of Chandraseni); Ganga Devi Par (the rhythm of goddess Ganga); Parvati Par (the rhythm of Parvati); Lakshmi Par (the rhythm of

Lakshmi); Boiravi Par (the rhythm of Boiravai); Buri Ma Par (the rhythm of Mother Buri); Patneshwari Par (the rhythm of Patneshwari); Samleshwari Par (the rhythm of Samleshwari).

16. For comparison with the Pano in Koraput, see Pfeffer 1994: 14–20.

17. Another example of the cultural idiom of social marginalization and spiritual specialization are the subaltern Sidhis in Gujarat (Basu 1994). Ritual ambivalence is also found in other regions and religions of South Asia as for example among the Korean Shamans, where the shaman—*mudang, mansin*— is a stigmatized unfortunate who has a story of social suffering before becoming a legitimized shaman (Kandell 1988: 31–46; 1996: 21), or in Japanese Shinto rites, where *burakumin,* the Japanese untouchables perform the ritual butchering of animals and tanning of leather for drums used in the most sacred Shinto rites (Alldritt 2000).

18. Locally, the identifications of rhythms and goddesses can vary.

19. For comparative ethnographic studies on ritual language see Demmer and Gaenszle 2007.

20. See transcription on p. 191.

21. For a transcription of a *dhunkel* song and narration presented during a *boil* ritual.

References

Assayag, J. and Gilles Tarabout, eds., 'La possession en Asie du Sud. Parole. Corps, Territoire. Collection', *Purusartha*, vol. 21, Paris: Édition de l'École des Hautes Études en Sciences Sociales, 1999.

Alldritt, L.D., 'The Burakumin: The Complicity of Japanese Buddhism in Oppression and an Opportunity for Liberation', *Journal of Buddhist Ethics*, online conference, retrieved online. <http://www.buddhistethics.org/7/alldritt001.html#barakumin>, accessed on 20 February 2010.

Bakker, H. and Alan Entwistle, eds., *Devi: The Worship of the Goddess and its Contribution to Indian Pilgrimage: A Report on a Seminar and Excursion.* Groningen: Institute of Indian Studies, State University of Groningen, 1983.

Basu, H., *Habshi Sklaven, Sidi-Fakire. Muslimische Heiligenverehrung im Westlichen Indien*, (Indus 1). Berlin: Das Arabische Buch, 1994.

Boddy, J., 'Spirit Possession Revisited: Beyond Instrumentality', *Annual Review of Anthropology*, vol. 23, 1994, pp. 407–34.

Bourguignon, E., ed., *Religion: Altered State of Consciousness and Social Change*, Columbus, Ohio: Research Foundation, 1973.

Carrin, M., *Enfants de la Déesse: Dévotion et Prêtrise Féminine au Bengale*, Paris: CNRS Éditions, 1997.

Csordas, T.J., 'Embodiment as a Paradigm for Anthropology', *Ethos*, vol. 18, 1990, pp. 5–47.

Csordas, T.J. and Elizabeth Lewton, 'Practice, Performance and Experience in Ritual Healing', *Transcultural Psychiatry*, vol. 35, 1998, pp. 435–512.

Daniélou, A., *Introduction to the Study of Musical Scales*, New Delhi: Oriental Books, 1979.

———, *Einführung in die Indische Musik*, Taschenbücher zur Musikwissenschaft [Hrsg. Richard Schaal], vol. 36, Wilhelmshaven: Heinrichhofen's Verlag Wilhelmshaven, 2004 (1975).

Demmer, U. and Martin Gaenszle, eds., *The Power of Discourse in Ritual Performance: Rhetoric, Poetics, Transformations*, Berlin: LIT Verlag, 2007.

Fischer, E., B.N. Goswamy and Dinanath Pathy, *Göttinnen—Indische Bilder aus vier Jahrhunderten* (Goddesses—Indian Images during four Decades), Zürich: Museum Rietberg, 2005.

Fox, J.J., *To Speak in Pairs: Essays on the Ritual Languages of Eastern Indonesia*, Cambridge: Cambridge University Press, 1988.

Guzy, L., R. Hatoum and Susan Kamel, eds., *From Imperial Museum to Communication Centre?* Würzburg: Königshausen & Neumann, 2010.

———, *Museumislands. On the New Role of Museums/Museumsinseln. Zur Neuen Rolle von Museen*, Berlin: Panama Verlag, 2009.

Hauschild, T., *Magie und Macht in Italien*, Gifkendorf: Merlin Verlag, 2002.

Helffer, M., 'Fanfares villageoises au Népal', *Objets et Monde*, vol. IX, 1 Printemps, 1969a, pp. 51–8.

———, *Castes de Musiciens au Népal*, Paris: Éditions de Département d'Ethnomusicologie, 1969b.

Hornbostel, E.M.V. and Curt Sachs, 'Systematik der Musikinstrumente. Ein Versuch', *Zeitschrift für Ethnologie*, vol. 46, nos. 4–5, 1914, pp. 553–90.

Howes, D., ed., *The Empire of the Senses: The Sensual Culture Reader*, New York: Berg, 2005.

Kendall, L., 'Initiating Performance: The Story of Chini, a Korean Shaman', in *The Performance of Healing*, ed. C. Laderman and Marina Roseman, New York: Routledge, 1996, pp. 17–58.

———, *The Life and Hard Times of a Korean Shaman: Of Tales and the Telling of Tales*, Honolulu, Hawaii: University of Hawaii Press, 1988.

Kinsley, D., *Hindu Goddesses: Visions of Divine Feminine in the Hindu Religious Traditions*, Berkeley: University of California Press, 1985.

Köpping, K.P. and Ursula Rao, eds., *Im Rausch des Rituals: Gestaltung und Transformation der Wirklichkeit in körperlicher Performanz* (Performanzen: Interkulturelle Studien zu Ritual, Spiel und Theater; Band 1), Münster, Hamburg, London: Lit, 2000.

Laderman, C. and Marina Roseman, eds., *The Performance of Healing*, London: Routledge, 1996.

Leiris, M., *La possession et ses aspects théâtraux chez les Éthiopiens de Gondar*, Paris: Plon, 1958.

Lewis, I.M., *Ecstatic Religion: A Study of Shamanism and Spirit Possession*, Harmondsworth: Penguin Books, 1971.

McLuhan, M., *Understanding Media: the Extensions of Man*, Cambridge, Massachusetts: MIT Press, 1994 [1964].

Needham, R., 'Percussion and Transition', *Man*, vol. 2, 1967, pp. 606–14.

Obeysekere, G., *Medusa's Hair: An Essay on Personal Symbols and Religious Experience*, Chicago: Chicago University Press, 1981.

Pfeffer, G., 'Music in Context: Ethnography and Meaning', *Beiträge zur Musikethnologie*, vol. 30, 1994, pp. 14–20.

Prévôt, N., 'How Musical is God? A Pantheon and its Music in Bastar', in *Religion and Music*, ed. L. Guzy, Berlin: Weissensee Verlag, 2008, pp. 75–88.

Roche, D., 'Music and Trance', in *Garland Encyclopedia of World Music: South Asia*, 2000, pp. 288–95.

Rouget, G., *La Musique et la Transe: Esquisse d'une Théorie Générale des Relations de la Musique et de la Possession*, rsvd. edn., Paris: Gallimard, 1990 [1980].

Sachs, C., *Musikinstrumente Indiens und Indonesiens*, 2. Aufl. Berlin/Leipzig: Vereinigung Wissenschaftlicher Verleger Walter de Gruyter & Co. (Handbücher der Staatlichen Museen zu Berlin), 1923.

Schlesier, R. and Agnes Schwarzmaier, *Dionysos—Verwandlung und Ekstase* (Ausstellungskatalog Pergamonmuseum Berlin), Regensburg: Schnell & Steiner, 2008.

Schoembucher, E., *Wo Goetter durch Menschen sprechen. Besessenheit in Indien*, Berlin: Reimer Verlag, 2006.

Schoembucher, E. and Claus Peter Zoller, eds., *Ways of Dying: Death and its Meaning in South Asia*, Delhi: Manohar, 1999.

Senapati, N. and B. Mahanti, *Orissa District Gazetteers: Sambalpur*, Cuttack: Orissa Government Press, 1971.

Smith, F.M., *The Self Possessed: Deity and Spirit Possession South Asian Literature and Civilization*, New York: Columbia University Press, 2006.

Stietencron, H.V., *Ganga and Yamuna: Zur symbolischen Bedeutung der Flussgöttinnen an indischen Tempeln* (Ganga and Yamuna: The Symbolism of River-Goddesses on Indian Temples), Wiesbaden: Harrassowitz, 1972.

Stoller, P., 'Sounds and Things: Pulsations of Power in Songhay', in *The Performance of Healing*, ed. Carol Laderman and Marina Roseman, New York: Routledge, 1996, pp. 165–84.

Tambs-Lyche, Harald, ed., *The Feminine Sacred in South Asia*, Delhi: Manohar, 2004 [1999].

Tingey, C., *Auspicious Music in a Changing Society: The Damai Musicians of Nepal*, London: School of Oriental and African Studies, 1994.

Wadley, S., *Shakti. Series in Social, Cultural and Linguistic Anthropology, No. 2.* Chicago: University of Chicago, 1975.

Wegner, G.M., *The Naykhinbaja of the Newar Butchers: Studies in Newar Drumming II*. Wiesbaden: Franz Steiner, 1988.

Wilke, A., Michaels, A. and Cornelia Vogelsanger, eds., *Wild Goddesses in India and Nepal. Proceedings of an International Symposium*, Bern and Zürich: Bern: Lang (Studia Religiosa Helvetica 2), 1994.

Zinser, H., 'Ekstase', *Handbuch der Religionswissenschaftlichen Grundbegriffe (HrwG)*, vol. 2, 1990, pp. 253–8.

8 Pioneers of the Plough
Aghria-Peasants in North-Western Odisha in an Anthro-historical Perspective

UWE SKODA

Introduction: Frontier and Middle Ground

After travelling through the princely state of Gangpur, forming the largest part of present Sundargarh District in Odisha, W.R. Gilbert, A.G.G. Hazaribagh, reported in 1825 to G. Swinton, Secretary to the Government:

> In the course of my march through Gangpoor the country I regret to say manifested but little appearance of prosperity. On my remarking this to the Raja Purssram Ram Sicher Deo, who accompanied me, he declared that although he had made by offers of grant of land in different directions rent free for 7 years, every effort to obtain settlers he was unable to procure any. This he conceived to arise from two fold cause the 1st the want for roads through the country, and 2ndly the devastation amongst aborigines by tigers, which infest the jungles. (*Miscellaneous Despatch Book from 26th September 1822 to 4th May 1826*, Archive of the Commissioner, Ranchi, Jharkhand.)

Gilbert's report does not just indicate how the Rajas were supervised by the colonial power, but more importantly here documents the abundance of available land, the want of cultivators in relatively scarcely populated jungle areas and the way peasants were actively encouraged by rulers of these emerging princely states to immigrate in view of land grants and revenue reductions as additional incentives. And as Gilbert continued to report, a military road from Calcutta to Sambalpur was

* I would like to thank the family of Khirod Kumar Patel, Prasanna Kumar Patel and Pramod Kumar Patel for accommodating me and supporting my project in every possible way. Moreover, I am grateful to Professor G. Pfeffer and Professor D.K. Behera for their comments and critical remarks as well for their encouragement and support in the field. Last, but not least, I am indebted to the German Research Council (DFG) for funding my research generously. Diacritical marks have been generally omitted here.

already under construction which, passing Gangpur, was intended to make the area more accessible.

These various measures certainly contributed to a migration process in nineteenth century and early twentieth century that resulted in a constant influx of settlers increasing the density of the population of the feudatory states of Western Odisha considerably in the following decades—for example, almost doubling between the censuses of 1881 and 1931 (Schwerin 1977: 48).[1] Members of the Aghria community, nowadays settling largely in Sundargarh District as well as in neighbouring Sambalpur District, or the former princely states of Gangpur and Bamra, seem to have made use of these new opportunities by migrating from a north-western direction, though they were not the only migrants.[2]

The area Gilbert passed through was, as he acknowledged, not a 'no man's land'. Though sparsely populated, a number of groups labelled 'aborigines' in Gilbert's text and considered autochthonous had already settled in the area prior to the arrival of these peasants. Their migration led to a new transitional, interstitial or crossover zone that can be characterized as a frontier combining British and American notions of the term. In the former sense it refers to 'remote backwoods regions (characterized by primitive living standards, uncertainty, coarseness, ruffianism) that differ significantly from areas of metropolitan refinement' as reflected in Gilbert's remarks. In the latter sense it also refers to relatively more positive connotations of 'pioneerism, dynamism and advancement' (Rösler/Wendt 1999: 3) taking into account, for example, that new generations of Aghria families often progressively ventured further into the area by procuring new villages for different sons. Characterizing the area as a frontier also implies that it has a lot in common with 'marches' in the sense that it lacks precisely defined and permanently fixed boundaries, but is by tendency rather shifting and extending.

As Thomson and Lamar (in Rösler/Wendt 1999: 4–5) argued a frontier can be seen as a 'zone of interpenetration between two previously distinct societies' and while this scenario may well describe an encounter between Aghrias and autochthonous communities, the empirical situation was further complicated through various migrations. Rather than a binary settlement situation a new multiple 'contact zone' (Pratt 1992) emerged and the social space at the frontier where various cultural 'trajectories' coincided involved at least:

1. autochthonous or 'first' settlers like Kondhs or Bhuiyans—or aboriginies in Gilbert's words;

2. Aghrias or other peasant immigrants, such as the Kultas being equally attracted by the migration incentives;
3. communities such as Mundas, Kharias and Orams migrating from Chotanagpur for the same reasons, but being classified today as Scheduled Tribes and claiming an Adivasi status like the 'original inhabitants' (group 1), but often not accepted by them;
4. castes such as Brahmins, Dalits or artisans—usually considered migrants as well though the migration process often remains rather vague.

Thus, several communities began to co-exist in newly 'opened' forest areas. Some of these communities like the Paudi Bhuiyans (under 1) appear to have been rather loosely linked, often only ritually, to certain Rajas in nineteenth and early twentieth century and offered only token payments or gifts to such 'jungle kings' like in Gangpur (see also Roy 1970 [1912]: 199; Gell 1992: 4).[3] They seem to have shared characteristics of Sahlins' 'tribesmen' (Sahlins 1968: 5).[4] By contrast, Aghrias not only migrating into the area but also clearing jungles, often taking up the headmanship of villages and becoming revenue collectors were more directly tied to outside powers, also reflected in their mythology, as well as to petty Rajas and by extension colonial rulers. Playing a major role in extending the reach and localizing the influence of emerging princely states, being more bureaucratic and centralized than previous 'little kingdoms', and being involved in 'asymmetrical structural relationships between producers of surplus and controllers' (Wolf 1966: 10–11) not only through the payment of taxes but by collecting and transferring them to a ruling or dominant elite, or to non-farming specialists makes it appropriate to speak of Aghria peasants in Wolf's sense (ibid.).

Examining the impact of the migration of peasants in western Odisha, I argue that they contributed substantially to an emerging frontier society not only by collecting revenue, but also by advancing plough-based intensive wet-rice cultivation in the surrounding of relatively independent slash-and-burn cultivators. The plough was not only a prime agricultural instrument, but also a symbol of power, for example as an early revenue measurement—the revenue being fixed according to the number of ploughs owned, i.e. as 'plough tax', before the land itself was more accurately surveyed. Contemplating the connection between the plough as a central agricultural instrument and new power structures Ernest Gellner (1993 [1988]: 1) referred to Prophet Mohammed who is said to have exclaimed that servitude came into the house along with the plough. It is perhaps not too far-fetched to see truth in this dictum in terms of the role of peasant castes in Odisha too, although these pioneers of the plough have been rather neglected in the literature in favour of 'tribal' groups or Rajas so far.

Analysing this frontier and contact area from the perspective of the Aghrias through a historico-anthropological approach[5] the chapter intends to look at how Aghrias established themselves as headmen on this frontier, at the ways Aghrias locate themselves in such as setting by narrating their myths, but also at interactional and integrative practices involving Aghrias and other communities and at transformations occurring in the sphere of kinship and life-cycles. Considering these practices I argue further, that there are indicators for a 'middle ground', to borrow White's concept (1991), having emerged in this crucial zone as a place 'in between' where no side was able to dominate or ignore the others completely. As White argued:

Perhaps the central and defining aspect of the middle ground was the willingness of those who created it to justify their own actions in terms of what they perceived to be their partner's cultural premises. Those operating in the middle ground acted for interests derived from their own culture, but they had to convince people of another culture that some mutual action was fair and legitimate. (1991: 52)

However, White also stressed the specific intricacies of such a situation, i.e. cultural encounters often lead to misinterpretations and distortions, which in turn lead to new, shared meanings and practices on the middle ground (ibid. 1991: x). Without presenting an over-harmonic picture (for conflicts and uprisings see, e.g. Pati in this volume) peasants like the Aghrias chose to—or had to—accommodate others, notably the 'first inhabitants'. For example, in the village I conducted my research Kondhs[6] were widely accepted as 'original settlers' having established the village and such claims to status were not disputed by Aghria peasants. Linked to this position of 'village founders' was the central role in the cult of the village goddess which also remained with the Kondhs and Aghria headmen, just like Rajas in the region, rather started to patronize the village goddesses.

Rather than dominating, Aghrias acted as 'power brokers'—or even as 'culture brokers'[7]—while establishing themselves as headmen or 'village kings'. Brokerage, as Kurin (1997: 19) noted, 'captures the idea that . . . representations are to some degree negotiated, dialogical, and driven by a variety of interests on behalf of the involved parties.'[8] Accordingly, certain local and regional symbols of rule in the frontier zone such as wooden posts or *khunt,* erected as symbols of divinity, dominance and ownership in the cognition of the more autochthonous groups of the villages, were shared though also modified by Aghrias who remained numerically a minority in the area.[9]

Co-existing on such a 'middle ground', however, does not mean that identifiable categories like Aghria peasants or autochthonous Khonds ceased to exist. Instead, practices of the 'middle ground' are not easily distinguishable as being either or, for example 'peasant' or 'tribal'. All sides were confident of their own status and cultural-religious practices, yet had to deal with others, who did not necessarily share their own values and ideas. Various forms of interaction, introduced in the following, offer evidence for a 'middle ground'—here explicitly not confined to a politico-economic sphere. Moreover, the frontier encounters intersect with other, social stratifications such as caste, class, or age. A multitude of ritual friendships on a personal level or the symbolic selling of children exemplify novel practices, newly evolved in often unexpected and unpredictable shapes and not just a simple mixture of diverse cultures.[12]

Such novel modes of interaction, being located on a cultural frontier, are often characterized as 'hybrid', but according to Werbner (1997: 4–5) taking clues from Bakhtin, two different kinds of hybridization must be distinguished. On the one hand an organic, unconscious hybridity relating to the commonplace that cultures should be understood as permanently open systems of interaction (Wolf 1982) always being foreign in origin and local in pattern (Sahlins 1999). By definition cultures are hybrids with new elements being constantly indigenized and perceived as 'own' rather than as threatening the social order. Such a mostly 'un-reflected' change seems to have occurred in the sphere of kinship and life cycle rituals presented below. Aghrias share kinship features with their neighbours, even though intermarriage is explicitly forbidden. Yet, the tendency to integrate everybody into the sphere of kinship (also described by Vatuk 1969 for north India) seem to have led to the establishment of fictive kinship relations on the village level with kinship categories and practices being reconfigurated or renegotiated. On the other hand, an intended hybridity as a disruption 'through deliberate, intended fusions of unlike social languages and images' (Werbner 1997: 5) may be identified as well, for example through ritual 'friendships' creating new alliances.

However, as Baumann (1997) stressed various levels of the discourse about the 'other' can be observed which is applicable for Aghrias as well. On the one hand, boundaries between communities or cultures may be deliberately transgressed in the process of seeking such ritual friendships and other cross-cutting ties—often on a personal level—a level Baumann characterizes as demotic. But on the other hand, the very same boundaries might be confirmed on another level, i.e. in a dominant discourse. Such a view reifying a clear cultural 'rootedness' and presenting a rather conservative image seems to be at the centre of the Aghria myths in which, though presented as 'Aghria history', neighbours are simply ignored, though a peripheral, frontier-like situation away from centres is indicated.

Positioning themselves on a frontier: Aghria mythology

Aghria mythology[11] is generally transmitted in two ways. On the one hand myths are passed on by the *Disandhri* acting as the Aghrias' bards and reciting mythological stories known as *mandla*[12] on special occasions. For their performance the *Disandhri* were ideally entitled to a gift of a cow or a buffalo. On the other hand accounts are published by the Aghria caste organization (*Aghria samaj*) founded in 1904. Thus, one finds oral and written traditions not only co-existing, possibly even merging in a process of canonization—but also occasionally deviating in certain details.[13] Without homogenizing and reducing the various mythological stories to a singular 'standard version',[14] dominant topoi can be extracted from the collected oral as well as the written sources.

Aghrias remember their origin in two phases: a very distant and undated mythical past and a more recent historical past linked to precise dates. The former contains a long list of mythical kings starting from the union between the moon and a star as the 'point of commencement' (Thapar 2002 [1978]: 758), thus claiming to be of *chandra/soma bansa* origin.[15] From there the line of ancestors leads to Bidur, as a mythological figure of the Mahabharat epic, to whom Krishna once promised that his descendants would never be poor. He is asserted to be the forefather of all Aghrias. His credentials as a Kshatriya are somewhat ambiguous, however, since in some versions (many of them put forward by Aghrias or *Disandhri* themselves) his mother and wife are said to be of Shudra or Vaishya origin. However, though the Aghrias believe to be descendants of Bidur, he does not play any role in the ritual cycle of the Aghrias.

In the second phase a more recent migration is narrated and the myths are metaphorically richer in the sense of containing more oppositions. It places the Aghrias somehow at the periphery between two centres and offers an explanation for their place and occupation in Odisha. To paraphrase the account told by a *Disandhri*:

The Soma–bansa Rajput were the inhabitants of Agra. When the emperor (*badshah*) told them to pay respect, the Aghria Rajput replied that the Aghria are bold heroes (*bira*), they are very strong and they should not bow down in front of the emperor. The emperor became angry and decided to tie a sword (*karat bata*) in the middle of the court. On hearing of this decree the Rajput would be frightened and bow down their heads, he thought. When the Aghrias came around 10–20 heads were cut off. Most of the caste died, but they never bowed down their heads. Coming to know about this conspiracy they decided to leave Delhi and Agra and vowed not to take water anymore in the absence of a cosmic order (*pane pine ka dharam nahi*). They left Agra and came to the Gajapati Maharaja [in Puri] and requested him to allow them some occupation. 'If you do not allow us any occupation, what will we do? We have come under the foot of the King [under your jurisdiction].' The Gajapati Maharaja constructed two sword covers. One sword (*khanda*) was made of iron, but its handle was of silver. Instead of constructing a second sword, he just kept a stick to drive the bullocks (*pachen badi*) with a golden handle. He kept them in front of Parmeshwar [Lord Jagannath]. Then the Gajapati said: 'You have to choose one among these two. Whatever is in your fate, that will be your occupation.' After listening Uros Raut, oldest among the Aghrias chose the sword with the golden handle. Then they started to take care of the land [started cultivation]. They made 10 shares and one share to go to the Dissondhri. That was the order of the Gajapati.[16]

Following this decision the Aghrias are believed to have moved towards north-western Odisha and stories differ according to their ultimate place of settlement in the former undivided districts of Sundargarh, Sambalpur and Bolangir. However, considering the main migration myth, one finds on the one hand Agra as centre of the Moghul Empire ('badshah'), left behind by the Aghrias. As reasoned in the myth, Agra is a place without *dharma* (religious or cosmic order). Their departure is caused by a trick at the ruler's court to make them bow their heads. Such a ploy is presented as incompatible with a *ksatra-dharma*, which prescribes conquest, warfare, and duels on the battlefield instead of playing tricks.[17] On the other hand, Puri is ruled by the Gajapati, or a Hindu dynasty, and associated with Lord Jagannath and as such a place of *dharma*. Thus, the migration is based on the oppositions as shown on next page.

While the Aghrias have to leave their place of origin after having revolted against orders to bow their heads, they readily accept the divine order of Lord Jagannath. Similar myths of divine interventions to legitimize rulers from outside—or 'intruders'—are also found in other parts of Odisha and the *vamsavalis* or chronicles of the royal family of Jeypore may serve as an example here (Schnepel 2002: 148f.). Without over-interpreting the myth it seems Aghrias rationalize in this way their

Agra (Delhi)	Puri
Moghul (*badshah*)	Gajapati (*maharaja*)
West (North–West)	East (South–East)
Muslim	Hindu
absence of Gods/dharma (cosmic order)	presence of Gods/dharma (cosmic order)
centre left behind	centre of destination
autochthonous	immigrated (newcomers)
revolt against orders	obeying of orders
negative centre	positive centre

presence at a frontier, explicitly as outsiders, without referring to their immediate neighbours and in particular those already settled at the time of their arrival. At the same time the myth might well be related to a social rise of the Aghrias to the position of headmen or even 'village kings' in a 'contact zone' and a subsequent process of 'Ksatriyaization'.[18] In this regard—and in order to legitimize their place and rank—Aghria myths may play a similar role as the chronicles of royal families (Kulke 2001 [1987a], 2001 [1987b]; Berkemer 1993; Schnepel 2002). Furthermore, within such a political arena the existence of deviating versions contesting their origin and Kshatriya status is not surprising.

It is significant to note that it is the divine order—combined with their greed, i.e. their own fault—which legitimates the decline in status: warriors turn into peasants or the stick replaces the sword, which, however, led to new wealth.

warrior	peasant
sword	stick

Aghria myths are not just the seemingly simple straightforward stories, which reflect only past 'grand events' (Thapar 2002 [1978]: 755) and offer an explanation for a conceived fall.[19] They are not simply representations of empirical facts, but rather characterized by various inversions. In my opinion, a central paradox of the myths concerns the relation between Aghrias and *Disandhris* or bards. On the one hand, Aghrias are presented as elder brothers of the *Disandhris*—a distinction linked in middle India to a difference in status: the elder being in a hierarchically higher position (Pfeffer 2000: 342). The superior Aghrias provide their younger brothers with their means to survive, offering ideally one-tenth of their harvest to them as their share (*bhag*), hence the name *Disandhri* is derived from ten (*dis* via *dos* = ten). A material dependence is clearly expressed in the myth and related to the elder-younger differentiation. On the other hand, the *Disandhris* are ascribed with the task of guarding the sacred thread (*paita*), which the Aghrias had to remove in order to turn to agriculture and to start ploughing. Aghrias believe that ploughing cannot be combined with the standards of purity required for wearing the sacred thread, which *Disandhris* are wearing to this day, while Aghrias are not. Therefore, a second conflicting hierarchy of purity is contained within the myth: the *Disandhris* as younger brothers are relatively purer but materially dependent:[20]

higher	lower
elder	younger
Aghria (eB)	*Disandhri* (yB)
materially independent	materially dependent
higher	lower
purer	more polluted
Disandhri	Aghria
sacred thread	plough

Without stretching an interpretation too far, the relation between the Aghrias and *Disandhris* resembles the Kshatriya/Brahmin or king/priest pair in a wider sense.[21] This seems to be confirmed by the fact that priestly functions are assigned to the *Disandhri* in the myth—though *Disandhris* do not fulfil them at present—while the Aghrias, by order of Lord Jagannath, receive a stick which is also seen as a symbol of rule, royalty and control in the world.[22] Aghrias appear as relatively impure givers in relation to the *Disandhris* as purer receivers. Thus, the myth seems to deal with a more general societal paradox, one which Trautmann (1995 [1981]: 285) once called 'the central conundrum of Indian social ideology'.[23] In the myth one finds the contradiction between two conflicting patterns of ordering society—or two hierarchies; one from the perspective of the king as the universal giver, the other from the perspective of the relatively purer priest. The myth reveals this paradox, though in a disguised form, and, following Lévi-Strauss, acknowledges an irresolvable paradox, an admitted practical antinomy (1992 [1973]: 197ff).[24]

This is further substantiated by another inversion of the myth: In most accounts it is the eldest among the Aghrias who is described as greedy by choosing the golden sword handle instead of the silver one, a mistake which proves to be so fatal for the Aghrias. Keeping the aforesaid in mind, it seems that the status as Kshatriya is opposed to greed here. When the eldest Aghria is tempted and overwhelmed by his greed, the Kshatriya status is lost and a decline of status follows. Thus, this part of the myth might be a symbolic reminder of a close link between the

Kshatriya status and generosity rather than greed. Only by generosity, by giving, such a status can be maintained and the *ksatra-dharma* be fulfilled, a point which seems to reflect the position of Aghrias as 'village kings' and givers at the centre of a redistributive system rather than as being warriors.

In some versions of the dominant myth, particularly in the accounts told by members of the Leunia clan,[25] as a subsidiary element one finds a peculiar link to Chamars instrumental in the survival of the Aghrias.[26] Chamars without children offer their help by hiding them in their home-cum-workshop, but ask the Aghrias to perform their last rites for them in return.[27] Other mythical stories explain why the Aghrias are served by priests supposedly in their exclusive service. These ritual specialists are known as Tiharis/Tiwaris and claim to be Kanyakubja Brahmins. At the same time there are indications that other Brahmins were rejected for not supporting the Aghrias as warriors.[28]

Turning to the peculiar link between Chamars and Aghrias (and also stressed by the Chamars for whom it is certainly prestigious to link themselves to the dominant caste) one might argue, as some Aghrias do, that the Chamars, sharing the same language as the Aghrias, may have migrated from the same area or at the same time as the Aghrias. One may also explain the relation by the fact that in former times Chamars used to produce special products necessary for Aghria techniques of cultivation.[29] By contrast, however, another opposition seems to be expressed here, the one related to the relative impurity of the Chamars. In the myth the Aghrias are endangered by the Moghul, but safe in the house of a Chamar. While Chamars are often associated with death, specifically death of cattle, in this myth they, from the perspective of Aghrias, appear as protectors of life—though they may sacrifice their own life. Thus, one finds the oppositions:

Kshatriya	Chamar
pure	impure
high	low
needing help	offering help
endangered	safe/surviving
status temporarily given up	status temporarily sought

Thus, being a Chamar or having an impure status in a wider sense may offer protection against life-threatening forces. Apart from stressing their roots in caste society in this way, the Aghrias may possibly highlight the relativity of purity and pollution in respect to their presence as well as their encounters in a rather devalued sphere conceptionalized as frontier or outside away from the centres like Puri.[30]

Aghrias as Headmen or 'Village Kings': Expanding, brokering and losing power

Leaving aside mythical constructions of the migration process and looking at specific family histories of headmen or 'Gauntias', one notices that the migration did not occur as a single wave, but should rather be understood as a long and drawn-out process. Aghrias taking up the headmanship in certain villages tried to secure separate settlements for their sons. Thus, many families moved in successive generations from a north-western direction towards the princely states of Bamra and Bonai. Only by the 1930s the progress of the Aghrias and similar peasant castes came to an end. By implementing new forest protection laws in the princely states the process of penetrating the jungle was severely restricted.[31] Particularly this end of migration as a viable option in the region, roughly 100 years after Gilbert's tour, seems to have intensified previous contacts with neighbouring communities as well as agricultural practices.

As headmen Aghria-Gauntias were embedded in a multilayered political structure in which Cohn (2001 [1962]) distinguished several levels of the political system ranging from the 'local level', as the lowest or most basic administrative stratum consisting of revenue collectors, indigenous chiefs and lineages, up to the imperial level—a structure or 'relational construct' (Berkemer 1993: 319) in which the position of a 'little king' was determined by his relationship to the overlord(s), in which he was subordinate, as well as to his subjects, in which he himself was in turn the overlord. As Cohn and later Stein (1975: 77) pointed out, 'little kings' did have power but needed the superior kings' authority or ritual sovereignty. Although these theories were developed with regard to kingdoms prior to British colonial rule, they may also be applied to the relations in the princely states of western Odisha, since the latter by and large remained internally intact in nineteenth and early twentieth century (Berkemer 1993: 321). Given the limited British interference the role of Aghria headmen may be understood in many ways as that of 'village kings' in a 'little kingdom' framework, even though they were also instrumental in transforming this very same political structure, for example, by extending an increasingly fixed revenue system, etc.[32] The idea of kingship as embodied in Gauntias (or in the Raja) remained and still remains alive, for instance in rituals, even despite the abolition of the Gauntia system after Indian independence, and despite a formally 'absented throne' Galey (1990: 129).

A *gaunti* headmanship or 'kingship' of the village could be acquired in various ways, most commonly, however, by clearing the forest. Rights to establish a village in this way were termed *khunt kata gaunti. Khunt* standing here for the stumps of the trees, which had to be cut (*kata* = to cut) in order to settle down and to create a realm as a *Gauntia.* Acting and styling themselves as clearers of the jungles Aghria Gauntias not just followed in the footsteps of earlier kings—the king's conquest of the wilderness being a well-known motif of ancient Hindu scriptures (Falk 1973: 2), but they also expressed this act, perhaps indicative of a 'middle ground', in an idiom rather similar to or shared with that of Chotanagpur communities further north such as the Mundas (Roy 1970 [1912]: 92) or Orams (Roy 1999 [1928]: 68, 204–5) or further south such as the Kondhs and the Gadabas (Bailey 1960: 28ff, 78ff; for the Dongria Kondhs and Gadabas see Hardenberg and Berger, personal communication), who all distinguish between the 'original clearers of the soil' and the later immigrants who are quite often affinal relatives of the former.

Munda case	Khuntkattidars (original clan of the village owning the land—clearers of the forest)	Parjas (outsiders—cultivating land particularly of their khunt–relatives—paying rent)
Aghria case	Gauntias (newcomers owning the land—having a khunt kata pata designating them as clearers of the forest)	Parjas (cultivating land allotted to them by the Gauntia or for the Gauntia to whom they are not related—paying revenue—having no rights to cultivate the land as such)

As a Gauntia could not cultivate all the land, many Gauntias, as soon as they had acquired landrights or rights to clear the jungle, started sharing their rights by inviting other members of their own caste as well as of other communities to settle and shoulder certain responsibilities, e.g. inviting Chamars to take charge of the dead cattle and to contribute to the revenue fixed for a village, thus reducing their own share.

Superior kings acknowledged these rights and formally documented them at least by the time of the establishment of more bureaucratic structures and settlements in the princely states from late nineteenth century onwards. In a landlord's *pata* or, land deed, issued to an Aghria–

Gauntia by the Raja of Bamra as late as 1942, this is expressed in the following way:

You or any recorded tenant of your village can occupy any wasteland within the area of your village by taking permission of the State except the revenue land that is measured and is being utilized for pasture (for cattle). If the tenants of your village cannot or will not occupy it, it can be given to tenants of other villages for occupation in the same system by taking due permission from the State.

Someone, who has occupied such wasteland, will enjoy five years without paying rent. Afterwards until the next settlement he will pay half of the fixed revenue rent and until then you will be enjoying that rent.

A Gauntia's most important obligation was the collection of revenue, which is fixed in point 2 and 3 of the *pata*.

2. You have to collect revenues from the tenants as per the rent roll or as per the newly made or as per the changed rent roll and you should always give receipts for each collection of revenues and cess from the tenants in the printed receipts books that are brought from the State.

3. You have to collect the fixed revenue and cess of [your] Landlord village as per the calculation of Touzi[33] instalments as given below: 1st instalment Rs.0 – Rs.40 1st June; 2nd instalment Rs.0—Rs.30 1st December; 3rd instalment Rs.0—Rs.30 1st March

After seven years, there will be a revised settlement. In that, the rate of the rent will be fixed in the presently fixed rate of all newly possessed or occupied land. Accordingly you have to deposit fixed rent collection of new land of your village.

If according to the fixed instalments the fixed revenue rents are not paid for each instalment, you will have to collect Rs.6% surcharge (extra) per year. If one arrear of three instalments is not paid up to ten years, you will be removed from the Landlord's right and the arrears revenue etc. will be collected by selling your movable and immovable property.

Though tenants—even those failing to deposit their rent—were formally protected in the deed, in practice, however, it seems to have been the Gauntia's privilege to distribute land in the village. Land not cultivated by anyone, could be given to tenants the Gauntia chose and sometimes villagers remember certain headmen with gratitude who allowed them to stay in their villages and offered them some land to cultivate. The paragraph to protect the tenants seems to have been of little relevance in practise as a powerful Gauntia could simply force some tenants to sell him their land or their best cattle.

Apart from collecting revenue, each Gauntia had other obligations particularly the duty to accommodate the King, members of his family or any government servant on their journeys through the kingdom. Usually a special room known as *baithak*—close to the entrance of the Gauntia's house—was reserved for such occasions. Pioneering also other new technologies in the area such as the use of limestone to construct temples and particularly prestigious solid two storey buildings, so-called *paka ghar*, Aghrias were not only able to offer suitable accommodation, this kind of village palace so typical for Gauntias in the region had other advantages as well. Inhabitants were protected against heat and cold in this extreme climate, could spot from a distance elephants destroying crops and could defend themselves more easily against the attacks of robbers and marauding soldiers. Guests, accommodated in the *baithak*, had to be served meals too. The ingredients and utensils which had to be provided were precisely listed according to the guest's status. Furthermore, Government employees had a right to be supplied with carriers or porters to the next village. In addition, food had to be allocated for royal weddings. However, these 'gifts' such as milk, paddy and others fixed prior to the function were not stated in the land deed.

At the same time, although not mentioned in the *pata*, Gauntia and villagers alike also remember the socage (*bethi*) they had to offer to the King. According to some people this forced labour for road construction, elephant hunts and the like was abolished two or three years before independence. In some cases the villagers also had to work for a limited time without wages for the landlord. Some villagers recollect that they had to offer their labour in exchange for the costs the Gauntia used to bear during festivals, where the Gauntia used to pay for dancers, meals and other entertainments. The Gauntia used the free labour or *bethi* to build ponds or wells, but also for urgent works like firefighting or in his personal fields—to plough, to sow and to harvest—if additional labourers were needed.

Apart from titles, cloths and other royal symbols received by the 'village kings', one of the most important privileges a Gauntia enjoyed—linked directly to the *gaunti*—was the right to cultivate land formally belonging to his superior King and known as *bhogra*. In most cases this land was rent–free and of a very high quality. As expressed in the aforementioned *pata*:

According to this appointment you will enjoy the free right of land tenancy. If there is no free land . . ., you will get rupees in cash. With this deed (pata) you will enjoy free land (bhogra jami) as per the tenancy calculation. Free land (bhogra) cannot be transferred, divided, altered, sold, mortgaged or given on loan in any respect. If for any reason there are changes in landlordship (gaunti) it will be completely transferred to the successors.

The *bhogra* land belonging to and representing the king, here the Raja of Bamra, has a counterpart in the so-called *guti buna*—rent-free land the Gauntia gave to Gutis—loyal servants and often bonded labourers, literally for sowing (*buna*), i.e. for their own purposes, but belonging to the Gauntia and recorded in the Gauntia's name. Both may thus be termed as the 'King's land' on different levels of the continuing 'little kingdom' framework, as they are structurally identical. As Dirks (1979: 177) noticed:

As decentralized as the little kingdom appears, the king was the symbolic head of the system of redistribution, which even as it allotted rights to local power configurations underscored the pre-eminence of the king and the king's rights.

Land—or rather entitlements to certain lands and sharing land rights—played a major role in this redistributive process, into which the Aghrias were integrated in order to integrate others in turn.

Older Aghria still remember that initially revenue was assessed according to the number of ploughs owned. Thus, it was appropriately termed 'plough tax' rather than 'revenue'. The number of ploughs did not just indicate the size of cultivable land, but was usually also equivalent to the number of *Guti* (contract labourers or servants—sometimes also referred to as *Halia* or ploughmen) and often with the number of pairs of bullocks and buffalos, although in some cases more pairs of bullocks or buffalos than ploughs were kept and ploughing was done with bullocks during the daytime and with buffalos during the night-time. In Kuchinda as a major village, the Gauntia is believed to have owned a maximum of 25 ploughs, while in a remoter village like Mundaloi, the Gauntia had around 15 ploughs at a time. Thus, the number of ploughs hinted at the number of cattle, labourers and acres of cultivatable land respectively and also indicated a ranking in terms of wealth in the same way as power tillers, tractors and other more 'modern' signs do today.

The various settlements introduced under colonial supervision in the princely states of north-western Odisha in late nineteenth and early twentieth century replaced the earlier plough-tax by a revenue collection system based on the size of more accurately measured cultivated fields— particularly those fields under wet-rice cultivation, while areas under slash-and-burn cultivation often remained un-surveyed for a longer period. In the region specifically Aghria headmen were also pioneers in transforming and intensifying agriculture. Related to intensive agriculture was the building of tanks to supplement water resources and to become more independent from rainfall. The Aghrias became masters in the art of tank construction, distinguishing between several kinds of ponds built according to a specific landscape.[34] Thus, they executed what Cohn (2001 [1962]: 493) once called the 'developmental function' of 'little kings'. The Gauntias did not just establish themselves as sacrifiers (*jajman*)[35] in hereditary relations to various service castes (priests, barbers, washermen), but also as masters (*sahu*) in opposition their different types of agricultural labourers (*guti, butiya*) closely tied to the most important economic modification, i.e. the spreading and intensification of plough–oriented wet-rice cultivation with an emphasis on transplanting.

As Thapar and Siddiqi (1997 [1979]: 426) have pointed out, a substantial surplus is required for the formation of a state. The economic changes as introduced by the Aghrias, occurring in conjunction with a change from millet to rice cultivation,[36] certainly generated more revenue, which was transferred to and appropriated by the state through various settlements— presumably the prosperity imagined by Gilbert. Aghrias were quite directly involved in the establishment of these more central systems of redistribution and kingship. Although it is uncertain whether the Aghrias did indeed introduce the plough in their villages or if it had been known or used in certain forms of axe—or shifting-cultivation before, it is clear that the wet-rice cultivation practised by the Aghrias differed markedly from the axe-cultivation (*podu*)—with or without plough—en vogue among their not so distant neighbours in the hills such as the Paudi Bhuyans.[37] For example, Bhuyans told Elwin touring the region in 1942 that axe-cultivation or slash-and-burn was 'their right; it was established by divine authority' (1942: 13). In contrast to these neighbours, only the Aghrias appear to have a very special symbolic relation to ploughing. On the one hand this is attested in their myth introduced above linking ploughing to the divine intervention of Lord Jagannath. On the other hand this special relation comes clearly to the fore in the annual 'plough rituals' (*nangala puja*).[38] In contrast to all of their neighbouring communities in the village, the plough is only worshipped among the Aghrias. Though other agricultural instruments such as yoke and hoe are venerated too, the plough remains the prime instrument as indicated by the name of the ritual.

While the plough ritual is practiced exclusively by Aghrias indicating the importance of the plough for them, other rituals and festivals are celebrated with other communities and Aghria peasants, also as 'village kings', did not just change the landscape, but acted as 'culture brokers' in a process of 'intensive propaganda' (Weber 1988 [1921]: 11) or 'inner colonization' (Pfeffer 1978: 426; Kulke 2001 [1978]: 3), i.e. they also initiated the setting up of temples, inviting Brahmins and offering land to them, building funeral memorials, introducing new technologies and methods and opening schools at a later stage. Acting as patrons of festivals such as Shivratri and temples—usually for Lord Shiva or Lord Jagannath—the Gauntias were involved in processes of 'Hinduization' (Kulke 1979: 18f; Thapar/Siddiqi 1997 [1979]), which was, however, never a one-sided affair.

One of the most important religious functions was and is the performance of the *rath jatra* for Lord Jagannath as practised by kings of Odisha on all levels. In sponsoring the festival, a Gauntia explicitly replicates royal functions on the village level by styling himself as the first servant of Jagannath or 'walking Vishnu' in the same way the Gajapati does (Hardenberg 1999: 153). However, as Dirks (1979: 188) observed, displaying royal emblems without proper permission has a certain 'double-edgeness', since taking over a role of an overlord implies that he is imitated and challenged simultaneously. It is also important to notice that in many villages Gauntias started to perform the *rath yatra* only after independence, thereby locally consolidating their central position via rituals at a time when it was often endangered by land reforms and by the loss of their role as revenue collectors. Deviating from the Puri ritual practice, villages Gauntias of western Odisha often did not perform the ritual sweeping like the Gajapati—a task associated with untouchability and often left to relatives or other dignitaries. They preferred to sprinkle water only. Like temples, religious altars (*mandap*—quite often just opposite the Gauntia's house) or memorial stones (*samadhi*), these rituals as symbols, as Burke (1993) and Assmann (1999: 21) argued, represent and belong to the social and cultural memory. Being closely associated with locality and memory, the landlord's power, his spatial and ritual centrality as well as the glory of Hindu-gods are inscribed in them.

Aghria Gauntias did not only share the authority of superior kings as in the *rath yatra*, they also established links to the important local deities—specifically the village goddess (*gram sri*) usually situated in a sacred grove—thereby proving a certain sovereignty as demonstrated by a privileged access to and position in the cult of the *gram sri*. While the sacrificer (Kalo) in most cases belongs to autochthonous communities such as the Kondhs, the Gauntia has a very exalted position in the cult being the prime donor to offer all ritual items for the worship, including the valuable animal sacrifices. Furthermore, as a Gauntia told me, without his presence, the ritual cannot be performed properly. Having a privileged access to the goddess effectively implies having access to the female power (*sakti*) as embodied by the goddess, which is also royal power.[39] However, by retaining those ritual specialists who belong to the category of village founders in the cult, Aghrias also acknowledge their specific autochthonous link to the soil in contrast to their own status as relative newcomers.

A centrality of the 'village kings' is furthermore demonstrated during the rituals of *Rakhi Puni*—a festival seen in many parts of India as an occasion for sisters to fast for the sake of their brothers and bind a *rakhi* around the latters' wrists asking for protection. In north-western Odisha various relationships of dependency are expressed: husbands, together with their wives, bind *rakhi* to the ancestors as well as to different Gods and Goddesses in the house. Furthermore, *rakhi* are offered to the Gauntia as a kind of amulet to show respect and loyalty as well as dependence and a need for protection. Like sisters, villagers such as temple priests and Gutis, coming to the Gauntia, pray for his well-being. In exchange for binding a *rakhi*, they receive some money and in some cases the raw food stuff or cloths. Thus, during *Rakhi Puni*, which appears to correspond to a durbar or royal assembly on the village level and may again be a specific practice on the 'middle ground', the Gauntia incorporates villagers who are literally bound to him, while he in turn acknowledges the superiority of ancestors.

A frontier situation seems to have also contributed to other forms of dominance and worship such as the 'village kingship of the wooden post' or *khunt Gauntia*. In some cases, when the village headmen had no issue, were poor or had other problems—or possibly other conflicts—they used to erect these wooden posts in order to rule on behalf of the *khunt Gauntia* as a kind of 'acting Gauntia'. In the few cases I found these *khunt*—often in villages with only a small Aghria minority—they were placed either in a separate mud house near the Gauntia's house or in his field. Various stories surround the poles. People claim that the acting Gauntia is protected by the wooden post, because Yama, the God of Death, is unable to harm it. Since it has been argued that such posts also represent aniconic 'tribal' gods or spirits (Roy 1999 [1928]: 10, 16, 50;[40] Eschmann 1994 [1975]: 214, 221; Kulke 1979: 22ff; Mallebrein 2001; Jena et al. 2002: 204, 214) or that *khunt* are synonymous with sub–clans or lineages among the Santals (Troisi 2000 [1979]: 30), Orams (Roy 1999 [1928]: 7, 16, 68ff) or Mundas (Roy 1970 [1912]: 361; Choudhury 1977: 33, 38) as mentioned above one may consider it as an element of 'Tribalization'[41] here on the side of immigrating Hindu settlers. However, the aspect of rulership and control seems to be equally important. For example, ancient Hindu texts link Asoka to the worship of certain trees (Falk 1973: 10ff) and a culturally transformed tree may well signify a conquest of wilderness. In both cases the erection of a *khunt* is somehow linked to the idea of protection and to a certain deification, but the meanings may differ depending on the perspective. Thus, the symbol of the post with its multivalence appears to be particularly apt on a 'middle ground' enabling Aghria village kings to fulfil their state functions by using a religious idiom familiar to their Adibasi-neighbours.

Nowadays however, after the formal abolition of 'village kingship', the worship of *khunt Gauntia* has been subjected to a significant process of decline. However, this does not mean that the institution of 'village kingship' is necessarily in decline everywhere. Many Gauntias managed to keep their economically influential position despite the land reforms. These leaders rather initiated and patronized additional rituals in the village or transformed their central role by engaging themselves in the setting up of schools and presiding over school committees or by venturing into new businesses. Wedding parties arriving at the village often still first call upon the Gauntia and usually offer a gift as a sign of respect and request for security referring to a Gauntia's role as arbitrator and protector. Gauntias used to be actively involved in settling disputes— also in punishing villagers found guilty of crimes like adultery or theft and calling the police was often—and still is—considered a *laj* or shame for a Gauntia as well as the village, because of the implication that a Gauntia was unable to maintain law and order in his respective realm. In this regard his position appears to have differed markedly from the role of headmen in autochthonous communities such as the Muria (Gell 1992: 9–10). However, after merger and particularly since the late 1960s or early 1970s, the way of settling disputes has changed considerably. Gauntias hardly settle disputes in the same manner any longer, but rather arrange village meetings, in which both sides can give their version, while a Gauntia or a Sarpanch usually preside over the meeting.

Interacting and integrating on a 'Middle Ground'

The 'middle ground' in north-west Odisha did not only comprise of common form of worship of deities, some of them being understood as 'hinduized tribal gods or goddesses' (Eschmann 1994 [1975]: 211ff; Sontheimer 1994: 117ff; Pasayat 1998: 103ff) and it is not only bound

218 Uwe Skoda

together by still reverberating power structures of former 'little kingdoms' (Kulke 2001 [1993]: 114ff, Schnepel 2001: 271ff). The 'middle ground' was and perhaps still is also linked by a subtle network of relationships as established and maintained, for instance, by a local caste hierarchy, by a symbolic selling of children and by personal 'ritual friendships'.

As indicated in their own mythology, Aghrias claim to have brought certain Brahmins into the region in order to serve them and there is also a close connection to the Chamars or 'Untouchables' as the second pole of caste hierarchy. Both links hint at a caste hierarchy having evolved at this frontier, which however, as I want to argue, is—in contrast to a pure/ impure distinction—commonly expressed in the idiom of *bhal/bad lok* (good/big or 'senior' people) versus *san/chot lok* (small, 'junior' people). This idiom has been described as being typical for the 'tribal society' (Pfeffer 1982, 2000) of Southern Odisha and linked to the value of seniority in middle India. Dichotomies such as *uncha* (high) versus *nicha* (low) and *bari* (big) versus *choti* (little) are, however, also known from UP (Kolenda 1983: 134)—though the semantic content may differ.[42] It might be precisely such a multivalence of an opposition such as 'big' versus 'little' which makes it so conducive on a 'middle ground'.

Hierarchy itself is always a very sensitive topic and if brought up in a group-discussion, locals often prefer to say that they do not know anything about hierarchy, which appears to be a rather convenient way to avoid these often difficult or awkward questions. Instead the village harmony or 'peace' (*shanti*) is often emphasized, which could be potentially damaged or disturbed by an articulation of questions on hierarchy. As such, hierarchical distinctions are often made implicitly by transferring food, by allowing or denying entry to the kitchen and similar markers, but verbally they are rarely expressed. Observing the possible acceptance of food and drink, as well as discussing these matters rather personally, a picture of a hierarchy, in terms of purity and seniority, emerges, which, however, should not be confused with rankings within the framework of kingship, i.e. based on land and patronage.

Hierarchy as expressed by the concept of *bhal lok* or *bad lok* has an absolute and a relative dimension. In absolute terms it articulates the status difference between the 'good/senior people'/*bhal lok* and the 'small people'/*chot lok*—the 'good castes' being those served by high status Brahmins, barbers, washermen, certain gurus (Kan Guru) and Kalo (sacrificer of the village goddess being important for marriage rituals and Gram Sri Puja). The concept in this narrow sense was indicated, e.g. in one village by the building of various *mandap*—temporary altars used for festivals. While one had been erected for the high ranking communities by an Aghria–Gauntia, a second one had been built with money given by the government for a community (Kisans) that remained excluded from the high caste *mandap*. Finally, a third *mandap*—also erected by the Gauntia—was exclusively used by the Harijans.[43] Here Chamars were excluded in the same way as Harijans were excluded from the Kisan *mandap*. It is noteworthy here, that Aghria peasants and similar communities like Chosas (classified as group 2 in the beginning) largely share the same position with Adivasi communities such as Kondhs, Bhuiyans or Gonds (group 1)—despite occasional finer distinctions—while communities of group 3 (e.g. Mundas) were usually not counted among the 'good people' by 1 and 2 in absolute terms.

However, the concept of *bhal lok* as a relative one also reflects processes of inclusion and exclusion as described by Pocock (1957) for the caste society of Gujarat. On the 'middle ground' *bhal lok* or *bad lok* signifies not only high status groups enjoying the services of Brahmins and others in opposition to all lower groups, which are *chot lok* or small people, but it may also be used by lower communities, who include themselves into the category *bhal lok* in certain circumstances, e.g. if asked from whom they might accept water. A Khadia may say 'it is acceptable from all *bhal lok*' which indicates that he could drink water from all communities higher than his, including Kisans and Mundas, while at the same time excluding all communities lower than his own. Again, verbalizations are avoided and it would be very impolite if not insulting to call someone else *chot lok* in his presence because of the negative connotations. However, lower communities could use it to describe themselves. For example, a Luhura (black smith), once asked if he would also perform certain rituals that the local landlord performs, replied: 'We are *chot lok*, that's why we are not doing such rituals'. Thus, some may apply it to themselves to underline a difference with people of higher status.[44]

Apart from food transactions, the symbolic 'selling' (*bikri*) and 'throwing away' of children appears to be another peculiar way of establishing, negotiating, yet also hierarchizing relations. Elaborating on the symbolic 'selling' (*bikri*) of children, a phenomenon hardly mentioned elsewhere,[45] may invoke images or thoughts of child bonded labour and the tragic fate of children in the carpet-knotting industry (e.g. Voll 1999) or elsewhere. However, in none of the cases described here any harm is done to them. In fact the opposite is more accurate, by selling them or throwing them away symbolically the parents hope to improve the health condition of their children and to help them to survive, i.e. they may either be ill or considered to be endangered in the sense that elder siblings already died.

For example, an Aghria girl, now an old lady of about 65 years, was sold when she was not even one year old. Before, her elder sister had died. She was often ill and considered to be weak. Her parents were afraid that she too would die. Subsequently she was sold to a Chamar family in the village of her maternal uncle. At the time of the sale she received a leather necklace from the Chamar family which she wore until she was repurchased. It was seen as her identification with the Chamars. She called the Chamars mother and father although she continued to live with her Aghria family. Later, she would visit the Chamar family occasionally and would have light snacks there, but no boiled rice. The old lady said that she was treated, to some extent, as though she did not belong to her original caste, e.g. she received less food at feasts, but she could, in contrast to 'ordinary' Chamars, enter the kitchen and use the same dishes. Years later, hours before her child marriage, she was repurchased. In order to sell her back to her original family, a *purug*[46] filled with parboiled rice was prepared and she was made to sit upon it. Her Chamar family had offered a sari which she wore while sitting there. In exchange, the Chamars demanded a new sari, a metal pot, a substantial amount of money (Rs.5 as silver coins—ten grams each at that time) and the *purug* filled with rice.

In other cases the child is deliberately made impure, e.g. the child is made to sit in the 'leftovers of a meal' (*aentha*) for a short while. An elder Aghria lady told me that her late husband was a case in point. He used to be called by the nickname *aentha* after 'being thrown away' symbolically. Again, the impure child remained in this condition until marriage. Immediately before the wedding a ritual purification and a feast for the *jati* is obligatory.

Considering the larger picture of selling, but also throwing and giving away within one's community, there are two overlapping intentions of these transactions. First, the child is transferred—into a family or house not affected by misfortunes and illnesses. Second, the child is made impure in the hope of diverting the evil eye, the attention of Yama or other evil forces to be deceived, but also to become stronger physically in a lower community environment. The sale of children, which people see as the most effective method of saving the children, obviously combines both aspects: the child is transferred to an impure setting. In being given away to a low status family and becoming impure at the same time, the child has the best chances to survive.

	Child is transferred	Child becomes impure
Giving away	X	
Throwing away		X
Selling	X	X

Marriott's transactional theory showed 'rankings established by food transfers' (ibid. 1968: 169–70) that expressed the value of avoiding pollution with regard to food as well as of the removal pollution in regard to services. But Marriott also observed, 'pollution is not dreaded as an absolute evil, instead it may be manipulated or even enjoyed' (1968: 143). A state of self-induced impurity might be a *protected* state—as elaborated in the Aghria myths too. In our case, it is attained deliberately—even though for a restricted purpose and a limited time. Furthermore, not only pollution—prior to marriage—but the act of transfer itself is valued.

One must also note that the child's transfer and temporary identification has no negative effect, i.e. neither on the high status of the giver at the time of sale nor on the receiver when repurchasing the child. The same is true in the reverse direction: the child's receiver of low status cannot improve it, when selling the child. The transaction does not affect the rank of giver or receiver—presumably because it is a market–like transfer. The child is first sold and then eats in the receiver's house. Money is acceptable from everyone and, contrary to Marriott (1968: 144), it seems that money does not even convey 'the slightest degree of subordination'. It rather seems to solidify the transfer of any substance-code.

The temporary identification of children establishes inter-group relationships that reflect a local hierarchy; at the same time, it creates and reinforces a hierarchy on a 'middle ground'. By giving amulets such as leather necklaces of the Chamars, this sale expresses a process of 'identifying differences' (Jeffrey 2000: 286) as well as essentializing differences between the categories in public, thus, ordering them hierarchically. Children are sold from groups of relatively higher status— like the Gonds or Kondhs (group 1 & 2)—to relatively lower status groups, such as the Mundas (group 3) or Harijans, and usually not the other way around—though all except the Harijans belong to the administrative category of Scheduled Tribes (though it is not formulated as a strict rule). Thus, the sale also shows that so called Scheduled Tribes—a rather heterogeneous category—are not always and exclusively integrated into the lower strata of the hierarchy, as sometimes assumed,[47] but on higher levels as well.

However, in the case of children, there is a fixed time-frame for the transaction and the deception. Every child must be repurchased and purified before marriage. In view of the Gods one could also argue that, at the time of marriage Laksmi, the Goddess of wealth and happiness, comes into one's house—in particular in the form of the bride—and this entry is expected to help checking the evil forces endangering family members.

Corresponding time-frame: Birth > Identified (Sold/Transferred) Child: Unripe (*apurnna*) Person > Marriage: Ripe (*purnna*) Person

However, the selling and even a temporary breaking of commensality do not endanger the separation of groups according to their relative purity, which is instead reinforced. Essential boundaries, like marriage, are maintained—therefore the identification remains incomplete and mainly restricted to childhood. For women, marriage initiates a new process of identification—the bride becomes integrated and henceforth identified with her husband's family and clan. The temporary identification of children shows that status as identity is not fixed permanently, but rather continuously negotiated and even voluntarily lowered for some time in order to benefit personally within a collectively constructed framework.

Apart from relations involving a symbolic selling of children another, quite different way of establishing or rather formalizing interactional patterns on a personal level may be described here as 'ritual friendship'. Very close friends, particularly school or college mates, often choose this way to create more formal and more permanent ties. Quite often parents also arrange the ritual for their young children in order to become friends. Such a relation can only be established between different communities, e.g. between Aghrias and Kisans (groups 2 and 3) or Kisans and Malis (group 3 and 4), i.e. they occur particularly on the intercommunity level. They stand in contrast to 'tribal society' of south Odisha or Chotanagpur, where relations of 'ritual friendship' might be forged on an intra-community level connecting, for example, various clans. Therefore one may find an adaptation or transformation of ritual friendship between a rather segmentary 'tribal society' in the south, and a more complex society having evolved at a frontier. While in the former society ritual friendship may balance a condition of latent hostility (Sahlins 1968: 4ff.), in the latter type of society it may occur as a counterweight to newly established hierarchies. Thus, various meanings might be attached to the same forms of 'ritual friendship'—the forms in turn are also hierarchized or influenced by hierarchies.

The phenomenon bears a resemblance to kinship ties in the sense that it is extended to other family members: the relationships created are not restricted to two persons, but rather involve their wider families as expressed in forms of address like *mita ma* (friend's mother) or *mita bua* (friend's father) for the close relatives of the ritual friends. This also includes an obligation to invite each other to festivals. In comparison with ordinary friendship, they have a more permanent character, most importantly because they are sanctioned in front of, and blessed by, various gods providing them with a sacred character. Ritual friends are said to support each other and to share everything as, ideally, brothers or sisters do, and some people joke that they would even share their wives; although in practice a ritual friend's wife should be avoided like a younger brother's wife. In fact, ritual friendship implies a 'total identification' (Pfeffer 2001: 138), a certain 'de-personalization', or the ideal of the merger of friends, as in the case of *mahaprasad*-friendship, whose life-spirits (*jiban*), it is believed, have become one. The idea, of sharing everything among ritual friends—you give to your ritual friend something of whatever you have—hints at the idea of a pure gift and of generalized reciprocity in Sahlins' terms (1965: 147). Ritual friends are cared for, and the greatest hospitality is shown to them. They usually do not demand anything, but they also know that a wish could never be refused. Therefore, apart from the balancing effect of ritual friendship in regard to an evolving hierarchy of ritual purity, ritual friendship may also have a certain counter-effect on, and stand in contrast to, the redistributive systems that have been historically established in the 'contact zone' by revenue collecting Aghrias.

This, however, should not imply an absence of hierarchy—even within ritual friendship. First, different forms of ritual friendship do not embody the same sacred character. Comparing the various types of ritual friendship one notices that some—like *mahaprasad, sahi* or *sahya*—can be forged every day while the others like *makra, bensagar* or *karamdal* can be created only during religious festivals usually held once a year. Thus, sacredness appears to be ranked. There is a clear difference between *mahaprasad* and all other forms. *Mahaprasad* is considered to be most sacred and irreversible. While a *mahaprasad*-friendship simply cannot be dissolved, it is unlikely that any other ritual friendship would break up either.

Second, in some high castes like the Aghrias the number of friends from lower status communities is rather limited and status considerations seem to be a reason behind it. Such a finding contradicts Choudhury's (1977: 68–9) argument that friendship should be understood as a concession to the individual in a close-knit, kin-based society. Though there is a degree of personal choice, this is also limited by the culturally determined forms. Although two friends form a new relationship in many cases, this does not mean that an individual decision is necessarily involved. Often the parents might be more interested in arranging a new relationship than their children.

Moreover, although friends are equal in many respects, this does not mean that restrictions regarding food are no longer valid in inter-community relations. Although ritual friends can feed each other *prasad*—and in fact the bond is created through the sharing of food—they cannot disregard the regulations of the communities they belong to in everyday life. On important occasions like *nua khai* or *rakhi puni* friends might send each other raw food as a sign of their special bond, but usually they are not allowed to share boiled food—hierarchy invades the sphere of friendship.

Apart from the various cross-cutting intercommunity links contributing to a 'middle ground' one can also recognize certain synthesises in the sphere of kinship and during life-cycle rituals. In ritual practises such as weddings and funerals Aghrias appear to differ less from their Adibasi neighbours than one might expect given the migration background and their mythical constructions.

The life cycle among the Aghrias is, to a large extent, dominated by two complementary sets of relations: that of father and son as well as that of mother's brother (*mamu*) and sister's son (*bhanja*). While the former appears to be a relatively common feature throughout India—at least in patrilinially structured communities—the latter, specifically the role of the sister's son or potential son-in-law during the funerary rites, seems to deviate from a more general north Indian caste pattern. Comparing the Aghrias to other north or south Indian cases (e.g. Bennett 1983, Conzelmann 1996, Kapadia 1996, Madan 1989 [1965], Parry 1994, Randeria 1999), one finds a similar role of a mother's brother in early life cycle rituals up to marriage, i.e. his presence and, perhaps more importantly, his gifts being required. However, the role of the sister's son in funeral rituals is not mentioned in any of these comparable cases, while among the Aghrias his presence is obligatory.[48] Thus, at the time of the *mamu*'s death, the *mamu/bhanja* relationship is somehow reversed. On the eleventh day—the main day of the funeral—the sister's son receives *bhanja dan*, i.e. a special gift for the sister's son. Moreover, the *bhanja* and sometimes also the *bhanja*'s wife are worshipped and fed by the family, for example the widow, and receive some money and cloths. Without an offering for the *bhanja*, without his presence during the funeral rituals, the soul (*atman*) of the deceased *mamu* cannot find peace (*shanti*). This hints at the high esteem in which a *bhanja* is held among the Aghrias. An Aghria-proverb says: 'To feed a Brahmin is more valuable than feeding

100 cows. But to feed a *bhanja* is more valuable than feeding 100 Brahmins.' This indicates that a *bhanja* is elevated to a position even higher than a Brahmin which may also hint at priest-like functions of the sister's son in a social context in which a Brahmin, representing caste society, has not as yet been fully established or in which both Brahmin and *bhanja* co-exist in their ritual roles.

Within the region, however, and particularly Adivasi communities—in contrast to north India—the role of the *bhanja* seems to be not as unique as it may appear at first glance. Elwin (1945) mentions in his description of funerary rites in Bastar the necessary presence of a *bhanja* among Bison-horn Maria Gond. Apart from a ritual specialist the sister's son is seen as the 'chief actor' (Elwin 1945: 95). As part of his obligations he 'climbs up to the roof and makes a hole which is intended symbolically to allow the message of death to spread out through the world' (ibid.); he beats on the drums and finally—and probably most importantly—'he sits on the *uraskal* [the memorial menhir—US] while it is being carried to its hole; he makes the appointed offerings before the stone; he kills the sacrificial and festal cow' (ibid.). In bringing the menhir for the ultimate peace of the deceased, it is the sister's son 'who plays a leading part' (Elwin 1945: 113) because he 'touches the stone and addresses the dead man. "In your name," he says, "we are bringing this stone; . . ."' (ibid.).[49]

The *bhanja* guides the deceased into the world beyond and transforms the mother's brother into an ancestor. His role in funerary rites is complementary to the role of his mother's brother in helping his *bhanja* into the world or to become a complete social person. Generalizing this result and combining it with the basic tetradic model suggested by Allen (1986), the diagonal link within the four sections or the relation to the closest affinal relative of the adjacent generation is certainly of the utmost importance in life cycle rituals not only among Aghrias, who might have adopted a pattern found among their neighbours, specifically the 'village founders'.[50]

The importance of a sister's son's presence in all these cases also seems to stand in contrast to cases cited by Parry and Bloch in which 'the avoidance of exchange constructs the image of permanence' (Bloch/Parry 1982: 32) and in which eternity seems to be symbolized by an 'end of affinity' (ibid.: 27). Among the Aghria the *bhanja*—or the presence of a close affinal relative of an adjacent generation in the wider sense—may hint at a continuity of kinship ties or affinal links beyond death, which is linked to the practiced cross-cousin marriage in which the sister's son is ideally the daughter's husband and son-in-law.

The rule of cross-cousin marriage has been widely practiced, with a preference for the matrilateral cross-cousin (MBD)—a custom the Aghrias share with many Scheduled Tribes in their immediate vicinity such as the Kondhs, being themselves one of the northernmost cases of peasants practising this type of marriage. Aghrias claim that apart from the *bhanja dan* the biggest gift a mother's brother can give to his sister's son is *kanya dan*, the gift of his daughter. By offering a daughter, a mother's brother earns not just religious merits (*puniya*), but the biggest merit possible—the *mahapuniya*. Earning this merit is regarded as a way to reach *mukti* or salvation, the ultimate goal of leaving the cycle of birth and rebirth.

However, given the frequent occurrence of the sickle cell anemia—a genetic defect which may lead to a potential breakdown of certain organs such as the heart and lungs (Dey 1997: 1–3)—many educated Aghrias try to avoid cross-cousin marriages today and prefer structurally and spatially rather distant marriages. Medical doctors tend to recommend non-kin marriages as well. This does not mean that cross-cousin marriages are arranged no more, but only that social change is imminent here and Aghrias no longer *prefer* cross-cousin marriage as they used to do in the past. Yet, cross-cousin marriages are possible and in no way prohibited as in most of north Indian.

Apart from matrilateral cross-cousin marriage, the empirical data show that another type of marriage, i.e. a delayed sister exchange or marriage with a *sangat* (ZHZ/BWZ), occurs frequently. In contrast to matrilateral cross-cousins, it is not formulated as a rule in the sense that someone can earn *mahapuniya*, such as a *mamu* (MB) giving his daughter for this kind of delayed sister-exchange. In this case marriage relations are not only repeated diachronically, but also in one's own generation or generation-set, or synchronically. Furthermore, marrying a certain *sangat* (BWZ) implies a repetition of the marriage direction, i.e. accepting a wife from a wife-giver family, as in the case of the mother's brother's daughter marriage or wife's younger sister marriage. Marrying a *sangat* (ZHZ) may also mean reciprocal exchange. However, while marrying a BWZ occurs in several regions of north India and even marrying a ZHZ is not uncommon, though often despised (Parry 1979: 287–8; Conzelmann 1996: 323), the Aghria difference is the fact that in their case a marriage preference is explicit and the category *sangat* equates BWZ and ZHZ.[51] Taking into account the case of the Juang who, as McDougal (1963: 162) pointed out, have a high rate of marrying into the SbSpSb-category, one may argue that a repetition of marriage relations within the same generation/generation-set is not just valued as affinity (Dumont 1983), but that this category of relatives—or SbSpZ, who might be termed co-sister-in-law in a male perspective—is of importance in the region and may even define a certain sub-regional pattern in this specific 'contact zone', i.e. in the northern Mahanadi area of Middle India (Skoda 2009).[52]

Apart from a continuity of affinal ties highlighted in the role of the *bhanja,* a continuity of the local line—lineality—is very prominent in the life cycle, e.g. in the role of the eldest son as chief mourner. This is illustrated by the construction of small tombs or *samadhi* for the deceased—to store their bones to be immersed into the Ganga later on. New *samadhi* are usually built next to the other tombs of the family symbolizing the descent group. Such a *samadhi,* built for each separately ancestor, stands in contrast to the postulated 'lack of individuality in Brahmanical conceptions of the after-life' (Michaels 1999: 127–8) or the destruction of the individual after death in Hinduism, 'where nothing of the individual is preserved which could provide a focal symbol of group continuity' (Bloch/Parry 1982: 36). By retaining an individual *samadhi* the deceased might keep a limited individuality, which is comparable to traditions of some autochthonous groups such as the Kondhs where 'shape and size of the memory stones are selected according to certain calculations on the basis of male/female and social–status considerations' (Nayak 2001: 44). Thus, the dead may keep individual aspects even after the final burial and their transition to the status of ancestors.

In addition to these central sets of relations—mother's brother/ sister's son and father/son from a male perspective—two oppositions are prominently expressed in life cycle rituals: adjacent versus alternate generation and *jati* standing for 'other clans' versus *bansa* or the category for 'own clan'. Particularly, the former is explicitly expressed during wedding rituals and in the kinship terminology (see Skoda 2005) and here Aghrias, once again, deviate from a rather well-known north Indian standard. They rather share life cycle and kinship practices with their neighbours in the 'contact zone' to which the overlapping ties and links between persons, families and communities described above certainly contribute. Some relations such as the services of the Brahmins, barber, etc., rather separate or hierarchise parts of the village or different groups of migrants and 'first settlers', while other links, such as ritual friendship, unite otherwise unrelated or particularized categories. However, it is noteworthy and perhaps a specific feature of a 'middle ground', that none of the relationships introduced here simply distinguishes or identifies communities—even the services of Brahmins bring together so-called 'good people' and excludes others at the same time, while ritual friendships unite persons across boundaries though the choice is partly influenced by the very same type of boundaries.

Conclusion

Having migrated into rather remote and sparsely populated areas of north-western Odisha Aghria peasants positioned themselves in their own mythology as on a frontier, i.e. away from or between two centres, the place of origin from where they had to escape after resisting orders and the centre of *dharma*, where Lord Jagannath resides and ruled that instead of being warriors, they should drive bullocks and turn to ploughing or more generally to agriculture. Moreover, they locate themselves between hierarchical antipodes of caste society, but completely ignore their more autochthonous neighbours. In this way, they firmly emphasize their 'rootedness' in caste society and claim a higher status in the past, while avoiding any statements on co-residents.

However, while establishing their rule on the village level, becoming Gauntia (headmen or 'village kings'), they patronized local deities and used symbols and idioms such as the *khunt* appealing to the 'village founders'. Accommodating earlier settlers as ritual specialists for the village goddess, rather than fully dominating appears to have been a feature of a 'middle ground' that evolved and seems to be reflected in ritual practices. At the same time Aghrias were more integrated into asymmetrical power relations in emerging princely states in nineteenth and early twentieth century, e.g. transferring revenue collected by them, than Adivasi communities which had already settled in the area and used to be rather loosely linked, i.e. through rituals to the 'little kings', while Aghrias rather replicated royal models on the village level occupying a central position in it.

The pioneers of the plough did not just promote new techniques of cultivation, but also forged and were entangled in a web of links cutting across the boundaries of communities: 'first settlers', migrating peasants, late-coming Adivasi, or service castes. More personal forms of interaction, e.g. ritual friendships or symbolic selling of children—often actively sought—co-existed and co-exist with a local caste hierarchy ascribing a relatively high status to village founding communities similar to the Aghria status being expressed in terms of purity and seniority. However, Aghrias did not just engage in a multitude of cross-cutting cleavages, their own practices in the sphere of kinship and life cycle rituals seem to have been altered in the process. The position of the sister's son or *bhanja*, being held in high esteem, not just as potential son-in-law, but almost in a priestly function, is highly unusual for peasants further north and may serve as a point in case here as a practice shared with many other communities in a 'contact zone'.

Under colonial and royal encouragement Aghrias commenced their migration into rather thick jungle areas of the former princely states in present north-west Odisha. Around 150 years ago they started as plough-wielding peasants—the plough being the first and foremost sign of more intensive agricultural technique, i.e. wet-rice cultivation, but also—at least initially—a measurement for revenue collected as plough tax. Thus, the plough is also a code for an administration trying to extend the revenue base and for a princely state itself increasingly penetrating remote areas with the help of pioneers such as the Aghrias, who also worship the plough as central tool. In the aftermath of this migration process a certain 'middle ground' emerged as a power balance in an early phase, but also as cultural practices shared in this 'contact zone' by various communities—autochthonous or immigrated; peasants, Adivasi cultivators or service castes.

Notes

1. Schwerin further argues that the autochthonous population did not decrease in absolute, but only in relative numbers. Similarly Rothermund (1978: 4) did not find evidence of a large-scale transfer of peasants from overpopulated areas to cultivable wasteland, but rather saw a spill-over from neighbouring areas.

2. I conducted my 18 months long field research among Aghrias in Kuchinda Block of Sambalpur District (formerly belonging to the princely state of Bamra) between 2000 and 2003 and visited Aghrias in Sundargarh District (former Gangpur State) frequently during this period. Besides, there is a large concentration of Aghrias in Bolangir district of Odisha and in neighbouring Chhattisgarh which I cannot include here.

3. The Paudi Bhuyans or 'Hill Bhuyans' in the neighbouring princely state of Bonai, site of my present research, may serve as a case in point. They are linked to the state by bringing their goddess to the Raja for a day during Dossehra, before returning back to the hills. Otherwise state influence remained limited and accurate settlements did not take place during state-time. However, in other cases such as the Mundas there have been tendencies of state formation.

4. He related this distinction tribe and state to the contrast between war and peace. War should be understood here in the sense Hobbes had attached to the term 'Warre'—that is, as the absence of an institutionally guaranteed peace, i.e. 'the right to use force and do "battell". . . is held by the people in severalty' (Sahlins 1968: 5). Feuds among the Dongria Kondh of South Odisha as described by Nayak (1989) seem to exemplify Sahlins's observations. The term 'tribe', however, appears to be particularly complex in India,

where analytical concepts, such as Sahlins', overlap with administrative categories such as 'Scheduled Tribes'.

5. As White (1991: xiv) pointed out such an approach is always biased in favour of a certain 'upstreaming', i.e. a stressing of continuity instead of historical ruptures.

6. Throughout the chapter I am using the spelling Kondhs, Bhuyans and the like as my Aghria hosts do. However, I am aware that there are other spellings depending on the regions, historical periods and other factors.

7. Concerning this term see Sinha 1966 (cited in Urhahn 1985: 58), Kurin (1997) and Pfeffer (1997: 13).

8. Kurin (1997: 19) had once described cultural brokerage as a 'strategic brokering': 'Strategic brokers are symbolic analysts—they manipulate symbols, they simplify reality into abstract images, which are rearranged, juggled, experimented with, communicated to others, and then transformed back into reality.'

9. In spite of these major changes in recent history, the region is still regarded as a predominantly 'tribal area' today as indicated by the fact that Sundargarh district forms a reserved constituency, since around 55 per cent of the whole population in Kuchinda Block belong to 'Scheduled Tribes'. For population figures see: www.Odishagov.nic.in/census, accessed on 12 March 2003.

10. For similar processes of creolization in the Caribbean see Glissant 2005.

11. I use the term mythology here—in the sense of myths as sacred narratives (Leach 1991: 66), since it is said that the *Disandhri*, as bards, traditionally used to tell these stories only in a ceremonial context and were entitled to gifts. However, there is no clear-cut distinction between mythology and history. Myths may very well contain a 'historical core' which might be termed historical if it can be cross-checked with other independent sources (ibid.).

12. On the term *mandla* and its use in Puri see Kulke (2001 [1987a]: 154).

13. This double transmission of mythology itself, written versus oral versions, may lead—or may have led to contradictions in the texts or, rather, express existing conflicts as Goody and Watt (1986 [1968]: 93) remarked. According to them, the emergence of a literal tradition is often related to the realization of contradictions between various texts, while an oral tradition might be more easily adaptable to changing conditions within society.

14. Lévi-Strauss (1996 [1980]: 171) had already emphasized the importance of retaining a certain heterogeneity of myths while presenting them in order to avoid any imposed homogeneity. A variety of mythical forms rather helps to understand their transformation.

15. One of the two important lines of Kshatriya-descent. For the Mahabharat as epic of the Candravamsa see Thapar (2002 [1992]: 788).

16. The various versions differ in details. See Skoda (2005).

17. For *ksatra–dharma* see, e.g. Zimmermann (1987: 184).

18. The term is borrowed from Kulke (2001 [1976]). For further examples of the widespread phenomena of caste mobility and castes aspiring a higher status

by adopting a Kshatriya-model see also Rowe (1968a, 1968b). For social mobility in the wider perspective see also Dumont (1980 [1966]: 196).

19. The theme of decline in low caste myths is quite frequent and occasionally combined with own decisions leading to the fall (see also O'Flaherty (1988 [1976]: 19–21).

20. For the Brahmanical ideal of non-dependence at which the entire ideal-typical life of a Brahmin is aimed, see van der Veen (1973: 47ff). For a similarly ambivalent relation between Rajput and their bards in western India see Basu (2004).

21. For critical remarks on the structural interpretation of myths see, e.g. Douglas (1988 [1968]: 61ff) who explicitly rejects reductions of meanings by imposing binary oppositions, or Burridge (1988 [1968]: 109) additionally advocating a meaningful dialogue between culture and myth.

22. For the stick as royal symbol see Hardenberg (2000: 21).

23. Trautmann related the conundrum to two types of exchange: sacred versus profane and noble versus ignoble. For multiple hierarchies resulting from these overlapping patterns of classification see also Basu (2004).

24. Lévi-Strauss (1985: 239ff) also argued that myths may express or 'communicate' options, theoretical solutions or models for certain societal problems out of which one may be chosen by the society.

25. Some Leunia rationalize the peculiar custom of their clan by stating that they were the leaders of the Aghrias trying to escape, but other Aghrias do not agree.

26. For a very similar myth see Rowe (1968a).

27. Interestingly, some Aghrias acknowledge that until recently their forefathers had performed funerary rites for their mythical supporters, but nowadays most Aghrias deny such a practice which they probably conceive as degrading.

28. Thus, I found an undated pamphlet, probably an early publication of the *Aghria samaj* titled 'Why Aghria do not accept food from Brahmins?' describing how the Brahmins let the Aghrias down by not supporting their fight against Muslims.

29. For example, leather buckets to pump water and to carry it to the fields.

30. For the values of inside and the potential pollution of being outside in present Odisha, see Strümpell 2006.

31. Schwerin (1977: 28ff) showed that by 1875 the British had started to take up measures to protect the remaining forests in Chotanagpur by declaring certain jungles as 'Reserved Forests'. Similar laws were passed in the princely states with a certain delay.

32. For a similar process, see Dirks 1992.

33. *Touzi* is understood as the process of revenue collection.

34. There are three different types of ponds constructed in relation to the environmental conditions. For a *bandha* type of pond four walls have to be built, for a *munda* only three artificial walls and for a *kata,* only one or two

walls have to be erected to dam up the water.

35. Pocock (1962: 81ff) noted, that prior to Wiser's work the term *jajman* was less accepted and never universally known or used in India, instead the neutral term client was en vogue. However, I use the term as an emic one.

36. For a change or perhaps continuum of rice and millet cultivation, see also Gregory (2003).

37. For various kinds of axe-cultivation see Elwin (1942: 9). In some, though not all types ploughs are used to mix the ash with the soil after burning, while in other cases it is taboo 'to lacerate the breasts of Mother Earth with the plough' (1942: 9). However, during his tour in 1942 Elwin diagnosed a harmful damage to the forest over the last twenty years 'because the Bhuiyas have learnt the use of the plough and begun to keep plough-cattle on a large scale' (1942: 10), i.e. they started rather recently then to combine shifting cultivation with the use of ploughs. Interestingly, Bailey (1960: 63ff) noted that Kondhs further south believe that they were axe-cultivators originally knowing nothing of irrigated rice cultivation, which like the plough was introduced by Oriya from the Mahanadi valley. Significantly in Bonai—a princely state sharing a border with Bamra—during the Settlement in 1910–13 it was noted, that the areas of the Paudi Bhuyans, i.e. those Bhuyans staying in the hills as the most inaccessible tracts of the state, were left out of the Settlement and the plough tax remained. Even after another Settlement 1930–4 only 27 villages were measured and assessed, while 39 villages were left as before. That also indicates that at least some ploughs must have been in use in those villages—though in some remote places villagers may have evaded taxation completely. However, the reason given for leaving out these areas of the Settlement even after 1934 was that they were 'not so well advanced in wet cultivation' (Final Report on the Nayabadi Settlement Operations of Bonai State 1962: 3). Thus, a few wet rice fields may have been cultivated, e.g. in riverbeds even in the hills and slash-and-burn cultivation and wet-rice cultivation may not have been mutually exclusive, yet shifting cultivation appears to have dominated largely even during the later Settlement and is—contrary to the best efforts of certain administrators—still practised. In contrast to that, Aghrias engaged—apart from a few other crops—almost exclusively in rice and specifically wet-rice cultivation. For them shifting cultivation was not an option, while for their neighbours it was rather a 'way of life' than a form of agriculture Elwin (1942: 20). To summarize, axe-cultivation and plough-cultivation was certainly not a clear-cut opposition, but in tendency Aghrias were apparently much more oriented towards ploughing and wet-rice cultivations than the Hill Bhuyans.

38. Two plough rituals are performed among Aghrias: one known as *Harli Uans* or *Nangala Puja* in the month of *Sraban* and the other one called *Akshya Trutiya* in the month of Baisakha. On both occasions the plough and other agricultural instruments are worshipped by the women of the house,

though only the former may properly called 'plough puja' locally. The instruments are placed under the eaves of the inner yard near the kitchen—a place also associated with ancestors.

39. As Marglin (1989 [1985]: 300) noted in relation to the Gajapati: royal power is sakti–power and every Gajapati is 'symbolically infused with the female procreative powers'.

40. Roy (1999 [1928]: 50) speaks particularly of nature–spirits. In contrast to that ancestor–spirits are represented by stones.

41. I borrowed the term from Kulke (1979: 18).

42. While Pfeffer argues that the opposition is linked to seniority with the seniors always being of higher status, but not primarily to purity, Kolenda links the first dichotomy, i.e. *uncha* (high) versus *nicha* (low) directly to pollution and the second one, i.e. *bari* (big) versus *choti* (little) to politico-economic power and force.

43. Though the term Harijan (literally 'children of god') as euphemism created by Gandhi is sometimes used to refer to all so-called 'Untouchables', in north-western Odisha the term Harijan more specifically designates a community that used to be engaged in weaving. In some cases people still use their old and very derogatory name Ganda. They consider themselves to be different from the leatherworkers or Chamars, who are sometimes also known by the name Mochi. Though both communities are regarded by others as 'untouchable', Harijans do not engage in leatherwork and therefore claim a superior status to the Chamars.

44. In yet another, very general sense *bhal lok* is used to signify all people, who are neat and clean, that is, all who keep themselves as well as their household spotless. So if one wishes to underline the observation that a certain member of a community keeps stricter standards of hygiene than another one, one could say that he is a *bhal lok* compared to the others. *Bad lok* may also denote material wealth, which was perhaps implied in the above mentioned remarks of the Luhura, since the performance of rituals—related to status—requires wealth. Most—though not all—high status communities are at the same time relatively rich.

45. Only Elwin (2000 [1936]: 18), Grigson (1991 [1938]) and Roy (1999 [1928]) have briefly hinted at such as custom.

46. Unstandardized measurement for paddy/rice—varying between 100 and 425 kg.

47. For example, see Kulke (2001 [1978]: 5).

48. If there is no close *bhanja* a distant, classificatory *bhanja* will replace him.

49. See also Fuchs (1960: 337) for the tribal Gonds and Bhumias and Fürer-Haimendorf (1979: 370ff) for Gonds of Andhra Pradesh. Similar ideas are also expressed among 'tribal' Rai (Gaenszle 1999) and Magar (Oppitz 1991) of Nepal, where the sister's son plays an important role which is comparable to the Aghrias.

50. However, significant differences may remain compared to other middle Indian tribal communities, for example, to the Sora as described by Vitebsky (1993).

51. Marrying a BWZ is often acceptable in several regions of north India and even exchange marriages (which in effect can mean marrying a ZHZ) are practised by certain communities, though despised by others (see, e.g. Parry 1979: 287–8; Conzelmann 1996: 323). However, there is a fundamental difference here related to the category. In Hindi BWZ belongs to the category *sali* (also WZ), while there is no term for ZHZ (see Trautmann 1995 [1981]: 94–101; also Parry 1979: 299 on the missing term for ZHZ, but apparently BWZ is absent in his list too).

52. Gell (1992: 136) mentions that in Muria Society 'direct exchange of sisters is forbidden' and thus hints at a different pattern south of the Mahanadi River crossing Odisha and Chhattisgarh from north-west to south-east.

References

Allen, N., 'Tetradic Theory: An Approach to Kinship', *Journal of the Anthropological Society of Oxford*, vol. 17, no. 2, 1986, pp. 87–109.

Assmann, J., *Das kulturelle Gedächtnis. Schrift, Erinnerung und politische Identität in frühen Hochkulturen*, München: Beck'sche reihe, 1999.

Bailey, F.G., *Tribe, Caste and Nation*, Manchester: Manchester University Press, 1960.

Basu, H., *Von Barden und Königen: Ethnologische Studien zur Göttin und zum Gedächtnis in Kacch (Indien)*, Frankfurt/M.: Peter Lang, 2004.

Baumann, G., 'Dominant and Demotic Discourses of Culture: Their Relevance to Multi-ethnic Alliances', in *Debating Cultural Hybridity: Multi-Cultural Identities and the Politics of Anti-Racism*, ed. P. Werbner and T. Modood, London: Zed Books, 1997, pp. 209–25.

Bennett, L., *Dangerous Wives and Sacred Sisters*, New York: Columbia University Press, 1983.

Berger, P., 'Gesellschaft, Ritual und Ideologie, Eine relationale Betrachtung der Gadaba des Koraput Distriktes, Orissa', *Mitteilungen der Berliner Gesellschaft für Anthropologie, Ethnologie und Urgeschichte*, vol. 21, 2000, pp. 15–28.

Berkemer, G., *Little Kingdoms in Kalinga: Ideologie, Legitimation und Politik Regionaler Eliten*, Stuttgart: Franz Steiner, 1993.

Bloch, M. and J.P. Parry, 'Introduction: Death and the Regeneration of Life', in *Death and the Regeneration of Life*, ed. M. Bloch and J. Parry, Cambridge: Cambridge University Press, 1982, pp. 1–44.

Burke, P., 'Geschichte als soziales Gedächtnis', in *Mnemosyne: Formen und Funktionen der kulturellen Erinnerung*, ed. A. Assmann and D. Harth, Frankfurt/M.: Fischer, 1993, pp. 289—304.

Burridge, K.O.L., 'Lévi-Strauss and Myth', in *The Structural Study of Myth and*

Totemism (A.S.A. Monographs 5), ed. E. Leach, London: Tavistock, 1988 [1968], pp. 91–118.

Choudhury, N.C., *Munda Social Structure*, Calcutta: KLM, 1977.

Cohn, B.S., 'Political Systems in Eighteenth Century India: The Banares Region', in *An Anthropologist among the Historians and Other Essays*, ed. B. Cohn, Delhi: Oxford University Press, 2001 [1962], pp. 483–99.

Conzelmann, E., *Heirat, Gabe, Status. Kaste und Gesellschaft in Mandi*, Berlin: Arabisches Buch, 1996.

Dey, A., 'Sickle Cell Gene: Its Pattern of Distribution and Association with Natural Selection', Ph.D. Dissertation, University of Sambalpur, 1997.

Dirks, N.B., 'The Structure and Meaning of Political Relations in a South Indian Little Kingdom', *Contributions to Indian Sociology*, n.s., vol. 13, no. 2, 1979, pp. 169–206.

———, 'From Little King to Landlord: Colonial Discourse and Colonial Rule', in *Colonialism and Culture*, ed. N. Dirks, Ann Arbor: The University of Michigan Press, 1992, pp. 175–208.

Douglas, M., 'The Meaning of Myth: With Special Reference to "La Geste d' Asdiwal"', in *The Structural Study of Myth and Totemism* (A.S.A. Monographs 5), ed. E. Leach, London: Tavistock, 1988 [1968], pp. 49–70.

Dumont, L., *Homo Hierarchicus: The Caste System and Its Implications*, Chicago: Chicago University Press, 1980 [1966].

———, *Affinity as a Value*, Delhi: Oxford University Press, 1983.

Elwin, V., *Leaves from the Jungle: Life in a Gond Village*, New Delhi: Oxford University Press, 2000 [1936].

———, *Report of a tour in the Bonai, Keonjhar & Pal Lahara States*, Mazagaon: The British India Press, 1942.

———, 'Funerary Customs in Bastar State', *Man in India*, vol. XXV, no. 2, 1945, pp. 87–133.

Eschmann, A., 'Sign and Icon: Symbolism in the Indian Folk Religion', in *Religion and Society in Eastern India*, ed. G.C. Tripathi and H. Kulke, New Delhi: Manohar, 1994 [1975], pp. 211–33.

Falk, N.E., 'Wilderness and Kingship in Ancient South Asia', *History of Religions*, vol. 13, no. 1, 1973, pp. 1–15.

Final Report on Nayabadi Settlement Operations in Bonai State, Berhampur: Sarada Press, 1962.

Fuchs, S., *The Gond and Bhumia of Eastern Mandla*, London: Asia Publishing, 1960.

Fürer-Haimendorf, C.V., *The Gonds of Andhra Pradesh: Tradition and Change in an Indian Tribe*, New Delhi: Vikas, 1979.

Gaenszle, M., 'The Making of Good Ancestors. Separation, Transformation and Exchange, in Mewahang Rai Funerary Rites', in *Ways of dying. Death and its Meanings in South Asia*, ed. E. Schömbucher and C.P. Zoller, New Delhi: Manohar, 1999, pp. 49–67.

Galey, J.C., 'Reconsidering Kingship in India: An Ethnological Perspective', in

Kingship and the Kings, ed. J.C. Galey, Chur: Harwood Academic Publishers, 1990, pp. 123–87.

Gell, S.M.S., *The Ghotul in Muria Society*, Chur: Harwood, 1992.

Gellner, E., *Pflug, Schwert und Buch. Grundlinien der Menschheitsgeschichte*, München: dtv, 1993 [1988].

Glissant, E., *Kultur und Identität. Ansätze zu einer Poetik der Vielheit*, Heidelberg: Wunderhorn, 2005.

Goody, J. and I. Watt, 'Konsequenzen der Literalität', in *Entstehung und Folgen der Schriftkultur*, ed. J. Goody, I. Watt and K. Gough, Frankfurt/M.: Suhrkamp, 1986 [1968], pp. 45–104.

Gregory, C.A., 'The Oral Epics of the Women of the Dandakaranya Plateau: A Preliminary Mapping', *Journal of Social Sciences* (Special Issue: 'Orissan Studies', ed. C. Mallebrein and L. Guzy), vol. 8, no. 2, 2003, pp. 93–104.

Grigson, W., *The Maria Gonds of Bastar*, Delhi: Vanya Prakashan, 1991 [1938].

Hardenberg, R., *Die Wiedergeburt der Götter: Ritual und Gesellschaft in Orissa*, Hamburg: Kovac, 1999.

———, *Die Ideologie eines Hindu-Königtums: Struktur und Bedeutung der Rituale des Königs von Puri' Orissa/Indien*, Berlin: Arabisches Buch, 2000.

Jeffrey P., 'Identifying Differences: Gender Politics and Religious Community in Rural Uttar Pradesh', in *Invented Identities: The Interplay of Gender, Religion and Politics in India*, ed. J. Leslie and M. McGee, Oxford: Oxford University Press, 2000, pp. 286–309.

Kapadia, K., *Siva & her Sisters, Gender, Caste, and Class in Rural South India*, Delhi: Oxford University Press, 1996.

Kolenda, P., *Caste, Cult and Hierarchy, Essays on the Culture of India*, Meerut: Folklore Institute, 1983.

Kulke, H., 'Ksatriyaization and Social Change: A Study in the Orissan Setting', in *Kings and Cults: State Formation and Legitimation in India and Southeast Asia*, ed. H. Kulke, New Delhi: Manohar, 2001 [1976], pp. 82–92.

———, *Jagann"atha-Kult und Gajapati-Königtum. Ein Beitrag zur Geschichte religiöser Legitimation hinduistischer Herrscher*, Wiesbaden: Franz Steiner, 1979.

———, 'The Chronicles and the Temple Records of the M"adal"a P"anji of Puri: A Reassessment of the Evidence, in *Kings and Cults: State Formation and Legitimation in India and Southeast Asia*, ed. H. Kulke, New Delhi: Manohar, 2001 [1987a], pp. 137–58.

———, 'Reflections on the Sources of the Temple Chronicles of the M"adal"a P"anji of Puri', in *Kings and Cults: State Formation and Legitimation in India and Southeast Asia*, ed. H. Kulke, New Delhi: Manohar, 2001 [1987b], pp. 159–91.

———, 'Tribal Deities at Princely Courts: The Feudatory Rajas of Central Orissa and their Tutelary Deities (istadevatas)', in *Kings and Cults: State Formation and Legitimation in India and Southeast Asia*, ed. H. Kulke, New Delhi: Manohar, 2001 [1993], pp. 114–36.

Kurin, R., *Reflections of a Culture Broker: A View from the Smithsonian*, Washington: Smithsonina Institution Press, 1997.

Leach, E., *Lévi-Strauss: Zur Einführung*, Hamburg: Junius, 1991.

Lévi-Straus, C.,'Die Geschichte des Asdiwal', in *Strukturale Anthropologie II*, Frankfurt/M.: Suhrkamp, 1992 [1973], pp. 169–224.

———, *Mythos und Bedeutung*, Frankfurt/M.: Suhrkamp, 1996 [1980].

———, *Der Blick aus der Ferne*, München: Fink, 1985.

Madan, T.N., *Family and Kinship: A Study of the Pandits of Rural Kashmir*, Delhi: Oxford University Press, 1989 [1965].

Mallebrein, C., 'Tribal Art: Continuity and Change', *Orissa Revisited*, vol. 52, no. 3, 2001, pp. 142–61.

Marglin, F.A., *Wives of the God-King: The Rituals of the Devadasis of Puri*, Delhi: Oxford University Press, 1989 [1985].

Marriott, M., 'Caste Ranking and Food Transactions: A Matrix Analysis', in *Structure and Change in Indian Society*, ed. M. Singer and B.S. Cohn, Chicago: Aldine, 1968, pp. 133–71.

McDougal, C.W., 'The Social Structure of the Hill Juang', Ph.D. Dissertation, University of New Mexico, 1963.

Nayak, P.K., *Blood, Women and Territory: An analysis of Clan Feuds of the Dongria Kondhs*, New Delhi: Reliance, 1989.

———, 'Jagannath and the Adivasis: Reconsidering the Cult and its Traditions', in *Jagannath Revisited: Studying Society, Religion and the State in Orissa*, ed. H. Kulke and B. Schnepel, New Delhi: Manohar, 2001, pp. 25–48.

O'Flaherty, W.D., *The Origins of Evil in Hindu Mythology*, Delhi: Motilal Banarsidass, 1988 [1976].

Oppitz, M., *Onkels Tochter, keine sonst. Heiratsbündnis und Denkweise in einer Lokal-kultur des Himalaya*, Frankfurt/M., 1991.

Parry, J., *Caste and Kinship in Kangra*, New Delhi: Vikas, 1979.

———, *Death in Benares*, Cambridge: Cambridge University Press, 1994.

Pasayat, C., *Tribe, Caste and Folk Culture*, Jaipur: Rawat, 1998.

Pfeffer, G., 'Puri's Vedic Brahmins: Continuity and Change in their Traditional Institutions', in *The Cult of Jagannath*, ed. A. Eschmann, H. Kulke and G.C. Tripathi, New Delhi: Manohar, 1978, pp. 421–37.

———, *Status and Affinity in Middle India*, Wiesbaden: F. Steiner, 1982.

———, 'Gadaba and the Bondo Kinship Vocabularies versus Marriage, Descent and Production', in *Contemporary Society. Tribal Studies, vol. 4: Social Realities*, ed. G. Pfeffer and D.K. Behera, New Delhi: Concept, 1999, pp. 17–46.

———, 'Tribal Ideas', *Journal of Social Sciences* (Special Issue: 'Asian World Views: Context and Structure', ed. R. Hardenberg), vol. 4, no. 4, 2000, pp. 331–46.

———, 'A Ritual of Revival among the Gadaba of Koraput', in *Jagannath Revisited: Studying Society, Religion and the State in Orissa*, ed. H. Kulke and B. Schnepel, New Delhi: Manohar, 2001, pp. 123–48.

Pocock, D.F., 'Inclusion and Exclusion: A Process in the Caste System of Gujarat', *Southwestern Journal of Anthropology*, vol. 13, 1957, pp. 19–31.

———, 'Notes on *Jajmani* Relationships', *Contributions to Indian Sociology*, vol. 6, 1962, pp. 78–95.

Pratt, M.L., *Imperial Eyes: Travel Writing and Transculturation*, London: Routledge, 1992.

Raheja, G.G., *The Poison in the Gift: Ritual, Prestation, and the Dominant Caste in a North Indian Village*, Chicago: University of Chicago Press, 1988.

Randeria, S., 'Mourning, Mortuary Exchange and Memorialization: The Creation of Local Communities among Dalits in Gujarat', in *Ways of Dying: Death and its Meanings in South Asia*, ed. E. Schömbucher and C.P. Zoller, New Delhi: Manohar, 1999, pp. 88–111.

Rösler, M. and T. Wendt, eds., *Frontiers and Borderlands: Anthropological Perspectives*, Frankfurt am Main: P. Lang, 1999.

Rothermund, D., *Government, Landlord, and Peasant in India. Agrarian relations under British rule 1865–1935*, Wiesbaden: Steiner, 1978.

Rowe, W.L., 'The New Cauhāns: A Caste Mobility Movement in North India', in *Social Mobility in the Caste System in India*, ed. J. Silverberg, The Hague: Mouton, 1968a, pp. 66–77.

———, 'Mobility in the Nineteenth Century Caste System', in *Structure and Change in Indian Society*, ed. M. Singer and B.S. Cohn, Chicago: Aldine, 1968b, pp. 201–207.

Roy, S.C., *The Mundas and their Country*, London: Asia Publishing House, 1970 [1912].

———, *Oraon Religion and Customs*, New Delhi: Gyan Publishing House, 1999 [1928].

Sahlins, M.D., 'On the Sociology of Primitive Exchange', in *The Relevance of Models for Social Anthropology (A.S.A. Monographs 1)*, ed. M. Banton, London: Tavistock, 1965, pp. 185–230.

Sahlins, M.D., *Tribesmen*, Englewood Cliffs: Foundations of Modern Anthropology Series, 1968.

———, 'Two or Three Things That I Know About Culture', *Journal of the Royal Anthropological Institute*, n.s., vol. 5, 1999, pp. 399–421.

Schnepel, B., 'Kings and Rebel Kings: Rituals of Incorporation and Dissent in South Asia', in *Jagannath Revisited: Studying Society, Religion and the State in Orissa*, ed. H. Kulke and B. Schnepel, New Delhi: Manohar, 2001, pp. 271–95.

———, *Jungle Kings: Ethnohistorical Aspects of Politics and Ritual in Orissa*, New Delhi: Manohar, 2002.

Schwerin, D., *Von Armut zu Elend: Kolonialherrschaft und Agrarverfassung in Chota Nagpur, 1858–1908*, Wiesbaden: Steiner, 1977.

Skoda, U., *The Aghria. A Peasant Caste on a Tribal Frontier*, Delhi: Manohar, 2005.

———, 'Delayed Sister-Exchange in Middle India: A Preliminary Sketching of Co-Sister-in-law- and Granddaughters-marriage among the Aghriaa and Neighbouring Communities', in *Tribal Studies*, ed. G. Pfeffer and D.K. Behera, vol. 7, 2009.

Sontheimer, G.D., 'The Vana and the Ksetra: The Tribal Background of Some Famous Cults', in *Religion and Society in Eastern India*, ed. G.C. Tripathi and H. Kulke, New Delhi: Manohar, 1994, pp. 117–64.

Stein, B., 'The State and the Agrarian Order in Medieval South Asia: A Historiographical Critique', in *Essays on South India*, ed. B. Stein, Hawaii: University Press of Hawaii, 1975, pp. 64–91.

Strümpell, C., *Wir arbeiten zusammen, wir essen zusammen*, Münster: Lit, 2006.

Thapar, R., 'Origin Myths and the Early Indian Historical Tradition', in *Cultural Pasts*, Delhi: Oxford University Press, 2002 [1978], pp. 754–81.

———, 'Clan, Caste and Origin Myths in Early India', in *Cultural Pasts*, Delhi: Oxford University Press, 2002 [1992], pp. 782–96.

Thapar, R. and M.H. Siddiqi, 'Tribals in History: The Case of Chota Nagpur', in *Social Stratification*, ed. D. Gupta, Delhi: Oxford University Press, 1997 [1979].

Trautmann, T.R., *Dravidian Kinship*, New Delhi: Vistaar, 1995 [1981].

Troisi, J., *Tribal Religion. Religious Beliefs and Practices among the Santals*, Delhi: Manohar, 2000 [1979].

Urhahn, M., 'Grenzen und Übergänge von Kasten und Stammesgesellschaft in Indien', Ph.D. Dissertation, University of Heidelberg, 1985.

Vatuk, S., 'A Structural Analysis of the Hindi Kinship Terminology', in *Contributions to Indian Sociology*, n.s., vol.3, 1969, pp. 94–115.

Voll, K., *Against Child Labour: Indian and International Dimensions and Strategies*, New Delhi: Mosaic, 1999.

Weber, M., *Gesammelte Aufsätze zur Religionssoziologie II*, Tübingen: UTB, 1988 [1921].

Werbner, P., 'Introduction: The Dialectics of Cultural Hybridity', in *Debating Cultural Hybridity. Multi-Cultural Identities and the Politics of Anto-Racism*, ed. P. Werbner and T. Modood, London: Zed Books, 1997, pp. 1–28.

White, R., *The Middle Ground: Indians, Empires, and Republics in the Great Lakes Region, 1650–1815*, Cambridge: Cambridge University Press, 1991.

Wolf, E.R., *Peasants*, Englewood Cliffs: Foundations of Modern Anthropology, 1966.

Zimmermann, F., *The Jungle and the Aroma of Meats*, Berkeley: University of California Press, 1987.

9   A Steel Town in the 'Wilderness'
Industry, State and Empire in Western Odisha

CHRISTIAN STRÜMPELL

Introduction

With around 550,000 inhabitants, Rourkela is the largest town in western Odisha.[1] It lies in the north-western border region of the union state, a mere 20 km. away from Jharkhand and roughly 60 km. from Chhattisgarh. It is an industrial town designed by government agencies on a drawing table. It was built in the 1950s to host the managers, engineers and workers of the Rourkela Steel Plant (RSP), India's first public sector steel plant. Political scientist Srirupa Roy emphasizes that the significance of Rourkela and other state-planned 'new towns' that have come up around the same time in Bhilai, Durgapur, Bokaro and numerous other places is the very fact that they were located in an 'elsewhere', far from the large metropolitan centres of colonial India. This peripheral location 'offered the nation-state an opportunity to realize its vision from scratch' (Roy 2007: 134). That vision was to establish steel mills and townships, considered as places of modernity par excellence, in India's internal peripheries and to thereby integrate these 'elsewheres' closer into the new-found nation-state; at the same time, these places would produce special people, modern industrial workers who transcend their many 'primordial' and allegedly divisive identities of caste, community, and language-based ethnicity, thereby setting an example of how the citizenry as a whole was to be integrated into the new nation-state.

In this chapter I also aim to critically engage with Rourkela's spatiality. Drawing on my ethnographic research in Rourkela[2] I will first show that the place was not merely an 'elsewhere', but that workers and engineers building mill and township in the 1950s remember the place as a wilderness that was to be modernized. Following that I will discuss why the Odisha state perceived this civilizing mission as a threat unless it could foster the assertion of an Odia nation within India, and how the local tribal people or Adivasis struggle since the 1950s against their reproduction as the wild 'other'. Hence, more specifically this article focuses on notions of wilderness prevailing in Rourkela, its (more implicit then explicit) opposites modernity or civilization and on the relations of inequality manifest in them.

Historians of South Asia and indologists have written extensively on Indian notions of 'wilderness' as well as the relations between the *jangal*, *vana* or *aranya*, the 'wild' world of forested hills inhabited by equally 'wild' people and the *kshetra* or *grama*, the 'civilized' world in the plains where states preside over sedentary castes (Heesterman 1985, 1989, 1997; Malamoud 1996 [1989]; Skaria 1997, 1999; Sontheimer 1987; Zimmerman 1987). In principal, these studies agree that in precolonial India these different spheres stood in a relationship of pervasive, agonistic conflict (Skaria 1999), and that they formed as such complementary parts of an encompassing whole (Heesterman 1985, 1997); but that British imperialism radically altered this relationship. The colonial state aimed at taming the 'wild' people behind the subcontinent's 'inner frontiers' (Skaria 1999: 131) thereby rendering relationships across them antagonistic and turning, as Ajay Skaria (1999: 268–81) shows, erstwhile forest chiefs in the course of imperial history into subaltern Adivasis. According to Jan Heesterman (1997: 117), the modern state is conceptually incompatible with inner frontiers and systems of shared sovereignties characterizing empires. Hence, the colonial as well as postcolonial state in India aimed at replacing permeable and dynamic imperial frontiers that connect as much as separate the complementary domains of the wild *aranya* and the settled *grama* by modern static boundaries drawn around nations, regions and communities separating them without any notion of complementarity. However, Heesterman emphasizes that though 'modern' boundaries gained pre-eminence only with colonialism they are in fact not modern at all, that their presence can be traced back even to ancient Indian history (Heesterman 1985: 67ff).[3] Furthermore, he argues that the idea of empire and frontiers periodically re-emerge even in a world divided into nation-states, but he leaves open the question whether this entails the return of a complementary 'wilderness'—as his argument would suggest (Heesterman 1997: 116). Though not directly addressing notions of wilderness, David Ludden (2011, 2012) reconsiders in a couple of articles the on going debate on the contemporary re-emergence of imperialism with regard to Asian contexts[4] and develops a general model on relationships between imperial centres and their frontiers as they unfold particularly in the *longue durée* of South Asian history. Ludden (2011: 135) argues for conceptualizing empire primarily as a process, as 'a kind of power dynamic operating in ranks of systematically patterned inequality' that pervades also contemporary nation-states, and that the frontiers these processes establish are the sites that best reveal specific imperial dynamics (ibid.: 133).[5] He broadly distinguishes in this regard between two modes of the imperial, fusion and fission. The former describes the incorporation of peripheries into a 'unitary framework of centralized imperial management' (ibid.: 139), usually by means of heavy central investments, and the latter denotes imperial processes that are propelled by 'frontier activists' acting largely independently from imperial centres and that leave local elites considerable clout on the trajectory of the imperial incorporation of a region. Ludden (2011: 139f) claims that the histories of China and India present classic examples for imperial fusion and imperial fission respectively, but that both also show temporary reversals of their paradigmatic process of empire. Hence, in India the prevailing pattern of imperial fission was reversed, e.g. after 1857 and 1947 when heavy central investments were undertaken in order to closer integrate internal peripheries into the British Empire or the Republic of India only to return to fissiparous practices later on.

The Rourkela Steel Plant (RSP) as well as Nehru's modernization project in general obviously exemplify the moment of 'imperial fusion' in early postcolonial India. However, the question remains in what ways imperial fission regains prevalence in the decades that follow, as Ludden's generalizing account suggests, and, concomitantly, in what ways contemporary imperial fission differs from its earlier manifestations. Ludden (2011: 140) argues that in the long run fission has always proven to be the dominant imperial process in India, only temporarily interspersed by Moghul, British and nation-statist attempts to pursue fusion, because it valorizes and well adapts to 'environments of extreme local diversity'. This argument, however, brushes over the impact of colonialism that— according to, e.g. Skaria and Heesterman—transformed agonistic relations between 'civilized' centres and 'wild' peripheries into antagonistic ones. Hence, more precisely, the question remains whether the present-day re-emergence of fission also entails the re-evaluation of wild peripheries as complementary parts of imperial or nation-statist centres. It is these questions that I will discuss in this article.

In the first section I will show that the ways construction workers, engineers and contractors remember the place at the time of their arrival in the 1950s reveal striking similarities with characterizations of the 'wilderness' Heesterman discusses in his classic Indological studies, but that this 'wilderness' is to be tamed by industrial modernity, i.e. that the relation to it is antagonistic. In the second section, I turn to the pivotal role the RSP played since its foundation in the late 1950s in the concerns of the government of Odisha to integrate the western hill regions into the state as well as to assert itself within the Indian republic. From the late 1960s onwards the government of Odisha succeeded in gaining decisive clout over people's access to well-rewarded and well-esteemed— and thus, highly sought after—RSP employment by establishing, in Heesterman's terms, a 'modern' boundary regime around it. Thus, imperial fission indeed gains momentum during this period, but, as I aim to show, this does not necessarily entail the valorization of diversity as Ludden suggested. Nevertheless, as I discuss in the third section, there persist in contemporary Rourkela articulate notions that the steel town's surroundings, and to some degree also its slums, constitute 'wildernesses' that are to be tapped, but—in comparison to the idea behind the RSP— tamed only as much as required to guarantee the smooth transfer of resources out of them. Yet the tribal people largely settling in these areas struggle against their 'othering' as 'wild', among other means by demanding the region's incorporation into Jharkhand, Odisha's neighbouring 'tribal'—and thus 'their'—state. This shows, as I conclude, that the idea of empire with its boundaries separating as much as connecting different realms, as Heesterman put it, or with its fissiparous modes of incorporation, as Ludden frames it, indeed returned to Rourkela. As my ethnography further shows, however, under the current conditions and power relations this process looks not as benign as suggested by Heesterman, but rather the contrary. This is at least the case from the vantage point of the tribals or Adivasis living in and around Rourkela, which confirms, I conclude, Ludden's argument on the importance of perspectives from peripheries for a deeper understanding of processes of empire.

The Frontier of Modernity in Rourkela

The Government of India reached the decision to build India's first public sector steel plant at Rourkela on 15 February 1954 after a consortium of West German companies contracted for that purpose had submitted its survey report (Röh 1967: 126). These companies had recommended the site because it had everything a steel plant needs: nearby abundant deposits of iron ore, dolomite, limestone and coal, nearby sufficient water supply, and a railway line that connected the then small settlement Rourkela already since the early twentieth century with Kolkata and Mumbai. Furthermore, Rourkela is situated in Odisha's Sundargarh district that was considered to be among the most underdeveloped and also among the most under-populated parts of India, hence one of her 'elsewheres'.

During my field research fifty years later I could still meet dozens of people who had come to Rourkela in the 1950s and their stories of what the place was like at that time were very similar. The general tone was that they all had come to Rourkela in search for work on or around the gigantic construction site the place had then been and that they had heard about it from official notifications or from relatives or friends who already had found a job here. Employment opportunities or business prospects were very good, or as they describe it, money was 'flying' (*uluchi*) around in Rourkela then. However, despite the abundance of money everybody described the living conditions in 1950s Rourkela as very harsh. People had to live either in one of the temporary mass accommodations the larger contractors provided or in self-built makeshift huts. Wherever they found shelter, they couldn't get much protection against the weather, be it during summer, monsoon or winter. Furthermore, food was then much more expensive than in the villages they had come from; and water was so scarce that people had to pay for it in hotels and had to walk long distances for bathing and washing clothes.

The elderly people who narrated about these times of early settlement had almost all been engaged either as *munzi* (low-ranking supervisors) or, more often, as manual labourers.[6] They all stressed, too, that work on the construction sites was a hard and arduous affair, but that as village-grown people they had been used to work hard for long hours, unlike the urban youth of today. People were of course engaged in different jobs. Thousands of male daily wage labourers, or *kuli*, were levelling the ground, laying rail tracks or concrete fundaments, erecting poles or chimneys or digging out the deep excavations required for ovens and furnaces while the *reja*, their female co-workers, were carrying away the earth in baskets on their heads; others were engaged in unloading material imported from West Germany at the railway station and still others were operating bulldozers or assembling equipment. A *munzi* normally just had to maintain the attendance register and had to see that people work. People were also switching jobs. Prakash C. Sahoo, e.g. worked on construction sites either on what has since then become the company township or where now the steel plant reaches into the sky. Once in a while he got retrenched and ran a small *pan* shop until he found another job as a wage labourer. During the first year of construction, in 1957/8, around 46,000 workers were employed in preparing the ground for the steel plant, township and other infrastructure (Sperling 1963: 22). The whole of Rourkela, at that time, resembled one gigantic construction site and I was often told that to endure life around such a place was not easy. Many people therefore left Rourkela after a short while, either because they couldn't find a job that would sustain their stay or simply because they couldn't bear life in such a place and far away from home.

People also describe Rourkela as a dangerous place then. Around the train station retrenched workers about to leave Rourkela were often lured into the surrounding *bustees* with the promise of further employment and then robbed of their savings. Many people died in accidents on the construction sites, fell off high steel structures, or were crushed by collapsing earthen walls of the excavations. Some elderly workers, like K.C. Panda, a Brahmin who had come to Rourkela in 1957 from a village in Odisha's southern Ganjam district, are convinced that these people died of their greed (*lobha*). To earn more money they worked too much, often also after dusk and were thus more likely to get involved in accidents. Some people also told me that fatal accidents had not always been mere accidents, but were often intentional acts of human sacrifice ordered by contractors to appease local deities. However, unlike in Bhilai, where RSP's sister steel plant was constructed at the same time with Soviet aid (Parry 2008: 233-262), in Rourkela human sacrifices are not a prominent topic when people discuss the steel plant's construction. In Rourkela people remember more vividly the frequent skirmishes between the different ethnic groups that regularly turned into ghastly mob violence. During 1958–9 mobs of Odia workers launched a series of attacks against Punjabi, Madrasi and Bengali migrants in redress for the exploitation and humiliation they suffered from. Odia most often found only employment as unskilled workers whereas their Punjabi, Madrasi and Bengali contractors or RSP officers employed their own countrymen as better-paid skilled workers or machine operators. The main perpetrators behind these riots were Odia *goondas* such as Subash Lenka who had come down to Rourkela from his native town Jamshedpur, India's first 'steel town' a mere three-hour train journey away in neighbouring Bihar (now Jharkhand). However, because of their discontent these *goondas* were easily able to instigate many Odia workers to join the mob. In fact, many Odias still remember the *goondas* as 'heroes' fighting for their cause, though others confided that they were often only racketeers threatening to instigate the crowds against the contractors in case they were not given protection money.[7]

All the trade unions active in Rourkela at that time tried their best to prevent violence and to organize workers across ethnic divides. However, the trade unions competed with each other for workers' support and often did so quite fiercely, which heightened social tensions. The then popular union leaders nevertheless were praised for their integrity and for the hardships they suffered in their fight for workers' rights and many of them are still nowadays venerated by most people in Rourkela. I was often told that Tapas Dutta, the long-time general secretary of a far left union, had given up the career of a grand artist and committed himself instead to face police repression, prison terms and lead a frugal life in closets next to his union office, all for his selfless revolutionary struggle. Similarly, people never tired to tell me that Dhuliswar Bastia, until his death in 1966 the general secretary of the once most powerful 'socialist' union and still Rourkela's most popular labour leader, sacrificed a life of comfort. He is said to have endured life in a shack nearby the RSP, where he sat in a wet, malarious place—'like Shiva on the burial ground' as some people put it—equipped with only a few essentials and his vigour to fight for the cause of the working class.

Elder workers thus describe Rourkela at the time of its birth as Odisha's industrial capital not just a place where Indian and foreign engineers and workers struggled hard to build a modern steel plant-cum-township but also as a place of robbers and protection-racketeers, of itinerant traders and of self-sacrificing unionists resembling renouncers.[8] In this sense, the depictions are remarkably akin to the notion of the 'wilderness', the *aranya*, that is, according to Heesterman (1997: 13), considered in classical texts as the 'world of the warrior, the robber and protection-racketeer, the mercenary, the itinerant trader, the caravaneer and, finally, of the renouncer'. The *aranya* is regarded as a 'wilderness' in relation to the *grāma*, the village or the world of a sedentary peasantry; a relation that is complementary and marked by an inner frontier connecting as well as separating two parts of a whole. This relationship is also complementary in political and economic terms: while the peasantry populating the *grāma* is obliged to provide regular revenues, the semi-independent chieftains making up the uncontrolled interstitial *aranya* pay irregular tributes (Heesterman 1997: 109), and as much as the former partly depends on 'the liquid resources' of the *aranya* '[t]he warrior and trader ... seek an outlet for their accumulated mobile wealth in the productivity of the peasant world' (Heesterman 1989: 13).

It is important to note that the elder workers I talked to never refer to Rourkela back then as an *aranya*. For them it was simply a 'foreign place', a *pardesh*, and it was also an empty place. As they always emphasize, when they arrived 'nothing had been here' (*ethire kichhi no thila*), and it was them who changed that with their hard labour. The wilderness they encountered around the massive construction site does not appear as complementary, neither to their villages of origin nor to the modernity that was to emerge in Rourkela. Rather in contrast, their relationship to this wilderness is antagonistic: it was to be tamed and civilized, and—as their narrative shows—they take great pride in having literally contributed to that with their own hands.

The Modern State in Rourkela

In Heesterman's terms, the events taking place in Rourkela in the 1950s can be described as a replacement of 'inner frontiers' or 'traditional' boundaries by 'modern' ones. The two stand, so Heesterman argues, in sharp contrast because a 'modern' boundary encircles, in a continuous line, a territory that is—conceptually—complete in itself and separates it from equally self-contained, external worlds without any notion of complementary. Despite this 'modernist' terminology, Heesterman (1985: 67f) argues, as already pointed out, the 'modern' boundary is, in fact, quite an ancient phenomenon that comes to the fore in the boundaries established by kings 'from outside the local community' aiming at controlling a given place and its people without 'becoming involved in the intricate web of local relationships'. In India, royal land grants to Buddhist monasteries, but also to Brahmins or temples, are a case in point. Monks of a monastery are individuals unrelated by ties of caste and family, so that the unity between them can only be established with reference to territory, and that requires this territory to be unambiguously demarcated (ibid.: 68). The same is true for the modern nation-state: also the latter is made up by individual citizens that are conceptually independent from each other and that therefore, inevitably require a closed and compact territory to provide their unity an 'actual, tangible form' (ibid.: 69). However, because the urge for a 'transcendent reference point mediating the unity of the participants' grows stronger 'once the little community had ceased to be the main basis of society' Heesterman (1985: 69) considers 'modern' boundaries as much more explosive than the 'traditional' separating and connecting boundaries.

Hence, in Heesterman's terms, public sector company towns like Rourkela, as well as the Nehruvian nation-building project as a whole, were about breaking down primordial arrangements and 'inner frontiers', about turning all places of India into integral parts of the nation-state and about providing citizenship to all people.[9] As discussed at the beginning of this article, Rourkela was in fact to become a central locus for the production of 'modern India', to serve as a reference point that would transcend the various 'little'—and often hierarchically ordered—

communities, and not only to produce the steel required for the country's economic modernization.

However, several 'modern' boundaries around Rourkela had already been established prior to the arrival of the RSP. On 1 January 1948 the princely state Gangpur to which Rourkela hitherto belonged was 'merged' into the province Odisha and the Republic of India. As in all the other twenty-three princely states stretching over the hills of present-day western Odisha, the *raja* of Gangpur resigned from his rule, the administration was reformed and universal suffrage was introduced. Together with its neighbouring princely state Banei, Gangpur turned into the modern district Sundargarh, that is subdivided into several *zilla parishads*, municipalities and *panchayats* governed by elected bodies; not anymore into estates ruled by *raja, zamindar* and *ganju* or *gauntia*.[10]

With merger the territory of Odisha state increased fourfold and its population doubled (Bailey 1963: 173), and soon after, the former kings, administrators and the lettered middle class of these princely states established the Ganatantra Parishad, a regional party in order to safeguard the interests of their former people against the *katakiya*, i.e. literally 'the people from Cuttack', the former capital of Odisha in the coastal plains, who after merger took over administration of the states in large numbers, with a mentality of conquerors as the hills-people alleged (Bailey 1959: 1471). Because the local tribes or Adivasis shared their former rulers' concern about the *katakiya* incursion the Congress party for long remained unable to win constituencies in the merged former princely states and to form stable state governments.[11] Nevertheless, the members of both the Ganatantra Parishad as well as the Odisha Congress shared a staunch Odia nationalism (ibid.) and both parties were equally agitating for the amalgamation of two further princely states, Kharswan and Seraikella, with Odisha (Mohanty 2006: 233–62). Like in Gangpur and the other twenty-three states that had been merged with Odisha in 1948, the educated middle classes in Kharswan and Seraikella were Odia. They felt threatened by the prospect of being permanently merged with Bihar instead of Odisha, because this would have put them at the whims of a Bihari administration that they perceived to be unsympathetic to their people. Still, after the States Reorganization Commission submitted its enquiry report the central government reached the final verdict to keep both states within the borders of Bihar in 1956 (ibid.: 257). Politicians in Odisha reacted by offering Odia living outside the state *cakri*, or government employment, in Odisha, as some people who had followed that call and had come to Rourkela told me. Quite a few tried their luck here, because the emerging steel town was just a 3–4 hours train journey away from these former states and because the place offered the best prospects to find suitable employment for these educated migrants of a 'middle-class' background. They were engineers, lawyers, or businessmen and were attracted by prestigious jobs that came up in and around the RSP. On realizing that in Rourkela, Bengali, Punjabi and Madrasi or south Indians also had a say, they felt disgruntled. Some of them decided to ship in the Odia *goondas*, that were behind the ethnic violence around the construction sites and many of whom came from Jamshedpur, India's first steel town established by the private Tata Company in 1907[12] adjacent to Kharswan and Seraikella.

The ruling Congress, the oppositional Ganatantra Parishad and other parties in the Odisha state assembly also became increasingly concerned about the employment prospects the people of Odisha had in Rourkela. In April 1959 the assembly appointed an enquiry committee to investigate into the ethnic composition of the then still small RSP workforce of 2,000 employees and this committee found out that people from Odisha formed only a minority within it (Sperling 1963: 25). The state government released its report amidst a series of attacks against non-Odia people in Rourkela mentioned earlier. The state government condemned the violence, but demanded preferential employment in the RSP for people from Odisha. In the end, they argued, the RSP was established in Odisha to generate employment especially for local people (Mardaraj Deo 1959: 10). The RSP management answered by pointing to the lack of qualifications of Odia applicants and continued to employ workers, clerks, engineers and managers from all across India. During 1959–66 the RSP workforce grew from 2,899 to 23,163,[13] and everyone in Rourkela agrees that roughly two-third of them came from outside Odisha.

It is only in 1968 that the Odisha state government gained significant control over the recruitment of labour for the RSP. The Government of India then made it obligatory for public sector undertakings to recruit manual labour via the local employment exchanges that are under the jurisdiction of state governments' labour departments (Weiner 1978: 339). In Odisha, a newly elected state government came to power in 1967, a coalition of the Swatantra Parishad, a larger, national party into which the Ganatantra Parishad had merged in 1962, and the Jana Congress. This government paid heed to the implementation of the amended labour laws. For registration with an employment exchange a residential certificate is required, for which the applicant has to satisfactorily show (most often with a school certificate) her continuous residence in a locality for the last ten years. Of course, by then many people from outside the state had lived long enough in Rourkela and would have been legally entitled to such a certificate, and even if not, they could have obtained it on the black market. However, as a high-ranking veteran of the then most powerful 'socialist' trade union revealed to me the new state government internally released the informal, but strict order not to issue certificates to individuals whose status as a citizen of Odisha is dubious.[14] And indeed I have met several people in Rourkela whose applications were bluntly rejected simply because of their Bihari or Bengali surnames.

In the late 1960s the RSP also expanded its production, and again recruited workers in large numbers. The workforce grew from 23,163 in 1966 to 35,531 in 1974 and the large majority of new recruits were, according to common sense in Rourkela, Odia. This trend has continued up to the present time and nowadays there are very few Bengali, Punjabi, Madrasi, and Bihari workers employed by the RSP.[15] The data I collected for several workgroups on different RSP shop floors confirm this popular perception: whether in the coke ovens, the rolling mills, the repair shops or the stores—in almost every group there are only one or two workers from West Bengal, Bihar or Andhra Pradesh. As a result the spacious, clean and green company township, looked after by the well-funded RSP town service department and endowed with well-equipped and subsidised quarters, schools and hospitals and meant to become a 'mini-India' is predominantly an Odia space. Accordingly, soon after I arrived in Rourkela for the first time in 2004 people told me to speak Odia in the company township and to switch to Hindi only in the boroughs around the railway station.

Language was a major concern for the Odia nationalist movement already in the late nineteenth century and the basis for the creation of a separate province in 1936 (Mohanty 1982). Until the 1980s in Rourkela also several associations for the promotion of Odia culture were formed that raised the language issue. One of their most prominent demands addressing Rourkela's large non-Odia citizenry was 'speak Odia, write Odia—if you want to stay in Odisha', as some Bengali friends remembered.[16] At that time many Bengalis lived in Rourkela and one of the major concerns for the promoters of these Odia cultural associations was to prevent them from dominating the 'culture' of the town. The violence unleashed by Odia mobs against Bengalis while the RSP was built never was to re-occur in Rourkela on a similar scale. Nevertheless, throughout the 1960s and 1970s the situation regularly turned dangerously volatile. This happened especially at the time of the Durga Puja when the Bengalis tried (as many Odias suspected) to control the organizing committees. Thus, the RSP did not develop into the 'melting pot' its planners had envisaged and neither did the company township housing the RSP workforce. As such, the Odisha state government, its state administration as well as many of its Odia citizens believed, it would have threatened the integration of Rourkela into Odisha. This, in turn, hampered the access to citizenship rights for the many non-Odias living in Rourkela, or as an elderly Punjabi once put it to me when discussing his life story: 'we are residents here, we will never be citizens!'

Political scientist Myron Weiner had pointed out long ago that despite her manifold constitutional provisions, in India ethnic minorities *de facto* often lack access to certain citizenship rights. According to Weiner, the reason for this lies in the fact that the reorganization of India's provinces along ethno-linguistic lines promoted within each state an urge for greater cultural-linguistic or ethnic homogeneity, and that this adversely affected the citizenship status of all residents who did not belong to the linguistic or ethnic community around whom the state's boundaries had been drawn (Weiner 1978: 325–48). These ethnic minorities are not denied citizenship as such, only when this comes into conflict with the interests of the ethnic majority of a certain state (Strümpell 2011: 485–98).

The boundaries between Odisha and its neighbouring states that are drawn by the effective citizenship regimes in Rourkela correspond to Heesterman's 'modern' boundaries. Though they form boundaries *within* a nation-state, they conceptually equal the ones between nation-states: they form continuous lines 'completely enclosing a compact block of territory' that is regarded as a 'complete, self-contained world' in the sense that the relations between Odisha and other union states of India are (ideologically) not complementary in Heesterman's sense. Furthermore, the unity of this world was mediated by a strong emphasis on its 'Odia-ness' that had to be defended against intrusion of or occupation by 'outsiders', and apparently this was particularly so because the fragile unity of the two parts of Odisha that were merged only in 1948 was a matter of serious concern for the Odisha state government and for many of its citizens. For them Rourkela was a place that was to be turned into an integral part of not just India but also of Odisha. Hence, the dynamics described in this section reveal that the imperial fusion the Government of India pursued in its internal peripheries such as western Odisha by means of heavy investment was only one side of the story. The other side were attempts launched simultaneously by the government of Odisha to incorporate this very periphery closer into the union state. And with regard to membership in the modern, prestigious RSP workforce it could succeed, because the centre allowed local Odia elites considerable leverage over its administration, or—in Ludden's (2011: 147) terms—because it allowed for a certain amount of fission. On the part of the local Odia elite, however, this did not entail a valorization of diversity with regard to the Bengali, Punjabi and other Indians from other states.

'Wilderness' in Contemporary Rourkela

'Modern' state boundaries are not the only boundaries prevailing in and around Rourkela. From the start of my field research in 2004 the Rourkela Police always strongly urged me not to venture into the town's hinterland. In Rourkela itself, everything is fine, they told me, but into the forested hinterland Maoist 'terrorists' had recently infiltrated in numbers so that my safety could not be guaranteed. My research assistant was from a village some 20 km. away from Rourkela and whenever he returned home from Rourkela after sunset he had to pass police check posts, as indeed anybody did who commuted between the steel town and its hinterland at night. For some time the night train service across the densely forested Odisha-Jharkhand border had been stopped for fear of Maoist attacks. The state is regularly conducting 'combing operations' against Maoist insurgents in the forested hills, but the latter's influence is growing continuously (Das 2012).

In Rourkela as well as in diverse media there are a variety of reasons given for the relative success the insurgents have in the region. It is either explained with reference to the state's neglect of Rourkela's hinterland, the poverty as well as the general ignorance of its largely 'tribal' population allegedly resulting from it, which, in turn, makes them susceptible to the agenda and luring promises of the Maoists. More cautiously, many concerned people in Rourkela from all walks of life also point to the large-scale industrialization that has gained enormous momentum soon after India began 'liberalising' her economy in the 1990s and that has led to the devastation of the environment and the displacement of whole villages around Rourkela.

Since the early 2000s various national and international corporations started exploiting the mineral wealth that lie beneath the forested hills of western Odisha and quite a few also established mills to process them into aluminium, steel or, more often, sponge iron.[17] Of course, the RSP, too, exploits the region's resources. However, the agendas behind the Nehruvian public sector steel plant and the private sector mining and manufacturing companies differ significantly. The private companies are concerned about their profitability, not about carrying modernity, urban life and citizenship rights into a wild, peripheral 'elsewhere' (cf. Parry 1999: 136f). As some old industrialists and entrepreneurs in Rourkela told me, they suspect many of these new undertakings to be only 'fly-by-night' companies, i.e. transient enterprises established to make quick profits during a boom, such as the current sponge iron companies, and closing down during busts. However, whether fly-by-night or not, private companies do not found townships or colonies to accommodate their staff near their factories. In fact, their actual, i.e. regularly employed, staff consists of managers, clerks and some skilled workers only and these are commuters residing in the established towns of the region like Jharsuguda, Rajgangpur or Rourkela. None of them want to live near the factories because the area is so heavily polluted. Unlike the RSP, the recently established private companies employ their manual workforces almost exclusively through labour contractors.[18] This means that several substantial labour laws do not cover them, and that they are cheap and easy to retrench. These workforces either come from nearby villages or, more often, they are tribal migrants from neighbouring Jharkhand accommodated in rented shacks that some villagers with an eye for business erected on their fields. Furthermore, many companies acquire the land for their factories in dubious cloak-and-dagger operations by bribery or force against which the local tribal villagers vehemently protest if they have not been entirely intimidated by the *goonda* such companies are said to deploy frequently.[19] The despair that grows from the loss of their land and the destruction of their habitat, it is said, makes the youth among these villagers likely recruits for the Maoist insurgents operating from nearby jungles (Das 2012).

In Rourkela I met many people with backgrounds in accounting, engineering or skilled trades who welcome the recent developments because of the employment opportunities they offer. At the same time, these people, like everybody else in Rourkela, consider the steel town's rural, hilly and still largely forested hinterland an unruly, scarcely regulated and controlled environment and are very much concerned about the increasing presence of the Maoist insurgents. Nevertheless, it is only because of this lack of regulation and control in Rourkela's hinterland that mines and mills, whose operation very often grossly violates environmental, land and labour laws, can generate the profits they do. In this sense, the relation between Rourkela's hinterland and the duly regulated steel town is complementary and hence resembles the 'traditional' relation between *grāma* and *aranya* according to Heesterman. Furthermore, in economic terms also the relation between Rourkela and its hinterland resembles the model Heesterman draws of the relation between *grāma* and *aranya* in significant ways. In that model, the *aranya* is the place where 'mobile wealth' is accumulated (Heesterman 1989: 13), and also the wealth accumulated in the mines and mills around Rourkela is skimmed off by company headquarters in Rourkela, Bhubaneswar, Delhi or any other urban centre. However, whereas in Heesterman's account it appears that it is people from the *aranya* itself who generate liquid resources, around Rourkela it is corporate houses from elsewhere that do so, by intruding into the 'wilderness' and dispossessing local tribal villagers. Hence, in terms of its political economy the relation between Rourkela and its surrounding 'wilderness' differ markedly from Heesterman's characterization of the relation between *grāma* and *aranya*. This confirms Ludden's argument that 'old imperial frontiers . . . form borders inside contemporary nations, dividing expansive national elites from rebellious subalterns', though 'not by reproducing the imperial structures of old, but rather by embedding imperial dynamics of power and authority inside national societies, cultures and economies' (Ludden 2011: 133). Such dynamics, Ludden argues, come to the foremost clearly if one looks at how the *process* of empire is experienced and takes shape at frontiers and peripheries, not at how its *structure* expands from imperial centres (ibid.: 135).

The way the moment of postcolonial imperial fusion was experienced on and around the RSP's construction sites I already discussed above. However, everybody in Rourkela knows that during the RSP's construction it were not only robbers and protection-racketeers, itinerant traders, labourers and self-sacrificing unionists or renouncers who dwelled here, but also people in dozens of pre-existing villages and hamlets. The villagers were in their large majority engaged in subsistence agriculture supplemented by petty trade or wage labour and they were Adivasis. In the eyes of the people quoted in section 'The Frontier' above, these Adivasis were very backward then: they didn't know how to wear cloths; they were very innocent, extremely shy and disappeared at sight. Nevertheless, despite the fact that Adivasis had settled in Rourkela before—or probably because it was Adivasis who had settled here—the industrial pioneers claim that there had been nothing. This notion that Rourkela was only an unruly 'empty space' at the verge of its modernization and civilization stands in stark contrast to the notions the local Adivasi villagers held of the process.[20] For construction of the steel plant, township and other infrastructure, the Odisha state government acquired, wholly or partly, land from 2,465 families or around 15,000 people and handed it over to the RSP (Ratha and Behera 1990: 10–23). The displaced people I could still meet during my field research between

2004 and 2009 remember their displacement as a violent, traumatising event. Mishra Mundari, e.g. an RSP worker from the scheduled tribe Mundari approaching 60 years of age, told me how officers arrived unannounced only to tell his family that they have to pack their belongings and leave instantly while bulldozers started to erase their village from the surface of the earth. And R.C. Sahoo told me that his uncle died out of grief over an insecure, most likely bleak future like quite some old people did.

The displaced people who wanted to remain farmers were allotted to so-called rehabilitation camps 40–100 km. away from Rourkela in the midst of the jungles that nowadays form the Maoist domains. The people preferring to become wage labourers in Rourkela were allotted to resettlement colonies adjacent to the steel town. In case it remained unoccupied some returned after a few years to their old village sites now lying waste somewhere between the township and the RSP. Most of the people living in such ex-villages and in the resettlement colonies adjacent to Rourkela did find regular employment in the RSP. They thus became part of India's postcolonial moment of fusion for which the RSP and the industrial modernity it encapsulates was to stand as a beacon. However, within the RSP they all ended up in the 'hot shops' such as coke ovens or blast furnaces, because as Adivasis the RSP management considered them especially well suited for bearing the hard working conditions there. Odias work there only as supervisors or in the RSP's—relatively speaking—cleaner and cooler mills. Furthermore, until recently, very few tribal RSP workers lived in township quarters, but segregated from them; after work, the Odias retreated into the steel township and tribal workers into the resettlement colonies or the slums into which their former villages had turned (Strümpell 2014, Behera 1996: 239–51).

By the time I started my field research in 2004 there were, in fact, not many people left in these resettlement colonies and slums that were still a regular part of the 'modern' RSP-workforce, and today there are even fewer. The first generation of RSP workers taken on in the 1960s in their early twenties started retiring in the 1990s, among them also the tribal workers recruited for the 'hot shops'. At the same time the RSP updated and cleaned up its production processes, and—complying with the new agendas set after economic liberalization—started reducing its manpower. Its regular workforce of then 37,000 has come down to 19,000 in 2007. This reduction was achieved by only partly replacing the retiring first generation of RSP workers with new recruits; and only with recruits who had at least passed matriculation, but preferably also a vocational training at an Industrial Training Institute. Of the sons of the first generation of tribal RSP workers who grew up in *bustees* and resettlement colonies very few meet these qualifications and they know that this excludes them from competing for RSP jobs on the labour market.

Economic liberalization affected the number of workers RSP regularly employs, not so much their wage scales, fringe benefits and overall job security. For people in Rourkela, employment in RSP hence remains the best working class job available locally. Their *de facto* exclusion from it is a painful, bitter experience for the youth that grew up in Rourkela's ex-villages and resettlement colonies. Over the course of the last twenty years they have often raised their protest by launching demonstrations and strikes. In several cases they also have been approaching courts to gain what they perceive to be their right by means of the law, though without much success. In all these contexts they claimed (and still do) that their land has not been rightfully acquired by the state, because they had not been properly compensated, either with money or with RSP employment, or because there never existed a legal basis for the acquisition, and that they have thus been betrayed and robbed. The failure of their political protest as well as their lawsuits convince many that the state of Odisha rules them by wild, brute force, by a *jungli raj*, and they therefore see the inclusion of the region into the neighbouring 'tribal' state Jharkhand that was carved out of southern Bihar in 2000 as the most viable way to restore justice.[21]

In Rourkela I met quite a few Odias who were more or less seriously concerned about the situation of the people in *bustees* and the resettlement colonies. However, almost all Odias met the protest and the claims that the largely tribal people there raised, with contempt. The claims for RSP employment were rebuked in a stereotypical manner by arguing that it is their own fault that the people in *bustees* and resettlement colonies remain uneducated and thus unfit for regular public sector employment. In the end these tribal people are simple souls, many added, content with little and actually more concerned about drinking and dancing than about 'progress', be it in the form of education or merely saving money. More irritation on the side of the Odia caused the demand for a separation of the Sundargarh district (along with two other districts in northern Odisha) from the province and its merger into Jharkhand that came along the protest for employment.

Many Odias often warned me not to visit local *bustees* such as Nag Nadi, a cluster of villages of around 250 houses right behind the housing colony where I had rented a flat soon after the start of my ethnographic research in Rourkela in 2004. Nag Nadi already existed before the RSP had come up and Mishra Mundari, the RSP worker introduced above, told me not only how this village was forcefully destroyed, but also how his parents and some of their co-villagers had re-built it later to reclaim and plough some old fields in addition to the regular work in the RSP they then still had. The colony where I put up was established only in the mid-1980s by the Orissa State Housing Board, which leased out its plots for 99 years, most often to retiring RSP workers. It is nowadays separated from Nag Nadi by a small strip of land covered by garbage that people from both the colony as well as Nag Nadi throw here. Places like Nag Nadi are not good, residents of the colony repeatedly told me, because the people there are 'uneducated' (*asikhita*) and 'wild' (*jungli*). They regularly get drunk and then misbehave. There are many *goondas* and ruffians roaming around in these places; in Nag Nadi they have even beaten up policemen recently. The people in the *bustees* or ex-villages (though not in the resettlement colonies) are anyway all illegal encroachers on government land, people in the colony emphasize, and would have been long evicted if self-interested politicians had not prevented it. Apart from politicians and 'party workers' during election campaigns, only drunkards go there. Respectable people avoid these unruly and uncontrolled places.

This avoidance does not mean that there are no social relationships between the people living in the orderly parts of Rourkela and the more unregulated, uncontrolled ones. The relationships to local politicians I have already mentioned. In addition, the people from *bustees* and resettlement colonies make their purchases on markets that normally are located outside these places, just like the hospitals, banks, offices they visit and the schools to which they send their children. The people in *bustees* and resettlement colonies also remain closely integrated into the local economy. A small number of people in the *bustees* or ex-villages support themselves largely with the small fields and gardens they still hold under occupation. However, these are exceptions and the vast majority of people who have dropped out of the RSP workforce and who live in places like Nag Nadi and in the resettlement colonies make a living from various activities: as contract workers in the RSP or other factories such as the sponge iron plants, as craftsmen or as daily-wage earners on construction sites, as petty contractors, illicit liquor distillers, or as *goondas*-for-hire, as drivers, watchmen or as maidservants, to name the most prominent ones. Thus, the people in Rourkela's unruly *bustees* and resettlement colonies are not only the wild 'other', but they also form that part of the town's informal economy that is valorized for its potential to be cheaply and insecurely employed. In this regard, the boundaries that separate as well as connect distinct spaces within Rourkela resemble the frontier that divides the steel town from its surrounding countryside, and, as I have shown, both of them rest on the idea of a complementarity between wilderness and modernity or civilization. However, as is apparent from the organization of work within the RSP, this idea never completely subsided, not even when the Odisha state government asserted its modern boundaries.

Imperial Structures and Processes

Even though traditional, imperial boundaries based on the notion of complementarity persist in the modern steel town as well as its hinterland, during periods of both imperial fusion and imperial fission, the relation between the *jungli* and the modern, civilized or settled domain do not quite resemble the relation between *aranya* and *grāma*. To recapitulate: in Heesterman's (1997: 110) model empires aimed to push out the inner frontier between regulated sedentary *grāma* and unregulated uncultivated *aranya*. The Mughal Empire which Heesterman takes as an exemplary case, pursued this through an elaborate system of concurrent rights, i.e. a co-sharing arrangement that granted several people, from the emperor down to the tiller, different shares in agrarian wealth. Under such circumstances the empire absorbed with relative ease invading newcomers from the *aranya* as well as conquered areas of the *aranya* (ibid.: 105, 109).[22] The co-sharing arrangements were of course laden with conflict: the exact shares someone was entitled to were a matter of serious dispute and there always existed the threat that peripheral areas could build up cumulative bases strong enough to become independent from imperial centres (ibid.: 105). Likewise, invaders from beyond the inner frontier at the periphery aimed to 'force a way into the imperial arrangement' by means of raids, ransom, rebellion (ibid.: 110). Thus, though Heesterman calls separating modern, nation-statist boundaries more explosive and risky than traditional ones, the connection—and not merely separation—traditional boundaries establish between *grāma* and *aranya* is in fact coined by a mutual exchange of violence and force (Heesterman 1985: 66), however agonistic in nature. And here, I conclude, lies one of the major differences between Heesterman's historical account and the contemporary ethnographic situation in and around Rourkela.

If one takes into account the presence of Maoist insurgents, even today, much of western Odisha experiences violent exchanges across these frontiers. However, most people in Rourkela's 'wild' *bustees* and hinterland experience violence as a one-sided affair, unleashed upon them by companies, their security forces and goons, by the state and its police forces. The 'traditional' boundary connects them to people and a state that displaced them in the mid-1950s and one that exploits them since then. It is for this reason that the people in the *bustees* and resettlement colonies as well as in the surrounding villages in the Sundargarh district demand an integration of the region into Jharkhand, the 'tribal' and therefore 'their' state. Many of them are convinced that it is only such a 'modern' boundary that could meaningfully protect them against the predatory actions by the Odia foreigners and that could provide them full citizenship. Hence, from their perspective the 'traditional' boundary or inner frontier looks less benign than it appears in Heesterman's model.

Of course, Heesterman never explicitly assumes that inner imperial frontiers persist unchanged in contemporary India. In fact, he hypothesizes on the re-emergence of 'empire' and imperial boundaries only by passing and without considering in detail the effects of this resurrection. Furthermore, the political economy on which the 'traditional' empires Heesterman primarily analyses rest, is long gone, and imperial frontiers—like empires themselves, in Odisha, in India as well as all over the world (Kumar 2010)—nowadays do not exist *de jure*, but only *de facto*. Nevertheless, the dominant narrative pursued most forcefully by Rourkela's middle-class, higher-caste Odia residents, and also by many others, on the *jungli* or 'wild' people of its hinterland and of its *bustees* in significant ways resembles Heesterman's historical model. The perspective put forward in this narrative is a 'centrist', 'imperial' one concerned with the structure of 'imperial' rule and expansion. This perspective abstracts from the way this process is experienced by people in the peripheries themselves, or, as Ludden (2011: 135) reminds us, from the fact that '[e]mpire looks different from different angles'.

Notes

1. This is the figure the 2011 Census gives for the population of the Rourkela Metropolitan Region that includes the Industrial Township, the Rourkela Municipality as well as several surrounding *panchayat*.
2. My fieldwork in Rourkela has extended over 30 months during the period 2004–11 and was supported by the *Deutsche Forschungsgemeinschaft* (DFG, German Research Council), the Free University Berlin and the Max-Planck-Institute for Social Anthropology, Halle/Saale, Germany. I gratefully acknowledge the invaluable research assistance of Rajat Singh, Zoober Ahmed and Ganesh Hembram.
3. Similar to Heesterman, also Kumar (2010) emphasizes the co-existence, at least for the last two centuries, of empires and nation-states and the different principles that define them ideally.

4. See especially Cain and Hopkins 1993, Mignolo 2000, Hardt and Negri 2001, Burbank and Cooper 2010.

5. Cf. Christoph Bergmann 2016: 88–98.

6. The engineers, managers, contractors and foreign technicians—on the contrary—lived much more comfortably in hostels or in bungalows that were constructed early on, and they employed domestic workers or were catered for in messes. However, also they describe these years in Rourkela as a time of enormous hardships.

7. For a more detailed discussion of ethnic violence in Bhilai as well as Rourkela, including an extensive discussion of the communal riot that blighted Rourkela in 1964, see Parry and Strümpell 2008: 47–57.

8. The unionist-cum-renouncer is a prominent figure in the history of the Indian labour movement, see Chakrabarty 1984: 116–52.

9. For more detailed accounts of the Nehruvian agenda behind the industrial mega projects, see Khilnani 2003 [1997]: 61–106, and Parry 1999: 107–40.

10. The late colonial and early postcolonial period in Rourkela I discuss in more detail in Strümpell 2014: 200–27. For a general historical analysis of the Gangpur state and the merger of the princely states see Nanda 2011: 149–74, and Pati 1993.

11. For a more detailed discussion of Odisha's political history during the period 1936–77 see Ghosh 1979.

12. For excellent historical and ethnographic accounts of Jamshedpur see Bahl 1994, Simeon 1995, Sanchez 2015.

13. The employment figures of the RSP for the period 1956–95 I collected from a local trade union office.

14. The trade unions in Rourkela and their links to other political and social movements in Rourkela I discuss in more detail in Strümpell 2014: 45–72.

15. The situation of the executive grades differs in this regard. They are recruited on an All-India basis and though the majority of them are also Odia a significant number comes indeed from all over the country.

16. This demand has lost much of its fervour nowadays because since the 1990s most Odias who can afford it send their children to English-medium schools.

17. The production of 'sponge iron', or direct-reduced iron, is cheaper than the production of pig iron and is hence the most viable feedstock for small private steel plants that have come up in India since the economic reforms in the 1990s.

18. The contrast presented here between the public-sector RSP and its private-sector counterparts is overdrawn in the sense that especially since the 1970s also the former employs contract labourers for the most menial tasks and since the 1990s the RSP has reduced its regular workforce by almost 50 per cent (cf. Strümpell 2014).

19. Some instances of these processes are described in detail in Blindt 2009, Mohanty 2006: 257.

20. However, though the displaced Adivasis in Rourkela routinely emphasized their regret of the loss of land to the RSP, the elderly Adivasis I spoke to never showed any regret for the abolition of kingship and all that it entailed, especially forced labour (*bethi*).
21. For a more detailed account of the displaced people's political and legal struggles see Strümpell 2012: 202–27.
22. See also Wink 1986.

References

Bahl, V., *The Making of the Indian Working Class: A Case of the Tata Iron and Steel Company, 1880–1946*, New Delhi: Sage, 1994.

Bailey, F.G., 'The Ganatantra Parishad', *Economic Weekly*, 24 October 1959.

———, *Politics and Social Change: Orissa in 1959*, Berkeley: University of California Press, 1963.

Behera, D.K., 'Plight of the Tribal Workers of Rourkela Steel Plant of Orissa', *Man in India*, vol. 76, no. 3, 1996, pp. 239–51.

Bergmann, C., 'Confluent Territories and Overlapping Sovereignties: Britain's Nineteenth Century Indian Empire in the Kumaon Himalaya', *Journal of Historical Geography*, vol. 51, 2016, pp. 88–98.

Blindt, U., 'Die Frage der Einmischung: Moralische Dilemmata und die Hilflosigkeit der Ethnologen' (The Question of Intervention: Moral Dilemmas and Anthropologists' Helplessness), in *Fieldwork: Social Realities in Anthropological Perspectives*, ed. Peter Berger et al., Berlin: Weissensee, 2009, pp. 85–118.

Burbank, J. and Frederick Cooper, eds., *Empires in World History. Power and the Politics of Difference*, Princeton: Princeton University Press, 2010.

Cain, P. and Antony Hopkins, *British Imperialism: Innovation and Expansion, 1688–1914*, London: Longman, 1993.

Chakrabarty, D., 'Trade Unions in a Hierarchical Culture: The Jute Workers of Calcutta, 1920–1950', in *Subaltern Studies III*, ed. Ranajit Guha, Delhi: Oxford University Press, 1984, pp. 116–52.

Das, P., 'Maoist Surge', *Frontline*, vol. 29, no. 7, 2012. Online version <http://www.frontlineonnet.com/fl2907/stories/20120420290703000.htm>, accessed on 1 June 2012

Ghosh, S., *Orissa in Turmoil: A Study in Political Development*, Bhubaneswar: Bookland International, 1979.

Hardt, M. and Antonio Negri, *Empire*, Cambridge, Massachusetts: Harvard University Press, 2001.

Harvey, D., *The New Imperialism*, Oxford, New York: Oxford University Press, 2003.

Heesterman, J., 'Two Types of Spatial Boundaries', in *Comparative Social Dynamics: Essays in Honour of S.N. Eisenstadt*, ed. Erik Cohen, Moshe Lissak and Uri Almagor, Boulder and London: Westview Press, 1985, pp. 59–72.

————, 'The "Hindu" Frontier', *Itinerario*, vol. 13, 1989, pp. 1–16.

————, 'Traditional Empire and Modern State', in *Dynamics of State Formations: India and Europe Compared*, ed. Martin Doornbos and Sudipta Kaviraj, New Delhi: Sage, 1997, pp. 100–21.

Khilnani, S., *The Idea of India*, London: Penguin Books, 2003 [1997], pp. 61–106.

Kumar, K., 'Nation-states as Empires, Empires as Nation-states: Two Principles, One Practice?', *Theory and Society*, vol. 39, no. 2, 2010, pp. 119–43.

Ludden, D., 'The Process of Empire: Frontiers and Borderlands', in *Tributary Empires in Global History*, ed. Peter F. Bang and Chris Bayly, Basingstoke: Palgrave Macmillan, 2011, pp. 132–50.

————, 'Imperial Modernity: History and Global Inequity in Rising Asia', *Third World Quarterly*, vol. 33, no. 4, 2012, pp. 581–601.

Malamoud, C., 'Village and Forest in the Ideology of Brahmanic India', in *Cooking the World: Ritual and Thought in Ancient India*, ed. C. Malamoud, Delhi: Oxford University Press, 1996 [1989], pp. 74–91.

Mardaraj Deo, R. et al., *Report on Rourkela*, Cuttack: Orissa Government Press, 1959.

Mignolo, W., *Local Histories, Global Designs. Coloniality, Subaltern Knowledges, and Border Thinking*, Princeton: Princeton University Press, 2000.

Mohanty, C., *Oriya Nationalism: Quest for a United Orissa, 1866–1936*, New Delhi: Manohar, 1982.

Mohanty, N., 'The Oriya Movement and Singhbhum', in *Interrogating History: Essays for Hermann Kulke*, ed. Martin Brandtner and Shishir Kumar Panda, New Delhi: Manohar, 2006, pp. 233–62.

Nanda, C.P., 'Between Narratives and Silence: Centering Gangpur State', in *Centres Out There? Facets of Subregional Identities in Orissa*, ed. Hermann Kulke and Georg Berkemer, New Delhi: Manohar, 2011, pp. 149–74.

Parry, J.P., 'Lords of Labour: Working and Shirking in Bhilai', *Contributions to Indian Sociology*, n.s., vol. 33, nos. 1–2, 1999, pp. 107–40.

————, 'The Sacrifices of Modernity in a Soviet-Built Steel Town in Central India', in *On the Margins of Religion*, ed. Frances Pine and João de Pina-Cabral, New York: Berghahn Books, 2008, pp. 233–62.

Parry, J.P. and Christian Strümpell, 'On the Desecration of Nehru's "Temples": Bhilai and Rourkela Compared', *Economic and Political Weekly*, vol. 43, no. 19, 2008, pp. 47–57.

Pati, B., *Resisting Domination: Peasants, Tribals and the National Movement in Orissa 1920–50*, Delhi: Manohar, 1993.

Ratha, S.N. and Deepak K. Behera, 'Displacement and Rehabilitation: Data from the Resettled Colonies Around the Steel Plant at Rourkela, Orissa', *Man in Asia*, vol. 3, no. 1, 1990, pp. 10–23.

Röh, K., *Rourkela als Testfall für die Errichtung von Industrieprojekten in Entwicklungsländern, (Rourkela as a Test Case for the Establishment of Industrial Projects in Developing Countries)*, Hamburg: Verlag Weltarchiv Gmbh, 1967.

Roy, S., *Beyond Belief: India and the Politics of Postcolonial Nationalism*, Durham: Duke University Press, 2007.

Sanchez, A., *Criminal Capital: Violence, Corruption and Class in Industrial India*, London: Routledge, 2015.

Simeon, D., *The Politics of Labour under Late Colonialism: Workers, Unions and the State in Chota Nagpur, 1928–39*, Delhi: Manohar, 1995.

Skaria, A., 'Shades of Wildness: Tribe, Caste and Gender in Western India', *The Journal of Asian Studies*, vol. 56, no. 3, 1997, pp. 726–45.

———, *Hybrid Histories: Forests, Frontiers and Wildness in Western India*, Delhi: Oxford University Press, 1999.

Sontheimer, G.D., 'The *Vana* and the *Kshetra*: The Tribal Background to Some Famous Cults', in *The Eschmann Memorial Lectures*, ed. Gayatri C. Tripathi and Hermann Kulke, Bhubaneswar, 1987, pp. 117–64.

Sperling, J.B., *Rourkela: Sozio-ökonomische Probleme eines Entwicklungsprojekts* (*Rourkela: Socio-economic Problems of a Development Project*), Bonn: Eichholz Verlag, 1963.

Strümpell, C., 'Law against Displacement: The Juridification of Tribal Protest in Rourkela, India', in *Law against the State. Ethnographic Forays into Law's Transformations*, ed. Julia Eckert, Zerrin O. Biner, Brian Donahoe and Christian Strümpell, Cambridge: Cambridge University Press, 2012, pp. 202–27.

———, 'Social Citizenship and Ethnicity around a Public-Sector Steel Plant in Orissa, India', *Citizenship Studies*, vol. 15, nos. 3–4, 2011, pp. 485–98.

———, 'The Making and Unmaking of an Adivasi Working Class in Western Orissa', in *Savage Attack. Tribal Insurgency in India*, ed. Alpa Shah and Crispin Bates, New Delhi: Social Science Press, 2014, pp. 200–27.

———, 'The Politics of Dispossession in an Odishan Steel Town', *Contributions to Indian Sociology*, n.s., vol. 48, no. 1, 2014, pp. 45–72.

Thapar, R., 'Perceiving the Forest: Early India', *Studies in History*, n.s., vol. 17, no. 1, 2001, pp. 1–16.

Weiner, M., *Sons of the Soil: Migration and Ethnic Conflict in India*, Princeton: Princeton University Press, 1978.

Wink, A., *Land and Sovereignty in India: Agrarian Society and Politics under the Eighteenth-century Maratha Svarajya*, Cambridge: Cambridge University Press, 1986.

Zimmerman, F., *The Jungle and the Aroma of Meats: An Ecological Theme in Hindu Medicine*, Berkeley: University of California Press, 1987.

Editors and Contributors

UWE SKODA is Associate Professor in India and South Asia Studies at the Department of Global Studies, Aarhus University. Currently, he is working on transformations of kingship in Odisha and is broadly interested in the fields of political anthropology and visual culture. He recently co-edited a volume on 'Contemporary Indigeneity and Religion in India'.

BISWAMOY PATI is a historian and is with the Department of History, University of Delhi. He works on the diversities of colonial and postcolonial India. At present he is a Research Fellow at the Nehru Memorial Museum and Library, New Delhi, where he is researching on the social history of exclusion of the Adivasis and Untouchables/Dalits.

PETER BERGER is Associate Professor of Indian Religions and the Anthropology of Religion at the Faculty of Theology and Religious Studies, University of Groningen. His published titles include *Feeding, Sharing and Devouring: Ritual and Society in Highland Odisha* (2015); *Ultimate Ambiguities: Investigating Death and Liminality* (2015, co-edited with Justin Kroesen); *The Modern Anthropology of India* (2013); *The Anthropology of Values* (2010); and *Fieldwork: Social Realities in Anthropological Perspective* (2009).

LIDIA GUZY is currently Lecturer in Contemporary South Asian Religions at Study of Religions Department, University College Cork (UCC), National University of Ireland, Cork; a Director of the Marginalised and Endangered Worldviews Study Center (MEWSC) at UCC; Board member of India Study Centre Cork, UCC; and Associated Researcher at the Centre d'Anthropologie Sociale (CAS-LISST, EHESS), Toulouse. She specializes in anthropology of South Asian cultures and religions, media anthropology with special focus on music, museum anthropology (religion and museum), comparative indigenous studies and marginalized and endangered world views.

ROLAND HARDENBERG is a Professor at the Department of Social and Cultural Anthropology, University of Tuebingen. He has done extensive research on the Jagannatha Temple of Puri, Odisha (India), on the buffalo sacrifices of the Dongria Kond, Odisha (India), and on the funeral rituals of the Kyrgyz people of Central Asia. He is Vice Speaker of the Collaborative Research Centre 'Resource Cultures' sponsored by the German Research Council (DFG). His interests include kinship, symbolic classifications, religious resources, and ritual economies.

GEORG PFEFFER is a retired professor of ethnology at the Free University of Berlin. He has a doctoral degree from the University of Freiburg and a post-doctoral degree ('Habilitation') from the University of Heidelberg in Germany. His ethnographic research includes work on the sweeper community of the Punjab and the highest Brahmin segment in Odisha. Between 1980 and 2002 he has regularly visited the tribal areas of western Odisha to study the ritual and the kinship structures of several tribal societies. Among the results are articles on 'Order in Tribal Middle Indian Kinship' (2004) and on 'Bondo Violence' (2008).

EVA REICHEL worked as a senior lecturer at the Institute of Enthnology at the Free Institute of Berlin. Her published titles include *Notions of Life in Death and Dying: The Dead in Tribal Middle India*, which is based on long-term fieldwork among the Ho, a tribal community in Jharkhand and Odisha.

CHRISTIAN STRÜMPELL is Assistant Professor of Anthropology at the South Asia Institute, Heidelberg University and also a fellow at the research centre Work and Human Lifecycle in a Global Perspective at the Humboldt University of Berlin. His main interest is in economic and political anthropology and he has undertaken long-term ethnographic research in various regions of Odisha. He is currently writing a monograph on the Odishan steel town of Rourkela.

Index